TRUE CRIMES

RODOLFO WALSH

the life and times of a radical intellectual

Michael McCaughan

True Crimes was first published in 2002 by
Latin America Bureau (Research and Action) Ltd
1 Amwell Street, London EC1R 1UL

The Latin America Bureau is an independent research
and publishing organisation. It works to broaden public
understanding of issues of human rights and social and
economic justice in Latin America and the Caribbean.

Editor: Marcela López Levy
Cover design: Andy Dark
Design: Sue Lamble
Printed by J W Arrowsmith Ltd, Bristol

A CIP catalogue record for this book is available from the
British Library.

ISBN 1 899365 43 5

This book is dedicated to the memory of my mother Alice McCabe

Acknowledgements

This book belongs to many people who gave it time and energy along the way but errors and omissions are entirely my own.

The supporting cast is numerous and some people deserve a special mention. Verónica Diz made me a present of *Operación Masacre*, a gift that changed my life. She also transcribed interviews, discussed each character, dissipated doubts then cajoled and threatened me every time I hinted at throwing in the towel. Her reward, with partner Leo, has been their beautiful child, Amanda. Marcela López Levy took on this book for Latin America Bureau and stuck by it with resilience and affection, offering key advice at every turn, particularly in the area of translation. Her reward, with partner Michiel, has been a beautiful boy, Ansel.

A strange pattern is beginning to emerge.

Lilia Ferreyra was a guiding light who answered every pestering detail with heroic patience. Patricia Walsh granted permission for the use of Rodolfo's work and kindly opened up childhood memories. Poupee Blanchard was funny and hospitable, even after my interviews turned into weekly visits. Rodolfo's brother Carlos welcomed me into his home on a dozen occasions, giving freely of his memories and his photos. His brother Héctor encouraged my work, as did the eldest of the Walsh brothers, Miguel.

Vicki Costa Walsh, Rodolfo's granddaughter, gave permission to use Rodolfo's work and put up with spontaneous visits at her work. Vicki's father Emiliano Costa foolishly invited me to his house in Tigre, where I plan to take up residence later this year!

Horacio Verbitsky talked me through the era in sentences sharp enough to cut and paste en masse into the text. Rogelio García Lupo encouraged me from the beginning and added crucial details to the story. He also lent me his complete collection of the *Semanario de la CGTA*, an irreplaceable treasure. Miguel Bonasso shared lively anecdotes. Cynthia Mansfield gave me permission to use her brilliant translation of "Nota Al Pie" (Footnote). Her death came as a terrible shock.

I thank Enriqueta Muñiz, Norma Leandro, Ricardo Piglia, Jorge Lafforgue, Pedro and Fari Roselli. María Isabel Orlando, alias "Nene" and her charming daughters, the wonderful Lilia Huljich and all the combative compañeros in Rosario.

Donald Yates gave kind permission to use two of Walsh's short stories which he translated himself. No book on the era can be written without the resources of Roberto Baschetti, a walking archive who traced material by and about Walsh and restored my faith in soccer. During the dictatorship, Baschetti preserved a mountain of documents by transporting them to safe locations inside his soccer kit bag, the perfect disguise in a dictatorship which prolonged its rule through the 1978 World Cup victory.

I also wish to thank Enrique Arosagaray for helpful hints, Pat Rice, Fatima Cabrera, Tununa Mercado, Laura Bonaparte, Marion, Rolando Villaflor, Juan Pedranti, Rosa Pedranti de Baude, Fr. Joe Campion, Alejandro Clancy, Susana Shanahan, Daniel Divinsky, Art Agnew, Sean Clancy, Martin Caparrós, Luis Bruschtein, Lila Pastoriza, Eduardo Jozami, Lilian Hezler, Elba Izarduy, Juan Fresan, Andrew Graham-Yooll, Carlos Bares, Gregorio "Goyo" Levenson, Roberto Perdía, Aníbal Ford, Gustavo Gordillo, Osvaldo Bayer, Enrique Pugliese, Claudia Barrera, Eduardo Kimel, Ana María Amar Sánchez, Marisa Araujo, Julio Alsogaray, Roberto Ferro, Juan Jacobo Bajarlía, José Valenzuela and Carlos Ferreira.

In Cuba I visited the offices of *Prensa Latina*, which remain virtually untouched since Rodolfo prowled the corridors over 40 years ago. Joaquín Crespo, who has worked there since it first opened, was on duty when I arrived. I was also helped by José Bodis, Pablo Armando Fernandez, Leo Acosta, Conchita Dubois and Alfredo "El Chango" Muñoz. Jorge Timmossi and Roberto Fernández Retamar, two important witnesses to Rodolfo's time in Cuba, declined to speak.

In Mexico I had the support and advice of Ramor Dagge, Lupita Miranda, María Ines Roque, Tim Russo, Javier and Tatiana, Elisa and Vic, Pepe Gil, Ana Valades, Cui and the people of the sun: compañeros and compañeras in Morelia and Siete de Enero, busy making the world anew.

In Ireland I salute my father, brother Gerard, sisters Aideen, Catherine, Susan and Mary. Gra Mor to Eamonn, Deirdre, Aoife and Siuan who contributed love and a roof over my head, Mairead ni Chiosain, Damian Brady, Jackie Bourke, Stephen Mahony and Barry Cooke.

Inside the evil empire I enjoyed the support and love of Tom and Susan, Adam and Emma.

The *Irish Times* newspaper has given me an opportunity to publish articles on some of the issues contained within these pages, an experience which has been challenging for both of us. I thank Paul Gillespie, Paddy Woodworth, Deirdre Falvey, David Shanks, Judith Crosbie, Angela Long, Peter Murtagh, Reggie Dwyer, Enda O'Doherty, Declan Burke-Kennedy and my friends on the switchboard.

The final acknowledgment goes to the great loves of my life, Lorraine and Yasmin, whose light makes the sun shine every day, even in the West of Ireland.

Last but not least *muchas gracias* Rodolfo Jorge Walsh – inspiration and margin-walker, whose work has changed my perspective on writing and on life – but that's another story.

Contents

Foreword

An historian of his own time

Eduardo Galeano

The specialists in wall-building and trench-digging tell us: This is as far as the novel goes, over there is the border of poetry, this here is the frontier which separates fiction from non-fiction. And most important of all: don't dare slip up or try anything on. There are zealous customs' agents busy separating literature from its lower reaches. Journalism is a suburb of the fine arts.

How do these soul stealers account for the fact that the best Argentinian narrator of his generation was basically a journalist?

In the bourgeois mindset, which breaks everything it touches, there would be no room for many of the best-written and beautiful literary works produced in Latin America.

The work of Cuban writer José Martí was written above all for publication in newspapers; the passing of time proved that it belonged to an instant, but also belonged to history. The same will happen with Rodolfo Walsh, protagonist and witness, this historian of his own time, who wrote, as he said and wanted, in order to bear witness.

There you have his words, his implacable lucidity, his ability to capture beauty. His works are of the highest quality, holding a flame-thrower to those responsible for the Argentinian tragedy. Walsh is one of those writers who restores one's faith in the profession at a time when it is wobbly and shaken; full as the road is with imposters and salesmen.

"Never underestimate how an exemplary life can persist in the imagination of others, how it can inspire beyond death."

Ariel Dorfman, *The Progressive*, May 1999

"It is important to remember that once upon a time in Argentina there were people with balls and ovaries, who decided that they had to change the country; they fought for justice and a sense of national identity."

Laura Bonaparte (interview with the author February 2000)

"...it is not only by shooting bullets in the battlefields that tyranny is overthrown, but also by hurling ideas of redemption, words of freedom and terrible anathemas against the hangmen that people bring down dictators and empires..."

Emiliano Zapata (*Katzenberger*, 1995, p.i)

A true crime story

March 25th 1977
10.30 a.m.

Clandestino took slow, measured steps along the dirt track which led from his modest home to the local train station in San Vicente, on the outskirts of Buenos Aires. The area was growing in sporadic bursts which left dispersed dwellings dotted loosely across the landscape, still undecided on whether to join the metropolis or declare themselves part of the surrounding countryside.

The stooped figure of Clandestino could have been taken for a retired schoolteacher, enjoying his well-earned leisure time. He wore a beige shirt which hung loosely over brown, corduroy trousers, while a straw hat covered his balding crown, shielding him from the intense glare of the morning sun. His pale face wore an expression of puzzled intelligence, a riddle waiting to be solved; his sharp features were concealed by a pencil-thin moustache and golden wire-framed glasses, their thick lenses suggesting myopia.

Clandestino was accompanied by a young woman, pretty and petite, with big round eyes and full lips, a certain shyness in her gaze, which never stayed longer than a split second on approaching strangers. The "old man" had just turned fifty years of age, his collection of disguises a constant source of amusement to his friends, who had difficulty identifying him at their regular meeting places. He took great pleasure in walking by other *compañeros*[1] then finding some excuse to tap them rudely with his walking stick before a sharp hiss of suppressed laughter broke the spell.

Only the Sobreviviente managed to turn the tables on Clandestino, surprising him one day as he got off the metro. In his pocket Clandestino carried the same false ID which he had used twenty years previously, when the implacable hunt first began.

The couple arrived at the local train station where they bumped into

---

[1] *Compañero/a*, a common term in Latin America for lovers, friends, colleagues and political contacts in left organisations.

the former owner of their house, who handed over the property deeds. The couple had been renting for several months but the Organisation had finally found money to purchase the property. In a rare breach of his own obsessive security, Clandestino pocketed the documents and proceeded into town. If he missed the arriving train he would miss the appointments set up for later that afternoon and it could take weeks to set them up again. The property deeds were hidden in the false compartment of his briefcase but the precaution would only delay discovery by minutes should a professional happen upon it.

The couple boarded the half-empty train at San Vicente and sat in silence until they reached Constitución station, in the heart of the city, a seedy market area. Outside the station hawkers touted fruit and clothes and dozens of dodgy hotels rented rooms by the hour.

He took the cyanide pill from his pocket and handed it to his compañera whose own pill had turned to dust inside her shirt. The only thing worse than sudden death in Argentina in 1977 was endless death on the torture table where electric prods and medical instruments achieved maximum torment. The Organisation prescribed cyanide pills for all their members, which they should swallow to avoid capture. The assassins responded by bringing medical teams out on their operations, with doctors injecting their prey with a powerful antidote before the pill could complete its fatal course.

12 noon

When the couple emerged from the train station Clandestino went to a telephone booth and called the Organisation's central telephone message system, where a receptionist confirmed the meeting planned for that afternoon.

He was relieved. "The meeting is on," he said, turning to his compañera, a smile on his face. He reminded her to buy meat for an *asado*[2] planned that weekend and added one final request: "Don't forget to water the lettuces." The couple had planted vegetables in their garden, part of a drive toward self-sufficiency, to lessen the need for dangerous trips into the city centre which had become occupied territory, as gangs of government assassins roamed the streets, disappearing people at will. He waved a final goodbye and melted into the crowd.

It was a long time since Clandestino had lived anything approaching a normal life. A week earlier he watched as neighbours prepared their own noisy *asado*, relatives pulling up the driveway to share the feast,

---

[2] An outdoor barbecue, a way of life in Argentina.

unloading children squealing with excitement. The men gathered around the smoke and gristle as slabs of meat and sausage cooked slowly, accompanied by the inevitable jugs of cheap and tasty wine. He sorely missed the sense of celebration surrounding the *asado,* a reminder of carefree evenings when friends gathered to shoot the breeze.

The enforced isolation of life on the run had a huge impact on Organisation members, blurring the ability of activists to interpret the desires of ordinary people in whose name they struggled. "Too long a sacrifice can make a stone of the heart," he said to himself, quoting his favourite Irish poet, WB Yeats.

Sobreviviente, a senior member of the Organisation, had instructions to send Clandestino out of the country. After two fruitless and dangerous weeks searching, a one-way ticket to Rome in his hand, a persuasive argument in mind, Sobreviviente finally abandoned the task.

The situation had become impossible. Every day brought news of fresh captures and unspeakable torture, of broken bodies revealing further information, which provoked further captures and further torture. Uprooted militants often rode the buses all night, lacking money or personal documents, unwilling to risk contact with relatives or friends, who faced certain death if they were even remotely suspected of helping the Subversives.

If that wasn't enough, dozens of broken compañeros collaborated with their captors, proving their loyalty by cruising the city streets "marking" former compañeros and revealing the location and time of regular meeting points.

"I was told I'd never recognise him, that he was disguised as an Irish priest," recalled the Sobreviviente, who had earned his moniker after three close brushes with death on his rounds of meetings with fellow fugitives, desperately trying to hold the Organisation together long enough to find militants a safe refuge.

12.30 p.m.

The Assassins moved into place along Avenida San Juan, between Entre Rios and Sarandí streets. San Juan is a long busy avenue running north–south towards the city centre, lined with opthalmologists' and cafés, crowded with people in the early afternoon. On Friday 25th March 1977, elderly couples strolled to nearby homes, while mothers wheeled children to the park or chatted with neighbours under the shade of apartment buildings. One of the killers idled at a newsstand, another pretended to read a newspaper and leaned against the bonnet of a car, weapons concealed. It would take a trained eye to notice anything amiss and all eyes were trained to look the other way. It was safer thus.

1.00 p.m.

Clandestino began walking, stopping to post five copies of the same letter, a way to get round the censors. His compañera had walked off in a different direction, to do the same; she felt an enormous relief when the envelopes were finally out of her hands.

After a short bus journey, Clandestino took slow, steady steps as he approached the designated meeting point, every nerve alive to the slightest hint of something out of place, a gesture or a sign that might indicate an ambush ahead. He turned into Avenida Entre Rios towards Avenida San Juan finding nothing out of the ordinary. He was a master at melting into the background.

Colleagues recalled how they often had the sensation that he had been absent from meetings and events, even when their notes confirmed his presence.

1.30 p.m.

When he reached the corner of Calle Carlos Calvo, still two blocks away from his rendezvouz, the trap was set and the Assassins were ready for their prey. Their boss had been emphatic – no unnecessary use of force. "Bring that fucking bastard back alive, he's mine," said the Admiral.

Clandestino walked past the Assassins, immediately sensing something amiss. No one knows for sure what happened next, the precise sequence of events blurred by the momentary adrenaline charge, the passage of time and the deliberate manipulation of events to diminish future responsibility. Someone may have shouted "Stop, police", for no apparent reason, giving Clandestino several crucial seconds to take out the pistol he kept hidden in his waistband. The Assassins opened fire but the first shots went wide of the mark. The cornered man ran into the street, hid behind a parked car and emptied his small Walther PKK calibre pistol at his would-be kidnappers. He managed to injure one of the Assassins, who was subsequently awarded a medal for bravery.

Seconds later Clandestino lay mortally wounded, his straw hat coming to rest under the wheel of a car while pedestrians hurriedly left the scene. "I fired at him, I fired again and again but he didn't fall," said one of the Assassins, years later, "he didn't fall, he still didn't fall. Blood poured out of him, more blood and I kept shooting and blood flowed, more blood and the guy didn't fall."

1.50 p.m.

The bloody, bullet-ridden body was dragged by the Assassins to a waiting car and dumped in the boot. They returned to their offices, preparing a credible story to justify the botched operation to their superiors. The corpse was left in a corridor of the *Escuela de Mecánica de la Armada*, ESMA[3] for twenty-four hours before it was set on fire and dumped on waste land near the River Plate.

Later that day

The Assassins found their way to Clandestino's home. They raided, looted and wrecked. A month later, the house had a new owner, a police chief who eliminated all traces of the previous occupants.

---

[3] Naval Mechanics School.

Introduction

The events that matter

Rodolfo Walsh's *Operación Masacre* (1957) is still a bestseller in Argentina today, not simply because the author uncovered a hidden episode of State terror but because the book is also a damn good read. The slim volume crackles with wit and literary style, driven by the genuine outrage which occurs when ordinary people are confronted by acts of injustice. Walsh carefully reconstructed the final hours, minutes and seconds of five executed men, weaving the stories together with the rigour of a forensic anthropologist. He never let his rising anger get in the way of the facts, which were all he needed to incite the reader to indignation.

Rodolfo believed in the transformational possibilities of journalism: "Events are what matter these days," he said, "but rather than write about them, we must make them happen." As he wrote up *Operación Masacre* Walsh found himself at the centre of events, seeking the truth behind a clumsy execution but also seeking justice for the victims at considerable personal risk.

In the twenty years which followed the publication of *Operación Masacre*, Walsh sculpted his sharp prose across short stories, poems, plays, letters, literary criticism and crime fiction. He lived up to his promise "to bear witness in difficult times" until a rake of enemy bullets stole his last breath on a hot Buenos Aires afternoon in March 1977.

There was no one left to investigate his death. The true crime of the military junta robbed the world of that rare species of individual: a passionate intellectual who lived out his commitment to social justice, not counting the cost.

This book was originally planned as an anthology of Walsh's work with only a brief introduction to the circumstances of his life and death. It soon became apparent that Walsh's life was his greatest work.

The search for Rodolfo turned into the reconstruction of a crime scene known as the making of modern Argentina. The harshness of rural life, the effect of military dictatorship on everyday life, the response from those who wanted revolutionary change in Argentina – all this was part of his personal experience.

Rodolfo Walsh was a first-hand witness to the geography of State terror, as it shifted from a spot of waste ground in 1956, where the badly executed murder of suspected dissidents left several terrified witnesses to Operación Masacre. In the 1970s, repression intensified into the systematic elimination of "subversives" and other undesirable citizens as Argentina was marched implacably toward "christian, western civilisation" by military rulers.

The writer

Rodolfo Walsh was still in his teens when he began writing tentative stanzas which he shared with María Isabel Orlando, known as Nene, his first girlfriend, in the mid-1940s. He also devoured crime fiction books from around the world, becoming an expert on the genre. He was only seventeen in 1944 when he started work at Hachette publishers, translating detective novels and short stories, as William Irish, Dashiell Hammett and Sherlock Holmes came to life through Rodolfo's creative pen. Walsh's work as a translator instilled in him a deep respect for the precision and ambiguity of words and language, sentiments he expresses in the short story included below, "Footnote": "He gradually discovered translating was quite a different thing from knowing two languages: it was a third domain, an entirely new field. And then, the hardest of all secrets, the true cipher of art: to erase his personality, to go unseen, to write like another without anyone noticing."

A fortuitous incident led Walsh to begin writing his own crime fiction, resulting in *Variaciones en Rojo*, a three-story collection, completed in 1950. Walsh's first stories won the Buenos Aires Municipal Prize in 1953, judged by two of the country's best-known writers, Jorge Luis Borges and Adolfo Bioy Casares.

Walsh's first full-length work was *Operación Masacre* (1957), heralding a new literary style, the 'truth-novel' or 'new journalism', pre-dating Truman Capote's *In Cold Blood* by nine years. The two books are constantly compared, but where Capote described an investigation already completed, the killers identified and hanged, Walsh conducted his own investigation into a massacre carried out by the government of the day, forcing an inquiry. At great personal risk he unmasked and denounced the culprits with all the vigour so notably absent from Argentina's justice system.

Walsh naïvely believed that the guilty parties, once discovered, would be punished.

He would never make the same mistake again.

In *Caso Satanowsky* (1958) Walsh applied the skills gleaned from his detective novels to a real-life whodunnit, in this case the murder of a prominent Jewish lawyer and newspaper owner. His investigation forced a parliamentary inquiry, his scoop won Story of the Year and his name was added to Argentina's Who's Who, anticipating a bright future.

Rather than build on his success at home, Rodolfo took off for Cuba in July 1959, into the heat of the revolution, where he helped launch *Prensa Latina*, an international press agency set up to counter the pro-US bias of international news agencies. Walsh witnessed the remarkable changes taking place on the island, with profound implications for his own future.

He also contributed to one extraordinary incident in which, as an amateur cryptologist, he decoded CIA messages detailing plans for the Bay of Pigs invasion. Walsh could have named his price for this scoop of the century, but instead he handed it over to the Castro government, giving Fidel crucial advance warning of the upcoming aggression. The incident is recounted by his *Prensa Latina* colleague Gabriel García Márquez (see pp. 113–14).

Rodolfo returned to Argentina in early 1961 where the media closed its doors to him, as Argentina's muzzled press had grown accustomed to its role as an apologist for the ruling class. Rodolfo took up work in his mother-in-law's antique business, quickly becoming a skilled buyer, learning basic Arabic and Chinese to help him decipher script on the objects.

His real passion still lay in his writing and he began to spend long weekends in Tigre, the maze of islands on the Paraná river delta less than an hour from the centre of Buenos Aires; there he began to write fiction, completing several short stories and plays.

Walsh's two plays, *La Granada* and *La Batalla* (1962), and two volumes of short stories, *Un Kilo de Oro* (1965) and *Los Oficios Terrestres* (1967), received critical and popular acclaim. By 1967 Walsh was on track to join the emerging Latin American literary boom led by Gabriel García Márquez, Mario Vargas Llosa and Julio Cortázar. Rodolfo's partner of the time, Pirí Lugones, a literary scout, persuaded publisher Jorge Alvarez to pay Walsh a modest monthly stipend to write a novel, a rare privilege among the legion of impecunious artists. Yet writing was hard to do when reality offered so much to do and change.

In January 1968 Walsh returned to Cuba, where he attended the World Cultural Congress, joining Julio Cortázar, Eduardo Galeano and hundreds more writers and artists in debates on the role of the intellectual in Latin America's rapidly evolving social struggles.

Rodolfo hit an extended period of writer's block, paralysed by the rising expectations surrounding his anticipated debut as a novelist. He was also deeply influenced by the lonely death of Ernesto 'Che' Guevara in October 1967 and the growing popular resistance to the Onganía dictatorship in Argentina, expressed through the combative independent labour movement.

Walsh decided to abandon his ivory tower and join the action.

Activist

Juan Domingo Perón, legendary president and exiled leader of the Peronist party, personally invited Walsh to take up the helm at a weekly newspaper launched by the Confederación General de Trabajadores de los Argentinos (CGTA), which broke away from the official pro-government CGT union. The *Semanario* published fiery accounts of State repression and economic exploitation while also taking a swipe at corrupt union bureaucrats.

The newspaper chronicled the rebirth of an independent labour movement, selling 40,000 copies a week as worker-led uprisings spread across the country.

The growing resistance to military rule culminated in the *Cordobazo*, when in May 1969 thousands of citizens took control of Argentina's second city, Córdoba, for two days, routing the army and police. The *Semanario* published 50 issues, including a series of articles by Walsh on the murder of union activists Domingo Blajaquis, Juan Zalazar and Rosendo García, killed by official union thugs in a Buenos Aires pizzeria, later published in book form as *Quien Mató a Rosendo?* (Who killed Rosendo?).

The government ignored the evidence uncovered by Walsh, which implicated CGT leader Augusto Vandor in the killings. Vandor was a useful government ally who willingly co-operated with the military rulers, defusing tension in the labour movement. Disaster struck when Vandor was shot dead by unidentified assassins on June 30th 1969, the very day that one of Walsh's critical articles appeared. Walsh had no idea that Vandor would be targeted for assassination but the timing of his article turned attention on him. The military government shut down the *Semanario* that day and Walsh went into hiding for several months.

Over the next two years Rodolfo contributed articles to various magazines and added fresh comment to a fourth edition of *Operación Masacre* (1972), a story which refused to go away. The intellectual authors of the massacre found themselves facing rough justice from a new revolutionary group, the Montoneros, a Peronist guerrilla movement, fourteen years after they got away with murder.

By then Walsh had moved decisively beyond the field of intellectual detachment, edging closer to the *Fuerzas Armadas Peronistas* (FAP, Peronist Armed Forces), working with local activists in a shantytown near Retiro in Buenos Aires. In October 1973 Walsh formally joined the

Montoneros. The Montonero leadership asked Rodolfo to join a talented team of radical journalists to launch a new daily paper, *Noticias*, financed through guerrilla bank heists. *Noticias* achieved a circulation of 150,000 copies per day, despite sabotage and bomb attacks on its offices. Walsh headed up the crime pages and monitored the work of cub reporters, among them his daughter Patricia.

Walsh also directed an intelligence team which infiltrated federal police and army ranks, or recruited sympathetic officers already on the inside; he was suspected of masterminding two of the organisation's most spectacular coups. The political climate deteriorated rapidly as *Noticias* was shut down in August 1974, less than a year after it was launched. Federal Police chief Alberto Villar stalked through the *Noticias* office until he stopped in front of Walsh's desk, addressing the empty chair. "I know you have a coffin ready for me," he said, "well, I have one ready for you too."

Meanwhile the State-sponsored Anti-Communist Alliance (Triple A) death squads roamed Buenos Aires at all hours, hunting down guerrillas and their suspected sympathisers. Villar was one of the co-ordinators of their actions.

Walsh went into hiding once more and focused his skills on organis-ing a mobile underground news agency, anticipating the military coup ahead. The result was ANCLA, Agencia de Noticas Clandestinas,[4] which consisted of a typewriter, a mimeograph, a handful of volunteers and hundreds of informants, ordinary people who witnessed the State terror apparatus in action. The ANCLA bulletins were sent to foreign and local media, embassies and international human rights organisations, breaking the silence of a country ruled by fear. The information also served the Montonero intelligence network.

The noose tightened around the Montoneros' exposed necks, with thousands of activists falling into the hands of the security forces in the weeks and months which followed the coup on March 24th 1976. The death of Rodolfo's daughter Vicki, who died fighting the regime in September 1976, was a crushing blow to Rodolfo and precipitated the events leading to his death six months later.

"In this atmosphere, you will understand that the only things one can or wants to write about, are precisely the things which cannot be written," wrote Rodolfo in a letter to his Cuban friend Roberto Fernández Retamar. "The only possible heroes, the revolutionaries, need silence." The strategic silence surrounding revolutionary struggle was compounded by the official silence imposed by tanks and censorship, as

---

[4] Argentina's Clandestine News Agency.

books were burned, school curricula revised, citizens disappeared and the exercise of memory considered treasonable.

The crime of the 'subversives' lay not in demanding the impossible, but in working night and day to make the impossible happen in their lifetime. They never accepted the myth of inevitable social inequality. Thousands of people were kidnapped by State security forces not only under cover of the night but also in broad daylight, in front of dozens of witnesses, sowing panic and terror among the entire population, who retreated into prudent silence. Argentina was an occupied country, taken over by its own military and police, comparable to Belgium under Nazi rule during the Second World War. The result has been the silencing of one generation and the paralysis of another, a collective and crippling trauma which has yet to be fully assimilated by the Argentinian people.

Sources

Searching for Rodolfo Walsh entailed going all the way back to his grand-parents, who fled famine and repression in their native Ireland to settle in rural southern Argentina. They arrived to the land General Roca had cleared for "civilised" European immigrants with his 1879 War of the Desert, a genocidal campaign against the indigenous population.

The mystery of Rodolfo's life slowly unravelled through family, friends and colleagues who opened their doors and their minds to me, dredging up memories covering eighty years of the twentieth century. An interview with Walsh's first girlfriend Nene was followed by a trip to his first home in Choele-Choel, southern Argentina, where 92-year-old Juan Pedranti still remembered Rodolfo's parents. Closer in time, his surviving relatives, colleagues, comrades and friends offered insights into different stages of his varied life.

For many interviewees the memories were extremely painful, excavated from the nation's darkest hour, re-opening old wounds which will not heal until the guilty are punished. "If you betray me I will tear your eyes out," said Lilia Ferreyra, scaring the life out of me when I announced my intention to write the book. Yet the threat was strangely reassuring as Lilia, the repository of Rodolfo's most intimate reflections during the last ten years of his life, could demand nothing less. Over the months and years of my investigation Lilia Ferreyra remained a guiding light and loyal friend.

Rodolfo's surviving daughter Patricia posed challenging questions on the relationship between men of action and their loved ones who are left behind to pick up the pieces. What happens when responsibility to children, partners and family collides with a life-threatening commit-ment to radical change? After his release from prison Nelson Mandela wondered "whether one was ever justified in neglecting the welfare of one's own family in order to fight for the welfare of others".

Even where the visible "results" of prolonged struggle fail to match yesterday's dream of a changed world, the dream itself propels people forward, even though we can never predict the outcome of our efforts. A savagely poignant case in point was Rodolfo's daughter Vicki, who followed his radical example all the way to her death. Walsh also suffered terribly when his old friend Paco Urondo and former partner Pirí Lugones fell to the death squads before him, but it was Vicki's suicide, to avoid capture, which killed something inside him, lowering his defences at a time of extreme danger.

Rodolfo's relentless pursuit of the truth had implications for children, partners, relatives and friends. At the time of *Operación Masacre* (1957), Patricia Walsh, then a small child, recalled how plain-clothes agents called to the door of her home in La Plata, looking for Walsh, whose wife, Elina Tejerina, ran a residential school for the blind. Patricia and Vicki, aged five and seven, appeared at the door, accompanied by several other children, baffling the agents, as no one appeared willing to answer their questions. They grew tired and embarrassed and soon departed.

Rodolfo's older brother Carlos had his navy career cut short in 1970, passed over for promotion due to his suspect surname. By a curious stroke of fate Carlos himself would have been next in line to junta leader Admiral Emilio Massera in 1976, had it not been for his premature retirement. Rodolfo inadvertently saved him from involvement in one of the most cruel aspects of military rule, as navy pilots tossed drugged and bound prisoners out of airplanes during the dirty war.

Legacy

Walsh's last piece of writing remains a powerful testament to his life. In his "Open Letter from a Writer to the Military Junta", he exposed the scale of damage being inflicted by the military on Argentina. The military rulers eliminated a generation of activists, and the economic consequences of the era are visible today, as Argentina carries the largest burden of debt ever defaulted upon.

Rodolfo Walsh's "Open Letter", posted on the day of his death, is a superb examination of military misrule which proved beyond doubt that information about the unfolding genocide was available at the time.

In June 2001 the government of Buenos Aires approved a city ordinance which directed all schools to read out Rodolfo's "Open Letter" every year on March 24th, the anniversary of the coup. The legacy of Rodolfo Walsh's life and work is still a bitterly disputed issue in Argentina today, just as the history and lessons of military rule are disputed between left and right and within the left itself.

In the 1990s the transformation of legendary guerrillas into business tycoons or tepid *arrepentidos* (repentant radicals available for chest-beating *mea culpas* at all hours) has disillusioned many former activists, who are still coming to terms with the horrific era and are still mourning their missing friends and relatives.

Rodolfo Walsh's life and death were exemplary in their coherence and integrity. But while one person exalts Walsh the writer and another Walsh the revolutionary few have identified the whole Walsh: ragged schoolboy in Fahy boarding school, impoverished proofreader, rigorous translator, distant father, fearless journalist, amateur spook, womaniser, pithy short story writer, playwright, union militant, implacable revolutionary.

It was difficult to establish precise dates for many of the events described in the book, as interviewees quickly tired of the constant nitpicking over dates and times: "We weren't looking at our watches back then," Elba Izarduy, an FAP activist, told me, "we were trying to make a revolution."

If Rodolfo J Walsh had been born in Michigan rather than Choele-Choel, he would have become a celebrated literary figure, admired and discussed, a candidate for the Pulitzer prize. His political activism might have taken him to death row, as with dissident US writer Mumia Abu Jamal.

"Our dominant classes have always tried to keep the workers from having a history, from having heroes and martyrs," wrote Walsh. "Every struggle has to start from scratch, with no connection to the previous ones: thus the collective experience is lost and the lessons forgotten. History then appears as private property, and those who own it, own everything else," he wrote in the "Open Letter".

This book tells the story of an unlikely hero who wrested history out of the hands of the oppressors and returned it to the people, paying for his bravery with his life.

Rodolfo Walsh in his own words

They call me Rodolfo Walsh. When I was small, the name didn't fully convince me: I thought it wouldn't do me, for example, if I was to be president of the country. Much later I discovered that it could be pronounced like two alliterated iambs and I liked that.

I was born in Choele-Choel, which means "heart of wood". Several women have held it against me.

My vocation surfaced at an early stage: at eight years of age I wanted to be an aviator. In one of those confusions which happen in life, it was my brother who achieved my ambition. I suppose ever since then I have lived without vocation and have had many professions. The most spectacular, as a window-cleaner; the most humiliating, as a dishwasher; the most bourgeois, as an antique seller; the most secret, as a cryptographer in Cuba.

My father was the foreman on a ranch, a transcultured individual who was called "Huelche" by the workers in Rio Negro. He studied as far as third grade but could *bolear*[5] an ostrich and leave his mark on the bowling field. His physical strength still seems of mythical proportions to me. He could talk to horses. One of them killed him in 1945, another he left us, his only bequest. That horse was called Black Sea and covered three hundred yards in 16 seconds: a lot of horse for the countryside. But that was already our doom, Buenos Aires province. I have one sister, a nun, and two lay daughters.

My mother lived among the things she hated: the countryside and poverty. In her implacable resistance she ended up being stronger than my father. The greatest upset I caused her was by not finishing my degree in literature.

My first literary efforts were satirical quartets aimed at sixth grade teachers and prefects. When I left secondary school at 17 years of age and started work in an office, the inspiration remained alive but I had perfected the method: now I put together a secret acrostic.

The most disturbing idea of my adolescence was that idiotic Rilke joke: if you think you can live without writing, you shouldn't write. My relationship with a girl who wrote far better than me reduced me to silence for five years. My first book consisted of three novellas, in the crime thriller genre, work which I detest today. I did it in a month, not thinking about literature but about fun and money. I stayed silent for four more years, because I didn't think I was capable of anything. *Operación Masacre* changed my life. In writing it I realised that beyond my own intimate perplexities, a threatening world existed out there.

I went to Cuba, witnessed the birth of a contradictory new order, epic at times, at others plain annoying. I returned and retreated into silence for six years. In 1964 I decided that of all the earthly professions, the violent profession of the writer was the one which most suited me. But I see no mystical purpose in this.

To tell the truth I have been pushed and pulled by the times: I could have been anything, even now there are times when I feel available for any adventure, ready to begin again, like so many times before.

If I should continue to write, what I most need is a generous dose of

---

[5] To lasso with heavy wooden balls on strings.

time. I am slow. It has taken me fifteen years to move from mere nationalism to the left; it has taken me five years to write a short story, to feel
a text breathing; I know I have a long way to go before I can say exactly
what I want to say, in an ideal form.

I think that literature is, among other things, a slow advance through
stupidity itself.   ●◆ (Walsh, 1996)

chapter one

Choele-Choel

Rodolfo Jorge Walsh was born on a cool summer morning in January 1927, in Argentina's southern province of Rio Negro. His mother wrapped the newborn infant in sheets of newspaper, after a neighbour told her that the ink would keep her child warm. "You see," he told his friends, years later, "I never had a choice, I was condemned from birth to be a journalist."

(author's interview with Poupee Blanchard)

Irish roots

"The Irish began to arrive en masse at the end of the Rosas government, at the time of the hunger in 1847. Today we imagine that they mixed well from the beginning, but that wasn't the case. They raised sheep and fenced off territory, which wasn't a job for the *criollos*.[6] They also married among themselves, at least until the 1920s, three or four generations of Irish married to each other. We are an example of this: we haven't an ancestor who is not Irish. But that's all over now. None of us – out of five children – married an Irish descendant. I suppose we began to get fed up with each other, fed up with cousin Sheila and cousin Maggie" (Walsh, 1996 p.194).

Mary Kelly left her native Ballymore, Co. Roscommon, Ireland, in 1851 at nineteen years of age, sailing aboard the *Isabella* to the port of La Plata beyond Buenos Aires. The potato famine had devastated Ireland over the previous decade, killing one million people and forcing the same number again to emigrate around the world. Within months of her arrival she married fellow Irish immigrant Edward Walsh; they raised a family of twelve children. Rodolfo's grandfather Miguel Walsh y Kelly, their ninth child, was born in 1866. Miguel married Catalina "Katie" Dillon and they lived together in Lobos until his death in July 1910. The couple had six children; their second, Miguel Esteban Walsh, would be Rodolfo's

---

[6] *Criollos,* people of European descent born in Latin America.

father, born in 1894 in the town of Lobos, south-west of Buenos Aires.

Walsh's paternal grandparents owned a sizeable farm, La Salada in Roque Pérez, beyond Buenos Aires, until Miguel gambled it away. The gambling bug reccurred with genetic precision throughout future Walsh generations. Rodolfo's grandfather died in 1910, crippled by debts, at the age of forty-four. The widowed Katie Dillon married again in October 1916, to Juan Merrin.

While still in his teens Rodolfo's father moved to Buenos Aires in search of work, becoming an administrator in a British-owned meat processing plant, the Armour company.

Meanwhile Irish immigrant Dora Gill secured a job as a telephone operator in the same meat-packing plant as Miguel, and the two began a romantic liaison which would eventually lead to the birth of Rodolfo.

The Gill family was dominated by Dora's father Christy, a temperamental man who was generous with his fists, according to the tales passed on through Rodolfo's mother to her children.

Rodolfo's brother Carlos recalled how his grandfather Christy used to tie up his eldest son Joe with a chain in the back yard of their house. A tough kid who excelled at boxing, Joe would untie himself and "threaten the rest of the family with death should they reveal the secret". As soon as he heard his father return Joe would put on the chains once more and sit in the patio, an anguished look on his face.

"That's the way I like to see you," Christy would say. Dora's brother William Walter Gill was a poet and champion whistler with an excellent ear for music. Uncle Willie set sail for Europe in 1914, fully intending to enlist in the movement for Irish independence, "as his bloodline demanded", wrote Rodolfo, who became fascinated by his life (Walsh, *Primera Plana*, 22/10/68).

During the First World War (1914–18) radical Irish nationalists subscribed to the slogan "England's difficulty is Ireland's opportunity," inspiring a group of rebels to launch an armed uprising against British rule in April 1916. Uncle Willie headed out to join them, but changed his mind halfway across the ocean, opting to fight the Germans for the British Army instead; he died tragically while on leave in Salonika, Greece, where he stepped on a land mine. Rodolfo wrote about him later, "…So my dear sister Dorothy, Willie wrote home, and my dear Lucy, and my dear Emma, and you so-and-so Tommy, and you Joe, son of a gun, here I am, all ready to go and tell the Germans, so you have lost the war, because a real man has come on the battlefield to put an end to all this stupidity which has kept the world on its backside for too long, so you may start surrendering, you big fat beer-inflated idiots" (Walsh, 1996, p.231).

On a subsequent visit to Argentina in 1927, the Prince of Wales presented Rodolfo's father with a heavy bronze medal for Willie: "He died for freedom and honour" reads the inscription on the medal, which still sits proudly in the apartment of Carlos Walsh. The story of heroic Uncle Willie was resurrected decades later by Rodolfo, in his short story "When Uncle Willie Went to War" which ended up among the work stolen by the military in 1977.

Born in Junín province in 1898, Rodolfo's mother Dora spoke faltering, heavily accented Spanish, which she had learned in her teens. She considered English the language of the civilised world and would nurse ambitions of social mobility among her children. Many Irish immigrants spoke a rarefied version of Spanish known as *Irish Porteño*,[7] with Rodolfo's parents the first generation to fully master the language of their new homeland. The Irish stuck closely together in their new country of residence, forming clubs and associations which assured inter-marriage within the Gaelic tribe.

When Miguel Walsh married Dora Gill the couple decided to become farmers in Lamarque village, a dot on the map beyond Choele-Choel, in Rio Negro province, southern Argentina. The land there is flat and limitless, marked by scrub bushes which blow like tumbleweed in the desert. The Walsh–Gill couple arrived in Choele-Choel in 1921, bringing their first son Miguel "Lito" Walsh, who was born the previous year in Buenos Aires.

Conquest and colonisation

"The bloody stain of the conquest was still fresh," Rodolfo would write, years later, in "Trasposición de Jugadas", a short story set in Choele-Choel, "the wind blew a pile of sand and the face of an Indian appeared, solemn and gaunt in death."

Argentina's Indian population had suffered successive extermination campaigns since Juan Díaz de Solís first sailed up the River Plate in 1516. They first came looking for a passageway linking the Atlantic and Pacific oceans, rather than land or gold, but that changed in the succeeding centuries. When the Spanish invaders disembarked they were met by Querandí Indians, who killed Solís and his party. The Spanish persisted and founded the first settlement at Sancti Spiritus a decade later. The Querandí held another meeting to discuss the new settlement and proceeded to destroy that too. By 1580 Buenos Aires had been "refounded", along with several other towns, by force of arms and larger contingents.

The new settlers ruthlessly cleared lands for cattle ranchers by waging

---

[7] *Porteño*, the noun describing inhabitants of Buenos Aires and their accent.

a war of extermination against the indigenous inhabitants. Argentina pursued an export-based economic model, in which leather was sent to Europe and dried beef was sent to keep slaves alive in Brazil. Further south in Patagonia, British immigrants wiped out, among others, the Ona people in Tierra del Fuego, reducing the native population from 4,000 in 1880, to just 200 people resettled in a reservation in 1950. The numbers of inhabitants in rural areas was never high, and began to decline at the beginning of the twentieth century, falling from 42 per cent to 32 per cent of the total population between 1914 and 1930.

The social and demographic make-up of Argentina began to change dramatically near the end of the nineteenth century, when General Roca came to power, leading a party which rallied support among provincial oligarchs. The Roca government facilitated business interests and welcomed European migrants, over three million of whom arrived between 1880 and 1910, constituting almost half the total population of the country. European immigration to Argentina slowed down during the First World War, but speeded up in the 1920s, when 900,000 more people arrived.

The combination of genocide and mass European immigration created a nation without roots or a common identity, constantly looking abroad for legitimacy.

Family life

As the federal government completed the bloody conquest of rural Argentina, lands were distributed to immigrant farmers, who paid the State an annual rent on the property. The Walsh family worked their plot of land in Choele-Choel as Dora Gill carried her second child, Carlos Washington, whose birth in 1922 coincided with the rising flood waters of the Rio Negro. The family farm was swept away and with it any hope of surviving on subsistence crops.

They were rescued by Victor Molina, rancher and politician, who offered Rodolfo's father Miguel a job as foreman on his sheep farm, called Saint Genevieve. The landowners visited only once a year, and it was the delight of Dora Gill, who craved 'good' company. The spacious ranch had fruit trees in the garden, a nearby river and a dozen horses to get around its 15,000 hectares. The Walsh family moved in and occupied several rooms in the elegant residence. Miguel Walsh was responsible for six full-time employees, while another two dozen workers were hired at shearing time.

Rodolfo's father was a quiet, introverted man, without formal education but with a great knowledge of crops and horses. His greatest pleasures were gambling and horses, the twin passions which would bring the family to ruin and take him to an early grave. Dora Gill constantly needled her husband over his lack of interest in literature and read to all her children at an early age. Irish settlers felt the lack of books available and often chaplains brought travelling libraries on their pastoral visits. The reading paid off with Rodolfo; at eight years of age he entertained fellow pupils in the school infirmary with his retelling of *Les Miserables*, chapter by chapter, each evening.

Dora pestered her husband to read books, but he preferred to spend his spare time with his horses. "One night after several conjugal disputes," Rodolfo wrote many years later, "Miguel gave in and accepted a new bet." Dora triumphantly delivered a book into Miguel's hands, challenging him to finish it. He picked it up, turned the first few pages, became absorbed and devoured the whole thing in three days. "It was the only book he would ever read," recalled Walsh. It was *The Gambler* by Dostoevsky.

Rodolfo's father enjoyed regular evening card games around a table shared with the local police chief, train driver and doctor. In a small isolated hamlet at the end of the country's railway line, the card-playing trio constituted a formidable power bloc.

The nearest town was Choele-Choel, connected by railway to the country's larger cities, as wool, fruit and cereals travelled out of the province and casual labourers drifted in.

Rodolfo's birth

Rodolfo Jorge Walsh was born on January 9th 1927. His mother wanted to call him Valentino after the great Russian actor, the toast of Buenos Aires at the time. It took the stubborn refusal of Rodolfo's father to persuade Dora otherwise. In the first five years of his life, Rodolfo enjoyed country life to the full, an adventurous, healthy and happy child, running wild with the children of other farm workers.

On October 28th 1934 Rodolfo received his first holy communion, dressing up formally for the occasion. Dora was loving and attentive to her sons but unhappy at finding herself in a remote corner of the provinces. The long-awaited daughter, Kitty, was born in 1935, the last of the five Walsh children.

Between Choele-Choel village and Victor Molina's ranch lay Lamarque, a handful of dusty streets, once the proud territory of native indians, since banished or massacred in extermination raids. Lamarque, home to about 500 people, would have fitted comfortably inside Molina's ranch several times over. The Saint Genevieve could only be reached by *balsa*, a wooden raft which could carry two hundred sheep in one go, the given measure of transport at the time. Foot passengers and an occasional car also found their way onto the island, but horseback was the most effective means of getting around.

The Walsh family enjoyed a decent income on the ranch, allowing Rodolfo's mother to read foreign magazines, dream of Europe and indulge her good taste by ordering clothes once a year from the prestigious Harrods department store in Buenos Aires.

In 1932, a city entrepreneur convinced Rodolfo's father to start his own *chacra*[8] in Juárez, a village in Buenos Aires province. The *chacareros* were small farmers with individual plots, who grew grains and raised a few animals. Miguel invested his savings in a small landholding, with crops rather than animals, producing wheat, flax and barley.

If the *chacarero* venture went well, the Walshes would increase their landholding and eventually employ others to administer the farm. The dream of prosperity was soon shattered as the entire country suffered one recession after another during the depression years. Rodolfo's father continued to labour at the farm but freak heavy winds carried everything away in 1936. The Walsh family left the land in 1937, moving to the nearby town of Azul, where Rodolfo's father fruitlessly scoured the town for work. It was the last year the entire family spent together.

Rodolfo's mother Dora was minded to play an occasional game of poker with her husband, for a few pennies at a time, but Miguel turned more seriously to chance as a means of improving his fortune. Even during the years on Victor Molina's ranch, Rodolfo's father sent away to Buenos Aires for lottery tickets, which arrived back on the daily train. By the time the family moved to a rented house in Azul, bankruptcy was imminent.

"My grandmother, the fool, paid off all her husband's debts, ending up penniless," recalled Héctor Walsh, Rodolfo's younger brother, musing over family history on the threshold of the twenty-first century. Héctor, aged 70 (b.1929), lives with his wife in a modest apartment in the resort town of Pinamar, 400 km from Buenos Aires, where he moved in 1958. Rodolfo and Héctor spent their formative years together, first in boarding school, then in cheap digs in Buenos Aires, where they began their working lives. Rodolfo nicknamed him *El Tahur*, the Gambler, as he kept up the passion which coursed through two previous generations of his family.

One fateful day in 1937, a year Rodolfo baptised "the year of misfortune", the Walsh household was invaded by bailiffs and auctioneers, who sold off every stick of furniture in the house, and left them, literally, on the street. "It was a terrible thing to watch," added Rodolfo's older brother Carlos, recalling the day which ended in the sale of the family furniture, as beds, chairs and the kitchen table, lovingly picked out by his

---

[8] A small farm.

mother, mercilessly went under the hammer.

Rodolfo, who was just ten years old, retained a vivid memory of the sudden downturn in family fortunes: "The decisive change in my life came when my father ceased to be the foreman on a ranch and became a *chacarero* and finally an unemployed labourer," Rodolfo told an interviewer in 1969. "I had been on the horse's back until then, in class terms. I belonged to a comfortable, bourgeois home until 1930. Back then the ranch foreman was a powerful figure, especially in Rio Negro."

The Walsh family responded to the crisis by splitting up, sending the four boys away while Kitty, still an infant, stayed with her parents. Miguel and Carlos, the two oldest boys, were dispatched to the home of their grandmother Katie Dillon, in Buenos Aires, where they continued their schooling. Rodolfo and Héctor, the younger boys, aged ten and eight years respectively, were sent to the *Capilla del Señor*, a boarding school run by nuns. The regime at the school came as a shock to the Walsh brothers but would soon be remembered as an easy ride compared to what awaited them in the Fahy Institute.

Childhood memories, 1937

Nineteen thirty six was the year of decline. It began with an auction and ended with an exodus, a secret wave of panic. My father had the bad luck to strike out on his own in the middle of a crisis. In 1932 he left his job as a ranch foreman in Rio Negro for a rented plot of land in Juárez and a house rented in the town. We were the reason for the move, we four children who would be five when my sister was born. We had to be educated. The demand – which he accepted unenthusiastically – came from my mother. In four years we were ruined. Then came the auction and the move, in virtual secrecy, to Azul, where we lost the little that remained: the piano and the car.

All this happened suddenly. They barely had time to see us safely dispersed. My two older brothers went to grandmother's house in Buenos Aires; the smallest stayed with our parents in a hotel on Calle Moreno; they didn't know what to do with us. Héctor was eight, I was ten. Someone told them that there was an Irish school for orphans and the poor in Capilla del Señor. My father took us. I remember the day: April 5th 1937.

The changes were so fast and so violent that they continue to surprise me, even today. Everything was bad, absurd and wrong. The first problem arose with the clothes which my mother had hastily got together, spending her last pesos.The school list said "overalls" and she understood and bought grey dungarees instead of a smock. When Miss Annie, in charge of the dormitory, called us into her office, we found her snorting contemptuously with anger and disdain, beside the open suitcases.

"What an idiot!" she kept saying, "What a country bumpkin."

She slobbered, her lips pursed, glasses sliding forward on her drooping face, with the same expression as old Te Mazawattee when her granddaughter broke the china.

I had never heard anyone speak about my mother that way. As the years passed, the difference between "overalls" and "smock" became a semantic one for me, as a translator. I reached for the Webster every time one of these words appeared. Back then I didn't speak English and I was in no position to prove that Miss Annie was the ignorant one.

The second confrontation came that night in the canteen. There I found the plate of semolina destined by providence to accompany me for years. A zinc plate, its immutable contents, a white circle, desert-like, covered by a tepid white scab. Salt of the soul, the rotting face of charity for two hundred nights of identical disinterest. I refused, I didn't eat. I refused the second night, then the third and the fourth. I recall the visceral rejection, the enemy hunger, the increasing astuteness at work in the knowledge that a battle was on. What I mean is, I pretended outwardly what I felt within – nostalgia, desperation – but exaggerating it, taking it to the limit, until I became a silent spectacle, arms crossed before the unacceptable.

On the fourth or fifth night they brought me a bowl of soup and a potato. It may not have been better than the semolina but I accepted it, I felt I had won and deep inside I laughed at the rosy-cheeked nun who presided over the canteen. From that night on there were one hundred and nine plates of semolina and one bowl of soup with a potato.

Beneath this authority there were other issues to settle. In the two Irish schools in which I have been, I discovered among the pupils a compulsive need to establish different levels of prestige, courage and strength. Behind the conventional reception of the first day, they were measuring me, slotting me tentatively into the hierarchy.

I suppose the hierarchy was inherited from year to year, with the necessary adjustments made when classes restarted. I had arrived late, the adjustments had been made, I interrupted the established order, provoking anxiety, an urgent need to know who I was, and so, without wanting it, I came face to face with Cassidy, in the backyard sun, a circle of people around me, to fight for the mythical third place which he occupied up until my arrival.

The first two were untouchables. Delamer, big, good-natured, inoffensive due to the general awareness of his strength; an old whale who no one dared challenge, nor did he himself think about it too much, a dark patriarch of eleven or twelve years of age. Delaney, who wasn't that big, a political creation, partly conjecture, partly the influence of his sister the caretaker, a sweet rose-coloured girl, desirable to the boys over five.

So we fought. Cassidy's face was covered in spots, it was painful to hit him. But there was no other way out. I beat him and took my place in the hierarchy, giving me the right to terrorise or protect the younger boys and the healthy right to abstain from bothering the stronger ones. I didn't challenge anyone for the rest of the year and no one challenged me, but an occasional triumphant act of rebellion exposed the semi-mythological nature of the ranking system.

The true winner of my first fight was Miss Annie. Someone told her about it and that night, when we went to bed, she came over to the bed and told me to take off the blankets. She held her favourite argument in her hand, a stick of solid, flexible bamboo. She gave me one hell of a beating. The next day my body was covered in bruises.

The hidings she administered under different pretexts were Miss Annie's nightly pleasure. I suppose her nights were sad when she was unable to re-establish the empire of justice with her bamboo stick. She was a miserable old sadist. I'm laughing as I write this, thirty years on, but it's the truth.

Miss Annie was not an oddball. The prefects and even the nuns beat us too. I remember the swing to the cheek with which sister Maria Angela decked Kelly beside the blackboard, in the middle of the class. It was a clean blow, brilliant; although it's also true that Kelly was very small and maybe quite weak.

All of this was quite disturbing. I wasn't hit at home, apart from an occasional clip on the ear. In Juárez I attended a religious school for three years. The nuns were Italian, fascist and ignorant, but they never punished us. At most they suggested we offer up some absurd mortifications to Christ. Outside of that they were affectionate and almost sweet. I suppose the difference was that that was a fee-paying school while in Capilla we were sons of small farmers and the unemployed.

In the midst of all these trials and tribulations, the greatest disaster of all hardly bothered me. I finished third grade in Azul, but in Capilla they didn't have fourth grade. The logical thing would have been to send me to Fahy school in Moreno, a priest-run school from fourth to sixth grade, but apparently my parents didn't check it out in time in those chaotic days in which our home fell apart. I had to repeat the year and Maria Angela's classes were one long exercise in tedium, apart from her occasional pugilistic showpieces.

The English classes, in contrast, fired me with enthusiasm. I was deeply fond of Mrs T. I think she was a widow with children who were separated from her. Her situation was like our own, uprooted. I see her now as a woman of thirty or forty years of age, sand-coloured hair, a broad nose, clear eyes. Not a particularly attractive face but a strong one. She had an innate sweetness, but on the outside she was cutting and sarcastic.

She was amazed that I didn't have a word of English, when my grandmother (she imagined) hadn't even learned to say hello in Spanish. And she would imitate my grandmother, without much success, as she had never met her, but with such imagination that she cracked me up. I worked hard to reply to her sarcasms. In two weeks I was at the top of the class, and in a month she admitted that I ought to move on to the following grade. A bitter triumph, which ended in separation.

Mrs T's affections were the centre of dispute in this desert, unfortunately. I suppose she missed her children and replaced them with ourselves. There were too many of us. Preferences emerged, and a fight developed, a replica of the competition for prestige, but I was prepared to go further in this case, unwilling to accept an external imposition.

My rival was a very handsome, innocent boy, younger than me. He was called O'Neill, a name for kings and heroes, and not only was he in Mrs T's class but he was in the dormitory she was in charge of while I suffered under Miss Annie's cane. I don't remember how I broke the rules of the game, I imagine I humiliated O'Neill in public. The next time I saw her (Mrs T) during recreation, she wouldn't speak to me. For days she walked by me as if she didn't see me. Afterwards I locked myself into a classroom and cried desperately until she came in, hugged me and consoled me as best she could. It was a reconciliation, but also an end. I gradually moved away from her without ceasing to love her.

My new English teacher, Miss Jennie, was an exceptionally beautiful girl, and somewhat stupid. In order to motivate us in life she drew heaven and hell on a big white card: above, to the left, was God the father, his floating beard and open arms; below, to the right, Satan shouted his head off among horrible flames.

In the space between, a group of twenty or thirty doves made their way, pricked with pins. We were the doves, and each of them carried one of our names and witnessed our progress and our failure, up toward heaven or downward to hell. It didn't take me long to take the lead in the celestial flotilla and I was touching the Creator's skirts when I committed some horrible crime, which I have forgotten. My dove fell head first into the fire. Doubting perhaps that the moral lesson would be enough, Miss Jennie decided to complement it with a physical one. She made me put my hand out and with one of those long black rulers, with the steel tips, she began to hit me on the knuckles, slowly, powerfully and methodically, counting each blow.

I think that if I had shouted, taken my hand away or curled up one of my fingers, the punishment would have stopped. But all I did was look at her and that drove her insane, tied her in knots and made her keep going. When she said "Ten!" and I felt the last ruler blow on the numbed knuckles, the lesson was complete. I had lost all respect for her: the story on the card wasn't a true representation of what happened, it was false, a version of heaven and hell which allowed it to be used against us. From then on my relationship with Miss Jennie was purely formal, based on disruptiveness and disrespect.

All these things happened in the first weeks. They were an initiation. Afterwards you got used to it, you didn't get caught out in visible sins. The absence of further anecdotes suggests I made a total retreat and the clearest symptom of that isolation is that I lost sight of my younger brother. I know he was with me, but I can barely remember him there or the things that happened. I didn't make friends, I was an outsider.

We didn't leave the school all year, not even to get to know the town. There it is, impassive, the building, the chapel where we attended mass, the bare trees whose roots swelled the yard, yellow floor tiles where we played marbles or *payana*, the grey smocks, the night-time whistle of the trains going back to my home. I don't know of a sadder sound than that.

One Sunday my father came to see us. They let us go to the field beside the school, to sit on the grass. He opened a package, took out bread and salami and ate with us. I suspected he was hungry and not just from that day. He talked football, Moreno, Labruna, Pedernera; he and I were fans of River.[9] Maybe he spoke about politics. He was a radical.[10] The first bad word I heard in the house was Uriburu. Then came others, like Fresco, Pinedo, Justo. I think that somehow I identified them with our circumstances, with the plate of semolina. We were happy for the longest time, although I sensed he was sad, anxious for us to tell him that we were well. And yes, we were well. Afterwards I found out how bad things were going for them. In reality he was down, unable to find work.

One day in November or December they came to get us. It's odd, but I don't remember it, maybe because I had waited so long for the moment. There were other changes, good and bad. Happiness wasn't lost for good; but it had to be treated with caution, never complaining when it suddenly disappeared. I began to get a taste of the era, and that was for the best. Without that you could go straight to hell, no longer mounted on a dove, but carrying a donkey on your back.

➥ (Walsh, 1996)

---

[9] River Plate, one of Argentina's most successful football clubs.
[10] A member or supporter of the political party Unión Cívica Radical, UCR.

chapter two

The end of innocence

The world breaks everyone and afterward many are strong at the broken places.
But those that will not break it kills. It kills the very good and the very gentle and
the very brave impartially.

(Ernest Hemingway, *A Farewell to Arms,* Chapter 34)

Fahy Institute

The large entrance gives way to a curving path shaded by overhanging
poplars and oak trees before reaching a grey building with a red-tiled roof
and green shutters. The bright colours fail to lift the bleak, austere
atmosphere of the place. Welcome to the Fahy Institute, founded and run
by Irish Pallotine fathers from 1930 to the day I arrived in December
1998. The supply of priests had dried up and the last Irishman, Fr Joe
Campion, was packing his bags. The school is located in Moreno, outside
Buenos Aires city limits, and has an elegant ornate chapel with football
and hurley fields attached, along with a small farm.

In the hallway of the Fahy school hangs a plaque to the founding
matrons, the Ladies of Saint Joseph, a charitable group that owns the
school and the 70 acres of surrounding land. Opposite the plaque is a
portrait of the mighty Father Fahy himself, gravely sizing up each new
boy as he stepped through the front door. Fr Fahy was a Dominican
priest, the first chaplain to the Irish community in Argentina, where he
became an influential figure in local politics.

The entrance hall leads into a courtyard the size of a football field,
where the cries of one hundred and thirty boys echoed across the school
at lunchtime each day. Tall, arched pillars punctuate the long corridors
facing onto the square. Classrooms, library and cobweb-ridden store-
rooms lead off from the quadrangle, while the tiny first-aid room still
houses the school records, a collection of yellowing documents dating
back to 1930.

Rodolfo and his brother Héctor, aged eleven and nine respectively, travelled by train with their father to Buenos Aires in March 1938, stopping off at their grandmother Katie Dillon's home, where they spent the night; they would later recall her faltering Spanish and how she would sing Irish ballads to her grandchildren. Her husband, Juan Merrin, spoke only English.

"It seemed like an adventure at first," said Héctor to me decades later, the prospect of new friends at a new school. The day after the two boys arrived at Fahy all thoughts of adventure ended, and the fight for survival began. The strict regimentation of boarding school life contrasted sharply with their early years in the rambling freedom of Lamarque. The boys discovered that they had to establish their place in the pupils' league of toughness, taking on fellow classmates with their fists. Héctor lived off Rodolfo's reputation as a willing fighter, enjoying the protection it afforded him among the boys. "If anyone wanted to start on me, they had to fight Rodolfo first," recalled Héctor, with evident relief.

Sixty years after the Fahy experience, Héctor Walsh's voice still bore traces of bitterness: "It was a military regime, the priests were complete bastards," he said. The boys were roused at 6 a.m., with a cold shower followed by mass. They drank *mate cocido*[12] for breakfast, then scrubbed floors and toilets, or cleaned up the dining room area. The food was "precarious and badly cooked", prompting extended and inadvertent fasts. "We used to pocket the food, put it in our smocks, then throw it away afterwards," recalled Héctor, still angry at the treatment inflicted on the young boys. The day's classes began at 8 a.m., continuing until lunch break at midday. Rodolfo played hurling and football at recreation time or engaged in an occasional round of boxing, until 1.30 p.m. Then came English classes, delivered by the Irish priests.

The arbitrary cruelty of the Pallotines obliged Rodolfo to face the reality of the harsh world beyond home and family, thrust into a strange and threatening world. The boys had just one outing each year, to the city zoo, while a handful of parents visited their children each Sunday, bringing vital food packages, which were consumed or traded.

The slightest transgression was punished with zeal, and sentences ranged from five or six pages of English text, to be learned by heart (all breaks suspended in the meantime), to several hours spent kneeling on the flagstoned courtyard floor. The gravest transgressions of school order were punished by a sentence of twenty-four hours locked inside an empty room, without food or water.

The boys felt more abandoned than afraid. "What am I doing here?" Héctor often asked himself, "when there is a school 300 metres away at home, and the headmistress is my mother's best friend?"

---

[12] A type of green tea popular in Argentina.

Irish boys after a cat

excerpt from Los Oficios Terrestres

The boy they later called 'the cat' appeared unannounced and unintroduced against the north wall of the playground, during the last break before dinner. No one knew how long he had been curled up beside the corridor window which connected the cloisters. He had no business being there because it was late April and classes had been on for a whole month, swallowing up the last light of an annoying autumn marked by long, boring periods of rain. It was growing dark and the courtyard was huge, eating up the very heart of the enormous building built in the 1910s by charitable Irish ladies.

The dusk, then, and the huge space which even 130 pupils caught up in their games were unable to fill, probably explains why no one saw him before. That and the dark nature of the new arrival, which gave him a distant, camouflaged appearance, his grey face and smock against the smudge of the wall farthest away from the dining hall meant that, numbly, the marbles, the hide-and-seek, the chat had carried on for the previous twenty minutes.

The boy seemed sick, his face was like an immature lemon with a sprinkling of ash. He hadn't turned twelve yet, deathly thin, and the first to approach him noticed his eyes shone brilliantly. He had a curious, unnatural way of moving, sudden bursts and sparks of passion, whatever it was, mixed with the most subtle slipperiness and evasiveness of a sinous body.   ➥ (Walsh, 1965 pp.71–2)

Lessons in life

The boys went home each summer (December to March in Argentina), basking in the freedom of the countryside, riding horses, swimming in the river, breaking loose after months of rigid discipline. The reluctant pupils led a chorus of protest against Fahy when the holidays came to an end, but it was fruitless, as Dora Gill determined that her boys would receive an education which would leave them ahead of the pack, with favourable career prospects.

It was not the absence of a local school which meant sending the Walsh children to Fahy. There was a school just three streets away from the Walsh home, yet Dora Gill wouldn't entertain the notion of sending her boys there, insisting that they be educated in English by Irish priests. "She had delusions of grandeur," recalled Héctor, speaking at a café in Pinamar beach resort. "She thought that the locals weren't up to our level, so she sent us hundreds of kilometres away to a worse school."

The years at Fahy left lasting marks, physical and mental, on both

Rodolfo and Héctor, who held the experience against their mother. "As a teenager I couldn't stay in the house longer than an hour, I felt like a caged animal," said Héctor, recalling the claustrophobic effect of life inside the school.

Rodolfo's inattentiveness in class drove the priests to distraction, but he never slipped up on the academic front. "He sat there all day, drawing war planes," said Héctor. "He was somewhere else." The priests would ask him a question on something they had just been studying, expecting to catch him out. "Rodolfo responded with three times more information than he had been asked for," chuckled Héctor.

The most important day of the year for the Fahy boys was not the annual outing to the zoo but the yearly visit by the Ladies of Saint Joseph, the aristocratic philanthropists who paid for the upkeep of the school. "Everything was first class that day," recalled Héctor, as fresh roast, scones, sweets and other unthinkable treats passed before the eyes of the astonished pupils.

The annual visit occurred on Corpus Christi, in early June, when a dozen women would stroll around the institute, listening to the pupils answer questions from a visiting bishop, "wanting to see everything at once, tenderly stroking the reddest head, or the blondest, asking strange questions, like what finally happened to Brian Boru when he prayed with his back to the battlefield?" recounted Walsh in his short story "Earthly Responsibilities", one of a three-part "Irish series".

Walsh described the food served up during the Ladies' visit: "The first person came in leading a team of six who served up the food, Dolan, with a tray of meat so big he could hardly carry it, and behind him came the others, with fresh trays of meat and mountains of bean salad [...] There was enough food to keep us alive for a week," noted Walsh, narrating the course of events through the wide-eyed gaze of the astonished pupils. The crowning moment came when fizzy cola bottles appeared, giving rise to "a spontaneous reaction by the people" who "rose up in a sudden wave from the white tables, acclaiming the dear Ladies".

Bishop Usher closed the festivities by praising the boys for the discipline and good order evident in their pristine turnout. "And that's as it should be, because none of us were born to a velvet cradle, and every honourable man must learn his earthly responsibilities, and the earlier the better, to be independent in life and earn the bread he puts in his mouth."

The bishop's closing words were accompanied by a general but mute panic, as each boy scrambled to pocket the remains of the *asado*, wrapping up lumps of meat in napkins, bits of paper or shoved straight into pockets, "ruining more than one Sunday suit". The afternoon waned and the inevitable departure of the Ladies occurred, "leaving us depressed and grey once more, superfluous and promiscuous, under the iron fist."

The speech by the visiting bishop proved prophetic on one count at least, as the years at Fahy gave Walsh a stubborn, determined independence and an ability to bear adverse circumstances with stoic pride. "Fahy came as a total shock to the two boys," recalled Carlos Walsh, five years Rodolfo's senior, who stayed with his grandmother in Buenos Aires on weekend breaks from his courses at a naval academy. Carlos remembered the tirade of abuse aimed at the Pallotine priests during holiday time. "Rodolfo was a very brave guy," said Carlos, "he would take anyone on." The lesson would stay with Rodolfo all his life, sustaining him through greater battles ahead. Carlos believed, however, that the very strength acquired from this experience would be the root of his future downfall. "To go from a normal life, in your home, with your family, to that college, it taught them to get by but it also destroyed them." Carlos considers Walsh's life a waste of genius, his literary career blocked by a "subversive instinct" born of resentment which began inside the Fahy Institute.

Curiously enough, from the opposite end of the ideological spectrum, Rodolfo's surviving daughter Patricia concurred with the former navy captain. "Rodolfo entered the world of politics the day he walked into Fahy," she said. The school provided a test of wills, where Rodolfo triumphed, giving him a solid footing for the days of combat ahead.

"The downside were the thumps," summed up Carlos, "the positive side was that they became tough enough to get by anywhere in the world."

The exam results from the end of Rodolfo's first year attested to the rigour and intelligence of the young pupil. Not only did he jump up a grade but he had also scored the highest marks in almost every subject on the curriculum, notably history, languages, mathematics, writing and reading skills, religion, physics, agricultural studies, zoology, geology, manual work and physical exercise. Most of the class were a year or two older than him. Rodolfo's lowest marks were for drawing and singing, hinting at a source of future disappointment. Five years after Rodolfo left Fahy he sat entrance exams for navy school but failed his drawing test, ending a youthful ambition to become an officer like his brother Carlos.

In his first year at Fahy Rodolfo didn't miss an hour of class, scoring 200 straight days of study, while in his second year he missed four days due to unspecified illness. Rodolfo had now turned thirteen, completing his first year of secondary school. He maintained his high marks, slipping slightly in physical education, which came as no surprise to friends, who testified to his clumsiness.

The Fahy experience ended in March 1940 when Rodolfo walked out of the drab institution for the last time, transferring to the Belgrano

Institute, in Buenos Aires city centre, joined once more by Héctor, who called the regime "totally different", a huge relief to the boys.

Former classmates complain that Rodolfo was unfair in his literary treatment of school life at Fahy. After all, they say, the Walsh brothers got a free education. It is not a widely held view, as Michael Geraghty of the Argentinian Joyce Society attests: "If it wasn't for Walsh, the Fahy Institute would be unknown."

By 1939 Miguel Walsh had recovered from the gambling debts which saw all the family possessions come under the auctioneer's hammer and his children spread to the four winds two years previous. The precarious days in Azul town, two hundred kilometres south of the capital, where the Walsh family reached complete financial ruin, had given way to happier times in Juan Blacquier, a large estate named after its owner, one of Argentina's wealthiest men. Miguel was hired as a foreman, quickly winning the trust of Blacquier, an absentee owner who rewarded his competent employee with a highly prized Ford Model T car in 1940.

After Fahy the two brothers studied in Buenos Aires and spent each Saturday with their grandmother, returning to the school on Sunday night. "It was our refuge," recalled Héctor, who enjoyed the family reunion of sorts: Miguel, the oldest brother lived in the same house and Carlos came to stay at weekends.

At the Belgrano Institute, Rodolfo tired of the academic life and hungered for a taste of the real world. On November 12th 1942, he asked to see school head Lachica Campoy and proposed that he study third year by himself and sit the exams the following month. "Impossible," said the head, nobody could cram a year's study into one month. The challenge was accepted when Walsh pledged he would repeat the entire year if he failed. Campoy chided Walsh for wasting his parents' money on a losing bet, but Rodolfo's instincts told him otherwise. "Let's make a deal," he said, "if I pass the exams I don't pay any fees," and the director agreed. A month later, at fifteen years of age, Rodolfo scored 10 in every subject bar one, a mere nine, perhaps in his Achilles' heel – drawing (Author's interview with Patricia Walsh).

The teenage Rodolfo finally broke the family's poor track record in the business of gambling.

Rodolfo stayed on at school for another year, finished his fourth year exams then left before completing his secondary education. He took up a job as an administrator on a farm in San Luis province, a job he got thanks to the father-in-law of his older brother Miguel. His employer never paid him for the work, and Rodolfo was soon back in Buenos Aires, anxious to find employment. A series of odd jobs followed, as Rodolfo moved into a downtown bedsit, washing dishes and cleaning windows to get by.

In 1944, at the age of seventeen, Rodolfo's life took a new and significant turn, when he acquired a job as a proofreader with the French publishing house Hachette, located in 745 Calle Alsina, in the heart of Buenos Aires.

Fahy today

The Fahy Institute seems frozen in time, back in the 1930s, with the same doors, windows, pipes, furniture and fittings. Fr Joe Campion accounted for the old world feel inside Fahy with a more practical explanation – not a penny had been spent on maintenance.

The tender but tight-fisted Ladies of Saint Joseph refused to invest any money in improvements for the school. The only new building inside the school was a gymnasium, funded after years of lobbying the school sponsors. The plan for the gymnasium was blocked at every turn until the priests got fed up waiting, dispensed with formalities and warned the charitable ladies that the boys were "doing things to each other" and needed an outlet for their physical energies. The money was immediately approved.

The Fahy Institute has two floors. Upstairs the dormitory stretches the length of one side of the building, ending in communal showers, twenty-four in all. Water drips constantly. The fittings are identical to the first day the school opened in 1930; the only concession to modern days is a boiler, hot water having replaced the cold water purgatory of yesteryear.

Downstairs are classrooms, reception rooms and a school library, renamed Rodolfo Walsh Library in 1997 in honour of the school's best-known pupil. In among the tomes on Benjamin Franklin and magazines like *Ecology Today* nestle Walsh's *Operación Masacre* and *Un Kilo de Oro*. A group of students read up Rodolfo's work in advance of the library inauguration and presented Walsh's daughter Patricia with a folder full of comments. "Rodolfo Walsh would have laughed his head off at the cover, it's great!" responded an emotional Patricia, impressed at the pupils' work. The cover bore the author's name, written in dripping red ink, an artistic tribute to Walsh's passion for detective stories and tales of the supernatural.

Not everyone agreed with the tribute to Walsh. At least two parents threatened to withdraw their children from the Fahy Institute if Rodolfo's name was honoured. Parents sent their children to school with old photos of police and soldiers maimed in guerrilla attacks. History is bracingly fresh in Argentina, where living memory repudiates the dictatorship but where the letter of the law grants equal status to repressors and victims.

chapter three

Earthly responsibilities

Rodolfo turned reality into his greatest work.
(poem by Mario Benedetti, Baschetti 1994, pp.322–3)

Military in power

Rodolfo's arrival in Buenos Aires in the 1940s coincided with a lengthy period of military rule which began in 1930, bringing General José F Uriburu to power. The nation's fragile civilian institutions crumbled before six hundred cadets and nine hundred soldiers, along with two trucks and six cars, thoughtfully provided by US transnational Packard. In what would become a familiar mantra to Walsh and his peers, the military dissolved parliament for "reasons so notorious they require no explanation," setting the tone for military uprisings which dominated the nation's history during the twentieth century. The Uriburu coup primarily served cattle ranchers, displaced from power during the presidential rule of Hipólito Yrigoyen (1914–28), a democratic reformist who belonged to the *Unión Cívica Radical*, UCR (Radical Civic Union).

The military enjoyed the support of conservatives impressed with the rise of Italian dictator Benito Mussolini. The newly created Special Section of the Federal Police specialised in torture, led by Leopoldo Lugones, who left his sad mark on the nation's history by introducing the *picana*, the electric baton, as a routine instrument of police interrogation.

The coup leaders held elections in April 1931 but the "wrong" side won so the nationalists simply called fresh elections for November of that year and applied what was called "patriotic fraud" to ensure victory for their candidate, General Agustín P Justo. Argentina's armed forces now constituted "a social class of its own, a country within another" (Ortiz, 1997 p.62).

The government passed legislation to improve the lot of the nation's large producers; the beef-led economy was seriously threatened by

Britain's decision to favour domestic production in the 1930s, forcing Argentina's new rulers to sign an agreement that gave Britain control over Buenos Aires public transport in return for buying Argentinian beef exports. The Second World War provided an unforeseen boost to the Argentinian economy, with European nations snapping up all available beef, ushering in a decade of economic expansion.

In 1944 a young colonel, Juan Domingo Perón, was appointed head of the National Labour Department, which he elevated to ministerial level. From there he began building alliances with the national labour movement. Perón had worked as an Argentinian military attaché in Mussolini's Italy in the 1930s, and had been impressed with Il Duce's "organised community".

The new military government, pressured by the Allies who bought most from Argentina, finally declared war on Germany and Japan in January 1944, taking advantage of the subsequent emergency legislation to repress opposition forces and confiscate "enemy property".

Speedy industrial growth during the war years created a working-class population of 1.2 million people in Buenos Aires alone, a new social sector lacking political representation; union membership climbed from 400,000 in 1941 to 1.5 million in 1947 and 3 million in 1951.

Street politics

Rodolfo's Irish ancestry and his experience in the Fahy Institute had equipped him with a street-fighting sensibility and a strong anti-English political bias, leading him to the Alianza Libertadora Nacionalista, ALN (Nationalist Liberation Alliance), between 1944 and 1945. The organisation was nationalist, anti-English, anti-communist and anti-semitic, attracting dozens of teenagers who would later make a mark on their nation's history.

"I didn't give a hoot about the latter," wrote Rodolfo in later years, referring to the Alianza's anti-semitism, "but I cared a lot about the former," referring to its anti-imperialist line. "Back then it was a youth thing," explained his brother Héctor. "You were in the Alianza or you were with the communists." Héctor worked two streets away from Calle Florida, where frequent street battles occurred between communists and nationalists who gathered at the Alianza headquarters.

Rodolfo quickly settled into his new life in Buenos Aires, enjoying the independence that came with his proofreading job and the room he rented in the bustling city centre. He lived by night, according to Héctor, once more his trusty ally, sharing a musty one-room flat in 474 Calle Lima, since demolished to make way for the giant Avenida 9 de Julio. Life was hard and there was little entertainment, his wages barely enough to cover his food and board. Rodolfo attended Alianza meetings each weekend in support of Perón, still only a rising star, who used his platform at the Social Welfare Ministry to consolidate a broad nationalist alliance between the working class, the military and the church.

Rogelio García Lupo, a close friend of Walsh's throughout his life, first glimpsed the writer at an Alianza meeting in 1945. García Lupo was fourteen years of age, while Rodolfo had already turned eighteen. "There were courses on economics and political ideas," recalled Rogelio, who met Rodolfo on an elementary economics course given by Cecilio Morales, who later became Argentina's representative to the Organisation of American States (OAS). "It was a feeling, not an ideology," he said. "We all sensed that this was a defining time in Argentinian history."

"The Alianza was the best invention of nazism in Argentina," reflected a mature Walsh, years later. "Today it seems certain that the leaders were paid a salary by the German embassy." Roberto Queralto, the Alianza leader, was "a comic type, simplistic, violent, lacking any finesse." Walsh conceded that the Alianza represented "the exaggeration of a legitimate sentiment" which soon was to find massive public expression in Peronism.

Perón to power

Argentina's traditional parties, conservative and progressive alike, felt threatened by the growing influence of the ambitious army colonel who had become War Minister. They demanded his dismissal and trial at a public rally held on October 9th 1945. Perón was subsequently arrested and held on an island off the coast of Buenos Aires.

The workers whose rights he had championed in the previous year downed tools and led by Eva Duarte, Evita, marched on the city centre, with hundreds of thousands of people converging on the Plaza de Mayo, in front of the presidential palace, on October 17th 1945.

In what became a watershed in the nation's history, the marginalised, forgotten, trampled-down masses, disparagingly referred to as *cabezitas negras* (literally black heads, alluding to their darker complexion), engaged their leader in a mass "dialogue", a vital pulse-taking exercise which cemented Perón's connection with the dispossessed.

Perón was gifted with remarkable political intuition and made his boldest gamble yet, agreeing to compete in democratic elections; his opponents put forward a unity candidate, pitting conservatives, radicals, communists, socialists and progressive democrats against Perón, who enjoyed church and military support, the advantage of State machinery and, above all, the hitherto invisible working classes.

On February 24th 1946 Perón swept into power, winning 52 per cent of the votes cast, decisively altering the course of the nation's history. Perón's wife Evita quickly established herself as a living legend, distributing State resources to the poor, styling herself mother of the nation. Five years later Perón consolidated his power, winning 62 per cent of votes in the presidential elections held in 1951.

Perón implemented sweeping social reforms for workers, who for the first time became political actors in a system which had permanently excluded and ignored them, enjoying paid holidays, health care and pensions, and above all, dignity. Inspired by Italian fascism, he sought a strategy of class alliance rather than class war, where the wealthy elite would continue to control the economy but would concede benefits to workers to ensure social stability. In the immediate post-war years the social benefits hurt little thanks to the export boom which lasted through Perón's first period of government.

While Perón encouraged the growth of trades unions and university organisations, they were all expected to pledge unconditional loyalty to the *caudillo*,[11] or face shutdown. Opposition newspapers were closed, dissidents were tortured and jobs were distributed on the basis of affiliation to the Peronist movement.

Perón established corporativist control over the country's largest union, the Confederación General de Trabajadores, CGT (General Confederation of Workers). He returned strategic industries to national ownership, to widespread acclaim. His wife Evita looked after their support base through her Evita Foundation which distributed mattresses, bicycles, jobs or homes to the faithful.

"It would be wrong to describe the Perón era as a dictatorship," wrote Rodolfo in a letter dated 1957 to his penpal Donald Yates, a literature student based in Michigan, USA. "It was probably the most perfect modern example of demagogy, the tyranny of the plebeya." Walsh explained Argentina's political system after the coup which deposed Perón: "Under Perón the workers enjoyed freedom and democracy while the middle class, intellectuals, artists, journalists, and the upper classes felt oppressed. Now the exact same thing happens but in reverse. The 'elite' and the middle class feels perfectly free and very well represented; and as it is precisely the 'elite' who express themselves through books, the media and art, anyone watching from the outside would get the impression that the most perfect democracy prevails here. In contrast, however, nine out of ten workers wouldn't hesitate to say they live under a military dictatorship."

---

[11] Originally a 19th century military strongman; in the 20th century, commonly used to refer to some Latin American political leaders, some of whom have emerged from the military.

"The only military aspect of Perón was his uniform," continued Walsh, "and a certain braggadocio." Perón could have resisted the coup which finally toppled him in 1955, but he fled into exile instead. When he faced a failed military conspiracy earlier that year, he opted not to execute the leaders. "Perón is afraid of blood," opined Walsh, "in all his years of government only two political assassinations took place."

"Perón's extraordinary power was built on words, basically. And words cost him nothing. He gave the concept of the word a new dimension, almost palpable and capable of feeling." The caudillo's speeches lacked literary spark but when spoken the words acquired an undeniable force.

"From home to work and work to home," was Perón's slogan for the working class. The average Peronist was expected to turn up at the occasional public rally and cast a vote on election day. In return workers had a sympathetic ear for their demands in the highest circles of power and the short-term prospect of a mattress or a bicycle dispensed by Evita's solidarity network.

The shallowness of Perón's nationalist rhetoric became clear in 1947 when he signed the Chapultepec Acts which brought Argentina into line with US foreign policy objectives, with oil concessions ceded to US companies. Walsh and other supporters of the ALN protested noisily on the streets. Perón's betrayal ended Rodolfo's flirtation with right-wing nationalism and he welcomed the coup which overthrew him in 1955.

The translator

In his spare time Rodolfo played chess, supported River football club and obsessively read any newspaper, book or magazine he could get his hands on. His knowledge of English stood him in good stead, and he was taken on by Hachette publishers, to proofread and translate crime fiction. He often took his work to the elegant surroundings of the National Library, where first love surprised him while still a teenager.

Rodolfo worked his way up through every area of Hachette's publishing operation, graduating from proofreader to translator, editor, anthologist and finally published writer. One of Walsh's most acclaimed short stories, "Footnote", was inspired by his time inside Hachette. They published the crime fiction series *Evasión* and *Serie Naranja*, with Walsh translating novels by Ellery Queen, Patrick Quentin and William Irish.

Rodolfo's wages didn't last the month so he supplemented his income by working overtime on book translations, spending long hours in the National Library, absorbing the different styles of authors scattered around the globe. Walsh achieved a remarkable speed in translating novels, but went somewhat further than his mandate as an accurate translator. Two or three chapters of each book would arrive by post, which he would complete and return, then wait for the next instalment. During the translation of William Irish's novel *The Bride Wore Black* two chapters went missing in the post. Rather than hold up production, and risk losing income for that week, Walsh invented the missing chapters, then pieced together the plot when the following chapters arrived.

"I told him he was wasting his time translating other writers when he clearly had the talent to write his own stories," said Héctor, who recounted the story of his brother's "creative" translation work. Rodolfo wrote poetry, often in English, but would soon be stunned into silence by his encounter with a talent he believed far greater than his own.

María Isabel Orlando, known to her friends as Nene, was cramming for upcoming Latin and Greek exams when a young man sat opposite her, sending amused glances her way. "I noticed this boy watching me and having a great laugh at my expense," Nene recalled, some fifty years later. "What are you laughing at?" she asked. "Here I am translating cheap detective novels and you're working on Latin and Greek scholars," he replied. Within five minutes Rodolfo had told Nene that he had yet to complete his secondary school education, an issue which was clearly on his mind. "From that moment on we had great fun, he was always clowning around," she said.

Rodolfo and Nene began to meet regularly, going for walks along the *costanera*, the city centre river front, reading their verses to one another. Nene's parents were educated lower-middle-class bureaucrats, while Rodolfo was off the class radar, a youth without education and with little prospects of a career. Nene studied at night and worked by day, in public health administration.

Rodolfo described himself as a "writer of novels for poor people" and a penniless translator of thrillers with literary ambitions. "It hurts to remember the way he lived," said Nene. "His trousers were falling off him, his shoes stank, he didn't have a change of clothes, his money ran out before the end of the month, he looked like a wretch."

It was an innocent friendship, neither of the two daring to take the mutual attraction beyond an occasional kiss. Soon after we began to chat Nene asked me if the tape recorder was rolling and immediately launched into one of Rodolfo's poems, written for her in 1947, which she recited by heart in the original English.

"To love a memory
nothing else
to be anchored in the past
not to know peace ever
to hunt shadows

to be hunted at my turn
it is a cruel fate."

Nene's memory was impressive enough but then her 35-year-old daughter dropped by for lunch, and proceeded to recite Walsh's poetry herself. "These verses were part of my childhood," she recalled, a hint of Nene's lifelong attachment to Rodolfo. Nene's own poetry was accomplished and confident, overwhelming the lovestruck Rodolfo who retreated into silence. "I told him he was utterly ridiculous, I loved his work," said Nene, but there was no shifting "obstinate" Rodolfo, who immediately gave up writing.

Rodolfo entered Nene's poetry into a literary competition run by the Cámara Argentina del Libro (Argentinian Chamber of Books) using a pseudonym. "Rodolfo got the forms, filled them out, took them to the office and dropped them in for me," recalled Nene, who was astounded to learn that she had won first prize. "Rodolfo was over the moon," she recalled, but she was too shy to collect the prize. Rodolfo was having none of it and escorted her to the prize-giving ceremony, while he waited outside. When she emerged, she told Rodolfo that the secretary of the Chamber had put her at ease, a nice young man by the name of Julio Cortázar. He came out and greeted Rodolfo. "He was a giant, twice my size," said Nene of Cortázar, who stood six feet six inches.

"I suppose Rodolfo was in love with me," said Nene, who felt trapped by the conventions of the time and fearful of her parent's reaction to Walsh. "I felt that I was heading nowhere fast with him, he had no future." The three-year age difference, with Nene 22 and Rodolfo 19, also played a part in her decision to discount the prospect of a long-term relationship. "I was also looking for someone older, someone who had lived a bit more."

Those were conservative times in Argentina, when courtship rules were demarcated with strict discipline: "First we addressed each other as *usted* [the polite form of "you"] then we talked about books, then we held hands, then a kiss, then another kiss and it was back home by 8 p.m."

Rodolfo adored Nene and invented an Irish nickname, "Sheeka", which Rodolfo claimed was her name translated into Irish, although it may have been *chica*, "girl" in Spanish, pronounced in English. Nene never saw the inside of his bedsit, as Rodolfo always found some pretext to meet her elsewhere. "The look of the place was enough," said Nene, who described it as a "wretched and depressing dump." When Nene arrived at her doorstep with Rodolfo she would bid a discreet farewell under the watchful eyes of her parents.

Once inside the house she would raid the family fridge, go upstairs and open the balcony window. With the aid of a blue basket and a length of string she would lower down ham and cheese sandwiches to the hungry Rodolfo, who waited below. The grateful Walsh would remove the sandwiches and return the basket, sharing the food with younger brother Héctor. In addition to the sandwiches, Nene hoarded her brother's worn jumpers and coats, destined for charitable institutions, and gave them to Rodolfo and Héctor. "One night the two of them were standing outside the house," recalled Nene, "they looked terrible, skin and bone."

The basket is now a family heirloom, enjoying pride of place in the home of Nene's eldest daughter.

On August 7th 1947 Rodolfo's father died from injuries he received after falling from *Mar Negro,* his favourite horse. Rodolfo returned home but arrived too late to say goodbye. He said his own particular goodbye when he saved his father's beloved horse, riding it 200 kilometres to the McCormack family ranch, where relatives took care of it.

Rodolfo returned to Buenos Aires where he told Nene of his worries for his mother Dora, anxiously trying to figure out ways to help her face the future alone. At one point Rodolfo inquired into the possibility of inheriting his father's job as foreman but the ranch owners refused the offer and Dora moved to Buenos Aires, where she lived with Miguel, known as "Lito", her eldest son.

Rodolfo joined Nene in amateur theatre recitals of Greek tragedies, but his off-key voice shattered the chorus and Nene's admirers made him jealous. She soon began a relationship with another actor, to Rodolfo's deep disappointment. "He cried, he suffered a lot over it," said Nene. "He was very sentimental and affectionate."

Everything we know yet everything we hide
behind a harmless smile/behind a garden grey
everything alive within us/and everything is dead outside.

Rodolfo's last poem to Nene anticipated the inevitable separation. The two remained friends until Nene left Buenos Aires to take up a new job, in September 1949. She quickly met the man who would become her husband, an authoritarian academic ten years her senior who prohibited her from seeing any of her previous friends. She never forgot Rodolfo though. "Loving someone means remaining faithful to them in your heart," she said, in a wistful, nostalgic tone.

It took Rodolfo several months to get over the loss of Nene before he began seeing Elina María Tejerina, a literature student and also a friend of Nene's. Elina was 25 years old, three years older than Rodolfo, just like Nene, and studied languages and literature. The two met in the house of the acclaimed writer Jorge Luis Borges at a literary event in 1949.

They arranged to meet the following evening and Rodolfo recommenced the evening walks which combined poetry and a stroll along the river front. Elina Tejerina was a woman of vast intelligence, who fell in love with Rodolfo but found him impossible to introduce to her family, hard-working immigrants who placed a special emphasis on formal study. Walsh had left secondary school unfinished and appeared to have little hope of a career beyond translation work.

Elina finished her degree in literature and began taking a special course in teaching blind children, an area in which she quickly established herself as a leading specialist. The couple announced their decision to wed in March 1950, to the mild disapproval of both families. Elina was pregnant and the marriage was held in a registry office. The Tejerina family was still in mourning for their father, who had died several months previously. It was a wedding without a father-in-law on either side.

The newly married couple went to live in a cheap hotel then moved to Rio Cevallos, in Córdoba, northern Argentina, where Elina's family had a house. The move was shortlived as the young couple found themselves in isolated, depressing circumstances with Rodolfo surviving on the translations he sent back to Hachette publishers.

The Córdoba months were quickly forgotten when an opportunity for advancement appeared to Elina later in the year. Just before she gave birth to her first daughter, María Victoria, Elina was offered the post of director in a new school for the blind in La Plata (then named Eva Perón City) an hour away from Buenos Aires. The Walsh couple jumped at the opportunity.

The new house was spacious, with two large rooms dedicated to the young couple and a further ten reserved for boarding pupils. The school for the blind was located right beside La Plata's police station, a detail which held no particular significance for Rodolfo when he first arrived.

The couple's first daughter, named after Elina's grandmother, was born in September 1950, as Rodolfo finished off his secondary school exams and entered La Plata university, taking up literature studies. Elina was following the same course but was several years ahead. Walsh continued to travel frequently to Buenos Aires, delivering proofread texts and crime fiction novels, translated from the original English or French.

Rodolfo was writing his own fiction by now, finally overcoming the self-imposed silence.

Walsh left Hachette in December 1950 but still worked with them on a freelance basis. He pursued his own writing career, combining fiction with journalism. His short story "Las Tres Noches de Isaias Bloom" appeared in the literary magazine *Vea y Lea* on August 17th 1950. He was 23 years of age. The same story won a mention from the First Crime

Fiction Prize jury, a competition set up by *Vea y Lea* and Emece publishing house.

Vea y Lea was a pocket-size monthly magazine which published short stories and miscellaneous news. Rodolfo contributed quirky news items, most of them unsigned, posing a challenge to future Walsh enthusiasts who still trawl through back issues in search of hidden gems. Walsh also contributed to *Leoplán*, a US-style magazine which published crime fiction and stories of general interest. His contributions included a biographical reflection on Ambrose Bierce, "The Mysterious Death of a Mystery Writer" (4/3/53) and "The Return of Sherlock Holmes!" (20/5/53).

Rodolfo and Elina's second daughter Patricia was born in 1952, named after an independence hero from Walsh's ancestral land. Patricia was to be called Patricia Celeste (literally sky blue) in honour of the Argentinian flag, but the baptismal agents refused to recognise the name, and she was called Patricia Cecilia instead.

In 1953 Walsh edited the Hachette crime fiction anthology *Diez Cuentos Policiales Argentinos* (Ten Argentinian Detective Stories), the first such anthology ever published in the country. Walsh selected Borges, Bioy Casares, himself and others, offering a brief introduction to each writer. Walsh praised the "master" Borges, whose "La Muerte y la Brújula" (Death and the Compass) "constitutes the ideal of the genre, a purely geometric problem, with a concession to human frailty: the detective is the carefully chosen victim."

In the same year Walsh published his own *Variaciones en Rojo,* also with Hachette publishers. Walsh acknowledged that *Variaciones en Rojo* obeyed "a definite need in modern life, the need to escape from predictable, uniform, routine things". The main protagonist in Walsh's three crime fiction stories was Daniel Hernández, a humble proofreader and amateur detective who solves each crime mystery. Walsh began his writing career at the most logical departure point – taking elements from his own life and working a story around them.

Variaciones en Rojo won the prestigious Buenos Aires Municipal Literature Prize in 1953, with Jorge Luis Borges and Adolfo Bioy Casares judging the entries. "There are several million readers of crime novels in the country and a dozen authors," concluded the jury, "Walsh is one of them and one of the best."

Rodolfo was enjoying the first extended period of stability in his life since his family lived on a ranch in Choele-Choel. In 1953 Rodolfo had turned 26, and was the father of two girls and a struggling writer; he combined poorly paid fiction with occasional journalism. His translation work helped pay the bills but it was Elina who managed the family home as children, pupils and Rodolfo all depended on her domestic and professional skills to support the household.

Rodolfo Walsh's early work turned up in the most unlikely places. An old friend, Pedro Roselli, a blind poet, rummaged through piles of old files to find a dusty yellow braille manuscript, dating back to 1953. His hands danced across the page, dictating "Quiromancia", an early short story, which he re-translated back from his original braille translation, reading it aloud into my tape-recorder. The original version had been dictated to him by Rodolfo himself.

Walsh remained aloof from party politics during this time, revealing only that he voted for the moderate Unión Cívica Radical in the 1952 presidential elections which returned Perón to power.

Chiromancy

I have come back to my country. My eyes didn't see the sky torn apart by artillery fire, my ears didn't hear the whistling sound of the bombs. I live in a tranquil house with a garden where the birds sometimes sing. Quigley predicted all of this, one almost-forgotten night, at a completely forgotten party which I imagine was dominated by that magical atmosphere which Quigley created around himself.

I don't know why I always remember him multiplied by mirrors, innumerable yet one in the mirrors, tall and blond, dressed in black in the mystery of the mirrors of hot sitting rooms, some of which had huge candelabra, solemn men with monocles and women with ill-defined smiles.

Afterwards I met him one evening laced with symbols and premonitions, an evening I have been reconstructing for years with devoted patience. Men in grey overalls were up in the trees, as far as the eye could see, pruning trees which seemed like huge tormented hands or unusual candelabra in the greyish light of the sunset.

The first anti-aircraft shelters were being built in the city centre streets, the workers laboured lethargically, as if they didn't believe in them. They raised the tram tracks and beneath the paving stones, the brownish-grey earth appeared, ugly as a corpse.

The city dwellers stopped in groups and remembered with surprise that below the streets and houses, below the monuments and cinemas and theatres lay always the great devourer, insatiable and indifferent.

Was it me or Quigley who came up with these vain precisions? He walked beside me, disdainful and indifferent. The sky, now a very dark, metallic blue, was sprinkled in the distance with small and tenuous pink clouds.

I – how inevitable to repeat it – have returned to my country. I haven't seen the war. I wouldn't have believed it if Quigley hadn't got his last prophecy wrong. But Quigley got it wrong and so we must resign ourselves to it.

Some rumours, certain uncertainties reached me through the dense fog of the great catastrophe. I don't know if they are sufficient material to reconstruct Quigley's feverish final days but I would like to pay Quigley back for the bold happiness he predicted for me. I would like to rescue his name from among the ruins and the ashes.

Francis Quigley – now I can say it, now that everyone has forgotten it – was a famous palm reader. The hands of princes, artists and adorable women, killers too, revealed their secrets to him. The future of men glided before him along the rivers of the hand as he unravelled them.

But then the war made everyone lose interest in his art, as everybody's hands turned tense with fear. As night fell the planes crossed the river at low altitude. All night long they danced like silver butterflies in the glare of the searchlights. The people heard them come and counted the seconds in hushed tones while the bombs perforated the silence.

Francis Quigley wandered, crazy, through the streets of London, among the ruins; he stopped at night to look at the sky dotted with grenades, in the daytime he sat on park benches, with his black frock coat, his sad expression and his irredeemable loneliness.

No one recognised him. Grave-looking men passed quickly by him, gloomy children fled from him. He thought that if he could practise his trade once more, delve into an unknown future, bring the future creation to the surface, recreate the past, he would become himself once more. If he did that then he could die, or at least he wouldn't mind living.

On the night of November 20th 1941 a bomb destroyed a nearby house. Dragged by an irresistible force, Quigley ran to the smoking ruins. His arms began to blindly dig among the ruins. Quigley, a grotesque sight, laughed in short bursts as the biting wind carried his laughter through dark, nameless side streets.

His hands buried themselves in the hot ashes as an unspeakable tenderness invaded his heart. It was there – he knew it – among the ruins, the goal of his search. Finally he found it. The hand was severed from the bloody, horrible, mutilated body, a teenage hand with delicate white fingers. By the light of the fires Quigley saw all the certain, inevitable details of the future stamped on the lines of that hand.

He named them, deranged and delirious as he was, suddenly understanding that the horror and the death meant nothing if he could reaffirm the miracle: "You have long years ahead, many years," he whispered conspiratorially, moved by the revelation. "You will have a wife, children and a house where the birds occasionally sing. Everything in your life is peaceful. Peace..."

The sirens wailed.

They found him crying, sitting on a rock.   ●◆

chapter four

Pulp fiction

I gaze at my fingers in astonishment. Walsh, "Footnote" (see p.76)

Crime fiction

Rodolfo's crime fiction debut *Variaciones en Rojo* won the prestigious Buenos Aires City Fiction prize in 1953 but he remained modest about his writing abilities: "I wrote it [*Variaciones*] in a month, thinking less about literature than about fun and money," he said. A decade later he "abhorred" the three stories in the collection yet they established him as a talented writer with a promising future.

Walsh devoured crime fiction from around the world, fast becoming Argentina's foremost expert on the genre. In February 1954 Argentina's daily *La Nación* published an article by Rodolfo on the origins of crime fiction entitled "2,500 Years of Crime Literature". Walsh began the article by acknowledging the "near unanimous" agreement among aficionados that the detective fiction genre had begun with five short stories by Edgar Allen Poe, between 1840 and 1845. Rodolfo then argued that crime fiction really dated back to the Bible, citing the Book of Daniel, where the protagonist proves the innocence of Susannah, accused by the elders of committing adultery. Daniel "solved" the mystery by questioning the elders in separate rooms, thus exposing contradictions between their different versions of events. Walsh moved on to examples from Greek and Roman classics, the Maya indigenous book of wisdom (the sixteenth-century *Popol Vuh)* and Sancho Panza's "inquiry" in chapter 45 of Cervantes' *Don Quijote*.

One of the key ingredients in Rodolfo's crime fiction was the battle of wits set up between writer and reader. In his introduction to *Variaciones en Rojo* Walsh playfully included the page number by which the reader had all the elements to unravel each mystery. Walsh divided crime readers into active and passive. The active readers tried to find the solution before the narrator while the passive reader was happy enough to go along with the story to the sudden revelation at the end.

Walsh adopted the "closed narrative" style, where the action takes place within a limited geographical area: an apartment building, a mansion in the countryside, with all the suspects gathered respectfully around the police chief.

"There are two types of narrative technique," Rodolfo noted in his prologue to *Variaciones en Rojo*. "In one, the author grabs the reader's attention in the first five pages, bores him in the next 30 pages, then blows him away in the last 15 pages, saving his virtuosity for the epilogue. In the second type of narrative the author never blows us away but neither does he bore us." The detective genre challenged Walsh's analytical mind; he loved riddles and distrusted crime writers who tricked the reader by adding unknown elements to a mystery. In his own stories Walsh always left elaborate hints behind, maps and diagrams, challenging the reader to solve the mystery by themselves.

In "La Aventura de las Pruebas de Imprenta" (The Proof's Adventure), the first story in the *Variaciones* collection, the plot was straightforward: Raimundo Morel, a translator and proofreader, was murdered, his body found inside a locked room. The story began with a description of a bookshop below a publishing house on the second floor where accountants in overalls "make incessant, mysterious annotations in ledgers." Daniel Hernández, a proofreader at Corsario publishing house, worked among "silent and engrossed" proofreaders, beside desks littered with mock-ups of covers and illustrations-in-progress; bookshelves that groaned under the weight of dictionaries; encyclopedias, foreign languages, idioms and synonyms. Employees eagerly eyed the clock, waiting for it to strike 6.45 p.m., when they hurriedly left the office, their duties over for another day.

Rodolfo set the scene from his own experience in Hachette publishers, where he worked as a proofreader on the second floor, above the publisher's bookshop. The murder occurred in such a way that the mystery could only be resolved by someone with an in-depth knowledge of the proofreading profession.

Police chief Jiménez took up the investigation but quickly ruled out murder. "The door was locked and the weapon belonged to him," he said, suggesting that Morel shot himself while cleaning his weapon. Hernández asked police chief Jiménez whether another pistol of the same calibre might have been used in the killing, at which Jiménez "smiled with the superiority afforded by his knowledge of the profession." The investigator patiently explained the intricacies of forensic science, a description which took up several pages. Jiménez then gave Morel's proofs back to Hernández, commenting wryly, "Maybe you'll find something in them that escaped our attention."

Daniel Hernández, the myopic proofreader, examined the galley proofs and solved the crime in a matter of minutes. The Jiménez–Hernández relationship quickly established itself within the classic crime detection couple, pitting an experienced but routine-bound police officer, whose job is to get things wrong every time, against a highbrow amateur with an intuitive grasp of human nature.

The dots and squiggles permitted Hernández to reconstruct Raimundo Morel's final hours, on a precise, minute-by-minute basis. The puzzle lay in the intermittent garbling of Morel's proofs, taken at first to indicate inebriation. Hernández realized that Morel had worked on the proofs while making a train journey, thus blotting a certain number of words every time the train pulled in and out of a station.

By counting the number of proofs corrected by Morel, Hernández was able to calculate the number of stations he had passed. "'These proofs talk,' he said, absent-mindedly running his hands over them," (Walsh, 1953 p.65). Hernández then measured the gap between stations and the distance travelled, consulted the train timetable and concluded that the only possible journey which Morel could have made was between Constitución station in Buenos Aires and La Plata. Hernández checked his hypothesis by making the journey himself, the very journey Rodolfo Walsh made each day, from Elina's school in La Plata to his job at Hachette publishers, a journey spent correcting proofs.

Walsh enjoyed spinning out the dénouement with all the relevant characters gathered in a room, stunned as Hernández painstakingly unravelled the mystery over thirty-five pages. It transpired that Morel's wife Alberta had plotted the murder with her lover Anselmo Benavidez, who had carried out the deed. "We shouldn't judge her too harshly," said Hernández of Alberta. "In a certain way she was defending her right to happiness, a right which Morel had neglected, blind as he was to everything outside of his vocation as a writer" (ibid p.71).

Crime fiction is widely regarded as escapist literature yet the entertaining yarns often had marginal characters at the centre of the narrative, down on their luck, sad and desperate. One of Walsh's favourite writers was Cornell Woolrich (alias William Irish), who wrote *Rear Window*, filmed by Alfred Hitchcock. The narrator, lying in bed after a leg injury, has nothing to do all day but watch his neighbours and observe their lives. There is a single woman with a young child, "sitting there motionless, with her head in her arms. Something about it, it used to make me a little sad."

While the forces of law and order invariably triumphed over evil, restoring harmony to the world, crime thrillers often painted an accurate picture of grim social reality, with a sympathetic eye for the underdog.

The Gambler's Tale [13]

Renato Flores, turning a little pale, passed his checkered handkerchief across his moist brow. Then, with a slow movement, he gathered up his winnings. As if determined not to be hurried, he smoothed the bills out, one by one, folded them lengthwise and wedged them between the fingers of his right hand, where they resembled another wrinkled and dirty hand entwined perpendicularly with his own.

With a studied slowness he dropped the dice into the dice-box, and began to shake them, a double crease furrowing his brow. He seemed to be wrestling with a problem that was becoming more and more difficult with every breath he drew. Finally he shrugged his shoulders.

"Whatever you say," he said.

I decided then to remain as a spectator solely – a role temperamentally congenial to me as a student of human folly, romantic or otherwise. No one had remembered the lateness of the hour. Jiménez, who ran the game, watched from a distance without attempting to remind Flores that a gambler could not afford to keep late hours. Very deliberately Jesus Pereyra got up and threw a wad of money onto the table.

"Luck is luck," he said with a menacing glint in his eye. "But you've got to be half asleep for this."

I dislike violence, and the instant I sensed the ominous implications of his words, I took possession of the corner nearest the door. But Flores lowered his eyes and feigned ignorance.

"You've got to know how to lose," said Zuñiga, with chill emphasis, laying a five-peso note on the table. And he added with meaningful sarcasm, "after all, it's only a game."

"Seven straight winners!" commented one of the viewers admiringly.

Flores looked him up and down.

"Gibbering fool," he muttered.

Afterwards I tried to remember the spot occupied by each person before the hubbub began. Flores was some distance from the door, against the back wall. At the left, from where the police had come in, was Zuñiga. Across from him, separated by the width of the billiard table, stood Pereyra.

When Pereyra got up, two or three of the others also rose. I thought it was out of interest in the game, until I saw that Pereyra had his eyes fixed on Flores's hands. The others were watching the green expanse where the dice would presently fall. But Pereyra was following only the movements of Flores's fingers.

The little pile of bets had grown. There were bills of all denominations

---

[13] From the anthology *Latin Blood*, translated by Donald Yates.

and even some coins thrown carelessly on the table by one of the outsiders. Flores seemed to be hesitating. Finally, he cast the dice with an exaggerated flourish. Pereyra wasn't even looking at them. His eyes remained riveted on Flores's hands.

"Four!" someone exclaimed.

At that moment – precisely why I don't know – I recalled all the points that Flores had made so far: the four, the eight, the ten, the nine, the eight, the six, and again the ten... and now he was shooting for the four again.

The cellar was hazy with rising spirals of cigarette smoke. Flores asked Jiménez to bring him some coffee, and that fiercely scowling little man went off upstairs, mumbling.

Zuñiga smiled maliciously, watching Pereyra's angered expression. Plastered against the far wall, a drunk roused himself from time to time to babble in a thick voice, "I'll lay ten against you!"

The dice rattled in the dice-box, and then suddenly, they were out bouncing on the table. Eight pairs of eyes followed their path.

At last someone exclaimed, "Four!"

At that moment I lowered my head to light a cigarette. Over the table hung an electric lamp with a green shade. I didn't see the hand that smashed it into a thousand pieces, throwing the cellar into smothering darkness. But I heard the gunshot, a single deafening report ringing out in the blackness.

I made myself small in my corner. *Poor Flores! He was too lucky!* I heard something come rolling over near me, and felt it touch my hand. It was a die. Groping in the darkness I quickly found its mate.

In the midst of the tumult someone remembered the neon tubes on the ceiling. But when they came on, it wasn't Flores who was dead. Flores was standing frozen with the dice-box in his hand, his eyes dark pools of horror. At his left, doubled up in his seat, was Zuñiga with a bullet in his chest.

My first thought was: *They missed Flores and shot someone else by mistake! Nothing can happen to him tonight. His luck is too incredible.*

Two of the outsiders picked up Zuñiga and laid him out on three chairs placed in a row. Jiménez, who had just come down with the coffee, refused to let them put him on the billiard table, for fear that an ineradicable stain would spread over its felt surface. Anyway, it was too late to do anything for unlucky Zuñiga. Stepping over by the table I noticed that the dice on its surface spelled out a seven. Lying between them was a gleaming, thirty-eight-calibre revolver with a pearl handle.

As inconspicuously as possible, I slipped over to the door and went slowly up the stairs. Out in the street a crowd of excited onlookers had gathered, and a policeman was elbowing his way through them.

That night I remembered the dice I was carrying in my pocket – I had completely forgotten them – and I began to play alone, just for diversion. I rolled dice for half an hour without hitting a seven. I soon realised that I was playing with dice which had been very unethically numbered. One of the "educated cubes" had the five, four and three repeated on opposite sides – the other the five, six, and one.

With such dice a man's luck could hardly fail to seem miraculous. You couldn't lose on the first throw because it would have been impossible to throw a seven, which is a loser *after* the first throw.

I remembered that Flores had made seven straight points, and almost all of them with hard numbers: the four, the eight, and ten, the nine, the eight, the six, and again the ten... And on the last throw he had come up with the four again. Not one single "snake-eyes" had he thrown – not one "boxcars." And in the forty odd times that I had tossed the dice, I hadn't rolled a single seven – and seven is the number that most often appears in the normal course of a game.

But, nevertheless, after the tragedy the dice on the table had read seven, instead of four, which had been the last number rolled. I can still see it clearly: a six and a one.

The following day I moved to another part of town and, perhaps with subconscious intent, misplaced the dice.

Whether or not the authorities came looking for me, I don't know. For a while I heard nothing more about the tragedy. Then, one afternoon, I read in the papers that Pereyra had confessed. According to his statement, he had realised that Flores had been cheating and had tried to kill him in blind rage. Pereyra had been losing more than he could afford, and everyone knew that the man was a bad loser. The rage had come upon him when Flores's winnings had reached three thousand pesos, and he had smashed the light with one blow. But in the darkness he had aimed poorly, and instead of killing Flores he had killed Zuñiga. Curiously enough, I had reached the same conclusion myself, at first.

As might have been expected, they had to let Pereyra go. He told the judge he had been made to confess under duress, and the authorities had to admit that many points remained vague. In the dark it is easy to mistake a target, but Flores had been standing directly in front of him at a distance of three feet while Zuñiga had been far over to one side. One detail especially favoured him: the broken fragments from the cellar light had fallen behind him. If he had been the one to smash the light the glass would have been found on the other side of the billiard table, where Flores and Zuñiga had been standing.

The incident remained without explanation. No one had seen Pereyra smash the light. Everyone's eyes had been glued to the dice. And even if the killer had been seen, nothing had been said. I, myself, who could have seen him, had lowered my head to light a cigarette which I never did light. No prints had been found on the revolver, nor could the owner be determined. Any one of the men around the table – and there had been eight or nine – could have shot Zuñiga.

Who more than anyone else had an account to settle with Zuñiga? Well if *I* had wanted to incriminate someone in a dice game, I'd sit on his left. And as I lost I'd exchange the honest dice for a pair like those I had found on the floor, put them in the dice-box, and pass them on to my victim.

The man would win once and be happy. He'd win twice, three times – and he'd go right on winning. No matter how hard his opening number might be, he'd always make the point before a seven came up. If Jiménez let him, he'd win all night, *because with those dice he couldn't lose!*

Of course I wouldn't wait around to see the outcome. I'd go home to bed and the next day I'd read about it in the papers. Try to chalk up ten or fifteen points in company like that! It's good to have a little luck; to have too much luck is not good; and to help your luck along is dangerous...

Yes, I think that it was Flores himself who killed Zuñiga. And, in a way, he did it in self-defence. Flores killed him so that Pereyra or one of the others wouldn't kill our lucky Flores first. Zuñiga – because of some old grudge, perhaps – had slipped the crooked dice into the dice-box, and had thus condemned Flores to win all night, to cheat without knowing it. He had condemned him to death, or to betray himself by giving an explanation so humiliating that nobody would believe it.

Flores was late in realising the deadly trick that had been played on him. At first he thought it was pure luck. Afterwards he got uneasy; and when he understood Zuñiga's evil intention, when he saw that Pereyra was ready for trouble, and was keeping his eyes on his hands to see if he'd change the dice again, he realised that he could save himself in only one way. In order to get Jiménez away from behind his chair, he persuaded him to go complaining upstairs for some coffee. Then he waited for the right moment. It came when the four showed up again, as he knew it would, and when everyone was instinctively absorbed by the dice.

Then he broke the light bulb with one blow from the dice-box, took out the revolver with his checkered handkerchief and shot Zuñiga through the heart. He left the revolver on the table, recovered the loaded dice and threw them on the floor. There was no time for anything else.

He didn't want it to be known that he had been cheating, even if it had been without his knowledge. So he fished in Zuñiga's pockets for the legitimate dice which the latter had taken from the dice-box and which, just as the fluorescent lights began to flicker on again, he threw on the table.

And this time he did roll with the odds, coming up with the number that most often appears – a seven, big as a house!   ●◆ (Yates, 1972)

Partners in crime

Rodolfo's first letter to Donald Yates was dated April 19th 1954, a reply to the student at Michigan University, who requested information on the origins and development of crime fiction in Latin America. Walsh told the thesis student that the difficulty in establishing the status of the crime novel outside Argentina and Mexico was its "apparent inexistence" as Latin American writers invariably located their stories in the US or Britain. Walsh criticised the prevailing orthodoxy which obliged Argentinian writers to invent English-sounding pen names to give their work street credibility.

Rodolfo's detailed two-page response to the student established the tone of the relationship, a cordial, chatty exchange of views which quickly expanded as magazines, books, business ideas and finally their own work was swapped, as Yates was also an aspiring crime writer.

In one letter Walsh expressed his preference for the stories of Leonardo Castellani, a Jesuit priest who doubled as a crime writer. He described Jorge Luis Borges as "the most talented and lucid Argentinian writer today." Borges had written *La Muerte y la Brújula* (Death and the Compass) which Walsh regarded as one of the finest crime stories ever written. "Entire books have been written to attack or defend Borges," wrote Walsh, back in 1954, while "personal abuse has reached even Congress!" Yates lapped up the information, later becoming a close friend and biographer of Borges. Walsh outlined the criticism of Borges, who was attacked for being "cold and intellectual", for not tackling social issues in his work, for the "European" influences evident in his work and for abandoning the task of "interpreting the national spirit." Rodolfo rubbished the "inept" critics, citing Borges's "unequalled dominion" of language which could only come about via an "intense working passion." Walsh approved of Borges's choice of literary themes, "time and eternity" which "permanently affect mankind's destiny."

Walsh's letters to Yates reveal a generosity of spirit toward fellow writers. In the case of his admired Castellani, Rodolfo spotted two stories which were lifted directly from Mary Coleridge and JD Beresford, yet Walsh held onto the opinion that there was no reason to divulge the truth about the "good father", thus preserving his reputation.

Donald Yates, whose own letters to Walsh were lost, urged his

Argentinian pal to take advantage of "local colour" in spicing up his work, particularly with the US market in mind. "In Buenos Aires it's difficult to find local colour," explained Walsh. "The investigation of a crime follows the same lines as in New York, London or Paris. The first thing that occurs to me in a story is the plot, then the characters and finally – if at all! – the atmosphere."

Walsh and Yates discussed ways to crack their respective markets, willing to sacrifice character and style in the bid for crossover acceptance. In one letter Rodolfo offered to "kill off" his amateur detective Daniel Hernández for the purpose of US translation. The replacement would be a more phlegmatic police inspector. Walsh was also flexible when it came to adapting his work in translation, in keeping with his own flexible approach to the discipline. He offered Yates total liberty to "suppress, highlight or add whatever he deemed convenient."

The two writer-translators also sought ways to market translated work by other writers, even discussing ways of "icing out" a Mr Smith who held a virtual monopoly on publishing rights to US authors in translation. Walsh plotted the end of Mr Smith's exclusive representation rights but the move was complicated by two factors: he appeared to be a decent guy; *and* he had offered to sell Walsh's work outside the country.

Walsh and Yates decided to form the New World Literary Agency which would represent US writers interested in publishing their work in Argentina, and vice versa for Argentinian writers interested in translation and publication in the US.

Argentina's currency laws prevented foreign writers from repatriating book royalties to their home country, a Peronist law which stimulated national literary production but dried up the steady supply of stories and novels of well-known authors from abroad. Walsh explained that the royalties were deposited in pesos into a local bank, where they waited for a future time when the laws would be repealed. The result was an increase in pirate editions and a decrease in authors willing to let *Leoplán* and other magazines publish their work.

The Walsh-Yates literary agency would offer a way around currency limits, as an agency or magazine would invest frozen royalties, part of which could be repatriated under foreign investment laws. Walsh's initiative would include a new detective story magazine published across Latin America, with a projected circulation of 100,000 copies.

As 1954 drew to a close Rodolfo wished Donald a happy new year, noting that Elina had been studying hard for an exam. "Not content with her blind and disabled students, she now wants to teach the deaf and dumb – there won't be any more room for me in this house before long," said Walsh. The mood was upbeat however, as Walsh and Yates signed the forms that formally launched the New World Literary Agency with its own logo, a map of the western hemisphere with a star in Michigan and another in Buenos Aires.

The new literary agency quickly ran into serious difficulties as issues of currency regulations, representational rights and start-up capital were compounded by a sudden decrease in sales of crime stories, as Spanish and Mexican publishers flooded the market with cheap imitations. The worldly Walsh advised Yates to treat the agency as "a hobby" for the time being.

The Walsh–Yates correspondence included the frequent exchange of books as Rodolfo expanded his general knowledge, requesting novels, short stories, tales of the supernatural, plays and books on scientific discovery. In return Walsh sent first edition copies of Argentinian writers, although Yates objected to the "complimentary" stamp which appeared on all the books, as they were obtained free from the publishers. Walsh was embarrassed by the complaint but could do nothing about it, as he couldn't afford to buy the books out of his own pocket.

The 1950s was a golden age for crime thrillers in Argentina, where, according to Walsh, "any halfway decent story is published the week after it is written."

Rodolfo asked Donald Yates to check out the possibility of publishing his work in the US, a favour he would reciprocate by publishing Yates in Argentina's *Leoplán* magazine and in an anthology of Argentinian detective writers. Yates was granted "honorary" citizenship for the purpose of the collection. Walsh sent Yates a copy of his *Variaciones en Rojo*, noting that the first story "can't have much hope of publication" while the third story, "Long Distance Murder" was closest to the style Walsh had read in US magazines and books. "Personally I prefer the second one," said Walsh, referring to the story that gave the collection its title.

Rodolfo spent a remarkable amount of time and energy on the letters, turning out four closely typed pages almost every fortnight until 1956, when extraordinary events turned his life inside out.

Rodolfo's letters reflected the frustrations of his work for Hachette publishers, "who pay their translators very little at the moment" leading Walsh to temporarily give up the work while inspiring one of his finest short stories, "Footnote".

Two months after his first letter to Donald Yates, Rodolfo revealed some family details. "María Victoria (Vicki) is three years and eight months old; the youngest, Patricia, will soon be two years old. They are a veritable cocktail of races: 50 per cent Irish by their father, 25 per cent Italian on their mother's side, 12.5 per cent Spanish and 12.5 per cent American Indian." Rodolfo sent regards from his wife Elina, who "writes poetry and sharply opposes my being called Rollo."

The letter signed off with hopes that the "exchange of ideas and books will turn into an exchange of visits." Rodolfo registered every book package he sent to the US, holding on to the post office slips and making a note of each book and magazine, a practice which proved useful when a package went missing en route to Michigan.

On one occasion Donald Yates referred a story of his own to Rodolfo concerning a communist sympathiser at the height of the McCarthy anti-communist hysteria. Walsh assured him that the communist theme wouldn't be a problem in Argentina. "I think most people agree with your veiled thesis that the repression of communism can lead to inconvenient situations, as you suggest."

Walsh was acutely aware of the ideological implications of different crime fiction styles; US crime writer Haycraft linked the development of the police novel with the growth of civil liberties, democracy and the perfecting of police methods. Walsh disagreed. "The most brilliant police machinery may be at the service of a dictatorship or serve to repress civil liberties," he wrote.

The definition of "democracy" was also a factor, noted Walsh, "whether it consists of the reign of civil liberties or the effective partici-pation of the people, of the masses, in government." Argentina under Perón offered a clear example of Walsh's argument, as the masses had enjoyed "unprecedented participation" in political and social events despite a parallel decline in civil liberties. This tendency corresponded with the "first serious manifestations" of the crime fiction genre.

The theory that the improvement of police institutions influenced the development of the detective novel "seems right to me" noted Walsh, who counted the Argentinian police as one of the most efficient in the world. In 1900 Juan Vucetich, an Argentinian, developed a fingerprint recording technique now used in most parts of the world, while the clarification of a killing by fingerprints first happened in 1892.

The "perfect crimes" published with fanfare by the evening papers each day, explained Walsh, "are resolved by the morning edition."

The writer

The year 1955 got off to a good financial start as Walsh received the 10,000 pesos (about US$800) for winning the Buenos Aires City Fiction prize. Rodolfo was now 28 years of age and had no political commit-ments, his flirtation with right-wing nationalism abandoned once Perón's anti-imperialist rhetoric was revealed as careerist cant. Walsh even applauded the coup which ousted Perón in September 1955. Walsh and Yates became firm friends, while their respective wives, Elina and Mary, also wrote notes to each other and by August 1954 a visit by the

Yates family to Argentina was in the offing. Rodolfo was interested in visiting the US, but lacked the funds. "I'll have to win a few more prizes before that will happen," he wrote.

Rodolfo and Elina took the two girls to Mar del Plata for the summer holidays in January 1955, enjoying the sea and relaxation at Argentina's most popular getaway spot, 400 km from the capital. "It's a pity we didn't have more time" said Walsh, writing once more to Yates. "It really is the most beautiful city in the country with a perfect summer climate, unlike Buenos Aires which is an oven."

It was difficult to recognise the Walsh who, inside two years, would be in hiding, hunted by the police chief of La Plata, his routine shattered by a snatch of conversation in a café in December 1956.

The first phase of Walsh's crime fiction career had reached its high point, as the 28-year-old writer had published *Variaciones en Rojo*, (1953), 20 more short stories, mostly crime fiction, and edited *Diez Cuentos Policiales Argentinos* (1953), the first collection of Argentinian detective fiction. Yet his earnings never reached the point where taxation began.

Walsh's detective fiction was "at the top of their category in Argentina, very successful," according to Yates, who subsequently became president of the US Crime Writer's Association,"but he knew it was hack work, a formula genre, written for a specific audience which expects a problem, an investigation and a solution."

In the early months of 1955 Walsh's letters expressed his hopes of obtaining authorisation to translate certain US authors and trying to end publishing piracy: "If Vickers gives me written permission," wrote Walsh, of one US writer, "I will visit the publisher who pirated his work and demand compensation."

Donald Yates was preparing an anthology of Latin American writers and asked Walsh for recommendations. Rodolfo noted that while Argentinians wrote detective stories, elsewhere in the continent it was social injustice and indigenous issues which dominated literature. "If you pick out Chilean or Bolivian authors," noted Walsh, "the best work won't be a tale of the supernatural but a book about life in a salt mine." In Ecuador Walsh had high praise for Jorge Icaza, whose *Huasipungo* he regarded as "the most brutal and moving testimony" of the exploitation of the Indians.

Walsh then described Yates's upcoming anthology of Latin American crime fiction as "the most substantial contribution to north–south cultural relations to date," his hyperbole undoubtedly fuelled by the growing friendship.

In April 1956 Walsh wrote that he was giving up translation work and taking up photography to increase his options as a working journalist. Argentina, like Walsh, had moved on from the days of detective stories;

the fall of Perón signalled the end of the mass market for escapist literature as readers turned to newspapers and magazines, hungry to uncover
corruption and keep up with political events.

Rodolfo's penpal received a Fulbright scholarship and travelled to
Argentina in 1962, when they finally met. He taught Latin American
literature in Michigan State University for twenty-six years, alternating
semesters at home with sabbaticals in Buenos Aires, where he taught
courses in US fiction.

Footnote[14]

by Rodolfo Walsh

In memoriam Alfredo de León
† circa 1954

No doubt León had wanted Otero to come and see him lying there naked and dead under the sheet, that is why he had written his name on the envelope and in it, he had put the letter which may explain it all. Otero has arrived and is quietly gazing at the oval of his face concealed like a silly riddle, but he has not opened the letter yet because he wants to imagine the account the dead man would give, if he could sit opposite him at his desk, and talk as they had so often talked.

A sad quiet purifies the face of the tall white-haired man who does not wish to stay, does not wish to leave, does not want to admit he feels betrayed. Yet that is exactly how he feels, because he suddenly gets the impression that they never got to know one another, that he never did anything to help León, that he never was, as both had so often admitted, a sort of father to him, and of course a real friend. Anyway, here he is and it is him, and no one else but himself who says:

– Well I never…

and then he hears the voice of Mrs. Berta who looks at him with her dry blue eyes on her wide sexless face, devoid of memory and impatience, muttering that the chief of police is on his way and why doesn't he open the letter. But he does not open it, though he can imagine its general tone of lugubrious apology, his first phrase of farewell and regret.*

---

* I am sorry for not finishing the translation the House entrusted me with. You shall find the original on the table, together with the one hundred and thirty pages I have already translated.

The rest shall be no trouble at all, and I hope the House finds someone to do it. Unfortunately, I have had to ignore your latest admonitions.

I could not recover the typewriter, so I'm afraid you shall get that text and the previous one in handwriting. I have tried to be as clear as possible, and I hope you are not too irritated with me, considering the circumstances.

---

[14] from his book of short stories *Un Kilo de Oro*, translated from the Spanish by Cynthia Mansfield.

What's the use of this? They could have gained so much more if they had both sat down and talked, and suddenly, Otero has the obscure feeling that it has all been deliberately aimed at him, that León's life had lately tended to make him into an astounded witness of his death. Why, León?

It is not very pleasant to be sitting here, in this unknown room, next to the window filtering humiliated dusty light onto the work table where he recognizes Ballard's last novel, the Cuyás dictionary published by Appleton, the sheet of paper half-way covered in handwriting, on which a final syllable quivers and goes out of its mind, then bursts into a blotch of ink. No doubt León has thought that by doing this, he had done his duty, and indeed, the white-haired and melancholy man who is looking at him has not come to reproach him for the work left unfinished, or to think of someone to take over. I have come, León, to accept the idea of your unexpected death and put you at peace with my conscience.

Suddenly, the other has become a mystery to him, in the same way that he has become a mystery to the other, and the best of it all is that he does not even know how he chose to kill himself.

– Poison, says the old woman, who remains very still on her chair wrapped in black and grey woollens.

Then she crosses her hands and whispers her prayers, without

Do you remember the sinusitis I had two months ago? It seemed so harmless, but lately the pains would keep me awake. I had to call the doctor in, so the few pesos I had left went on medicines and treatments.

That's why I pawned the typewriter. I think I've told you already, but during these twelve years I have been working for the House to our mutual satisfaction, I have always tried to comply with the House rules, except for some instances I shall refer to further on. This is the first assignment I am leaving incomplete – I mean unfinished. I am very sorry but I have simply had enough!

One hundred and thirty pages at one hundred pesos the page makes thirteen thousand pesos. Would you be so kind as to give them to Mrs. Berta? Ten thousand pesos will pay for my lodging until the end of this month. I'm afraid the rest won't be enough for the expenses that are to ensue. Perhaps by retrieving the typewriter and selling it, some more could be raised. It is a very good typewriter. I was very fond of it.

The only snag is the plastic keys, they wear away, but by and large, I don't think they make typewriters like the 1954 Remington anymore.

I'm also leaving some books, though I doubt you'll get much for them. There are other things: a radio, a heater. I beg you see to the details with Mrs. Berta. As you well know, I have no relatives or friends other than

shedding a tear or even suffering, except for a general, abstract sorrow about so many things: the passing of time, the dampness on the walls, the holes in the sheets and the trivial habits that make up her daily life.

There is a patch of sunlight and clothes hung out on the patio, below the perspective of floors with iron-sheeted verandahs, where a feather duster sticks out like a joke swaying on its own in a cloud of dust, a faceless turban parades along, and an old man leans out, looks down and spits.

Otero sees all this in a snapshot, but the image he wants to shape in his mind is quite a different one: the elusive face, the character of the man who worked for more than ten years for him and the House. For no one can live with the dead, it is necessary to kill them within, to reduce them to a harmless image locked away forever in one's neutral memory. A spring moves, a curtain is drawn, and we rush to judge and sentence them, and anoint them with oblivion and pardon.

The old woman seems to be cradling the empty space between her arms.

– He always paid on time,

and the memory of the dead man emerges in meagre anecdotes: how badly he ate and the noise he made when he wrote by night, and how he fell ill afterwards, and became melancholy and speechless and

---

those from the House.

I am so sorry to put you to all this trouble and change right at the last minute such a friendly relationship, so fruitful in a certain way. When the question with the typewriter cropped up, for example, I thought that if I asked you for some money in advance, the House would not say no. But I had not done that in twelve years; I imagined you might disapprove of me, that something might change between us, so finally, I just decided not to ask at all.

I would like you to keep the Appleton. It is a rather old edition and it is pretty thumbed, but I have nothing else as a token of my feelings towards you, sir. One acquires a special intimate relationship with objects of daily use. I think that recently I had almost come to know it by heart; nonetheless I never stopped referring to it; I knew every time what I would find and I knew which words it was useless to look up. Perhaps you'll smile if I admit to you that, literally, I carried on conversations with Mr. Appleton.

I would say, for instance:

– Mr. Appleton, what's the meaning of "prairie dog"?

– "Aranata," was the answer

I see. And "crayfish"?

– Same as "crabfish".

did not want to leave his room any more.

– Afterwards he went nuts.

Otero almost smiled when he heard the word. It was easy enough to say now that León had finally gone mad, and the report would probably say so. But nobody would know what had triggered such madness, even if his oddities were quite obvious to all.

So, for instance, during the last months, he was bent on writing by hand, alleging vague mishaps with his typewriter, and Otero had allowed him to, in spite of complaints by the press; he had overlooked other things, as well, because he felt they were not deliberately done against him, they were part of the suicide's struggle against something impossible to decipher.

Surely, that loose page would still be lying in one of the drawers of his desk, the one that had been intercalated in León's last translation. There was nothing but a single word – shit – repeated from beginning to end in a sleepwalker's handwriting.

The woman enquires about who is to pay for the expenses of the burial, and the man answers:

– The House.

which must be the company León worked for.

Having cleared this up, she feels freer and brings a handkerchief to

---

– All right, but what does "crabfish" mean?

– "Crap".

– Mind your language!

– Oh, don't get annoyed. You can translate it into Spanish as "bogavante de río".

– That's better. Thanks.

It's funny, isn't it? One came to know how to say something in two languages, and even in different ways in each language, but one never got to know what the thing really was.

In the fields of zoology and botany, entire flocks of mysterious animals and spectral flora have crossed my pages. What on earth is a "bowfin"? I wondered before setting it free to navigate the Mississippi and imagined it was equipped with huge antennae with a light at each end, gliding in the submarine fog.

I wonder what the song of a chewink is like and then I would listen to the crystal notes rise unconfined in the quiet of an ancient forest.

I have not forgotten that I owe all that new world to you. That afternoon, when I walked down the stairs of the House holding the first novel you asked me to translate tight against my chest, is probably lost in your memory. In mine it is always luminous and pink. Look, I remember I her eyes and wipes a scanty string of tears, partly for León, who was poor after all, and did not bother anyone, and partly for herself, for all the things that have died within her, after so many years of solitude and hard work among mean rough men.

Otero's look roams the grey palm trees of a huge oasis where camels drink. In fact there is only one palm tree repeated ad infinitum on the wallpaper, only one camel, only one little puddle, and the face of the dead man hiding among the arching branches looks at him with the thirsty eye of an animal and finally dissolves, leaving him with the aftertaste of a wink and the misgiving of a sneer. Otero shakes his head to avoid being carried away, to recover León's true face, his huge mouth, his black eyes (were they black?), while he hears the officer's voice in the hall saying on the phone "the Courts" then he hangs up, dials and enquires "the Courts?" and hangs up and walks around with his hands behind his back among doleful hat-trees and bronze flower-pots.

Perhaps León's behaviour meant to convey his was a hard life, a fact not easily denied if one took a look at the bare walls, the flannel winter and summer suit hanging on the wardrobe mirror, the men in their undershirts waiting for their turn at the bathroom door.

But then who doesn't lead a hard life, anyway? And who else but

———————————————

was afraid of losing the book, I held it tight with both hands and the 48 tram, crawling into the dusk along Calle Independencia, seemed slower than ever: I wanted to bury myself, as soon as possible, into the new matter of my life. But even that neighbourhood, with its low houses and long cobble-stoned roads, seemed beautiful to me for the first time.

I ran up to my room, I opened the hard cover book, with those strong smelling pages which became a very white paste, solid cream, on its front edges. Remember it? No, maybe not, but the opening phrase stuck in my mind forever: "This, said Dan O'Hangit, is a case of a fellow who got taken for a ride. He was in the front seat of whatever kind of car he happened to be in. Somebody in the back seat shot him in the nape of his neck and pushed him onto Morningside Park."

Yes, I do admit it sounds rather idiotic today. Even the novel (that one about the cinema actor who kills a woman who discovers he is impotent) seems quite bad, after so many years.

The truth is that at that point my life changed. Without further thought, I quit the garage, burnt all my ships. The boss, who'd known me since I was a kid, refused to believe it. I told them I was going to the interior, it was hard to explain to them I would not be a worker any more, that I would stop sticking rubber rectangles on brush strokes of fluorine.

him chose that ugliness that explained nothing at all and that he very likely could not see?

This may not be the right time to ponder upon such matters, but what excuse would he give himself if faced with death he was not very honest as he has always been? Was the dead man honest with him? Otero suspects he has not. Right from the very beginning he had detected a streak of that kind of melancholy disguised in joviality that was pointing to the outstanding feature of his character. He talked a lot and laughed too much, but it was a bitter laugh, a jolliness that had rotten and Otero often wondered whether deep down, even if León himself could not realise, there was not a hint of perverse mockery at it all, a subtle indulgence in misfortune.

– He had no friends – says the old woman. That's tiring.

The visitor is no longer listening to her. He is carried away along paths of old memories, seeking the lost image of León. And once and again, he finds him hunch-backed and small, with that bird-like air of his, pecking at words on long sheets of paper, cursing correctors, refuting academies and inventing grammars. Yet still, it is a smiling face, the face of the times when he used to love his craft.

It took a keen eye to tell there was a potential translator behind that young boy walking out of a service-station – or was it a garage? – with

------

I had never, ever told them about the evenings spent learning how to type at the Pitman school, month after month, year after year. Why did I choose English, and not shorthand or accounting? I don't know. That's life. When I think of how difficult it was for me to learn, I conclude I was not cut out for languages, from which I derive some obscure pleasure, I mean that I did it all by myself, with the help of the House, naturally.

I never saw them again. Even today, when I go past Calle La Rioja, I take a detour so as not to meet them, as if I had to justify that lie. Sometimes I feel sorry for old Mr. Lautaro, who was like a real father to me, which does not mean he paid me well, but he did love me and hardly ever shouted at me. But leaving that place meant progress in every sense of the word.

Need I speak of how fervently – almost fanatically – I translated the book? I used to get up very, very early. I did not stop working until they called me for lunch. In the morning I made a rough copy, assuring myself at every step, that if it was necessary, I could do two, three or ten draft copies: that no word was definitive. On the margins, I wrote possible choices of each passage where I had doubts. In the afternoons, I would correct and make clean copies.

This is when I started my relationship with the dictionary, which was

his acceptable Spanish and his eager English he had learnt by mail. He gradually discovered translating was quite a different thing from knowing two languages: it was a third domain, an entirely new field. And then, the hardest of all secrets, the true cipher of art: to erase his personality, to go unseen, to write like another without anyone noticing.

– Don't go in – says the old woman.

Otero stands up and takes the coffee cup the girl reaches out to him, he sits down and has his coffee.

Another kind gust of the past lights up his face: León's look of surprise that morning when he saw the first novel he had translated. He had turned up the next day with a new tie and had given him a copy with a dedication, as a token of a certain innate loyalty. There had been other translators temporarily working for the House, who had learnt however much or little they knew, and then left for a few pennies' better pay. But at times, perhaps many times, León could intuit what the mission of the House was, he obscurely grasped the sacrifice involved in publishing books, in fuelling people's dreams and building up a culture for the people, even against their will.

On the night table, the alarm clock is now going off, shaking on its nickel legs, and by its side a photograph in a frame is trembling, the impudent and plebeian effigy of a girl roaring in laughter, her flowered

---

brand-new at the time and had a clean brown paper dust jacket.

– Mr. Appleton, what is the meaning of the word 'scion'?

– "Vástago"

– And "cruor"?

Annoyed:

– "Cruor" is "crúor"!

I even looked up the simplest words, even if I was sure of the meaning. I was so afraid of making a mistake... That novel by Dorothy Pritchett, that very bad pot-boiler novel sold in the newsstands for 5 pesos, I translated it word by word. I might tell you, I didn't think it was bad at the time, because I kept finding new depths of meaning in it, more and more subtleties in the plot.

I came to be convinced that Mrs. Pritchett was a great writer, not as great as Ellery Queen or Dickson Carr (because I was now frantically reading the best detective literature you recommended to me), but well, she was in the process of becoming great.

When the translation was ready, I corrected it again, I wrote out a clean copy for the second time. This method explains my taking forty days, even though I worked twelve hours a day, and even more, because even in my sleep, I would sometimes wake up to surprise someone inside

dress dancing too, her wide hips…
– Women?
– Not anymore – and the clock has another fit of alarm, and the snapshot has another fit of dance and laughter.

Otero sighs, and confesses it was such a heck of a long time ago León had started to be different; it was with the Scarlet Series, the volume of the Andromeda Collection (aligned on the only shelf there was like a secret calendar) that this man had said no, he had even forgotten the childish pride he took in his works:

– Guess how many entries I've got at the National Library – his balding head sunk into the lapels of his suit.
– How many, León?
– Sixty. More than Manuel Gálvez has.
– Marvellous.
– Phew! I'm only half-way through it.
Or otherwise:
– This translation is unique. It has one thousand words less than the original version.
– Did you count them?
He sneers:
– Every single one.

---

my head who was rehearsing variations on a tense or subject-verb agreement, and merge two phrases into one, indulging in ridiculous cacophonies, alliterations and inverted meanings. All my strength went into that task, which was more than a mere translation: it was – I realised much later – the change of one man into another man.

What is so strange about the fact that this job should finally turn out to be faulty, pedantic, scleroticised for attempting to bring exactness into the heart of every single word? I could not see it then, I was so pleased, I even knew some paragraphs by heart.

I was trembling and perspiring the day I took the manuscript to you. My fate lay in your hands. If you rejected my work, I would have to go back to the garage. In my exaggeration, I fancied you would read the novel right there on the spot, whilst I waited, regardless of how long that took. But you just glanced at it and put it away in your desk.

– Come in a week's time – you said.

What an atrocious week! I fluctuated mercilessly from the most insane hope to the uttermost abjection of spirits.

– Mr. Appleton, what is the meaning of "utter dejection"?

– It means melancholy, it means low spirits, it means grief.

I came back. You were slowly going through the manuscript at your

Later – but when? – a hidden spring leaped. It is necessary to admit that lately, he was not very pleased to see León at the office. He poured out all his problems and regrets, which often had nothing to do with him, but rather with the general state of affairs, the bombings in Vietnam or the Negroes in the South, subjects he disliked discussing, even if he did have his own opinions on them. Of course, León ended up agreeing with them, but deep down, one could see he disagreed, and such pretending was hard to forebear without their being mutually irritated. When he left, one felt like sweeping away all the scum of sadness and excuses. What was the matter, León?

– I don't know – said the tearful voice. It's that world is so full of injustices.

The last time he had come, Otero had asked his secretary to see him.

There's no point, anyhow, in remembering that small incident, which would obscure Otero's constant interest in León's matters, even in the trivial details:

– This month, you've translated two books. Why don't you get yourself a new suit?

It was like asking him to change his skin, and then Otero forgot his secret plan of inviting him out to lunch some day, of introducing him to the manager, and offering him a steady job with the House. He resigned

---

desk. I peeped with a start on the corrections in green ink you had heavily strewn on the pages. You did not say a word. I must have looked pale, because you suddenly smiled.

– Don't be afraid, you said handing me the pile of pages put back into order. There's a table for you over there. Look through the corrections.

Most of them were fair, some made no difference, and a few of them I would have liked to discuss with you. With a gush of blood rising to my face I understood that "actual" is not translated as "current" into Spanish, but as "true". (Sorry, Mr. Appleton). But what filled me with embarrassment was the relentless crossing out of about fifty footnotes my anxiety had riddled the text with. That's when I gave up that abhorrent habit for good.

All said and done, you saw in me a potential that no one would have guessed. That is why I accepted, with no resentment whatsoever, your final reproach to me, which, in other circumstances, would have made me cry.

– You've got to work harder.

You signed the payment order: 220 pages at 2 pesos each. That was less than I got for forty days work at the garage but it was the first fruit of intellectual work, the symbol of the transformation I had undergone.

himself to abandoning León to his listlessness, to his vague day-dreaming, to the unhealthy ideas leisure breeds; sometimes he even envied him because he could sleep in or decide to call it a holiday, while he lay awake worrying about the House's remote plans. Perhaps, his kindness had been misguided after all, perhaps he should not have left León to his own devices in facing the fantasies of an intelligence, which – let's face it – was not very vigorous.

But it's hard to know how far one's duties unto the other should go, and impinge on someone's freedom in order to be good to him. And then, what excuse could one give? Once or twice a month, León would come along, hand in his pile of translated pages, collect and leave. Could he have stopped him and told him his life was all wrong? And then, wouldn't he have had to do likewise with the rest of the fifty people working for the House?

Otero stands up, walks over to the door onto the hall, looks out at the blinding light coming from the patio, listens to the noises the dead man must have heard: metallic noises, taps, brooms. As though León had never even existed, because nothing stops. The soup in the pot, the goldfinch in its cage – voice of the old woman saying it's eleven o'clock already and I wish the chief of police were here any minute.

For a moment, the visitor shares the same wish, he has so much to

---

When I left, I was carrying under my arm the second book I was to translate.

– Unspeakable joy, Mr. Appleton?

– That is the joy you feel.

Three hundred pesos went on lodging for that month. One hundred, on the second instalment for the Remington. I savagely dived into 'Forty Whacks', that story of the old woman they kill with an axe on the beach, remember? I was very happy when on page 60 I guessed who the murderer was. I never read the book I translated beforehand, so that I could share the tension being built up, I took on a part of the authors' so that my work could have a minimum of... inspiration, let's call it. This book took five days less and you had to admit, I had learnt what you had taught me. Of course it takes years and years of daily work to acquire a craft. Progress is reached almost unobtrusively, as though it were the growth from the cotyledon to the Christmas tree.

Comparing a page translated today with another from a month ago, you will notice no difference, but if you compare it with one I did a year ago, one could exclaim in astonishment: That is the progress I have made!

Of course there were more important changes. My hands, for example, lost their stiffness, they became smaller and cleaner. I mean, it was easier

do at the office: budgets to decide on, letters to be answered, and even a long-distance call, besides lunch with his wife Laura, to whom he would have to explain what had happened. But before, he must know what León was like, and why he has killed himself: before the chief of police comes along and lifts the sheet and asks him if that was León.

Perhaps the mystery lay in his childhood, in old memories of humiliation and poverty. Did he ever tell him he never got to know his parents? Perhaps that was the reason why he felt dispossessed and could never love the world order. But except for that fortuitous incident he undoubtedly exaggerated, nobody had dispossessed him.

The House had always been fair – sometimes even generous – to him. When two years ago, out of their own free will, they had chosen to grant half a bonus to one of the ten translators, it was León who got it.

It is true that lately, he had shown a certain strange phobia of certain kinds of books – the ones he liked most at the beginning – and he even had a secret (and funny) desire to have a say in the publishing policy of the House. But even this last whim was about to happen: he would be transferred from sci-fi to the "Landmarks in Time" series. That was a definitely risky step for a man of scanty learning, picked up here and there, and full of gaps and prejudices.

Nothing was enough, quite obviously. León never came to realise

----

to wash them, I did not have to struggle against leftovers of acid and scales and traces of tools. I have always been very thin, but I became finer and more delicate.

With my fifth book (The Bloody Missal), I gave up the second rough copy and gained another five days. You were beginning to be happy with me, though you never showed you were, because of that kind of shyness that is born from the best friendship, a certain delicacy I always admired in you. As for myself, I was still not earning as much as at the garage, but I was not far from it.

Meanwhile, that extraordinary event took place. One morning you were expecting me with a special smile, and the light coming through the window haloed you, and gave you a paternal aureole.

– I have something for you – you said.

I already knew what it was, and I put on the same excitement that I felt, and would feel, while you drew your hand towards the drawer of your desk and with three movements you seemed to have rehearsed, you laid before my eyes the bright red copy bound in hard covers of Mortal Moon, *my first work, I mean my first translation. I took it into my hands with devotion.*

– Look inside, you said.

what his true status within the House was: the best paid and most considerately treated detective translator, who was never left without work, even in the hardest of times, when some thought the whole publishing business would go to pot.

Otero has not seen the men in white arrive and chat outside with two lodgers, or the stretcher leaning on the ochre patio wall marked with the dripping of so much sun and so much rain and so many clothes hung out to dry. With his hands behind his back, the officer sticks his nose into the room and announces, as if he were whispering a secret:

– He's coming,

which is the verbal form the chief of police uses.

Faced with the imminence of the arrival, Otero suddenly saw things more clearly. León's suicide was no act of greatness, nor was it an unconscious fit. It was the form of escape typical of a mediocre man, a symbol of the disorder of the times. Resentment and lack of responsibility nestled in everyone; but only the weak enacted them like this. The rest refrained from that, broke things, attacked order, questioned values, the very destructiveness León had turned against himself: that was the metaphysical disease corroding the country and those who were cut out for construction found it more and more difficult to face this disease.

It is useless for Otero to carry on his quest. He does not want to find

————————————————

– *Inside, that flash of lightning:*

Translated into Spanish
by L. D. S.

which was me, in short, in font size 6, but me, León de Sanctis, for whom the linotype had stamped once and the printer had repeated ten thousand times as bells toll ten thousand times on an auspicious day of largesse, me, me ... I went down to the salesroom. Five copies cost me 15 pesos with the discount: I had a need to show, give away, dedicate. One was for you. That evening I bought a bottle of Cubana and for the first time in my life I got drunk, reading aloud to myself the most dramatic passages of Mortal Moon. *Next morning, I could not remember at what point I had dedicated a copy "to my mum".*

My situation improved little by little. From a bedroom for three lodgers I moved into one for two. However, there were still difficulties. The rest were annoyed by my banging on the typewriter, especially by night. They were – and still are, as you are likely to see for yourself – workers. I never befriended them: they reminded me of my past and I suppose they envied me.

In May 1956, I managed to translate in fifteen days a 300-page himself guilty of any omission, lack of love or neglect whatsoever. And yet he is guilty, in the worst terms, in the words Laura always reproaches him for: too good, too lenient.

Finally, he is trapped, he wriggles and defends himself and answers himself. It is not that he is good, the fact is that he did not have to wait for human relations to be invented to treat working people as they deserve to be treated; after all, they are the ones who make possible whatever greatness there is in the country, in the House.

But, Otero, did you fail with León? Yes, with León I failed, I should have done something, I should have admonished him in time, I should have prevented him from following that path. The admission bursts into a final sigh, and León is beginning to stop moving among the paper palm-trees, the evidences of his earthly occupation, the saturated ruts of memory. It is time, anyway, to feel some pity for him, to remember how thin he was and how humble his origin was, and the old woman is surprised to hear him say:

– Far too much.

When the chief of police arrived, it was not even necessary for him to look at the things in the bedroom. The things seemed to be looking at him in that split of a second when all was comprehended, classified, understood. Neither did he need to introduce himself, his blue overcoat,

---

novel. The price had gone up to 6 pesos per page. Unfortunately, my lodgings had also increased threefold. The House's good intentions were always countered by inflation, demagoguery and revolutions.

But I was young and still full of enthusiasm. Every month one of my books appeared and my name as a translator appeared now in full form. The first time my name appeared in a press release of La Prensa *newspaper, I was totally overjoyed. I still keep that clipping and all the many others that appeared subsequently. According to those testimonies, my versions have been correct, good, faithful, excellent and on one occasion, magnificent. It is also true that other times, they did not remember me or they ticked me off as irregular, inconsistent and dissolute, according to the moody sway of the critics.*

Shall I confess I joined the game of vanity? I compared myself with other translators, I read them with the eye of an insomniac, I found out their age, the number of works they had translated. I remember their names: Mario Calé, M. Alinari, Aurora Bernárdez. If they were worse than I was, I dismissed them for good, and as for the others, I promised myself to outdo them with time and patience. Sometimes, my fantasy took me far away: I dreamed of emulating Ricardo Baeza, although we cultivated different genres and I finally resigned myself to leaving him on

grey hat, wide face and wide moustache. He simply opened his hand at the height of his hips, and Otero stretched out his.

– Have you waited for long?

– No, said Otero.

The chief of police had just shaved and perhaps he had just got up. Under his dark skin, you could see a healthy pink hue, and although the three steps he took in the direction of the bed and the dead man were quick and precise, in the saturated air of the bedroom a trace of tiredness, of tedium, of déjà-vu remained.

The chief of police's hand took one of the corners of the sheet and gave it a tug, to discover a small bluish naked body. Mrs. Berta did not look away, perhaps because she had already seen him like this when she came to wake him up on summer days, perhaps because in her world with no hope and no sex, she was beyond those forms of subtle embarrassment.

Otero finally found what he was expecting all the time, and tried to bite the bullet. When he wanted to look elsewhere, he stumbled with the chief of police's face.

– Did you know him?

Otero gulped.

– Yes, he said.

———————————

his own in his old glory. I started to read other things. I discovered Coleridge, Keats, Shakespeare. Perhaps I never quite understood them, but some lines have stuck with me forever:

The blood is hot that must be cooled for this.

Or

The very music of the name has gone.

When I asked you to try me out with other Collections of the House, you refused to: it is more difficult to translate detective stories than historical or scientific works, even if they are not paid so well. The implicit praise in that phrase was a consolation for some time. The change that had come about in those four years was already spectacular and definitive. Some strong headaches led me to see an ophthalmologist. When I saw myself wearing glasses, I thought once and again of Mr. Lautaro's garage.

The greatest transformation took place inside me. Neglect and dispiritedness were settling in me insidiously. Even I did not realise from one day to the next, slowly falling like tedious sand inside those old-fashioned clocks. Isn't one a fearsome clock that suffers with time? Around me, no one could really grasp the true nature of my work. I had already achieved that skill that allowed me to translate five pages an hour, and four hours' work were enough for me to survive on. They thought I was lazy and

The chief of police covered the corpse and the way was cleared for non-committal phrases no one rehearsed, consolations which had already been pronounced, gestures of superfluous memory.

León had stopped moving. The spring had leaped, the curtain was drawn, the image was ready to be filed away. It was a sad image, but it had a serene air about it that it had lacked while it was alive.

Otero said goodbye and was ready to leave. At the last minute, he remembered the envelope in his pocket.

– There is a letter, he said. Perhaps, you …

But the chief of police said the letter León de Sanctis wrote and signed for the judge was enough.

– That one's yours, he said.

---

privileged, they who handle winches, blenders, lathes. They ignored what it was to feel inhabited by another, who is often an idiot: only now do I dare think of this word; to lend one's head to a stranger, and recover it when it is wasted, empty, without a single idea in it, useless for the rest of one's day. They lent their hands, and I hired my soul. The Chinese have an interesting expression to name a servant: they call him Yung-jen, used man. Am I complaining? No. You always kindly helped me. The House has never committed the least injustice against me.

It was very likely my own fault, that morbid tendency to solitude I have since I was a boy, fostered perhaps by the fact that I never got to know my parents, by my ugliness, by my shyness. This is a touchy subject I have come to here, that of my relationship with women.

I think they find me horrible and I'm afraid of them rejecting me. I never approach them and so that's how I spend months, years in abstinence, wanting and abhorring them. I can follow a girl for blocks and blocks, plucking up courage, but when I am next to her, I walk right past her and look down. Once I had made up my mind. I was desperate. She turned round (I'll never forget her face) and said: "You idiot!" She was not even pretty, she was no one, but she could say idiot to me. Three years ago, I met Celia. One night the rain embraced us in the narrow entrance hall of her house. She was the one who spoke. It's silly, but I fell in love with her in five minutes. When the rain stopped, I brought her to my room and next day I made arrangements for her to stay. For a week, everything went fine. Then she got bored. She was unfaithful to me with other fellows in the same house behind my back. One day, she left without a word of notice. That is the closest to love I've ever come.

I often argued with you about whether it was the fall of Peronism that put an end to the enthusiasm for detective novels. So many good collec-

tions! *Traces, Evasion, Orange*: swept away by sci-fi. The House, as usual, had good foresight and created the 'Andromeda Series'. Now our gods became Sturgeon, Clark, Bradbury. At the beginning my interest was kindled. Then it was the same. Visiting the landscapes of Ganimedes or tuning in to Jupiter's Red Stain, I saw the colourless spectrum of my room.

I don't know when I started to get distracted, to skip words, then phrases. I solved difficulties by omitting them. One day I lost half a section of a novel by Asimov. You know what I did? I made it all up. Nobody realised. After that, I fancied I myself could be a writer. You dissuaded me, you were right. I calculated how long it would take me to write a novel and what I would collect for it: I was better off as a translator. Then I cheated deliberately. My pages had more and more white spaces, fewer lines. I no longer bothered to correct them. Mr. Appleton watched me sadly from a corner. I hardly consulted him any more.

– What is the metre of the dictionary?

– That is not a question.

Here, you might be expecting a spectacular revelation, an explanation for what I shall do when I finish this letter. Well, that's it. I'm alone, I'm tired, I'm good to no one, and what I do is no good either. I've lived to perpetuate in Spanish the essential lineage of idiots, the specific chromosome of stupidity. In more than one way, I am much worse off than when I started. I have one suit and one pair of shoes as I did then and I'm twelve years older. During this time, I've translated for the House one hundred and thirty books of 80,000 words each, at six letters per word. That makes sixty million strikes on the keys. Now I certainly understand the keys being worn, each key being sunken, every letter erased. Sixty million strikes are too much, even for a good Remington. I gaze at my fingers in astonishment.

●◆ (Walsh, 1967)

chapter five

Operación Masacre

There was a long break in the Yates–Walsh correspondence during 1956 until a breathless Rodolfo dispatched the first instalment of his ground-breaking investigation: "This is no short story, even if it sounds like one," wrote Rodolfo in January 1957. "Perón was a son of a bitch but these people seem no better," added the indignant writer turned detective. "Innocent people are being tortured and killed – again – by our police."

Walsh asked his US friend to send the story to a US paper or magazine as it seemed unlikely to find a publisher at home: "Everybody seems to think it's too dangerous. But I don't. I want it to be known."

Introduction

The first news about the secret executions of June 1956 reached me in a casual way, at the end of that year, in a café in La Plata where we played chess, where discussion was more likely to be about Keres or Nimzovitch than Aramburu or Rojas, and where the only military manoeuvre with any credibility was the bayonet attack in the Sicilian opening gambit. Six months earlier, in the same place, a nearby shootout took us by surprise one midnight, signalling the start of the attack on the army's Second Division and the police station, in Valle's failed rebellion.

I remember how we piled out in a group, chess players and locals, to see who was celebrating what, and as we got closer to San Martin square it all became more serious and there were fewer of us, then I crossed the square and realised I was alone.

When I went into the bus station there were a few of us again, including one guy with the uniform of a security guard who had barricaded himself behind some tyres and said revolution or not, they weren't taking his weapon from him, a fine Mauser from the year 1901.

I remember I found myself alone again, in the darkened 54th street, three blocks away from my house, where I wanted to get to, and where I finally made it two hours later, among the scent of the lime trees, which always made me nervous, more so on that night.

I remember the uncoercible autonomy of my legs, the preference they demonstrated at each street corner for returning to the bus station, where they returned on their own two or three times, until at last they didn't need to return because we had crossed the line of fire and reached my house.

My house was worse than the café or the bus station because there were soldiers on the rooftops and in the kitchen and the bedrooms, but mainly in the bathroom, and ever since I've had an aversion to houses which face barracks, a commando unit or a police station. Neither will I forget, as I hid behind the shutters, hearing a conscript dying in the street, not to the cry of "Long live the fatherland" but "Don't leave me here you fucking bastards."

I don't want to remember anything after that, not the voice of the radio presenter at dawn announcing the execution of eighteen civilians in Lanús, nor the wave of blood which soaked the country up until the death of Valle.

I have had enough for one night. Valle doesn't interest me. Neither does Perón, nor the revolution.

Can I go back to my game of chess please?

I can. Back to chess and the supernatural fiction that I read, back to the detective stories I write, to the 'serious' novel which I plan to work on within a few years, and other things I do to earn a living, which I call journalism, although it's not journalism.

Violence has spattered my walls, there are bullet holes in the windows, I've seen a bullet-riddled car, and inside was a man with his brains blown out, but it's pure chance which placed me in front of these things. It could have happened 100 km away, it could have happened when I wasn't around.

Six months later, on an asphyxiating summer night, in front of a glass of beer, a man approached me:

"One of the executed men is alive."

I don't know what it was that drew me into that diffuse and distant story, spiked with improbabilities. I don't know why I asked to speak to that man, or why I am talking to Juan Livraga.

Afterwards though, I know why. I looked at his face, the hole in his cheek, the bigger hole in his throat, his mouth smashed, his dull eyes where death's shadow still hovers. I feel insulted, the same way I felt, without knowing it, when I heard that terrified scream from behind the shutters.

Livraga told me his incredible story. I believed it on the spot.

That is how this investigation began, this book. The long night of June 9th came back to me, pulling me away from "the gentle, peaceful seasons."

Now, for almost a year, I won't think of anything else, I will leave my home and my work, my name will be Francisco Freyre, I will carry a false ID, a friend will loan me his house in Tigre, I will spend two months living in a freezing ranch in Merlo, I will carry a revolver and every minute the characters of the drama will spin obsessively around my head. Livraga, soaked in blood, walking around that endless back street where he cheated death and the other guy who saved himself by running between the bullets, and others who somehow escaped and others who didn't escape.

Because Livraga knows that there were several of them taken away to be executed, that there were ten of them taken away and that Giunta and him are alive. That's the story I heard repeated before the judge, one morning in which I am Livraga's cousin and for that reason I can enter the judge's office, where everything suggests discretion and scepticism, where the story sounds a little more absurd, a degree more tropical, and I can see the judge hesitate, until Livraga's voice climbs that steep slope behind which only tears can hide and he makes a gesture as if to take his clothes off, so they can see the other bullet. Then we are all ashamed, the judge is moved and I am moved once more by my cousin's misfortune.

That is the story I write as I hear it, in one go, so that no one would beat me to it, but time passed and it became worn and creased in my pockets, day after day, as I walk it all over Buenos Aires and no one wants to publish it, or even find out what it's about.

The thing is, you start to believe the detective fiction you have read or written, you feel sure that with a story like this, with a talking corpse, they'll be fighting over it at the news desks, you fancy yourself racing against the clock, because any minute now an important daily paper is going to send round a dozen newshounds and photographers, like in the movies. Instead you find only many people passing the buck.

It would make you laugh, twelve years on, looking back at copies of the newspapers at the time, realising that the story never existed then or now. So I wander through suburbs more and more removed from journalism, until finally I end up in a (Avenida) Leandro Alem basement, where a small union sheet is produced and I stumble upon a man who is willing to take a chance. Trembling and sweating, because he isn't a movie hero either, just a man willing to take a chance and that's better than a movie hero. So the story gets out, a fluttering of yellow pages on the newsstands. It is published without a signature, badly laid out, the sub-headings changed, but it is out. I look at it affectionately as it

disappears into ten thousand anonymous hands.
  ●◆ (Excerpt from the Introduction to *Operación Masacre*, 1972)

All change

In 1956 Rodolfo Walsh enjoyed a stable, settled existence in La Plata. He lived with Elina, Vicki and Patricia in a large house which served as a residence for a dozen interns at the blind school, plus staff. Rodolfo followed a long-established routine, commuting by train to Buenos Aires each day, dropping by the offices of Hachette publishers to leave finished work and collect new books for translation.

Walsh spent most evenings playing chess in Capablanca, a café which still looks out onto the main square in La Plata fifty years on; the city has an air of relaxed provincialism, despite its proximity to Buenos Aires.

On the night of June 9th 1956, shots were heard a short distance away, as a Peronist uprising began. Rebel generals Juan José Valle and Raúl Tanco, along with civilian supporters grouped in the Movimiento de Recuperación Nacional (Movement for National Recovery) led an uprising against General Pedro Aramburu, who had seized power from Perón in 1955. Aramburu knew about the uprising in advance, but allowed it to proceed before exacting his vengeance.

Walsh wrote passionately of the events of that bloody June evening, an uprising which began at midnight and still echoed across the nation fourteen years later. He left his game of chess and walked toward the sound of gunfire, advancing and retreating with great caution, taking two hours to reach his home which was just a few streets away. Walsh found 40 frightened soldiers barricaded inside his house, uncertain about whether to proceed with a military attack on their captured headquarters across the road, or hide out and stay alive.

The uprising failed and the panic subsided, the troops vanished and Walsh returned to his interrupted game of chess. Walsh had no political commitments in 1956 beyond an intuitive sympathy for the underdog. On December 18th 1956, six months after the dramatic events of the failed June uprising, Walsh was enjoying another game of chess when a man approached him and quietly dropped a bombshell.

"One of the executed men is alive."

The failed Peronist uprising left a death toll of 27 people, killed in different skirmishes around the country; but there were 11 more victims, unarmed and uninvolved in the uprising, executed in absolute secrecy on waste ground. Walsh didn't hesitate. He immediately began investigating the remarkable tale, sucked into the unfolding story through his indignation at the State-sponsored terror and his vocation for unravelling crime mysteries.

The executed men had spent their last evening listening to a boxing match and playing cards in two adjoining houses in the working-class Florida neighbourhood in northern Buenos Aires. The property was owned by Horacio di Chiano, en electrician, who lived with his family in one house, while renting a smaller flat at the end of a passageway to Juan Carlos Torres.

The voice that whispered to Walsh as he played his habitual game of chess in Capablanca café told him that more than one of the executed men had survived. Walsh caught up with Juan Carlos Torres in the Bolivian embassy, where the frightened survivor had sought refuge after escaping his would-be executioners. Torres acknowledged his intention to participate in the seditious events of June 1956 but said he was waiting for a signal to join the rebels, a signal that never came. "Everyone and anyone used to arrive at my house," said Torres, explaining why there were a dozen people there when a joint army and police patrol kicked the door in. "A few minutes more and everyone would have gone home," said Torres, "and nothing would have happened." When the arrests occurred, no one but Torres (who managed to run off through neighbouring gardens when the police arrived) and Gavino knew what rebel generals Valle and Tanco were planning to do that evening. The rest of the detainees had arrived at the house to listen to a boxing match, which ended with a knockout in just ten minutes.

Outside on the street, three more people were arrested, innocent passers-by who happened to be in the wrong place at the wrong time. When the group arrived at the police station, the detainees still didn't know why they had been arrested although one person suspected that the police had nabbed him for gambling offences.

Only Gavino knew the real reason for his detention and even then he only anticipated a year or two in prison for himself, on charges of distributing leaflets several months prior to the uprising. The suspects were questioned and statements were written up and signed by each of the detainees. Gavino and Carranza, a political ally, admitted they knew about the planned uprising, but maintained that they had only gathered to listen to news of the events, not to participate in them.

The process lasted until 3.45 in the morning. An hour later police chief Lt Col Fernández Suárez transmitted the final order regarding the detained men: "Take them somewhere and execute them." The regional police chief Rodríguez Moreno had his doubts, believing that at least half the men were innocent.

Rodríguez Moreno knew that if he disobeyed the orders he faced execution himself. The three men detained on the street outside Juan Carlos Torres's home had their documents and personal belongings returned and were released without charge. Rodríguez Moreno later claimed that he released the three on his own initiative even though they were also included in the execution orders.

The freezing, shivering prisoners were loaded onto a police truck. San Martín police chief Cuello came out of the police station and called to Giunta, a personal friend, conferring with him away from the rest of the prisoners. "Giunta… were you really inside the house?" Giunta knew instinctively that he could get out of the situation with a simple no, that he was being thrown a last-minute lifeline, one he was incapable of accepting. Giunta didn't lie, Walsh would later explain, because "he didn't know why he needed to lie."

The condemned men sat on the truck: Carranza, Garibotti, Diaz, Lizaso, Giunta, Brion, Rodríguez, Gavino, Livraga, Troxler, Di Chiano, eleven men in all, guarded by thirteen police officers armed with old Mauser rifles, a fact which proved decisive in allowing six of the men to escape the firing squad.

The two police trucks took off, driving round and round, searching for a suitable location for the execution, eventually arriving at waste ground in José León Suárez, a lonely spot close to a neighbourhood dump. Most of the prisoners still had no idea they were about to be shot, clinging to the official version, that they were simply being transferred to a detention centre outside Buenos Aires.

When the trucks stopped, six prisoners were ordered to get down. A voice barked from the second truck: "Not here, further on." The prisoners took their positions in the truck once more, travelling another 300 metres before coming to a final halt.

The same six prisoners got out of the truck, looking around them at the unlit waste ground behind. The guards prodded them with their rifle butts, ordering them to walk toward the dump; they set out "like a terrified herd" as the headlights of the truck illuminated their steps. Rodríguez Moreno watched from behind, pistol in hand.

Livraga, one of the prisoners, dressed in black, drifted slowly to the left, eventually finding himself out of range of the powerful headlights, ready to run at the first sound of gunfire. Another prisoner had opened up slightly to the right, but the others walked straight ahead.

The second group of prisoners waited inside the truck.

"Stop!" ordered a voice.

The click of the safety catches sealed the prisoners' fate. One of them turned around and kneeled before the guards, begging for his life.

Back at the parked truck, two of the prisoners, Troxler and Benavidez, overpowered two officers left guarding them, smashed their heads together and escaped. A third prisoner, Lizaso, reacted too slowly and was immobilised and shot dead by another guard.

Gunshots rang out across the waste ground, instantly killing three of the prisoners. Rodríguez, a fourth, was mortally wounded. "Kill me," he cried desperately, "don't leave me like this." "Only then did they finally have mercy on him and finish him off," Walsh wrote with bitter irony.

Six of the "executed" men survived, by running away into the darkness or playing dead; one even survived a follow-up bullet delivered to his head at close range. One of the massacre victims immediately sought asylum in the Bolivian embassy, another was recaptured but survived thanks to the swift action of relatives, who registered his re-arrest before he could be executed for a second time.

The final death toll for the botched execution was five men dead and six survivors, one of them seriously injured. The survivors went into hiding, fearing for their lives should they be discovered by the authorities.

Walsh faced an uphill battle when he followed the café tipoff and retraced the events of that night, as victims and assassins alike had good reason to lie low and stay silent. "I left my house, my job, acquired a new name and carried a gun for protection," said Walsh, launching a dangerous vocation for exposing State terror.

El Tigre

One of the places where Walsh hid out during the *Operación Masacre* investigation was the huge delta area close to Buenos Aires, known as *el Tigre*, a sprawling swampy maze of rivers described by some as a "lost continent". The regular *lanchas* or river boats travel down canals and around countless islands where people live; they are also dotted with holiday homes, huts on stilts and recreation centres, where *porteños* relax on weekend escapes from the city.

The vast refuge, much of it still unexplored, would shelter Rodolfo Walsh for two decades, affording him isolated conditions for his writing and a safe haven when the city became too dangerous.

"I've had a hell of a time these three months. Most of it away from home. But I'm doing just what I've always wanted to do, working on a *real* case and succeeding too. This thing grows more sensational every day [...] but please don't think I am crazy" (letter to Donald Yates 1/3/57).

Despite the remarkable nature of the June 1956 events Walsh faced no competition from local or international media: "I have talked to some foreign correspondents, including *AP*, but they ain't interested or don't believe the story. Hell, they do nothing but drink and sleep," wrote Walsh, in English, to Yates.

It took five months to piece the story together, as Walsh, the enterprising journalist-detective, delivered a powerful *j'accuse* to the Aramburu dictatorship, which had hitherto cloaked itself in the ennobling title of the "Liberating Revolution".

The key to the investigation lay in the precise time at which martial law was declared, the emergency legislation which allowed the State to legally kill suspected dissidents. Once the law was announced on national radio, any citizen who engaged in subversive activity knew what could await them. Any suspect detained before the announcement of martial law could not be retroactively executed.

Walsh examined the log book at the national radio station, which provided him with irrefutable proof that shattered the authorities' claim that the executions were legal and valid. The executed men were arrested before midnight, well before martial law was officially declared on national radio at 12.32 a.m., confirming the illegality of the procedure.

Two sleuths

Rodolfo had uncovered a true crime committed by the State and nothing would ever be the same again for him. He found a crucial ally in Enriqueta Muñiz, an attractive 20-year-old proofreader who worked atHachette. The youthful Muñiz accompanied Walsh everywhere during the five-month investigation, at considerable risk to herself. Enriqueta conducted interviews, analysed each chapter of the book in progress, suggested rewrites and fell in love.

Rodolfo felt the same way, his marriage drifting into habit, his feelings for Elina ebbing toward friendship. A new world beckoned at Rodolfo as the pages of his beloved crime fiction tales came to life, drawing him into a world of suspense, danger, intrigue and romance. María Victoria and Patricia, Rodolfo's children, were aged seven and five years respectively. In the early months of 1957 their father became a visitor to their home rather than a resident. Nothing was said but the lengthy absences hinted at the separation which lay ahead.

Meanwhile Enriqueta was forced to keep her relationship with Rodolfo a closely guarded secret, as her strict, authoritarian father, of Spanish origin, would have disowned her had he known what was going on. The dilemma was emblematic of gender relations in Argentina at the time as Walsh, a married man with two children, could abandon home and participate in a full-time adventure whereas Enriqueta was under her father's authority, even at the age of twenty while making her own living.

"It's difficult to do her justice in a few lines," wrote Rodolfo of Enriqueta in the prologue to *Operación Masacre*, which was dedicated to her. "I only want to say that if anywhere in this book I wrote 'I did', 'I went,' 'I discovered', it should be understood as 'we did', 'we went', 'we discovered'.

Forty years later, Muñiz was a reticent witness to the events of that intense period. Sitting in a café around the corner from her workplace, a state-of-the-art printing press, it was difficult for her to return to a time when she made irrevocable choices that shaped her future. "He used to stop by at the publishers, hand in his work and chat for a while," said Muñiz, going back to the beginning. "Then he asked me to join him for a coffee on the way home from work," she said, marking the start of a casual friendship. When Walsh heard about the startling untold events of June 1956, he went to Enriqueta Muñiz and asked her to work with him on the investigation.

It was December 1957.

She didn't hesitate.

Enriqueta finished work each day and joined Rodolfo across the road from the Hachette offices, in the Victoria café, to plan the evening's work over coffee and *media lunas*.[15] Neither of the two could afford anything more lavish. Enriqueta checked newspaper archives and the civil register, or accompanied Rodolfo to poor neighbourhoods on endless train and bus journeys to the outskirts of the city, as her second workday often stretched past midnight.

The two sleuths played chess together on the train, using Rodolfo's mini chess set, which he carried with him everywhere he went. "I had to perform acrobatic stunts to hide the whole thing from my parents," recalled Muñiz, who called up friends to confirm phantom cinema dates and non-existent dinners, even escaping on Christmas Day.

Muñiz also kept Walsh's morale up, when interviewees got cold feet and an exhausting day turned up nothing of interest. Few people wanted to talk, knowing that the military regime had all the resources to pursue and kill witnesses, while Walsh was a lone investigator who could be locked up on the slightest pretext.

Muñiz also applied her intelligence to practical issues, knowing when to resort to theatrical diversion. On one occasion she feigned a fainting fit to gain entry into the home of a reluctant witness. On another occasion she pretended to be out on a picnic with Rodolfo when their lingering presence at the scene of the executions seemed to raise suspicions in a passing pedestrian "with a sombre dog". The mock lovers required little effort to carry the scene off convincingly.

Together they pieced the various trails and clues to the massacre, revisiting the crime scene, conducting exhaustive interviews with participants and witnesses, finding important independent experts who reinforced the shocking revelations; they worked together each evening, then continued at weekends.

The intensity of the shared experience took their relationship to a new level, where only Walsh's married status held the two back from

---

[15] Small croissants, ubiquitous in Argentinian cafés.

launching into a passionate relationship. "He was my great love," said Muñiz, fumbling for words to describe the extraordinary moments she shared with the disappeared writer. "He was the great love that never was." Muñiz suddenly jumped forward twenty-two years, unable to resist a comment on Walsh's death. "If I had been around it wouldn't have happened," she said. "I would have taken him out of the country."

Muñiz recalled how Walsh carried a small pistol around with him during the investigation: "not to shoot anyone else," Walsh told Enriqueta, "but to shoot himself if he found himself in danger of being captured." The situation was an eerie anticipation of the difficult years ahead when Walsh faced the same dilemma on the streets of Buenos Aires, where death waited around every corner.

At sixty-four years of age Enriqueta Muñiz is an accomplished novelist and poet and has also written a chess book for children. She is also alone. "I could see no point in settling for second best," she said, referring to the "impossible dream" represented by her "tragic Irishman". Walsh spoke constantly of his Irish roots back then, a factor Muñiz described as "a major attraction" and may have been the reason she agreed to meet me when she had turned down all previous requests for her collaboration on Walsh-related projects.

Publishing a true crime

By the time Walsh had finished his investigation, he had not only unmasked the truth behind the massacre but he had also revealed the truth behind the State's repressive apparatus, run by a military junta which many Argentinians had initially welcomed as a break from Perón's authoritarian rule.

The next problem was to find a publisher. This proved harder than convincing the massacre survivors to speak out on the events of June 1956. Potential editors faced immediate shutdown, prison or worse.

Walsh found his man in the basement of an apartment in 282 Avenida Leandro Alem, where a four-page broadsheet was published each Tuesday, *Revolución Nacional*. The weekly appeared under the auspices of the 'Voice of the Workers' Cultural Institute,' promoting a culture of workers' resistance. The paper's mission statement was bold and ambitious: "the tenacious effort of a group of Argentinians who see clearly the future of the country, the future that awaits you and so defy everything (hunger, prison, torture) to tell the truth so that the Argentinian people understand the flimsy threads of power. Are we alone? No! We count on your sympathy, on your silent support. But that isn't enough, if you are a true Argentinian you can collaborate and help us. We need reports from your union, true silenced stories about repugnant events. This is your publication, send us your thoughts, we will give them shape."

This one-man bulletin, struggling against the grain to speak out about everyday repression, was a sneak preview into Walsh's own efforts, twenty years later, to achieve precisely the same goal, with his "information chain".

Walsh could hardly believe it when the first part of his hard-hitting *j'accuse* appeared in *Revolución Nacional* on January 15th 1957, even if it was a poorly designed pamphlet which did not include Walsh's full name.

The published document was a reprint of Juan Livraga's statement made before a judge the previous month in which he had nervously recounted his dramatic tale. In the statement Livraga denounced the police for attempting to take his life and held the government responsible for any harm that might befall him as a result of making his case public. The accusation was calculated to persuade other witnesses to come forward and give their version of the story, thus helping to protect Livraga from police reprisals.

The authorities began to take a keen interest in the unfolding events and went looking for the author, RJW, whose initials featured at the bottom of the first article. At 2 a.m. on a freezing winter's morning, a dozen weapons roused a sleeping man. The startled journalist was dragged from his bed, shoved into a helicopter, still in his underwear, taken to police headquarters in La Plata, then brusquely sat down in front of Fernández Suárez.

"So, you wanted to interview me, go ahead," barked the military man, dressed in impeccable white shirt and starched uniform, relishing the discomfort of the groggy, near-naked man sitting opposite him.

"I can't," said the prisoner, at which Fernández Suárez laughed mockingly.

"Why not?" he asked, confident now that the investigation would end as soon as the frightened journalist left the room.

"Because I'm not Rodolfo Walsh," explained RJW.

The journalist patiently explained that he wasn't Rodolfo Walsh but happened to share the same workplace and same three initials with the wanted man, whose mother he cursed loudly.

"Take him away," shouted Fernández Suárez, forced to release the unwitting imposter.

Walsh stayed one step ahead of his hunters, who began to visit his home in La Plata.

A number of plain-clothes members of the security forces called on Elina's school, where she lived with her interns and two young daughters. Between the interns, staff and children, each group of thugs was dispatched without ceremony, unable to locate Rodolfo's latest residence.

Rodolfo's fighting spirit was evident shortly after another house visit by State hoods: in June 1957 he wrote a letter to Fernández Suárez, taking advantage of a lapse in the state-of-siege legislation. "It was my turn to threaten the police chief," said Walsh, in an interview published years later (Walsh, 1996 p.120). "I told him I knew he was secretly looking for me, with no legal warrant, and that if he or his men caught up with me I would resist with all the means at my disposal."

The intimidatory visits stopped.

It would be a further twenty years before a police chief would catch up with him again, with more serious consequences.

The story came together piece by piece, as five of the survivors of the June 1956 massacre gave detailed testimony to Walsh, who illustrated their stark account with gripping descriptive detail and dry gallows' humour.

The final version was published in extracts by *Mayoría* magazine between May and July 1957, sub-titled 'A book without a publisher' and augmented with fresh information, disclaimers, replies and other comments, which dragged out the work until April 1958. When it came to naming the book, Walsh had considered "The Rubbish Dump Crime" but felt that the word 'dump' was too weak.

Rodolfo found a better title in the pages of *Leoplán* magazine, which published descriptions of World War Two "operations", a term which referred to any meticulously planned action during wartime. The concept grabbed the writer in search of a title. Walsh's book would have triumphed anyway but the difference between 'The Rubbish Dump Crime' and 'Operation Massacre' showed the close attention to detail which marked every aspect of Walsh's literary output.

Muñiz kept a sharp eye on the developing manuscript: "I corrected his writing, which he would bring, chapter by chapter, from La Plata to Buenos Aires. I don't think there was another copy of it." Enriqueta used to tell Walsh that he would be famous one day, that pupils would study his work in school and films would be made about him. "He used to laugh hysterically at the idea," said Enriqueta, but time proved her right.

Operación Masacre was handed over in nine instalments and printed up in Avenida Rivadavia. Rodolfo and Enriqueta would go to the historic Tortoni Café in downtown Buenos Aires to correct each set of proofs as they arrived from the printing press. The bored proofreader who corrected endless pages of other people's prose on the second floor of Hachette publishers finally began correcting a book which really meant something to him.

chapter six

The end of airships[16]

I've got a taste for adventure, the thought of going back to my usual routine is
unbearable, maybe I'll appear up there before you make it down here!

(Letter, August 1957)

A changed man

In August 1957 Rodolfo wrote to Donald Yates, announcing his plan to
take off around Latin America, hooked on the prospect of unforeseen
adventures and the open road ahead. Rodolfo had spent the previous year
living inside a real crime fiction novel and nothing would ever be the
same again.

The nine-month investigation into *Operación Masacre* turned
Rodolfo's life upside down, as his marriage fell apart along with his view
of the world as a safe and predictable place. The old life revolved around
his family in La Plata and work in Hachette publishers: a stable,
unchanging universe. A whole new world had since opened up, one that
offered endless possibilities to a man ready for adventure.

"One very positive aspect of the case [*Operación Masacre*] is that I have
shown that a crime fiction writer can investigate a real case and solve it.
And what an ending! The guilty party is nothing less than the chief of
police!"

Rodolfo was elated, he had solved the riddle of the year: a group of
executed men had come back from the grave to finger the police chief
who signed their death warrant. Here was a real murder case with an
ending which no fiction writer could have dreamed up.

The pace of events and the presence of Enriqueta Muñiz hastened
Rodolfo and Elina's separation, although the break-up was already on the

---

[16] *El fin de los dirigibles*, the title of a short piece written by Walsh under the pseudonym
Daniel Hernández (Walsh 1995, pp.58-64).

cards. Rodolfo and Elina remained lifelong friends, encouraged by their daughters, Vicki, then almost eight years old and Patricia, aged six. The two girls insisted that Rodolfo and Elina maintain the fiction of their relationship to avoid embarrassing situations at school.

Rodolfo's relationship with Enriqueta Muñiz ended soon after the publication of *Operación Masacre* as she changed jobs and consciously put Walsh to the back of her mind. "I've suffered enough," she told him, when he tried once more to talk her into gambling on a romantic relationship. She feared she would suffer a similar fate to Walsh's wife Elina, left behind in the whirlwind that accompanied the unexpected twists and turns in Rodolfo's life.

Walsh barely had time to draw breath after finishing *Operación Masacre* when he began investigating the murder of a prominent lawyer and newspaper owner, Marcos Satanowsky, at the request of the murdered man's family.

Vicki and Patricia

"Rodolfo was like another child in Elina's house," said Fari Roselli, then a young resident teacher at Elina's school in La Plata, where Rodolfo now arrived each weekend to see his daughters and snatch some rest. The busy sleuth made no time for washing dishes or taking care of the children. When Elina announced her intention to go to neighbouring Chile for a one-year course in 1958 she left the girls in Rodolfo's care; the budding detective had taken on the Satanowsky case and had no time to dedicate to his two girls. History repeated itself as tragedy and farce combined as Rodolfo packed off Patricia and Vicki to a boarding school run by nuns.

Patricia was excited at the prospect of going to a new school, which, she was assured, would be like a holiday camp, holding out the promise of new friends and extra playtime. New clothes and toys were bought for her and Vicki, increasing the buzz of excitement. The two girls gripped their father's hand when they arrived at the school gate, just as Rodolfo and Héctor held on to their own father's hand when they first passed under the portrait of Father Fahy and entered their boarding school in 1938, imagining a fun-filled universe of football and ice cream.

Reality proved to be a cruel disappointment; hours before they left for the school, the girls were told that they couldn't take any toys with them. Patricia and Vicki walked through the doors of the María Auxiliadora primary school, in Buenos Aires, where the stern Silesian nuns immediately advised them that henceforth they would be identified as "22" and "56" respectively, the numbers attached to the standard-issue smocks handed out in the school laundry room.

As the youngest girl in the school Patricia was allowed an extra half hour in bed in the morning, while she also arranged the flowers in the chapel and put out the candles on the altar after mass. "The weight of religion was overwhelming," she recalled. These minor privileges did nothing to lessen her unhappiness and Patricia spent most of the year in the school infirmary, sick with loneliness.

Every Sunday Rodolfo would arrive at the school gate and take the two girls to 2393 Calle Canning, the home of their grandmother, Dora, leaving them there for the afternoon. "He would take us to the door of the house, then leave," said Patricia, an unhappy memory of a busy father, passionately dedicated to the investigation of crimes but pitifully unavailable for his young daughters.

Patricia's grandmother Dora was "a stiff, unaffectionate woman" who greeted the two girls formally, "Hello Vicki, hello Patsy" and spent the first hour talking to them in English, a language they didn't understand.

While Rodolfo told the girls about their Irish roots, Dora considered herself English, firmly believing Britain to be the centre of the civilised world. She stuck to her habits of five o'clock tea as if her life depended on them. Out came the finest china, the napkins, scones, teapot and tea cosy, affirming another triumph over barbarism. The formality of Dora's behaviour convinced Patricia that her grandmother must have had exquisite taste and the wealth to match it but she came to realise that the fancy appearances masked her precarious financial condition. On closer inspection the furniture was old and shabby, the house short on maintenance.

When tea was over each Sunday the tablecloth was carefully shaken out, then turned over and a deck of cards was produced. In a nostalgic touch that recalled her departed husband, the indebted gambler who turned the entire family onto the street, granny Walsh taught six-year-old Patricia how to play poker. When the afternoon was over the girls had to shine their shoes to a spectacular finish before returning to the care of the nuns.

On the occasional Sundays when Rodolfo didn't turn up for the girls Patricia suffered fits of anxiety and had to be consoled by her older sister Vicki. Young Patricia's other abiding memory of the time was a campaign run by the nuns in favour of State-maintained religious teaching. The girls were given badges to wear when they left the school, indicating they supported the church campaign. "We hadn't even got outside the school gates before Rodolfo had taken the badges off," said Patricia, who carefully put her badge back on before returning to the school later in the day.

Poupee Blanchard

Poupee Blanchard, a delicate, petite woman with fine features and a warm sense of humour, first met Rodolfo at El Platero bookshop in downtown Buenos Aires in 1958. Poupee was friendly with the owner, Jorge Alvarez, who knew Walsh and would publish his work several years later. One evening Poupee and Rodolfo were pottering around the bookshelves as Jorge prepared to close up. "We went for a drink then I invited them back to my apartment," recalled Poupee in 1999, a slim, energetic 80-year-old woman whose memories of that era unfolded over a dozen lengthy interviews.

The trio played charades until three in the morning, beginning a regular Friday night reunion which gradually turned into a literary happening, as actors, politicians and writers turned up and cut loose, leaving behind the stuffy bourgeois manners of the time. The informal gatherings were held in the home of Poupee's mother, adjacent to the family antique business in downtown Buenos Aires. Juan Fresan [17] was a regular guest at Poupee's soirees and he recalled the spontaneous fun which drew more and more people to her home each weekend. The visitors used to dress up in clothes taken from Hollywood Bazaar, one of two antique shops owned by the Blanchard family, and pose in the shop window, waiting for people to stroll by and look in. "People spotted something odd about the mannequins," said Fresan. "When the passers-by were about to move on, we would move a finger or an eyebrow and the person stopped again, trying to work out what the hell was going on."

Poupee opened her house to writers and artists, introducing a whole new world to Rodolfo, who was too shy and ashamed of his poverty to invite anyone around to his home. "He was a solitary man, an utter orphan," recalled Poupee, attracted by his undefined "Irishness" and a certain air of vulnerability.

Another regular visitor to Poupee's home was Ricardo Vitanni, her mother's partner, a police chief who surprised everyone, particularly Rodolfo, with his broadminded attitudes, unheard of in a profession where torture was used more commonly on crime suspects than handcuffs.

Vitanni became friendly with Walsh, and a crucial ally during the Satanowsky investigation, teaching Rodolfo how to mount or avoid

---

[17] Fresan, a PR genius, directed the successful marketing behind Jaime Lusinchi's presidential bid in Venezuela in 1966. Among his ideas, he convinced the candidate to wear shirts which were two sizes too big, which forced him to look up, his neck outstretched, as in the classic images of Simon Bolivar.

surveillance. He invited Rodolfo to accompany him on police operations, teaching him the tricks of the trade. The apprenticeship was a golden opportunity for Walsh, who refined his skills and made useful, lasting contacts in the police force. The lessons also proved valuable in later years, helping Rodolfo stay one step ahead of the police as they ruthlessly hunted him down.

Vitanni was known for his democratic leanings but he was also sharp enough to recognise the radical side of Rodolfo, marking distances even at the relaxed, Friday night social gatherings. "If you guys take power," he said once, gesturing at Rodolfo and friends, "the first person you'll execute will be me." The awkward moment passed quickly, helped no doubt by the flow of alcohol and the apparent absurdity of the comment.

Fresan spotted Rodolfo's addiction to detail, an aspect of his character which shaped his commitments in the years to come: "Rodolfo was so demanding of himself," recalled Fresan, impressed at the rigour surrounding Walsh's every move, "he would spend three months figuring out the precise meaning of an adjective. [...] Rodolfo really relaxed at Poupee's fiestas," added Fresan, "he lost his fear of public ridicule, he had a great laugh, but he needed to be inspired by the company." Fresan eventually fell out with Rodolfo over personal and political issues and harboured mixed feelings about his legacy. "Rodolfo went from writing crime fiction to investigating true crimes, he craved action, he was a sort of Quixote who lost touch with reality, a suicide in the making, like Che Guevara," he explained.

Poupee quickly became a close friend and romantic companion to Rodolfo, intrigued by the "Irish orphan" with three brothers and a sister. "His mother much preferred the navy son (Carlos) to him (Rodolfo), sending him off to that wretched boarding school," said Poupee of Walsh's mother Dora. The two women met on one occasion in Buenos Aires; "she was completely depressing, one of these rrrrrrigid (sic) women, always serious and grave in manner."

Rodolfo visited La Plata once a week, taking Vicki and Patricia out each Sunday to the park. Poupee always bought the presents for the girls. "Rodolfo was incapable of choosing the children's presents," said Poupee "but he loved to take them something."

Rodolfo was reticent about discussing his childhood but told Poupee about an incident which happened when he was about ten years old, leaving a lasting imprint on his consciousness. His father bought him an air gun on his birthday and the proud boy wandered around the farm, his fingers itching at the trigger. He spotted a bird's nest, pulled aside a branch and came face to face with a stricken chick, beak open, feathers standing up in terror. "What did he do but shoot the gun, blasting the bird," said Poupee. He felt terrible afterwards and wrote a poem in an effort at atonement. "He would recite the poem, a lament, marking out the rhythm of each verse with his steady steps, something he learned at school, da dum da da da da," said Poupee, imitating Rodolfo's heavy tread around the room.

One aspect of Rodolfo's character which remained strong in Poupee's mind was his "exaggerated concern for the fate of defenceless insects and birds," a preoccupation which didn't always extend to defenceless people in public situations.

In 1959 when Poupee accompanied Rodolfo to Cuba, their apartment suffered a plague of cockroaches. "At great personal expense I came across a spray," recalled Poupee, but Rodolfo wouldn't let her use it. "What have they ever done to you?" he would ask, as Poupee fumed quietly, waiting for Rodolfo to leave the house before beginning the cockroach genocide.

When it came to people though, it was a different story. One afternoon in Argentina, as Rodolfo and Poupee returned home on the train, a young boy sat down opposite them. "An enormous youth gave the boy a shove and sent him flying from the seat, the boy fell on top of us." Poupee told off the bigger boy but Rodolfo appeared unmoved by the shameless act of bullying: "He watched all this in absolute silence, never got involved and just drew his own social conclusions." Poupee was bewildered. "He cared more about the death of a cockroach than he did about the bully shoving a small boy out of a seat right in front of him."

Full-time sleuth

"Everyone remembers the basic facts. Three men went into the office of a well-known lawyer, spoke briefly with him, shot him dead and left in front of the astonished gaze of twenty witnesses," wrote Walsh in *Caso Satanowsky* (Walsh, 1958 p.221).

On June 13th 1957, wealthy and influential lawyer Marcos Satanowsky was shot dead by assassins who entered his office in broad daylight, making no attempt to conceal their identities. The killers left behind several important clues, while witnesses later recognised the suspects from photos. The murder weapon was recovered months later, after the girlfriend of one of the suspects gave it to a friend who turned it over to the Satanowsky family.

The ballistic tests offered scientific proof that the gun owned by chief suspect José Americo Pérez Gris had been used in the killing. In the twenty-four hours which followed the killing the papers were full of leads and speculation, while the police said they were "optimistic" about an early resolution to the case. The initial flurry of information and activity came to a sudden halt, as terms like "hermetism" appeared in print. "No one knows who used the terms, but the newspapers registered it," wrote

Walsh, fresh from his success in exposing *Operación Masacre*. The Satanowsky affair suddenly faced "impenetrable reserve" before the final implacable barrier came down on press reports: *sub judice*.[18]

Satanowsky was a 64-year-old Kiev-born Jewish immigrant, who defied anti-semitic sentiment to make it to the top of his profession. Satanowsky opposed Perón but was a low-profile member of the intelligentsia, committed to his family law business. On the fateful day of his murder Satanowsky allowed three visitors into his office on the pretext of their wanting an autograph of his two-volume *Studies in Commercial Law*.

The phoney visitors planned to intimidate Satanowsky into abandoning a case in which his client laid claim to the Buenos Aires afternoon newspaper *La Razón*. The government's intelligence service *Servicio de Información del Estado* (SIDE), acting under orders from dictator General Aramburu, wanted to regain control of the paper. Satanowsky's representation on behalf of his client had already cost him his professorship at the law faculty of the State university, after an article sponsored by the US State Department accused him of being a crypto-communist infiltrated inside the university.

His murder was quietly sidetracked into a dead end of recriminations. Noted Walsh, "those who went to testify were detained and those who were arrested as suspects walked free" (ibid).

A year later, no advance had been made in the case. The crime was now described as "a mystery" while a few hotheads even went as far as to suggest it was "the perfect crime", a lie which incensed Walsh. "Any crime involving more than one person is imperfect, everyone knows that," wrote Walsh, in a scholarly treatise which poured scorn on the official version. At least three men participated in this crime, with at least one more in the shadows, as the material authors of the crime didn't know their victim.

"Any crime in which the killer is seen by one or more witnesses is also imperfect," continued Walsh, "and there are 20 witnesses in this case, watching in broad daylight," (ibid). This was clearly a case for supersleuth Rodolfo J Walsh, who accepted the challenge and the risks.

The murder had taken place within Satanowsky's office: legal staff saw the visitors arrive, heard muffled sounds of a struggle inside the lawyer's office, then a gagging sound on the office intercom. The three visitors left the office, guns drawn, covering their retreat as Satanowsky lay dying, blood pouring from his heart.

The Satanowsky family offered Walsh every facility to assist in solving the murder, beginning with access to all the workers in the building at the time of the assassination. Walsh interviewed them one by one, writing

---

[18] English: Under judicial consideration.

up lengthy comments on their facial expressions, gestures and character traits, re-enacting the work of detective Laurenzi in his fictional tales.

The results of the single-handed investigation were published in a series of articles in *Mayoría* between June and December 1958, the same magazine which first published *Operación Masacre* in May–June 1957. The first article hadn't left the printing press when the death threats arrived, a recurring occupational hazard for Walsh.

Rodolfo continued to work on the Satanowsky investigation, quickly discovering that the trio responsible for the killing were hired by General Juan Cuaranta, who had filled government intelligence with anti-Peronists and common criminals. One of the participants in the crime was Marcelino Castor Lorenzo, who had killed anything between 8 and 19 men in his shady career as a professional strikebreaker and pimp – and he had served no more than 15 days in prison thanks to his friends in high places.

The detailed evidence of State responsibility in the crime and the cowardice of the judge handling the case led Union Cívica Radical deputy Agustín Rodríguez Araya to formally request a special parliamentary commission of inquiry. Ricardo Vitanni was selected to sit on the commission, the police official well-known to Walsh.

By mid-October 1958, the investigating commission demanded the capture of José Americo Pérez Gris, identified as chief suspect in the Satanowsky killing. Yet Pérez Gris had a long record of protection by State security services, who had rescued him from countless scrapes with the law, as he stole, cheated and killed with impunity, always carrying an ID which accredited him as an agent of Argentina's army intelligence.

In his characteristic brash style, Walsh gathered the evidence which irrefutably linked Pérez Gris to the crime, then published his photo on the cover of *Mayoría* magazine, under the banner headline, "Wanted for the Murder of Marcos Satanowsky". While the State dragged its heels or protected the criminals, Walsh unmasked the guilty and put his case to the people. Hundreds of posters went up around the city, advertising the Walsh accusation.

Hours later a man visited Walsh. He had just arrived back from Paraguay and handed over a piece of paper with Pérez Gris's address in Asunción, where he was apparently working as a mechanic. As soon as he could, Walsh jumped on a cargo plane carrying fireworks to Asunción in advance of a visit by the Argentinian president, Arturo Frondizi (1958–62). When he arrived the local papers carried a front-page photo of Pérez Gris, while an INTERPOL arrest warrant secured his detention by Paraguayan police.

Walsh spoke with Paraguay's Interior Minister, who told him that the Satanowsky case was a secondary issue in the Pérez Gris arrest, as the

Argentinian spook was now linked to an alleged invasion plan by 60 guerrillas. The Paraguayan government uncovered arms and ammunition supplied to the rebels by Pérez Gris, along with details of an assassination plot against Argentinian president Arturo Frondizi, during his upcoming visit.

Walsh went directly to the police where he studied a copy of the confession that Pérez Gris had made to the Paraguayan police. The accused claimed that he had fled Argentina due to his involvement in the Satanowsky killing, carried out "under the express orders of General Cuaranta." The imprisoned agent also confessed to accepting money to plot the assassination of Argentinian president Arturo Frondizi and buying weapons for Paraguayan rebels, all the while collecting his monthly cheque as an agent of the Argentinian secret service.

A day later, Walsh talked his way into prison to visit Pérez Gris, who looked far different from the cocky criminal described by associates. He had a long beard, cotton earplugs and "reddened, insomniac eyes". Walsh offered him a cigarette, which he feverishly accepted. "Afterwards he finished off six packets," wrote Walsh. In one of the brief absences of the watching prison guard, Walsh asked him if he had been tortured.

Pérez Gris assured Walsh that he hadn't been tortured.

In a document dated October 26th 1958, Walsh typed up a second confession, a four-page account of Pérez Gris's involvement in the Satanowsky killing, implicating General Cuaranta as intellectual author of the crime and naming several accomplices to the killing: notably Oscar Allende, Rodolfo Ladislao Palacios and Marcelino Castor Lorenzo. Pérez Gris claimed that Palacios had taken them to Calle San Martín, where Satanowsky's office was located. Palacios, like Pérez Gris, followed Allende's orders and went up to Satanowsky's office, where Allende fired the fatal shots.

Walsh returned to Buenos Aires where he wrote up part of the confession and an accompanying article, holding off on the story of the assassination plot, as part of an agreement with Argentina's Interior Minister.

Someone leaked or sold Walsh's scoop to a rival paper, revealing the undisclosed part of the Pérez Gris confession. The rivals then handed the bombshell on to deputy Rodríguez Araya, precipitating a public announcement. The Interior Minister was forced to address the nation on television, denouncing the assassination plot.

The next day, all the daily papers had the story of the Pérez Gris confession (and details of the assassination plot) twenty-four hours before the magazine which had dedicated five months of investigation to getting the story.

Walsh was not impressed.

Walsh blamed the Radical party for leaking the story prematurely to divert attention from the following day's parliamentary debate on the thorny issue of oil company concessions. By then, however, Walsh was on a plane back to Asunción, where he confronted Pérez Gris again.

"You're in a fix," the imprisoned agent told him, "because I'm innocent."

Pérez Gris told him his confession had been obtained through torture, despite his previous denial. Walsh prepared a fresh confession, but caught him out on key details, such as his alleged date of leaving Buenos Aires, supposedly before the Satanowsky killing took place.

If Pérez Gris's interrogator had been any other journalist, he would have written up the story without further delay. Walsh the devoted sleuth, though, tracked down hotel records which demonstrated that Pérez Gris had checked into a hotel in the Argentinian city of Córdoba on June 16th (three days after the murder) and meteorological records which recorded the tremendous rainstorm that surprised Pérez Gris on his way to Paraguay: 47 millimeters of rain on Buenos Aires at dawn on June 14th – the day after the killing.

The Satanowsky case raised political hackles across the spectrum: the Argentinian Communist Party published their opinion of the Satanowsky events, writing in their daily paper *La Hora* that "it has been suggested that Walsh was linked to the SIDE from before 1955." Walsh dismissed the insinuation in a derisive footnote: "Obviously no one 'had suggested' any such thing," he said. "The suggestion came from the Communist Party itself."

The Satanowsky case occupied the front pages of Argentina's press for weeks on end, establishing Walsh as a journalist of national prominence and earning him a place in the 1958 *Who's Who*.

In November 1957, General Cuaranta implicated three navy captains in the Satanowsky killing, forcing the investigating commission to censure Satanowsky's brother Isidro, who had released the information. A government minister then issued an order prohibiting the media from mentioning the Satanowsky case. The measure was formally directed at State-controlled media outlets but the private media got the message too.

The tide turned against Walsh's investigation, as the parliamentary commission limped to a halt, its efforts dissipated on political infighting. The media meekly observed the government gagging order and doubts were cast on the validity of Walsh's information. Two of the navy captains accused by Walsh of involvement in the Satanowsky killing, Mario E Campodonico and Carlos E Arteaga, published articles in the daily *La Razón* newspaper, (28/10/58) discrediting Walsh, accusing him of being unpatriotic. Judge Alvarez Prado got the message, quickly releasing the two remaining suspects, Rodolfo Palacios and Castor Lorenzo.

Mayoría defended their controversial contributor, describing him as "honourable and brave" while readers also wrote letters to the editor, defending Walsh (6/11/58). The issue sparked a national debate while fellow journalists honoured Walsh's bravery. "Tribute to RJ Walsh" read an announcement in *Mayoría* in December 1958: "Argentinian journalists from across the spectrum have organised a tribute to their colleague for his brilliant, high-minded series of articles *Operación Masacre* and *Caso Satanowsky*".

The Satanowsky case demonstrated once more that despite having public opinion on his side and the support of media colleagues, a solid investigation was not enough to secure justice in Argentina. By November 5th 1958 a headline in *El Mundo* newspaper summed up the situation: "No detainees left in the Satanowsky case."

The paper at the centre of the Satanowsky crime, *La Razón*, was awarded to the assassinated lawyer's client but the shares ended up in the hands of the Argentinian army. "From 1957 on *La Razón* was absolutely faithful to its real owner – the army – especially the army intelligence sevices," wrote Walsh. "In each political crisis, during coup preparations, the army chief sent envelopes to *La Razón*, which published their contents without modification. The much-praised editorial talent [...] was limited to choosing a disastrous typeface, deciding where it [the story] would go on the front page, or picking an unsettling headline" (Walsh, 1958).

The Satanowsky case drew to a close in late 1958, although the book-length version would have to wait fifteen years for publication. A pirate edition was published on November 21st 1958, angering Rodolfo, who received no royalties or payment for the work within. By then he had more important issues to deal with. Walsh was now ready to embark on a fresh adventure.

Pedro Roselli

In 1958 Walsh had no fixed abode, staying in the homes of friends around Buenos Aires, among them Pedro Roselli, who was a teacher at Elina's school. Forty years later I tracked down Pedro through a chance encounter in the back of a taxi in south-east Mexico. It was a dark and freezing dawn when the shared car took off from San Cristobal de las Casas to Tuxtla Gutierrez airport, following a gathering of Zapatista supporters in Chiapas.

I recognised the woman in the back seat of the taxi, as she had played the piano and sung at the closing event the night before. It turned out that my fellow passenger was Argentinian, so I told her about the Walsh project, wondering if she had heard of the disappeared writer. "He used to come round to our house, tell stories and bounce me on his knee when I was a child," said the startled singer. Hebe Roselli, a musician exiled during the dictatorship, was the daughter of blind poet Pedro Roselli, an old friend of Rodolfo's. Pedro first met Rodolfo at the school for the blind where he graduated from pupil to teacher under the watchful eye of Elina Tejerina. In 1958 Pedro lived alone in the Chacarita neighbourhood of Buenos Aires, having split up with his partner. Rodolfo was in a similar position and asked Pedro if he could move in for a while. "I agreed immediately," Pedro told me. "Rodolfo used to lend me his eyes." When they began to share an apartment Rodolfo would read to Pedro, and he organised his books and papers in a way which made them more accessible to him.

Roselli, now a cheerful octogenarian, currently lives with his wife Fari in a comfortable second-floor city apartment. The couple looked back with nostalgic affection on that era. Pedro married Fari ten years after they first met in La Plata, where Fari was also a teacher at Elina's school. "Elina invited Pedro along to the poetry evenings that she organised," recalled Fari, as Pedro fetched me a book of his poems, which includes a homage to Walsh.

Rodolfo installed himself in Pedro's apartment, where the sitting room soon turned into an obstacle course with cigarette ends and coffee cups everywhere, while newspapers were carelessly strewn on chairs and magazines and books were left open, signalling work in progress. "It was a total disaster for me," said Pedro, laughing now at the craziness of it all. Roselli was less put out by the domestic disorder than by the lethal consequences of the mess for a blind man. "I needed to know where everything was in order to function," said Pedro, his contagious laugh echoing through the corridors of his home and onto the patio beyond.

Rodolfo had an erratic lifestyle; at times he was up before Pedro and out to work, other times he arrived in as Pedro was leaving for work at the national library for the blind. After several weeks spent dodging life-threatening obstacles Pedro reluctantly drew attention to the chaos which had built up around his friend's presence. The next day Rodolfo moved out, leaving a characteristically brief note: "Sorry for getting in the way," he wrote, promising to stay in touch.

Pedro was saddened by Rodolfo's sudden departure, having intended only to call attention to the mess. "I missed him and hoped I hadn't offended him," recalled Pedro, running his fingers across a braille file with a Walsh manuscript encoded within. Walsh's sudden departure was characteristic of the shy, introverted investigator, who could blag his way into a Paraguayan jail at a moment's notice but found it next to impossible to discuss his feelings.

Every year after that, even through the final years of terror, the first phone call of the new year came from Rodolfo. "It didn't matter where he was," said Fari, who took the calls and passed them on to Pedro, "come midnight Rudy was on the line, wishing us all the best." Pedro and Fari never knew where he lived, "for obvious reasons," yet the friendship remained.

chapter seven

The Cuban revolution

*Rodolfo was really warm and affectionate, always hugging me, very
demonstrative.*   Pablo Armando Fernández, Cuban poet

Walsh was a cold fish, always distant, difficult to read.
                                              Leo Acosta, Cuban journalist

On the road

A long-distance person-to-person call came for Rodolfo as he sat down to
eat dinner with Poupee in May 1959. The Cuban revolution was on the
line. Jorge Ricardo Masetti, the Argentinian journalist who visited Che
Guevara and Fidel Castro during the war of liberation against dictator
Fulgencio Batista, had a job offer for Walsh: to join the press agency of
the new revolution, *Prensa Latina*.

Rodolfo hit the road just four days after Masetti's call, stopping off
briefly in La Plata to say goodbye to Elina, Patricia and Vicki. In Buenos
Aires Poupee recalled Walsh packing a meagre bag of clothes and belongings, including a beginner's book on cryptography.[19]

Rodolfo's first task was to open up a *Prensa Latina* office in Rio, Brazil,
a job he expected to complete within 48 hours. "I had to find an office,
rent a telex machine and appoint a Brazilian chief correspondent, three
simple things which posed no legal obstacles," he wrote. However, "forty-
eight hours became forty-eight days" as problems mysteriously cropped

---

[19] In 1957 Walsh wrote *3120-5699-1184 Lenguage Universal Cifrado*, an article about a
proposed new language based on numbers rather than letters, (Walsh, 1995 p.51).
Each number corresponded to a letter or word, enabling people in different countries
to communicate with each other in writing despite speaking a different language.
The language was sustained by a pocket-size 'decoder' dictionary that contained all
the letters and words of a language and their equivalent numbers. The subject
fascinated Walsh, who visited the inventor of the language, Salvador de Luca, who
lived in La Plata.

up, problems "which couldn't be explained within the idealised frontiers of press freedom, free competition and other fantasies."

Someone somewhere was throwing a spanner in the works.

Walsh noted that US news agency *United Press* acknowledged losses of one million dollars in their Rio office that year. "It cost far less to block a licence application in the Ministry," said Walsh, suggesting malicious intent from a rival.

The Brazilian bureaucracy was the most imaginative that Rodolfo had ever come across. Delays and obstacles cropped up in all twenty Latin American countries where the Cuban press agency attempted to set up offices, even though the agency was registered in Mexico City, with phantom directors, to give the impression that its directorial control lay outside the feared island.

Poupee Blanchard met up with Rodolfo en route to Havana, where they arrived on July 26th 1959, on the sixth anniversary of the heroic but doomed assault on the Moncada barracks. The attack was a military fiasco but marked the beginning of armed resistance to dictator Batista.

The day was marked by huge street parades and military processions, with Rodolfo quickly swept up by the feverish mood: "This revolution cannot survive alone, it must spread elsewhere," Walsh told Poupee less than twenty-four hours after they arrived.

Guerrillas to power

The Cuban revolution marked a historic turning point in Latin American history. A small, ragged band of poorly armed rebels launched a guerrilla war which defeated the national army of a US-backed dictator. The rebels became national heroes, fêted on the streets of Havana. "Everybody wanted to take one of the bearded men home," wrote Reinaldo Arenas, a teenage rebel and poet who lamented his youthful inability to grow a beard and take advantage of the euphoria," (Anderson, 1997 pp.378).

Few people knew much about the intentions of the rebel movement, or their plans for government. The Miami Pact (November 1957) was a public statement of principle by moderate anti-Batista forces, calling for the resignation of the dictator and a return to constitutional rule. Castro publicly rejected the terms of the pact, accusing the signatories of treason: "The leadership of the struggle against tyranny is, and will continue to be, in Cuba and in the hands of revolutionary fighters." Castro was determined to implement a radical new programme of government with particular emphasis on agrarian reform and other urgent matters of social justice.

In the first year of the Cuban revolution, Fidel Castro's government put a supplementary stamp on letters to the United States with the following words printed in English: "Our Revolution is not COMMUNIST. Our Revolution is HUMANIST. We Cubans want only the right to an education, the right to work, the right to eat without fear, the right to PEACE, JUSTICE, FREEDOM."

A contagious, open spirit of inquiry prevailed amongst the revolutionaries, even if the evolving process now looks like a deliberate march toward tropical socialism. The Cuban revolution was a year old before Cuba's communists, grouped in the *Partido Socialista Popular*, PSP, merged with Castro's inner circle, purging militants considered ideologically unsound. The battleground would be Cuba's nascent State institutions, the engine which drove the popular revolution, including *Prensa Latina*, a crucial propaganda tool for airing Cuba's attitude to unfolding events at home and abroad.

"Castro had no intention to go the Communist way until events, pressures, perhaps necessity, drove him that way," wrote Herbert L Matthews, a *New York Times* journalist who travelled frequently to Cuba. "It was not a previously calculated or inevitable development," he concluded (Matthews, 1961).

The shadow of Guatemala also hung over the Cuban revolution. The Guatemalans overthrew their dictator, General Jorge Ubico, in 1944, installing a government which was liberal and nationalist. The government's modest efforts to promote social justice and limit the power of the United Fruit Company met with aggressive US opposition, culminating in a US-backed coup in 1954 which installed another dictator, Colonel Castillo Armas.

The lesson was not forgotten.

The Cuban revolution was an uprising without a doctrine but one with a keen sense of history and a pragmatic approach to ensuring its own survival.

Into the fire

The fortuitous arrival of Walsh in Havana on July 26th reminded me of my own arrival in Nicaragua, on the eve of July 19th 1985, the sixth anniversary of the Sandinista revolution. The anniversary fiesta was a riot of black and red flags, t-shirts and face-paint, as hundreds of thousands of cheering people celebrated the triumph of democratic socialism over dictatorial fascism. It was an unforgettable experience.

I imagined Rodolfo, 32 years old, living abroad for the first time in his life, plunged straight into historic circumstances, eyes wide open. Cuban writer César Leante described the first months of the revolution as "a dream made real [...] a perpetual exaltation" (Leante, 1999).

Walsh's reputation as a hard-hitting journalist preceded him. "Masetti told us about him," said Joaquín Crespo, then a young Cuban working in *Prensa Latina*. "We were impressed that someone with so much experience would come here and work so hard, for so little in return."

Rodolfo and Poupee had an apartment reserved for them on the 21st floor of the Focsa building, a towering seafront housing complex completed by US engineers (allegedly with mafia money) shortly before Castro and Guevara marched triumphantly into the capital. The building quickly filled up with foreign technicians and other guests of the revolution, its cool, breezy bedrooms a welcome respite from Havana's crushing heat.

The *Prensa Latina* office, though, was located in a stuffy, cramped space opposite Che Guevara's Ministry of Industry, its offices a boxed-in furnace which turned especially unbearable during power cuts. "When you tried to get up from your seat it came with you, stuck firmly to your backside," recalled Poupee, who began work as a French translator for the fledgling agency.

The Argentinian Ernesto Che Guevara recognised that the military defence of the revolution was not enough; Cuba had to show the world that with honest management of national resources and disinterested foreign aid, the island could achieve better basic levels of health, education, food production and general wellbeing than any other country in Latin America.

Guevara and Castro also recognised the importance of information in building support networks around the world to counter the influence of the US-dominated mass media. The launch of an alternative Latin American news agency had been on their mind ever since they began their guerrilla war in the Sierra Maestra mountains. It was there that Argentinian journalist Jorge Masetti had demonstrated his bravery and initiative during the guerrilla years, getting to the rebel army and eluding Batista's police, a feat which led to his appointment as the director of *Prensa Latina*.

The first counter-propaganda effort organised by the infant revolution was Operación Verdad (Operation Truth) in which 300 journalists and 'notables' from around the world were invited to Cuba in February 1959, to witness for themselves what was happening. Soon after, a budget was approved for *Prensa Latina* the news agency; competitive salaries were offered to lure journalists to Cuba, agency cars were purchased, offices and equipment were installed.

Jorge Ricardo Masetti

Jorge Masetti, an Argentinian journalist and friend of Walsh's, made a daring trip to the Sierra Maestra, Cuba, in March 1958, at the height of the revolutionary war. "His contacts were weak, his resources scarce, his objective – Fidel in the hills – way beyond his means," wrote Rodolfo in a prologue to Masetti's classic text on Cuba's guerrilla struggle *Los que luchan y los que lloran* (Those who fight and those who cry).

In the lazy afternoons in Café La Paz, situated along Buenos Aires's bustling Avenida Corrientes, Masetti and Walsh had shared a regular table with Rogelio García Lupo and other journalists, all of whom made solemn promises to join Masetti in Cuba if the revolution triumphed, little thinking the dream could possibly come true.

Masetti managed to interview Castro, Guevara and other members of the rebel army, despite a ruthless security sweep designed to keep journalists away from the battlefield. Masetti swapped his dark *porteño* street clothes for the peasant *guayabera*, a long, loose traditional shirt, the uniform of the rebel army. "But this act of journalistic ingenuity was also a dark rite of passage, an authentic transformation," wrote Rodolfo. "He went there full of doubts, caution and prejudice, all of which disappeared before the remarkable collective experience of a people forging a revolution." Masetti's interviews were broadcast through rebel radio transmitters, the first time that the Cuban people heard the voices and words of the rebel leaders.

In a stroke of monumental bad luck, Masetti's taped news package never reached his editors at Radio Mundo in Buenos Aires, forcing him to repeat the treacherous journey back to the Sierra, this time in the knowledge that his presence had been detected. One day Masetti was a German tourist, the next an Italian or the husband of a Cuban peasant woman. Masetti's daring deeds exceeded the wildest adventures dreamed up by Walsh in his days of writing crime fiction. "The article is, in my opinion, the greatest individual feat of Argentinian journalism," wrote Rodolfo. Masetti promised the rebels that he would return when the revolution triumphed, to begin an information service.

True to his word, Masetti took up the reins at *Prensa Latina* in June 1959, launching an international news agency to counter-balance the pro-US bias of agencies like Associated Press and Reuters.

In his prologue to Masetti's book, Walsh explained the background to the setting up of *Prensa Latina*, which stood accused of being a Castro mouthpiece. Walsh accepted that it was a partisan agency, "as official as United Press, Reuter or France-Presse: there isn't an agency in the world which doesn't answer to the interests of a particular State or a financial monopoly closely linked to that State".

The difference between *Prensa Latina* and the other agencies, "is that the dominant countries of the western world deny such a luxury to dependent countries." Walsh blamed news agencies like United Press and Associated Press, which monopolise the world news market, for "launching that torrent of informational rubbish which [...] paved the way for the chain of aggression and Playa Girón (Bay of Pigs)."

Prensa Latina quickly assembled a talented team of journalists, including Colombia's future Nobel prizewinner Gabriel García Marquez and Uruguayan writer Juan Carlos Onetti. "Wherever they had to fight for the news in equal conditions, they got there first and wrote it better," said Walsh, with evident pride.

Masetti and Walsh had a good relationship in Cuba but clashed on occasion: "Rodolfo would come home from the office, cursing Masetti," recalled Poupee, with disagreements usually arising over Masetti's habit of announcing his decisions without explanation. "It drove Rodolfo wild because he had the habits of the decadent bourgeois world where the employee must follow directives but always has the right to question a decision or pull a face over it."

They lived tense times, defining times, in the run-up to the decisive Bay of Pigs invasion, (April 1961) when Cuba would face its hour of truth and emerge victorious. The imminent threat of invasion also fomented a mood of paranoia, as the revolution kept a vigilant eye on potential enemies. Masetti was totally committed to the revolution, while Walsh remained an outsider, settling into the rhythm of work and life in Cuba but never belonging in the way Masetti did. Walsh's critical hour was still a decade away.

Walsh was impressed by Masetti's unflinching commitment, his belief in the notion of *entrega* (self-sacrifice) which would lead him to fight in Algeria and later in Argentina, where he formed a guerrilla in Salta, in the north of the country. In 1964 Masetti secretly organised his *Ejército Guerrillero del Pueblo*, leading a rebel column into Argentina via Bolivia, with the support of several Cuban veterans. Masetti styled himself "Comandante Segundo" with the maximum leadership post reserved for Che Guevara, who hoped to join them at a later date.

Masetti's group attempted to recruit local *campesinos*[20] but a combination of betrayal, harsh conditions and lack of support led to a series of deadly ambushes by the security forces. Masetti, "the devil with the red beard," as the security forces called him, was last seen in April 1964.

Years later, Walsh met Masetti's compañera Conchita Dubois again; she took Walsh to task for a cutting piece on the failed Masetti mission published in Uruguay's *Marcha* newspaper. "He told me that what he most regretted about Masetti was that his old friend didn't trust him enough to confide in him about the planned guerrilla movement," Dubois told me, speaking at her home in Havana in 1999, where she lives

---

[20] The term *campesino*, "small farmer", is often used of all rural inhabitants across Latin America.

and works as a tourist guide.

Masetti's example bore singular weight for Walsh, as the transformation from journalist to guerrilla operative mirrored Walsh's own future.

Prensa Latina

"There was one thing we all understood," said Joaquín Crespo, a Cuban citizen and founding member of *Prensa Latina*. "We had emerged from a social process and it was our job to refute the lies and distortions broadcast against Cuba."

The downside of Cuba's speedy social advance was that in achieving their modest goals of food, health and education for all, the embattled island became an ever greater threat to US interests in the region, as news of its achievements spread like wildfire through the continent.

Sympathisers of the Cuban revolution criticised the US government for portraying the tiny island, where the US still has a military base, as a threat to its national security. The real threat lay in the prospect of a dependent, impoverished State transforming itself into a functioning socialist nation, albeit with enormous Soviet support.

Walsh stayed clear of the political manoeuvring which gripped the country, as the infant revolution groped toward definition. "He devoted himself to the office," recalled Joaquín Crespo, the sole founding member of the PL team still working at the agency in 1999. "Walsh watched the grammar, the style, the focus of each article." The description matches the image of Walsh in Buenos Aires, the obsessive proofreader who could spend three weeks contemplating an adjective. Walsh turned thirty-three in January 1960, an ageing veteran compared to his youthful Cuban counterparts, most of them just out of their teens, who picked up the craft on the run. "I used to think Rodolfo was twenty years older than me," laughed José Bodis, another colleague. The impression was heightened by Walsh's austerity and self-discipline.

Walsh appropriated two offices for his Special Services department, which produced in-depth reports written by Walsh or commissioned from correspondents scattered across Latin America, including Gabriel García Márquez. Rodolfo combined this with rapidfire cables providing two-sentence "flashes" on breaking world news.

After several weeks at the bustling office Walsh seized a third office for himself, the agency's projection and conference room, justifying the extra space by claiming he needed somewhere to work alone. Conchita Dubois, Walsh's assistant and future partner of Jorge Masetti, had the task of rearranging the room when it was required for a conference meeting. "She would pack away all his papers, the radio, his revolver and bullets and hide them behind a curtain," explained Poupee, "taking good care to remember the order in which each item had been left on each chair."

US-backed counter-revolutionary attacks had already begun when Walsh arrived, as planes took off from Florida to bomb civilian targets in Havana, piloted by exiled Cubans with the full knowledge of US authorities. The windows and office partitions at *Prensa Latina* were shattered so often that an open plan system was established. No one sat too close to the windows, for fear of a surprise decapitation.

One of the reasons that Masetti imported experienced journalists from abroad was the difficulty in persuading well-established Cuban journalists to leave their posts. *"Prensa Latina* was a shot in the dark," said Rogelio García Lupo, Walsh's friend from Buenos Aires. The Cuban press was vibrant and free of censorship in 1959, with journalists earning higher salaries in jobs they had held since before the revolution. "A year later they were all shut down," added García Lupo, who left Cuba in 1960, worn out by the sectarian tensions which had taken root in Castro's revolution.

The assault on press freedom began in earnest in 1960 when a *coletilla* or "tag" was attached to articles considered hostile to the revolution: "This article is published by virtue of Cuba's commitment to freedom of the press. But the workers on this newspaper wish to make clear that the content does not in the least correspond to the most elemental principles of journalistic truth," read the obligatory tag attached to certain articles. The conservative daily *Diario de la Marina* produced its own *contracoletilla* or counter-tag: "We trust that our own readers will know how to judge this," it read.

The information war continued, with Masetti coming under fire for his "liberal" opinions. His friendship with Che Guevara delayed the inevitable ouster. Armed journalists in militia uniforms turned up at the offices of the newspaper *Información* on January 16th 1960, demanding the insertion of the tag into foreign news agency reports. Two days later Cuba's *Avance* newspaper opted not to publish that day rather than submit to the bullying. The paper was taken over by the Association of Reporters, a loyal party vehicle, in what was a clear statement that critical media faced shutdown by the authorities.

In the first year of *Prensa Latina*'s existence Cuba's political forces co-existed in relative harmony inside the agency office, as moderates, nationalists, socialists and communists focused on the urgent tasks before them: creating a news agency which would compete with international rivals.

What *Prensa Latina* lacked in financial resources they made up for in ingenuity, as when its correspondent Angel Boan succeeded in getting an interview with Dominican Republic dictator Rafael Trujillo (1932–61): "Boan simply called him up on the phone and claimed to be from a rival news agency," recalled Walsh.

The mood was upbeat and humour prevailed in the office, despite deadline pressures. "At that time humour was a revolutionary credential," recalled Plinio Apuleyo Mendoza, a Colombian writer who worked as a correspondent in Bogotá before spending time in Cuba. Mendoza quickly spotted the "bureaucrats" in the agency offices, noting their solemn attitude toward anyone who dared to make fun of the revolution.

Prensa Latina was home to all sorts of journalists, some of them fairly relaxed old-guard communists; there was also a nucleus of more conflictive communists, who believed that the selection of jobs at home and abroad should be decided according to the criteria of loyalty to the local communist bureaucracy.

Some of the staff members jockeyed for position and political favour, many of them members of the Partido Socialista Popular, PSP, which consciously set out to expand its influence in government ministries. The PSP cadres paid particular attention to the regime's political police, the G-2, subsequently called State Security. Once they occupied the top posts inside the security apparatus, the party "bureaucrats" installed their people in all corners of revolutionary authority. The launch of Cuba's Union of Writers and Artists (UNEAC) in August 1961 saw the PSP entrench itself as the guardian of the State's new cultural organisation.

The office was a noisy, bustling place where people shouted to each other to be heard above the general din. Fidel was the word on everyone's lips, the unquestioned leader of the revolutionary process. Journalists volunteered for militia duty just like plumbers and dentists, as the entire nation rallied to defend the revolutionary process. A healthy dose of irreverent humour prevailed, where an audience always tuned in to hear the latest Castro impersonator get up on a table and imitate *el caballo*, "the horse", as the Cuban leader was affectionately known.

The foreigners working in the agency office tended to be hand-picked Masetti loyalists, who stood by the agency chief when disagreements began over editorial policy. PSP party hacks pointed to his background in the anti-communist Alianza Libertadora Nacional in Argentina, an organisation he joined briefly, as Walsh had.

On one occasion Masetti spotted a light on in the office in the early hours of the morning, as he locked up and prepared to go home. He retraced his steps and discovered a secret meeting of party conspirators. "Go home," he barked, sending them packing. But they would return, armed and authorised to "retake" the agency from the "woolly liberals".

The tensions which exploded inside *Prensa Latina* first manifested themselves abroad, where the appointment of agency staff reflected bitter rivalries between feuding left-wing tendencies. A late-night visit to Masetti's office by Chilean senator Salvador Allende, in 1959, highlighted the problem. "Do you realise that your office in Chile is in the hands of enemies of the revolution?" asked Allende. Masetti was astounded by the news and roused the sleeping García Lupo out of bed, as he had just returned from Chile, where he had opened the agency branch and appointed the local correspondent.

It turned out that Rafael Otero, appointed correspondent in Chile, had backed a Communist Party candidate critical of Allende in recent elections. Otero had visited Cuba during Operation Truth and on his return home he wrote a sympathetic book, which sold out all fifteen editions. "He was a well-known professional at home and a friend of Cuba," said García Lupo, defending his decision.

On another occasion Che Guevara passed on a secret letter he received concerning the two correspondents in Colombia, Gabriel García Márquez and Plinio Apuleyo Mendoza. "What's with the assholes you appointed there?" asked Che. On closer investigation the correspondents' "crime" had been to call the Cuban ambassador to Colombia a "lout". Masetti was fascinated by the choice of words. "Lout? [Cafre?]" he repeated, while on a working visit to Bogota. "Why on earth did you call him a lout?" he laughed, more interested in the choice of word than the matter of the insult itself.

Masetti grew accustomed to the irate calls which invariably followed the appointment of an agency stringer in Latin America. If the journalist was close to the socialists, he was an "enemy of the revolution" in the eyes of local communists, and vice versa if the opposite was the case.

Special services

Walsh's Special Services section produced 44 reports in August 1959, its first month of activity, a figure which increased to 70 in September and 81 by October, an astounding output from a desk dedicated to in-depth analysis and lengthy features.

In a letter written around the same time, Poupee put the Special Services' high productivity down to "Señor Walsh's severe military discipline, which consists of dishing out precise orders in a Cuban accent, sticking his nose into everything and dispensing with the services of one employee each month, again with a Cuban accent."

Rodolfo's team of assistants was made up entirely of non-communist revolutionaries, including Heberto Padilla[21] and César Leante. They

---

[21] Padilla was arrested and imprisoned by the Cuban regime in 1971, for his alleged crimes as a "counter-revolutionary author", precipitating a sudden break with the revolution by dozens of sympathetic European intellectuals. Che Guevara was a fan of Padilla's poetry, likewise Rodolfo, who included his verses in an anthology of Cuban literature, *Crónicas de Cuba*, published in Argentina in 1969.

became easy targets when sectarian divisions surfaced. Padilla, a young Cuban poet, was a regular breakfast companion at the Focsa apartment. "He used to come round and complain bitterly about the revolution," said Poupee. "The poor thing suffered terribly, he was a bourgeois by-product, he wanted his books, he wanted to read, the revolution could be a real pain in the backside, those four-hour speeches, who could stand them?"

Each working day lasted well into the early hours of the following morning, with Masetti, Walsh and other Argentinians relaxing to the sound of tango records after the telex machines had finally ground to a halt. In their precious free time most *Prensa Latina* journalists trained with the militia or joined the national literacy crusade, eager to advance Cuba's ambitious defence and development plans.

News by numbers

On a November evening in 1960, as Walsh sat working at his desk, sending out the breaking news, the nearby telex machine began to spout yards of indecipherable letters, paragraphs and pages of it, all of which ended up in the wastepaper basket as pointless nonsense. Rodolfo stared at one of the messages as it came out of the machine, looked at it awhile, then carefully gathered up all the discarded sheets. He took them home, where they formed a two-foot pile in his living room.

Once more Rodolfo's years of reading, translating and writing detective stories provided the key to solving a real-life mystery. He dug out the cryptography manual which he had casually packed in Buenos Aires, one of a series of French DIY manuals: *Je le sais tout.*

Walsh contemplated the neat rows of figures during a week of sleepless nights, establishing patterns of frequency among the letters, finally converting the garbled crypt into ordinary letters, revealing startling news of global importance.

In an absurdly modest retelling of the incident Walsh noted that *Prensa Latina* had "signalled months ahead of time the exact location in Guatemala – the Retalhuleu ranch – where the CIA prepared the invasion of Cuba." If Walsh had worked with the major news agencies, he would have rushed the story to press, basking in the glory of a sensational journalistic coup, with promotion and Pulitzers guaranteed. He chose instead to pass the story on quietly to the Cuban government, increasing their chances of resisting the aggression ahead.

Cuba was ready and waiting for the invaders, who were routed within 48 hours of disembarking, in April 1961. The prisoners were subsequently swapped for medicines, a fitting humiliation for the US government.

Stealing a march on the CIA

by Gabriel García Márquez

It was Rodolfo Walsh who first discovered that the United States were training Cuban exiles in Guatemala to invade Cuba at Playa Girón in April 1961. Back then Walsh was chief of *Prensa Latina*'s Special Services desk, based in head office, Havana. His fellow countryman Jorge Ricardo Masetti, a founding member and director of the agency, had installed a special room with telexes so that he could receive and analyse information from rival agencies and discuss it at editorial meetings.

One night, due to a technical error, Masetti found himself sitting in his office with a roll of telex paper which contained not information but a very long message in a complex code.

It turned out to be a message sent from the Tropical Cable telegraph agency in Guatemala.

Rodolfo Walsh, who disowned his old crime stories, attempted to decipher the message with the help of some DIY cryptography manuals that he bought in a second-hand bookshop in Havana. He cracked the code after many sleepless hours, without any training and never having done it before.

What he found in the telex was not just a sensational scoop for a militant journalist but also a perfectly timed windfall for Cuba's revolutionary government.

The message was addressed to Washington by the head of the CIA in Guatemala, listed as a US embassy staffer in that country, and was a detailed report on the preparations for the landing in Cuba with the help of the North American government. It even revealed the location where the recruits were training: the Retalhuleu ranch, an old coffee plantation in northern Guatemala.

A man of Masetti's temperament could not sleep in peace without taking the discovery further and from that moment on, he set about planning to send a correspondent to the training camp. For many nights afterwards, meeting in his office, I had the impression that he couldn't think of anything else. One night as he sat thinking, he saw Rodolfo Walsh approach through the narrow passageway with his firm stride and short, fast steps.

He had clear smiling eyes behind the tortoiseshell frames of his thick-rimmed glasses, incipient baldness with solar patches like the skin of a hunter in repose. That night, just like every night in Havana, he wore dark corduroy trousers and a white shirt with no tie, the sleeves rolled up to his elbows.

When he saw him coming, Masetti asked me who Rodolfo Walsh

resembled and I told him he had the face of a protestant preacher.

"Exactly", responded Masetti, smiling as he added, "a protestant preacher selling bibles in Guatemala."

Besides, as a direct Irish descendant, he was perfectly bilingual. So Masetti's plans had every chance of success: Rodolfo Walsh would go to Guatemala with a black vestment and a white collar, preach the horrors of the apocalypse, which he knew by heart, and sell bibles door-to-door until he infiltrated the training camps.

It would have been the greatest news story of the era, we thought with enthusiasm. Only the Cuban government had already made plans to send its own agents to Retalhuleu, putting an end to Masetti's plan.

●◆ (Baschetti, 1994)

Cuba days

Shortly after their arrival in Havana, Poupee began writing letters to her mother Leonor, letters also addressed to her mother's partner Ricardo Vitanni. "My dear family," she began in August 1959, transmitting her first impressions of Havana and an early fruitless attempt to communicate directly by telex. Poupee was still writing her first letter at 2 a.m. that morning when her "implacable boss" (Rodolfo) "expropriated my biro for 'reasons of service'" forcing her to turn to a typewriter.

In her second letter Poupee lamented another Saturday morning which had turned into a working day, as a heavy shower prevented the couple from walking around the city. "The office has a domestic feel to it," she said, "the radio is on, work is light, there is coffee and chitchat." In the agency office that day, a 23-year-old aspiring Cuban apprentice was sent off to interview Fidel, his first mission in the writing world. "Good luck, *hijo mio*," Poupee said tenderly, while Walsh dispatched him with a gruffer "Get going and see if you can come up with something."

"Rodolfo got up early but took his time waking up," said Poupee of their daily routine. "You could see he was thinking about the day, piecing it together, before he showered and headed out to *Prensa Latina*." Walsh also enjoyed regular long baths, which became a source of domestic teasing.

On arrival in Cuba Rodolfo began target practice, often spending three hours a day perfecting his aim at a shooting range. At their usual breakfast spot, a café close to the central Habana Libre hotel, Rodolfo and Poupee would watch guerrilla hero Camilo Cienfuegos, his gun idly balanced across his legs, his broad laughter greeting some comment about the day's events. "We always picked a seat out of range of his gun barrel," laughed Poupee, who expected the forgotten weapon to loose off a few bullets at any time.

Walsh combined his afternoon and evening shifts in *Prensa Latina* with translation work at home. "Rodolfo's concentration was remarkable," noted Poupee. "He worked with the radio on, the telephone ringing, people chatting."

Rodolfo had one public row during his time in Havana, a dispute with Leo Acosta, a former UNESCO worker who set up the agency bureau in Mexico City. Leo returned home and spent time in the office, seconded to work in Rodolfo's section. "I had built up a reference library which I left in the agency," said Acosta, a renowned saxophonist and Cuban jazz historian. One day Leo noticed that several books were missing and tracked them down to Walsh, who had left the office for the day.

"I left a note asking him to register any books he removed from the office, as otherwise they might get lost," said Acosta, smiling at the innocence of his gesture. "Well, the next day there was a strident note, telling me that he was the boss of that section and he would take any books he damn well wanted." The war of the notes continued until Walsh asked Masetti to deal with Acosta. "Sort it out for god's sake," Masetti told Acosta, passing the buck. The beleaguered agency director had enough in-fighting to deal with throughout the Americas without adding a minor book dispute to his troubles.

The row was resolved at a birthday party for the agency, where Leo's jazz band entertained the crowd. "Rodolfo was a jazz fan," said Leo. "He came up to me, smiling, using that ironic tone: '*Che*', he said, 'I could forgive anything for the way you play,'" thus putting an end to the disagreement.

In true Walsh fashion he didn't borrow any more books either.

In her letter of September 30th 1959, just two months after their arrival, Poupee advised her mother to visit as quick as possible, as *el jefe* (the boss) Rodolfo, "has already begun to get tired of being a foreigner and beyond nationalising himself a Cuban I think this means he would like to return home".

Poupee went back to Argentina at Christmas in 1959, then returned to Cuba for several months before going home definitively in 1960, several months ahead of Rodolfo's departure.

Revolutionary stopover

Havana was a busy stopoff point for outsiders anxious to get to know the revolution.

A friend who passed through Havana at that time was radical Argentinian historian Osvaldo Bayer, author of the epic three-volume *Patagonia Rebelde*, an account of a worker uprising savagely repressed in 1919. Bayer arrived with a union delegation on the first anniversary of the revolution, in January 1961. Bayer and Walsh enjoyed verbal sparring over their respective political positions, as Walsh had sympathised with Perón, who had imprisoned Bayer, an anarchist, during his first period of rule, between 1946 and 1955.

Bayer believed that Perón was a shallow demagogue, great for talking up social change but the first to shut off anyone who disagreed with him. "Where is the working class?" countered Walsh, showing off Perón's trump card – his unwavering working-class support.

When Bayer got to Havana he phoned Walsh, who invited him over to his house, where Pirí Lugones, visiting correspondent for *Che* magazine, was staying at the time. Bayer's delegation had a meeting planned with Che Guevara that evening.

"Great," said Lugones, "I'll tag along."

Bayer told her it was out of the question, looking to Rodolfo for back-up, which never came.

Bayer stayed until the evening, then headed off, making a last plea to Walsh, as Pirí prepared to leave with him. The two walked along the street, hurrying toward the meeting, when a shootout began, as anti-Castro dissidents were trapped by an elite military unit in an alleyway. Bayer and Lugones were forced to take cover and arrived late to the hotel. The doorman whisked them off to the appointed meeting place, where Bayer once more made it clear that he was on his own, but the two were ushered into the room where Che was chatting to the other Argentinians.

Guevara described how the revolution would be won in his native country, requiring twenty or thirty youths to take to the hills, adapt to local conditions and then attack a police outpost. The local people would gradually join the group at which point they would occupy a village, attracting media attention and more recruits.

The process would continue in this vein, finishing with the triumph of the revolutionary forces. Bayer was the sole dissenting voice in the group, arguing that the police would come, then the *gendarmería* and finally the armed forces, to flush out the rebels, while media access and crucial contacts with other social movements would be aggressively denied.

Guevara stood firm on his prediction, dismissing Bayer's comments on the security forces with just three words, delivered with the standard piercing glare: "*Son todos mercenarios*," he said. They are all mercenaries. Bayer had never felt as petty and mean-spirited in his life.

Shortly after the meeting Bayer was hauled in before Cuban security forces, who berated him for allowing Lugones into the meeting. "What if she had been carrying a gun or a knife in her handbag?" they asked. "Well, she wasn't," he replied, reminding them that he had told them she had followed him without his consent. Bayer was ordered to leave Cuba the next day. It would be 25 years before the respected radical author and activist would be invited to return.

A journalist in Cuba

Walsh never wrote anything of length on his time in Cuba, "a rich and particularly important period of his life," said Rogelio García Lupo. "Maybe because he never quite managed to dispel his remaining doubts about the process," he speculated.

One night in Havana airport, Walsh conducted the shortest interview of his life, just twelve words long. "*Vamos a ganar*" (We're going to win), said Ernest Hemingway, the heavy-set, bearded author of *For Whom the Bell Tolls*, passing briefly through Havana airport. "*Nosotros los cubanos vamos a ganar*" (We Cubans are going to win), he added, before concluding in English, "I'm not a yankee, you know."

In his efforts to boost subscription to *Prensa Latina* Walsh secured the Latin American rights to the prestigious French magazine *L'Expresse*, whose regular contributors included Simone de Beauvoir and Jean-Paul Sartre. Some mainstream Latin American newspapers subscribed for the *L'Expresse* service alone, also receiving free the news stories.

"It was a great sales tool," said García Lupo, who opened offices in Ecuador and Chile before visiting Walsh in Havana. "You got papers interested in material which fell short of being an ideological flame-thrower and then they got the rest of the agency package with it."

The *L'Expresse* relationship was terminated in 1961 on orders of the Cuban authorities, who justified the prohibition on the grounds that the magazine was "bourgeois leftist" and "deviationist". By then the tensions between notions of communist orthodoxy and the concept of a lively, competitive news agency had led to the dumbing down of the agency.

The ideological straitjacket was imposed in Bogotá, where Gabriel García Márquez was reproached by a visiting Cuban press monitor, who criticised his choice of language in news reports; from that day on he had to substitute "imperialist agent" for "US diplomat" and "repressive forces" for "armed forces" in his copy.

Rodolfo Walsh was seen as a close ally of Masetti's, but he appears to have stayed out of the ideological battles being waged around him. "If you wanted to attack Walsh you had to go through Masetti and he had a broad back," said García Lupo, a reference to Masetti's excellent relations with Che Guevara. Walsh contemplated another year in Cuba as a literacy teacher but the idea was dropped and he followed Poupee Blanchard back to Buenos Aires weeks before the Bay of Pigs invasion, sometime during February 1961.

"Cuba was divided between communists and christians, democrats and socialists," explained Leo Acosta. "The communists themselves had left, centre and right within the movement, while Rebel Army veterans were divided between people of the Sierra and those who had fought in the plains."

Shortly before the Bay of Pigs invasion (April 1961), the growing tensions inside the agency spiralled. "Everyone went around armed at the time," explained Acosta, who had left the agency by then, weary of the feuding, but who still stopped by the office to chat to friends. Journalists used to set up makeshift targets in the newsroom, taking potshots with weapons they carried into work. Masetti would eventually shuffle out of his office, wondering what the noise was about, but by then the journalists, like errant schoolboys, had hidden the evidence, blaming the noise on disturbances in the street outside.

Masetti had also organised a militia branch among the news agency workers, but many of his employees received defence training in their own neighbourhoods. The permanent tension boiled over one evening, sparked by a row between a translator and a photo lab technician who came to blows. Work immediately stopped, guns were flashed and filing cabinets were transformed into improvised barricades. "A tragedy was narrowly averted," recalled Acosta, as the Interior Ministry sent police to surround the building and disarm the staff. From then on, no one was allowed into work with a gun.

Masetti made one final effort to get the bureaucrats off his back by transferring several of those he called *comisarios* (a term for party bureaucrats) to postings in Eastern Europe. The office regained its original atmosphere of conviviality but Masetti's days were numbered.

The Labour Ministry was now in party hands and word was sent down that the displaced bureaucrats were going to be reinstated. Masetti sent a letter of resignation to Fidel, who didn't respond. Masetti trusted in his special relationship with Fidel, established during the days in the Sierra Maestra. The Cuban leader still phoned Masetti at the end of each night, chatting about the latest news from around the world.

But the Bay of Pigs, when it came, changed everything; it hardened attitudes inside the Castro government. In the aftermath, Fidel sent word to Masetti that he was invited to join a panel of journalists for a televised questioning of the captured prisoners, raising hopes that Masetti would be reconfirmed in his post. But all became clear days later when armed militia members arrived at *Prensa Latina* offices, took control of each department and ordered everyone there to leave the building. The purge was brief but painful. That same evening there was a new face at each typewriter, a reliable party hack, ready to follow the party line down to the last adjective.

"When Walsh left Cuba," said José Bodis, another founding member of the agency, "he left motivated by the same logic which had brought him: as a curious traveller who wanted to know more about the revolution. Once he knew what was going on, he moved on, but the experience left an indelible mark on his political formation."

Perhaps Rodolfo grew tired of the tensions, the arbitrary decisions that saw colleagues "transferred" without due cause, sidelined not for journalistic ineptitude but because they fell foul of superiors belonging to rival political tendencies. His exit was as quiet as his arrival, in early 1961, with a small informal gathering of friends, who expected him to return within a year or two.

On the day after Rodolfo was killed, in 1977, Joaquín Crespo was at his usual post in the news agency office when the news came through. "It was almost like losing a brother," he said, "because we loved him, he came here and gave everything for nothing, and when someone has that sort of attitude you never forget them."

Never trust a special correspondent

From old man Repetto to Rogelio Frigerio, all those who believed it politically opportune to come out against Cuba, until recently, spoke *ex cathedra*.

This method had its disadvantages, requiring theoretical generalities which were, to say the least, redundant. I suppose it was around then that the idea occurred to someone to send special correspondents who could say, at least, that they had been in Calle Zanja, or eaten at the Bodeguita del Medio. With that and a few postcards from the Morro, they achieved the minimum requirements to lie with the impunity granted by the phrase "I was there."

The first to come was a Spanish writer based in Argentina. Strangely, what he wrote for a magazine where I worked in the past reverted to a vast sea of cheap generalisation: communism, the church, all that stuff. By which I worked out that on a personal level, he had nothing against what was happening in Cuba. What could be held against him was the special correspondent bit. Even the reference to Fidel Castro's "Marxist education" seemed less an act of malice than a funny distraction; as everyone knows, Fidel was educated by Jesuits.

But then another one turned up who could – this one definitely – be defined as an outright liar. I refer to a Mr Chirusi, or Ciruzzi, thanks to whom I have just found out, after a year and three months in Cuba, that there are "Red Clouds in the Cuban Night." Such was the title of an article he published in *Clarín* on October 11th, and which it seems is part of a series.

With great interest in witnessing this meteorological phenomenon and taking advantage of the night, I had a look around the city. I looked at the smooth curve of the Malecón,[22] its green lights, I made out the half-hidden shape of the bay, Vedado's skyscrapers and the lights of the Old City, some buoys in the Gulf of Mexico, the reflection of Morro's lighthouse. Nothing. All I could think of was something I've thought many times before: if there was ever a city in the world which was easy to love, it must be Havana.

I can't see the red clouds that Chirusi saw. I wonder if he saw them in the neon light which says "Two Twelve" in Calle Consulado, where I think they took him. I wonder vaguely whether the red cloud thing might have been a metaphor. I thought that type of metaphor was passé by now. Then I wondered to myself if Chirusi mightn't be a liar. Then I read him more closely.

Yes, now I get it. The man was impressed from day one. They told him that things were dreadful here, and he felt like a film hero. He had only left the airport when he saw alarming signs, which he imagines are directed against him, "Flash Gordon" Chirusi.

Let's lend an ear to his exciting tale:

"We had only just left the airport when a disheartening poster appeared: 'Don't trust a stranger.' From then on, we came across these words in the most surprising places. Four words which, like other locks, kept our mouths shut every time we decided to begin a conversation with our host, a rebel officer. The you-know-which warning reminded us of other countries at war, where an attempt is made to create an awareness to prevent, within what is feasible, the action of spies and saboteurs."

"*Joñó!*" as they say here. A tough experience for our Flash Gordon Chirusi, in Cuba on a special mission, only off the boat and he is up against threatening posters stuck there no doubt by INIT in cahoots with the NKVD, along with Gosplan and G-2,[23] by god.

Chirusi was obsessed with the poster, why else would he have used it as the sub-title of his piece?

Chirusi went out to eat and ran into Czechs and Chinese people, naturally enough. This encounter allowed him to draw sinister inferences and a fortunate forgetfulness: that 30,000 Chinese people have been living here for years. But the totalitarian theme haunts him: "We left the cafeteria and could only smile when we saw the reddish light on a propaganda poster which read: 'Don't trust a stranger'."

He had worked it out now.

---

[22] The broad seafront promenade.
[23] INIT, *Instituto Nacional de la Industria Turística*; NKVD, one of Russia's intelligence organisations; Gosplan, Cuba's State Planning Commission; G-2, Cuba's intelligence organisation.

"The car kept going. All during the trip one poster followed another with similar messages: 'homeland or death', 'we will overcome', 'don't trust a stranger'."

By now, I admit, I was intrigued. In the time that I've been here, I think I've seen every poster in Havana. But this one, don't trust a stranger, don't trust an ace reporter, don't trust Chirusi, here to uncover the secret of Cubanacan, this one I swear I've never seen.

So I asked a friend.

"What's that *Don't trust a stranger* business about?"

"What do you think! It's a film."

I bought the paper and finally I discovered the advertisement which disturbed Chirusi so badly: "Columbia Pictures presents: Don't Trust a Stranger, in megascope, with Gwen Watford and Patrick Allen..."

Need I say more? Need I explain that the article, the series, everything this Mr Chirusi writes about Cuba is the fictionalised version of an imaginary adventure?

Mind you, he does say as much every time he tearfully repeats: "This isn't Havana."

Of course it isn't.

Tell us another, man. We've heard this one already.

●◆ (Walsh, 1995 pp.122–4)

Street of sorrow

The human condition has an unshakeable vocation for nostalgia, forever hauling past experience into the present day in a vain attempt to reconstruct what is irreparably gone. Or at least this was my excuse for taking a plane out of Mexico City and into Havana in February 1999, forty years after Walsh first blinked in the intense Havana sunlight.

I planned to retrace Walsh's steps between July 1959 and February 1961, a period which crucially influenced his perception of revolutionary struggle. Unlike Mexico City or Buenos Aires, where old buildings, city centre residences and open spaces have been ruthlessly transformed into car parks and luxury shopping centres, Havana has been spared the demolition "development" policy applied under "free market" neoliberal rules.

On my first evening in Havana I wandered down the narrow streets of the old district, strolling beyond Parque Fraternidad before arriving at the dimly lit Calle Amargura, a street which featured in one of Walsh's agency features, *Calle Amargura 303*, published in 1960.

The doorway at 303 leads into an unlit hallway and a broken lift. I climbed the staircase in complete darkness, feeling my way along, before the sound of conversations, television sets and salsa music revealed flickering lights inside several apartments. I knocked on a few doors before meeting the Pérez family, an all-woman household occupying an apartment on the third floor.

The following day I visited *Prensa Latina*'s offices, still located in their original spot close to the Habana Libre hotel, in the Vedado neighbourhood. It was a terrible disappointment, as archivist Margarita took a good look at me, wondering if my naïvety was a product of cunning or ignorance. "Time waits for no one," she said, softening me up for the truth, fixing me a sympathetic get-real smile. She deflated my fantasy of seeing Walsh walk through the corridor on the fifth floor to take up his usual post at the Special Services department, just to the right of the general news desk, where I waited.

Memory grows fuzzy over time. There were colleagues who placed Walsh at the head of Operation Truth in February 1959, five months before he set foot on the island. On another occasion, 1976 became 1970, 1963 became 1959, and all information had to be corroborated with several sources to ensure its accuracy.

Months before I called into the archive, agency veteran Gabriel García Márquez had stopped by on a similar mission, hoping to track down early archive material, as *Prensa Latina*'s 40th anniversary approached.

Once more Margarita, my archive ally, patiently explained *that there simply was no archive from the early days*. A long search yielded an original copy of the Montoneros's version of Walsh's "Open Letter from a Writer to the Military Junta" from March 1977.

Further investigation would reveal that the archive had been destroyed sometime in 1962 by order of incoming agency director Fernando Revuelta, a Mexican, in a bid to lay the agency's inconveniently free beginnings to rest and focus on transforming the agency into a loyal vehicle of revolutionary orthodoxy.

Calle de la Amargura número 303 [24]

I'm reading the vivid, colourful, almost enthusiastic story of the annihilation of the invaders of Haiti, in that great magazine *Time*. I'm thinking how good it would be to be able to write like that, with such precise adjectives. So perhaps to try myself out, to assimilate some of that mastery, I returned to my old trade of translator.

"Last week one of Duvalier's tactical units stealthily approached the invading force of thirty men which arrived from Cuba two weeks

---

[24] Walsh was writing about the first Argentinian war correspondent who died in action, in 1959, in "Papa Doc" Duvalier's Haiti. The original version of the article was found by Rogelio García Lupo.

earlier." Full, sated, gorged – the magazine uses just one word, "gorged", but me, a poor translator, I needed three words to convey the entire meaning, "gorged on a feast of roasted goat, most of the invaders died on the spot cut down by the overwhelming fire of the automatic weapons."

Here I stop, wondering if it is the poverty of the Spanish language, which does not have words such as "gorged" (which in six letters suggests so many things, gluttony, need, and general satiation) which prevents us from writing so well, as damn well as *Time* magazine.

Just as I promised myself I will study the issue further, a small, curly-haired man appeared. He spoke sadly and said too much, but the fact of the matter is that everyone talks too much today, in this heat, and to top it all I have to write about someone I never knew, who (I had been thinking) probably was a nobody, but he is someone because he died. His name was Jean Pasel and I don't know why I always have to deal with things like this.

But the small, curly-haired man opened a cardboard bag as he spoke, taking out a sky-blue shirt, the cuffs slightly dirty, and a light check jacket, which he fearfully dangled by the tips of his fingers.

The tag on the shirt read Raitor, Corrientes 572.

Then I look at him and he says,

"Jean's things."

Under the shirt and the jacket were two big files, packed with papers. The first which came to hand said,

Jean Pasel
Calle de la Amargura 303

Jean Pasel owed ninety dollars in the Nueva Isla de la Habana hotel, another fifty-eight in the Nueva Luz, in Calle Amargura. In the first they have his winter clothes, which he must have left in hock, and the rest of his things served the same purpose in the second.

I am asking myself whether it makes sense to publish these details, then I think I have no reason to lie. I have no reason to say Jean Pasel was an extraordinary journalist who arrived at the summit of success. The truth is that he was totally broke and opted to go and die on an island of fevers and blacks, where the vultures ate him. At any rate one of his articles, published in some Caribbean newspaper, says among other things, with tremendous honesty: "I believe in journalism, a noble profession which, if practised with altruism, allows you to give back to society a small part of what society has given you."

If he believed that then maybe he isn't sorry about the way things ended.

There was a photo of him in another envelope, which confirmed that

Jean Pasel was too thin, too skeletal and thin, to gorge himself on *Time* magazine's goat. He had a beautiful face, a little sad and old-looking, the face of a *porteño* who had been around the block and back again.

Then the package yielded an image of Our Lady of the Charity of Copper, patron saint of Chile. Then a photo of a girl appeared and a collection of newspapers, letters, articles, and future ideas for articles, items which no journalist will part with even if he has to let go of his clothes first.

Among the letters are three from Arturo Frondizi, dated October 1955, June 1957 and November 1957. They are brief, formal messages, acknowledging receipt of some articles which Jean Pasel had sent to the then presidential candidate.

"Thank you for your ideas on Oil and Politics," read the November 1957 note. "It's good to know that I have contributed to the best of my efforts in improving Latin America's economic reality..."

Other papers testify to the unlucky path followed by Jean Pasel in his final years, when he toured the newsrooms with a typed CV and a list of his work experience. And experience he had, all of it worthy, although it didn't do him much good in the end, as tends to be the way in this profession.

In Argentina he suffered the stupid persecution inflicted by Peronism on opposition journalists. From 1946 he was director of the daily paper *Bragado* in the town of the same name, where he was born. In 1949 the paper was closed down. He began another paper called *Por Todos*, which was also shut down, in 1951.

Juan Carlos Chidichimo Poso (for that was his real name) came to the attention of the authorities and was sentenced to five years in prison. He escaped into exile in Montevideo, where he worked on Radio Ariel and *El Espectador* and the dailies *Acción* and *La Calle*. He went to Brazil, to the fiery *Tribuna da Imprenta*, edited by Carlos Lacerda.

From there he went to Venezuela. The Pérez Jiménez dictatorship expelled him to Colombia, where he also suffered hardship and persecution. Seeking refuge in Panama, they held his passport until other journalists interceded on his behalf.

Jean Pasel came to Cuba to breathe freer airs. He managed to get a job in television, gave lectures in Havana and in Cienfuegos. Some Cuban papers wrote stories about him and opened up their pages to him. All of this wasn't enough to live on in one of the most expensive cities in America. Besides, Jean Pasel probably harboured a sadness in his soul. A man who had a passion for Latin America, he had seen only pain and misery in his lengthy pilgrimage throughout the region. This may explain one of his planned articles: "Looking for meaning in life is not only useless, it is unjust and almost indecent." Other phrases of his, which we leaf through at random, have a similar tone.

Nonetheless in his final days he was again presented with the holy grail of any journalist worth his salt, the article which takes their name to every corner of the continents in a single day, the one for whom the telex machine vibrates. He found out, God knows how, about a daring expedition taking off for Haiti. Wearing only the clothes he had on, the trousers and shirt saved from the hotel owners, he took off.

He passed by this newsroom before he left, or so I'm told. He was going to send us a great story about something very important, which he didn't even want to discuss. The daring expedition was doomed before it set off. It compromised Cuba, the departure point, on the international stage, even though it had nothing to do with it, to the point that Fidel Castro felt obliged to denounce it as soon as he got wind of it.

Afterwards came the annihilation, taking advantage of the "gorging" produced by the goat feast, according to *Time* magazine's historic phrase. Nothing of what was said can touch Jean Pasel. As a journalist his duty was to be where the news was. And he was there.

Even if he never did send us the great story or write so well, as damn well as *Time* magazine.

Havana 1960   ●◆ (Baschetti, 1994 pp. 283–7) chapter eight

Antiques and short stories

In 1999, 68 contemporary Argentinian writers, critics and publishers were asked to select their favourite Argentinian short story of all time. Competition was fierce, with literary giants like Jorge Luis Borges, Julio Cortázar and Adolfo Bioy Casares in the running. After counting the votes, the publishers announced the winning story: "Esa Mujer" by Rodolfo Walsh.[25]

Back home

At their home in La Plata Vicki and Patricia were euphoric at the prospect of their father's return after almost two years of absence. "It was all you heard up and down the stairs, day in day out," recalled Fari, then a young teacher at the school where Elina lived with her two children. Elina hoped that Rodolfo's Cuban sojourn might have yielded some financial gain, hopes which were dashed when Rodolfo turned up penniless as ever.

Patricia and Vicki, aged nine and seven, were demanding children who generally got their way. "Patricia used to stand at the top of the stairs and shout orders down below, for something to eat or drink," recalled Fari, who studiously ignored the constant requests for room service. The young sisters ingeniously set up a credit account at the local shop, spending liberally on their mother's account, buying sweets and magazines. "It was insane," recalled Fari, "they had half their mother's salary spent at the shop each month."

Rodolfo made no contribution to the family household beyond criticising a lack of towels in the bathroom, or some other domestic inconvenience. Elina was sloppy around the house, acknowledged Fari, who remembers her mentor as a brilliant, scatty woman, warm-hearted

---

[25] Olguín, S. ed. (1999) *Los Mejores Cuentos Argentinos: los cuentos más votados por escritores y críticos,* Alfaguara: Buenos Aires.

and devoted to the cause of education for the blind. In the evenings Elina would organise poetry readings in the school, her own verses jotted down on scraps of paper. Once, a favourite poem turned up on the back of an Education Ministry bulletin, having been forgotten for years.

On his return from Cuba Rodolfo had difficulty finding work as a journalist, stigmatised by his association with Castro's revolution. He published "Guatemala, una diplomacìa de rodillas" (Guatemala, diplomacy on bended knees) in March 1961, revealing the depth of Guatemala's subservience to US policy demands. "The documents I reveal are taken from correspondence telexed between 14/11/60 and 26/1/61 between the Guatemalan government and its ambassadors in Washington and the OAS [Organisation of American States]. These messages weren't stolen, as in the classic espionage novels, they were intercepted somewhere in the Caribbean and they came to be in my possession by means I cannot yet reveal."

Walsh explained how he deciphered the coded messages: "An old passion for cryptography and a certain dose of patience allowed me to crack the code that was being used by the Guatemalan government and which will be in use until the moment this article appears." Rodolfo reprinted secret cables in which Guatemalan diplomats planned ways to isolate Cuba and blame Castro for a failed army mutiny over the use of Guatemalan territory for training Cuban exiles.

Rodolfo was criticised by Masetti and others in Cuba for making public the story. "Rodolfo presumed that the codes were changed frequently," explained Poupee, by way of justification. The report was published in *Che* magazine. By then a major act of US aggression against Cuba was inevitable and imminent. Walsh never commented on this breach of security which annoyed the Cubans and Jorge Masetti. It may explain why Walsh wrote little about Cuba for nearly seven years, undoubtedly relieved when he received an invitation to sit on the jury for the annual Casa de las Americas[26] literary prize in January 1968.

Then President of Argentina Arturo Frondizi (1958–1962) sent a delegate to Cuba on the eve of the Bay of Pigs invasion, to take the pulse of political events there. The delegate, Ricardo Rojo, was an old friend of Che Guevara's, who confirmed the socialist path pursued by the revolution. Guevara flew secretly to Buenos Aires in August 1961, where Frondizi sought a pledge of peaceful co-existence from the Cuban emissary. The request was granted. News of the Guevara visit soon leaked to the press who ran stories highlighting the "concern" of the armed forces over the secret trip. Argentina's Foreign Minister was forced to resign while Frondizi himself was thrown out of office seven months

---

[26] The most important cultural centre and foundation in Cuba.

later, the Guevara visit a catalyst for the subsequent military coup. The military junta shut down the *Prensa Latina* office in Buenos Aires and broke off diplomatic relations with Cuba in February 1962.

Walsh divided his time between his old home in La Plata, his hideaway in Tigre and Poupee's home in the city. She still hosted the Friday evening get-togethers, in addition to a Saturday morning brunch, where dozens of friends would drop round between 11.30 a.m. and closing time at the antique shop, at 1 p.m.

Shortly after his return from Cuba, Rodolfo and Poupee paid a visit to his older brother Carlos Walsh at the Bahia Blanca navy base, where they enjoyed two weeks of relaxation. "It was great fun," said Poupee: "everyone clicked their heels and saluted at us when we walked by."

Rodolfo's brother was rising steadily through the navy ranks and the presence of his dissident brother was noted: "I got a lot of stick from some people who questioned me about bringing a communist to the base," acknowledged Carlos, who didn't take the comments too seriously. "I had nothing against the communists," he said.

The main enemy continued to be Perón, the exiled populist who flirted with every political faction bar the communists. Perón remained the single most powerful political influence in Argentina; his support for Frondizi guaranteed him victory in the 1958 presidential election. In return the Peronist labour movement secured a 60 per cent wage hike and a general amnesty for activists accused of plotting the *jefe*'s return.

The tactical alliance collapsed amidst declining salaries and increased strike activity, as six million work days were lost due to stoppages in 1958 and eleven million in 1959. Once in power, Frondizi renounced the nationalist colours acquired on the campaign trail, signing eight contracts with US oil companies and privatising the Lisandro de la Torre meat-packing factory, once a symbol of national industrial pride. According to one estimate, Peronist activists used 1,022 explosive artefacts of one type or another in their actions against the State between 1956 and 1961. Fires were started, industrial sabotage occurred and police officers attacked, in an era known simply as La Resistencia.

In the absence of a regular income Rodolfo began working in Poupee's antique shop, Bazaar Hollywood, where he quickly acquired formidable buying and selling skills. "You would think he had worked at it all his life," said Poupee, who accompanied him to auctions and showed him the ropes. "Within two months he'd learned everything there was to know about the business," she said, objecting only to Rodolfo's tendency to under-price items. Walsh believed that a better volume of sales was preferable to higher profit on single items. "Everyone knows that in hard times you price higher and rely on a more discerning customer," Poupee told me, in teacherly fashion.

Donald Yates paid a visit to Buenos Aires and stopped by the antique business, located at a busy city centre junction. "Rodolfo wandered around, picked up a nice paperweight and gave it to me," recalled Yates, who sensed little interest from Walsh in the profit-making aspect of the business. In the two years he spent buying and selling antiques Rodolfo took a strong liking to just one item: a fitted gun wardrobe with a dozen rifles inside. "He hauled it back to the house with great care," said Poupee, "but it didn't fit into any of the rooms so he gave it away."

In his rigorous determination to learn every detail Rodolfo taught himself basic Arabic and Japanese, deciphering letters and drawings on antiques from around the world, hoping to happen upon some priceless treasure. Walsh made his weekly pilgrimage to Tigre, the delta area beyond Buenos Aires, where he found time and space to write and think. Each Thursday he set off by train and boat to his cottage Lorerey, where he holed up for the weekend, surrounded by silence, without electricity or newspapers. There he began writing fiction.

While he was on duty at the antique shop he would receive regular visits from activist friends hoping to recruit him into one of many political groupings inspired by the Cuban revolution. Yet Walsh was firmly focused on his writing craft. "He sometimes used to hide in the back of the shop when his political friends came," recalled Poupee, leaving her to make his excuses. Rodolfo was more interested in literature and antiques than guns and revolution at the time. His time with the Cuban revolution had placed Rodolfo in the eye of the hurricane, with daily personal and professional challenges. Now he needed time to assimilate the lessons of those remarkable days.

The boom period for Latin American literature was just beginning, led by Gabriel García Márquez, who published *One Hundred Years of Solitude* in 1962, catapulting the young journalist to world fame. When Gabo visited Buenos Aires to launch the book in 1963, a farewell dinner was arranged for him by Rodolfo, Poupee, Rogelio García Lupo and Lilian Hezler. "It was one of the most remarkable nights of my life," recalled Hezler.

The evening began inauspiciously as a broken oven forced Gabo to take to the streets and find somewhere else to cook dinner. It ended six bottles of wine later, at which point everyone's memory of the night became understandably fuzzy. "It was anecdote after anecdote, each one funnier than the last," said Lilian, before Gabo fled to the airport at dawn, back home to Colombia.

The military stood down from power in 1963, allowing elections in which Perón and his candidates were excluded. Arturo Illia was elected with just 25 per cent of voter preferences, as Perón called on supporters to spoil their ballots. In 1964 the Peronist Confederación General de

Trabajadores (CGT) organised a "plan of struggle" which called on almost four million workers to occupy 11,000 workplaces. Many Peronists turned to armed resistance, considering all other avenues of legal opposition exhausted. Argentina enjoyed a brief period of press freedom and a growth in university activity under President Illia, a well-meaning but ultimately weak leader, who ceded power to the military in 1966, unable to combat a deepening recession.

Rodolfo's relationship with Poupee came to an end the same year, soon after the JFK assassination in November 1963. "He sent me a beautiful letter from Tigre," she said, adding that they remained friends.

The post-Cuba work drought soon came to an end as Walsh recovered his place in the world of letters. "Work offers have rained down on me," wrote Rodolfo, who was finding his literary feet in Tigre. There was a job offer from *Primera Plana*, an editorial post at a new magazine and work as a stringer for *Newsweek*, where John Gerassi, an old friend, was then working. "It was hard to say no in the beginning but I've got used to it," wrote Walsh.

Walsh continued to write crime fiction stories in the early 1960s, stories which demonstrated a growing maturity in his writing. The crime fiction tales dried up as Walsh searched for a narrative to express his widening perspectives. On a wet evening in 1964, on the doorstep of Jorge Alvarez's bookshop, Walsh announced to his friends Donald Yates and Juan Jacobo Bajarlía that he was finished with the crime genre. "I won't be writing any more of that," he said, influenced perhaps by Bertolt Brecht's comment that "after Auschwitz the crime story as we know it could not continue to exist" (Lafforgue, 2000). Walsh needed to formally break with the genre, releasing himself from any sense of commitment to a bygone era, as he prepared to bring forth a new identity, groping toward new literary and political horizons.

Writing, centre stage

"I live by the riverbank," wrote Walsh in 1964, in what would be his last letter to Yates. "In a place like this, time changes, you have the feeling of swimming in vast oceans of time. I am forced to write or die of boredom but I have also rediscovered the fun of it. I'm not here for the sake of isolation but, as I have given up all remunerative work, I couldn't live in Buenos Aires, whereas here I can live with relatively little money." The Walsh–Yates correspondence dried up but the friendship continued, renewed each year during Yates's annual visit to Buenos Aires.

In May 1964 Walsh finished his first play, *La Granada*, an accomplished and hilarious yarn about a super-grenade new on the market which was in the process of being tested by a platoon of soldiers.

One unfortunate soldier removed the pin from one of the grenades. He stuck his finger into the hole to prevent it blowing him to pieces, beginning a series of comic scenes which made army discipline and regulations the butt of irreverent humour.

It was performed in the San Telmo theatre in April 1965 and resurrected several times in the 1990s. In addition Walsh began writing three short novels for an annual literary competition. In *Leoplán*'s comedy supplement *Gregorio,* he published several witty and insightful pieces: "They owe a distant debt to Borges," wrote Walsh "but more so to Macedonio Fernàndez, the father of all Argentinian humourists."

The news

She was a blonde woman, about 40 years old, probably German. Her name was Gertrudis. This is what she said:

"I have been eaten seven times by the dragons, but they always had to throw me up and out again…"

"Aha", said the journalist politely, closing his notebook, "And why was that, madame?"

The medical student accompanying the journalist smiled at the word madame.

"Because I am a goddess," said madame Gertrudis.

"A goddess…" said the journalist.

"Yes. Look at this," confided madame Gertrudis, waving her arm around, in a very delicate movement. "All the autumn leaves fall because of me. Look how they fall."

The journalist watched. The backyard of the mental institution was full of trees and from the trees fell thousands of dry leaves. Behind the walls there were other trees and leaves were falling from them too, in a silent, endless flood. The journalist saw how they fell, all over, at the same time, all over the world perhaps and he wondered how he was going to tell this story.

He said, "Please madame, put your arm down."

Madame Gertrudis lowered her arm apologetically. The air became clean and pure once more and the journalist was happy that he wouldn't have to write up such a strange story.

➻ (Gregorio, 5/2/64, reprinted in Walsh, 1996 p.44)

Rodolfo was invited to pick a story for an anthology called *El libro de los autores* (The book of authors), edited by Pirí Lugones. True to form he picked a brief vignette, little more in length than an extended Chinese proverb. "I'm in favour of short, sharp literature," he wrote in his diary, "I'm talking about the return on words, the rate between what is expressed and the raw materials required to say it. My second motive is a bias toward useful literature."

In Rodolfo's opinion, "The Wrath of an Individual" offered a perfect demonstration of the relationship between power without limits and the individual; and by extension between that power and the sum of individuals who make up a people. "It reveals the beginning and the end of the conflict," continued Walsh, where "ordinary people found themselves forced to become angry," like T'sang Tsu, the protagonist of the tale.

The wrath of an individual
(by an anonymous Chinese author)

The king of T'sin sent word to the prince of Ngan-ling: "In exchange for your lands I want to give you another property ten times bigger. I beg you to accede to my demand." The prince replied: "The king bestows on me a great honour and an advantageous offer. But I received my land from my princely ancestors and I wish to keep it until the end. I cannot agree to the exchange."

The king became furious, so the prince sent T'ang Tsu as an emissary. The king said to him: "The prince is unwilling to swap his land for another one ten times greater. If your lord still has his little holding when I have conquered great countries, it is because up until now I have considered him a venerable fellow and I haven't taken any interest in him. But if he turns down what's good for him now, then he's making a mockery of me."

T'ang Tsu replied: "That is not it. The prince wants to hold on to the legacy of his forebears. Even if you offered him lands that were twenty times bigger than his own he would still turn down the offer."

The king grew angry and said to T'ang Tsu: "Do you know how the wrath of a king is?" "No", said T'ang Tsu. "It is millions of corpses and blood flowing like a river for a thousand leagues," said the king. T'ang Tsu then asked, "Does your majesty know how the wrath of a mere individual is?" The king replied, "It is like losing the badge of dignity and walking barefoot while banging your head on the ground." "No," said T'ang Tsu, "that's the wrath of an ordinary man, not the wrath of a man of courage. When a man of courage finds himself forced to become angry, there will be no more than two dead bodies and the blood flows only a few feet. Yet all of China will be in mourning. That day has arrived." And he rose and unsheathed his sword.

The king's expression suddenly changed, he made a gesture of humility and said: "Master, sit down, why take things so far? I have understood."

●✪ (Gregorio 3/6/64, reprinted in *El Libro de los autores*, 1967)

"The rhetoric of State power has changed little in 25 centuries," concluded Walsh, explaining why he chose the anonymous Chinese text, "but in the area of individual decisions T'ang Tsu's epigram still shines with compulsive brilliance: 'There will be no more than two dead bodies here.'" In a prologue to the anthology Rodolfo compared T'sang Tsu's resolve to the determination of the Vietnamese people, resisting napalm and razed-earth terror tactics in their war of national liberation.

The second edition of *Operación Masacre,* published by Continental Service, appeared in 1964. Walsh's thinking was still evolving from the original investigation, with fresh evidence added to the book. Walsh's letters and diary entries of the time were peppered with references to his first investigation, which seemed destined to accompany Walsh throughout his life as he added or removed passages, quotations and commentary over a period of 25 years. "Fernández [the police chief] came out with more statements saying he wasn't responsible for *Operación Masacre,*" wrote Walsh on 15 January 1965 in a letter to his daughter Vicki, who was twelve years old at the time, "so I had to give him a few verbal clouts. This is the year of the battle axe," he added, signing off.

A law to indemnify the *Operación Masacre* survivors passed through parliament, using Walsh's book as evidence. "It seems my small Dreyfus case is about to close," wrote Walsh in 1965. The case closed seven years after it began, although the prospect of a film version kept the story alive, and Peronists remembered the massacre on June 9th each year.

Another edition was in the making; Rodolfo was friends with Daniel Divinsky, owner of *Ediciones de la Flor* publishing house. They drew up a book contract containing an unusual clause: "Walsh demanded that it be written into the contract that the cover price of his books could not exceed a certain amount," said Divinsky. The budget-price publisher put out a no-frills version of *Operación Masacre* with a black and white reproduction of Goya's *The Executions on the Mountain of Prince Pío* on the cover. The economy edition sold steadily over the years; it was obligatory reading for Peronists. Even today the same version is still available, costing less than ten dollars, true to Walsh's wishes.

Rodolfo's literary output included a second play, *La Batalla* (1965) and a collection of short stories, *Los Oficios Terrestres* (Jorge Alvarez, 1965). His work launched him onto the national literary stage; he attended book launches and cocktail parties, but he never appeared entirely at ease among that social set.

Rodolfo continued his old trade of translator, for financial reasons, tackling *La Crisis Brasileña* (Jorge Alvarez, 1965, foreword by Leonel Brizola) and Ambrose Bierce's *Diccionario del diablo* (Jorge Alvarez, 1965). It is impossible to tell just how many books Walsh translated over the years; long after his death, Poupee Blanchard came across a book called

How to Diet while Eating, written by a French author. "It was so well translated that I looked at the back and sure enough it was Rodolfo who had done it," she said.

Rodolfo published his short story about Eva Perón's missing corpse, "Esa Mujer", in 1965 to widespread critical acclaim. While the story is about Evita, her name is never mentioned, even though the whole text prowls around her figure. "The unspoken word was at that moment the perfect description of the body which had disappeared," said Tomás Eloy Martínez, whose book *Santa Evita* hit the US best-seller lists and was the basis for the Alan Parker film *Evita*.

In 1966 Rodolfo entered a new phase in his journalistic career, writing features for a *Newsweek*-style magazine called *Panorama*, between April of that year and December 1967. He spent several weeks travelling around the country with photographer Pablo Alonso, producing a series of in-depth social portraits; in north-eastern Argentina he delved into the myths and characters of *Argentina profunda*, the hidden depths of the nation's lost soul. He befriended lepers and farmers whose lifestyles had remained unchanged since the 19th century. One of the stories was about life on a leper island in the Chaqueña jungle ("La isla de los resucitados", June 1966), another followed the route of a provincial train journey, ("El expreso de la siesta", July 1966) while a third, ("San la Muerte", November 1966) investigated the popular myths surrounding a pagan saint.

"I deliberately set out to work on these articles with the same care as if I was writing a short story or a chapter of a novel, dedicating maybe a month to a single piece [...] this was exceptional within the norms of journalism, because it wasn't considered possible for a journalist to spend a month on a single article of twelve to fifteen pages, or twenty at the most."

Once more Walsh challenged the boundaries of journalism and fiction, chronicling the forgotten people of his country, telling their stories in their own language. In "La isla de los resucitados" Walsh painstakingly recreated the atmosphere inside the isolated leper colony, allowing an elderly local man to give a lengthy introduction in his rural Spanish phrasing, confidently establishing the mood of the place. "Walsh wanted to establish the precise record of the narratives he gathered, as though they contained the trail, the meaning that the written text is after," hazards Roberto Ferro, an academic and editor of Walsh's work. Walsh was edging closer to his true voice, a style which would not be limited by self-referential literary artifice or pulpit-bashing political pamphletism. Rodolfo called it "the breathing text."

"Every single report should be based on a particular investigation at the chosen place [...] Journalistic practice teaches you that when you begin an investigation on a particular subject, it leads to other subjects or sub-subjects that hadn't been considered before and so it leads to a general investigation that you never give up," confided Walsh to his diary, "or to put it more simply, sometimes you go out looking for something and find something else that may also be important." For most journalists the "general investigation" into social reality ends when the story is published. Rodolfo however, was determined to infuse his literary work with social responsibility. His journey into an in-depth Argentina led him away from the pursuit of the great Argentinian novel and toward a collective organising effort aimed at permanently altering power relations between rich and poor.

That man

"How many necrophiliacs have you met in your life?" Enrique Pugliese asked me, his wild-eyed expression exaggerated by the stray wisps of grey hair which sprouted from his unshaven face. I thought of an old friend who allegedly had his way with several corpses in Glasthule cemetery in county Dublin. "How can anyone be aroused by a corpse?" mused Pugliese. The veteran journalist was still in his teens when he became friendly with Argentina's best-known necrophiliac, Moori Koenig, the army colonel who kidnapped Eva Perón's body from the workers' federation office in 1955. "I wanted to screw every woman I could, but they had to be alive at least," said Pugliese, marking differences of style from his old friend.

In the 1950s Koenig was director of Army Intelligence Services and kept Evita in a coffin inside a flower van parked beneath his office, where he had his way with her as frequently as indecency permitted. Soon after his "relationship" with Evita began, Koenig's life began to fall apart, a tailspin which ended in a haze of alcohol, separation from his wife, a transfer to Berlin, a mysterious further scandal which no one talks about and finally prison.

Koenig boasted to army colleagues about his 'conquest,' which he shared with el "Mudo" Frascoli and Nuñez Cremades, two officers who had accompanied him to the Confederación General de Trabajadores (CGT) office to steal the corpse. Frascoli and Cremade went insane within a couple of years while Pedro Ara, the gifted Spanish embalmer who turned Evita's corpse into an eternal vision of perfect beauty, also took advantage of the corpse and joined the growing list of Evita handlers rendered insane by the enormity of the task.

Pugliese was a regular visitor to Koenig's third-floor apartment in Avenida Callao, in the heart of Buenos Aires. He would stop by at two o'clock in the afternoon and shoot the breeze. "We disagreed on almost everything," recalled Pugliese, "but he was an intelligent, jovial type, who enjoyed a good argument." Koenig worked his way through a tumbler of whisky while Pugliese sipped on his coffee, anxious to preserve his lucidity for the evening's work ahead – he was a leading political columnist for *La Razón* newspaper.

Alvarez Pereira, a friend of Pugliese's, approached him one day in 1961 on behalf of Rodolfo Walsh, who wanted to interview Koenig about the fate of Evita's body. Pugliese put the proposal to Koenig, telling him that Walsh was a talented writer, "maybe better than Borges." Koenig was taken aback, "you're joking, better than Borges?"

Pugliese had suggested that the meeting take place in the historic Aguila café but Walsh wanted to meet Koenig in his own habitat. Koenig read *Operación Masacre* and was duly impressed. "That Walsh guy is quite a writer," he said, agreeing to the interview.

Pugliese and Walsh arrived at 2.30 p.m., entered Koenig's apartment and took their places at his long, elegant desk where a tumbler of whiskey and a jug of beer were drained rapidly as the conversation progressed. Koenig said he drank the whiskey to piss away the beer.

Marie Márquez, Koenig's wife, pottered around the house, unhappy at the intrusion, still thinking of the bomb which had gone off outside their apartment some months before, probably left by a rival secret service faction. "She was blonde, pert and lively, she dished it out to Koenig but obeyed him, a typical army wife," said Pugliese. Koenig was fat and generous, "a seducer" whose broad laughter and military bearing contrasted sharply with Walsh's calculated reserve. "Walsh shrivelled up, making himself seem small and insignificant," recalled Pugliese; it was a strategy Walsh used to put Koenig off his guard.

The meeting lasted awhile, as Rodolfo pushed and prodded from all angles, trying to decipher the mystery of the whereabouts of Evita's body, Argentina's best-kept secret at the time. Walsh took no notes yet his reconstruction of the dialogue was "one hunded per cent accurate," according to Pugliese.

When Walsh got up to leave, Pugliese showed him to the door, then returned to Koenig. "Well?" he asked, wondering what Koenig thought of the meeting.

Koenig didn't hesitate.

"That guy is going to screw me," said Argentina's top intelligence chief.

In the introduction to his short story "Esa Mujer", published in *Los Oficios Terrestres* (1965), Rodolfo Walsh explained that he wrote it between 1961 and 1964.

"It didn't take three years," he clarified, "just two days."

One day in 1961 and one day in 1964.

Walsh blurred the strict boundaries between fiction and non-fiction, challenged the role of the intellectual and questioned the "sacredness" surrounding literary production. It is fitting therefore that his most acclaimed short story seems little more than the transcription of a press interview. In a preface to an edition of Walsh short stories, Horacio Verbitsky described "Esa Mujer" as the first synthesis of Walsh's evolving obsessions, as he turned a journalistic investigation into a crime mystery with a political point, written creatively with unmistakable style.

Evita was called Argentina's first *desaparecida*, her corpse kidnapped and disappeared in an effort to minimise the cult which grew up around her image. The effect was the exact opposite, as the missing Evita turned up everywhere, revered by the poor, who secretly lit candles in her honour and knelt in front of her image, carefully cut out of popular magazines, smiling out of home-made altars.

Walsh's story never mentions Evita's name, even though the entire story invokes her memory and highlights the immense absence left in her wake. Walsh coquettishly invented a Coca-Cola sign outside the apartment window, which said *beba*, "drink" in Spanish, a word pronounced almost identically to "Eva". This was the closest he got to mentioning her name.

That woman[27]

The colonel praises my punctuality.
    – As punctual as the Germans – he says.
    – Or the English.
The colonel has a German surname.
He is a stocky man, grey-haired, a wide face, bronzed.
    – I have read your work, he offers. Congratulations.
As he serves two big glasses of whisky he lets me know, by the way, that he has spent twenty years in the information services, that he has studied philosophy and literature, and is curious about art. He doesn't emphasise anything, he simply establishes the terrain in which we can operate, a vaguely common ground.

From the high window on the tenth floor you can see the city as the sun sets, the pale lights of the river. It is easy to love Buenos Aires from up here, however fleetingly. But nothing like love has brought us together.

The colonel is looking for some names, some papers I might have.
I'm looking for a dead woman, a place on the map. It still doesn't

---

[27] From his book of short stories *Los Oficios Terrestres* (1967) translated from the Spanish by Marcela López Levy.

amount to a search, it's barely a fantasy: the type of perverse fantasy which, others suspect, occurs to me.

Some day (I think in a moment of wrath) I will go find her. She doesn't mean anything to me, yet I will chase the mystery of her death, follow up her remains which are rotting slowly in some distant cemetery. If I find her, sudden high waves of anger, fear and frustrated love will rise up, powerful vengeful waves and for a moment I will no longer feel alone, I will no longer feel like a dragged-along, bitter, forgotten shadow.

The colonel knows where she is.

He moves with ease among the pompous furniture, ornate with ivories and bronzes, Meissen and Canton silvers. I smile at the false Jongkind, the doubtful Figari. I imagine the expression on his face if I told him who makes the Jongkinds but I praise his whisky instead.

He drinks with vigour, with health, with enthusiasm, with joy, with superiority and with contempt. His face changes and changes, while his fat hands slowly make the glass turn.

– Those papers, he says.

I look at him.

– That woman, colonel.

He smiles.

– Everything is linked, he reflects.

A porcelain Viennese vase is missing a sliver at the base. A glass lamp is cracked. The colonel, his eyes misty and smiling, mentions the bomb.

– They left it in the hall. They think it's my fault. If they knew what I've done for them, scum.

– Much damage? I ask. I couldn't give a shit.

– A fair amount. My daughter. I have left her in the hands of a psychiatrist. She's twelve, he says.

The colonel drinks, with anger, with sadness, with fear, with remorse.

His wife comes in, with two cups of coffee.

– You tell him, *Negra*.

She leaves without replying; a tall proud woman, with a neurotic expression. Her disdain floats in the air, like a small cloud.

– The poor thing was deeply affected, explains the colonel. But that doesn't matter to you.

– Of course it matters to me! I heard that something awful happened to captain N and major X after that.

The colonel laughs.

– People's fantasy, he says, see, it works. But when it comes to it they don't make anything up. All they do is repeat what they hear.

He lights up a Marlboro, leaving the packet within my reach on the table.

– Tell me some joke, he says.

I think. Nothing comes to mind.

– Tell me a political joke, any you want, and I will show you that it was invented twenty years ago, fifty years ago, a century ago. That it was used after the defeat at Sedan, or about Hindenburg, Dollfuss or Badoglio.

– And this?

– Tutankhamun's grave, says the colonel. Lord Carnavon. Rubbish.

The colonel dries his sweat with his fat hairy hand.

– But Major X had an accident, he killed his wife.

– What else? he says, tinkling the ice in his glass.

– He shot her in the early hours.

– He mistook her for a burglar, smiles the colonel, these things happen.

– But captain N…

– He had a car crash, it could happen to anyone, especially him, who can't see a thing when he's had a few.

– And you, colonel?

– It's different in my case, he says, they've sworn to get me.

He stands up, walks around the table.

– They think I'm to blame. That scum doesn't know what I did for them. But one day the story will be written. Maybe you will write it.

– I would like to.

– And I will be cleared, thought well of. Not that it matters to me that that scum think well of me but I want to go down well in history, you understand?

– I wish it depended on me, colonel.

– They came prowling. One night, one of them plucked up the courage. He left the bomb in the hallway and ran off.

He puts his hand into a glass display case, taking out a polychromed porcelain figurine, a shepherdess with a basket of flowers.

– Look.

The shepherdess is missing a tiny arm.

– Derby, he says. Two hundred years.

The shepherdess is lost among his suddenly tender fingers. The colonel has a steely look in his nocturnal, pained face.

– Why do they believe that you are to blame?

– Because I removed her from where she was, that much is true, and I took her to where she is now, that is also true. But they don't know what they wanted to do, that scum, they don't know it was me who prevented it.

The colonel drinks, with ardour, with pride, with ferocity, with eloquence, with method.

– Because I have studied history. I can see things with an historic perspective. I have read Hegel.

– What did they want to do?

– Dump her in the river, throw her out of a plane, burn her and throw the remains down the toilet, dilute her in acid. How much rubbish does one have to hear! This country is covered in rubbish, you can never tell where so much rubbish comes from, but we're up to our necks in it.

– All of us, colonel. Because at the end of the day we agree, don't we? The time has come to destroy. Everything must be broken down.

– And piss on it.

– But without regrets, colonel. Happily raising the bomb and the *picana*. To your health! I say, raising my glass.

He doesn't respond. We are sitting beside the high window. The lights of the port are shining mercury blue. From time to time you can hear the car horns, dragging themselves far away like voices in a dream. The colonel is barely the grey stain of his face upon the white stain of his shirt.

– That woman, I hear him murmur. She was naked in the coffin and seemed a virgin. Her skin had turned transparent. The metastasis of her cancer was visible, like lines drawn on steamed glass.

The colonel drinks. He's tough.

– Naked, he says. There were four or five of us and no one wanted to look at anyone else. That navy captain was there, the Spanish man who embalmed her and I can't remember who else. And when we took her out of the coffin, the colonel wipes his hand over his brow, when we took her out, that disgusting Spaniard…

It gets dark by degrees, like in a theatre. The colonel's face is almost invisible. Only the whisky shines in his glass, like a fire which slowly burns out. Distant sounds reach us through the open door of the apartment. The door of the lift closed on the ground floor, then opened somewhere nearer. The enormous building gossips, breathes, gurgles through its pipes, its incinerators, its kitchens, its children, its televisions, its servants. And now the colonel has stood up, holding a machine gun which appeared out of nowhere and on tiptoe he walks toward the hallway, switches the light on quickly, looks at the ascetic, geometric, ironic emptiness of the hallway, the lift, the stairway, not a soul there and he slowly returns, dragging the machine gun along.

– I thought I heard. That scum are not going to catch me unawares, like the last time.

He sits down, now closer to the high window. The machine gun has disappeared and the colonel muses once more on his time in the spotlight.

... He jumped on top of her, that disgusting Spaniard. He was in love with the corpse, he touched it, felt up the nipples. I threw him a punch, look, the colonel looks at his knuckles, that threw him against the wall. It's all rotten, they don't even respect death. Does the darkness bother you?

– No.

– Good. From here I can see the street. And think. I always think. In the darkness one thinks better.

He serves himself another whisky.

– But that woman was naked, he says, arguing against an invisible rebutter. I had to cover her pubis, I put a shroud on her and the Franciscan belt.

He laughs suddenly.

– I had to pay for the shroud out of my own pocket. One thousand four hundred pesos. That shows you, huh? That shows you.

He repeated 'that shows you' several times, like a mechanical toy, without saying what it was that it showed me.

– I had to get help to change coffins. I called on some workers who were there at the time. You should have seen their faces. To them she was a goddess, I don't know, the ideas they put into people's minds, poor people.

– Poor people?

– Yes, poor people. The colonel fights against a slippery anger inside him. I am Argentinian too.

– Me too, colonel, me too. We are all Argentinians.

– Ah, good, he says.

– Did they see her like that?

– Yes, I told you already that that woman was naked. A goddess, and naked, and dead. With all her death showing, you know? With everything, with everything...

The colonel's voice is lost in a surreal vision, that little phrase, ever more faint, framing his lines of escape and the lowering of his voice keeping a divine proportion or something. I also pour myself a whisky.

– She is nothing to me, the colonel says. I am used to seeing naked women. Many of them in my life. Dead people too. Many in Poland, in '39. I was a military attaché, remember.

I want to remember, I add up naked women plus dead men, but the total doesn't add up, doesn't add up, doesn't add up... with a single body movement I sober up, like a dog shaking water off itself.

– I couldn't be shocked. But they...

– Were they very affected?

– One fainted. I woke him up with a few slaps. I said to him: "You poof, is this what you do when you have to bury your queen? Remember Saint Peter, who slept while they killed Christ." He thanked me afterwards.

He looked out onto the street. "Coca," says the sign, silver on red. "Cola," says the sign, silver on red. The huge pupil grows, red circle after concentric red circle, invading the night, the city, the world, "*Beba*" (Drink).

– Drink, says the colonel.

I drink.

– Are you listening?

– I'm listening.

– We cut off one of her fingers.

– Was it necessary?

The colonel is made of silver, now. He looks at the tip of his index finger, marks it with the nail of his thumb and raises it up.

– This tiniest bit. To identify her.

– Did you not know who she was?

He laughs. His hand turns red. "*Beba*".

– Yes, we knew. Things had to be legal. It was a historic act, you understand?

– I understand.

– The fingerprint doesn't take properly if the finger is dead. You have to hydrate it. We stuck it back on, later.

– And?

– It was her. That woman was her.

– Had she changed much?

– No, no, you don't understand me. The exact same. It seemed like she was going to speak, she was going to… The finger business was to keep everything legal. Professor R. oversaw everything, he even took x-rays.

– Professor R?

– Yes. It was not something just anyone could do. It had to be someone with authority, scientific, moral.

Somewhere in the house, remote and faltering, a bell rings. I don't see the colonel's wife come in, but suddenly she's there, her voice bitter, impregnable.

– Shall I switch on?

– No.

– Telephone?

– Tell them I'm not here.

She disappears.

– It's to harass me, explains the colonel. They call me at all hours. At three in the morning, at five.

– Wanting to bother you, I say brightly.

– I changed the telephone number three times. But they always find out.

– What do they say to you?

– Wishing my daughter will get polio. That they're going to cut my balls off. Rubbish.

I hear the ice in the glass, like a distant cowbell.

– I held a ceremony, riled them. I respect ideas, I said. That woman did a lot for you. I am going to bury her as a christian. But you have to help me.

The colonel is on his feet and drinks with courage, with exasperation, with great and lofty ideas flowing back over him like great and lofty waves against a cliff, and leave him untouched and dry, wizened and black, red and silver.

– We took her out in a van, I had her in Viamonte, then 25 de Mayo, always taking care of her, protecting her, hiding her. They wanted to take her away from me, do something to her. I covered her in tarpaulin, she was in my office, on top of a wardrobe, up high. When they asked me what it was, I told them it was the transmitter from Córdoba, the Voice of Freedom.

I can no longer tell where the colonel is. The silvery reflection seeks him out, the red pupil. Perhaps he has gone out. Perhaps he is wandering amongst the furniture. The building smells vaguely of soup in the kitchen, cologne in the bathroom, nappies in the cot, medicines, cigarettes, life, death.

– It's raining, says his strange voice.

I look at the sky: the Syrian dog, Orion the hunter.

– It rains every other day, says the colonel. It rains every other day in a garden where everything rots, the roses, the pines, the Franciscan belt.

Where, I'm thinking, where?

– She is standing! shouts the colonel. I buried her standing, like Facundo, because she was a real man!

Then I see him, at the other end of the table. And for a moment, when the purple glare shines over him, I think he's crying, that thick teardrops slide down his face.

– Don't take any notice of me, he says, sitting down, I'm drunk.

And it rains long on his memory.

I stand up, I touch him on the shoulder.

– Huh? he says, huh?

And he looks at me with mistrust, like a drunk waking up in an unknown train.

– You took her out of the country?

– Yes.

– *You* took her out?

– Yes.

– How many people know?

– TWO.

– Does the Old Man know?

He laughs.

– He thinks he knows.

– Where?

No answer.

– This has to be written, published.

– Yes. Some day.

He seems tired, remote.

– Now! I'm exasperated. Doesn't history mean anything to you? I write the story and you come out well, looking good forever, colonel!

His tongue sticks to the roof of his mouth, to his teeth.

– When the time comes... you will be the first...

– No, right now. Think. *Paris-Match, Life.* Five thousand dollars. Ten thousand. Whatever you want.

He laughs.

– Where, colonel, where?

He stands up slowly, he doesn't know me. Perhaps he is going to ask me who I am, what I'm doing there.

And while I leave defeated, thinking I will have to return or that I will never return. While my index finger begins already its tireless itinerary through maps, linking lines, probabilities, complicities. I know that I am no longer interested, that I won't move a finger, not even on a map, and then the colonel's voice reaches me like a revelation.

– She is mine, he says simply. That woman is mine.

●◆ (*Esa Mujer* in *Los Oficios Terrestres*, Walsh, 1986)

Santa Evita

In July 1970 Rodolfo spent ten days in Paris, where he bumped into Argentinian writer Tomás Eloy Martínez, stopping to chat at a café beside the Champs-Elysees. The subsequent conversation helped unravel one of the country's greatest unsolved mysteries – the final resting place of

Evita's corpse.

Years later Eloy Martínez turned his attention to Walsh, recalling his appearance that day in Paris: "I remember his glasses with tortoiseshell frames, the solitary wisp of hair growing above his bulging forehead, his lips as thin as a knife gash."

When Perón's wife Evita died of cancer in 1952, aged 33, her funeral turned into a national outpouring of grief. If Peronism offered the people a faith then Eva was its saint. The Evita Foundation's free mattresses and bicycles did little to alter the balance of economic power in Argentina but her rags-to-riches life story inspired adulation and hope for all the poor.

"By bloody means or not, the race of oligarchic exploiters of men will die without doubt in this century," she once said, scorching the ears of the nation's wealthy elite. Even Che Guevara applied to Eva's Foundation for a motorbike when he planned his road trip through Latin America as a teenager. When Perón was ousted in 1955 Evita's body disappeared and 15 years would pass before anyone picked up the scent again.

There was wild speculation that the body had been dragged along the pavement on Argentina's Ruta 3 until it had no skin left, that it had been embedded in cement or thrown into the Atlantic ocean, horrifying fantasies which would become everyday reality for other Argentinians when the military seized power in 1976.

Rodolfo approached the Evita case as if he were investigating another unsolved crime story, picking over Colonel Koenig's every word, looking for clues. Walsh learned that the corpse had been buried standing up "in a garden where it rains every other day."

In Paris, Eloy Martínez recounted a conversation he had had with the secretary to the president of the World Jewish Congress. In a curious anecdote he told the writer that for the past ten years the Argentinian embassy in Bonn had closed down during the first weeks in August, for building work.

"They tore down the coal shed and planted a garden, and the next year, the garden was dug up so the coal shed could be rebuilt. That was all: the story of the stupid wastefulness at the embassy of a poor country," explained Eloy Martínez.

Walsh leaned forward, a sudden spark of recognition in his eyes, and dropped a bombshell.

"Evita is in that garden," he said, "that's where they're keeping her."

Eloy Martínez was baffled but Walsh had finally tied together the loose ends of her grim travels. "So they took her to Bonn," mused Walsh, "I always thought as much."

Lilia Ferreyra, there with Walsh, added that the colonel in charge of the body, Moori Koenig, had been military attaché in Bonn in 1957. Walsh had previously concluded that the body was in an Italian convent and that Moori Koenig was sent to Bonn to throw people off the scent.

"I suppose they rebuild the coal shed so that the wood of the coffin won't decay," said Walsh, "then they redo the garden and bury it again, out of fear that the body will be discovered."

Eloy Martínez discovered that Colonel Koenig had died a few months previously, taking his secret to the grave. Eloy Martínez suggested that the three of them take off for Bonn that afternoon and verify the story, but Walsh had lost interest. "I've already written that story," he said, "ten years have gone by and I've moved on to other things," (Eloy Martínez, 1996).

Evita's remains were repatriated on November 17th 1974, by Perón's widow and successor as President, Isabel Martínez de Perón.

chapter nine

True romance

Walsh worked on his memoirs, organising them into three themes: his relationship with literature, his relationship with politics and a third section simple called "Horses" which represented "the countryside, the land, his friends, his childhood, his women, that is, the emotional aspects of his life".

(Lilia Ferreyra, 1997)[28]

Emotional life

Since his days in the Fahy Institute Rodolfo had learned to cope with life's difficulties alone, building a giant wall around his feelings, resisting emotional outbursts. Rodolfo rushed impetuously away from emotional confrontation, his relationships fading away rather than burning to a dramatic finish.

The women in Rodolfo's life were talented achievers who organised him and provided the space for him to pursue his own literary and political ambitions. Nene, his first girlfriend, complimented his poetry but wrote verses "infinitely superior" to his own, recalled Rodolfo, a realisation that drove him to silence for five years.

Elina Tejerina, mother of Patricia and Vicki, encouraged him to finish school and study literature at La Plata University, introducing him to the classics. Elina won the *Buen Decir* prize in secondary school, a special award for the best all-round pupil of each school. The winner had to stand in front of the entire school and recite a poem. Elina also won the coveted Buenos Aires City poetry prize, giving her a lifetime artist's pension; moreover, as a renowned educational specialist, she lectured throughout Latin America.

Rodolfo and Elina remained friends after they separated, sharing the bond of parenthood which kept them in constant contact until Walsh's

---

[28] *Página/12* Sunday supplement *Radar*, 23/3/97, Año 1, No. 32.

death in 1977. Even when he lived in La Plata, Rodolfo remained a distant if loving figure to daughters Vicki and Patricia, the burden of childcare falling entirely on Elina. Rodolfo kept his own hours, often working late into the night on translations. "I remember we had to be quiet in the morning, because daddy was sleeping," recalled Patricia.

When it came to domestic arrangements Rodolfo was relaxed to the point of dereliction. In La Plata, the family furniture consisted of a double bed, a table, a chest of drawers and a stout bookshelf. "Anyone else would have bought kitchen furniture or an easy chair," said Patricia, but the home was inspired by literary rather than domestic concerns. Rodolfo may also have held onto the unsettling memory of the bailiffs showing up at his parents' home in 1937, removing the family furniture when they hit bad times.

"Rodolfo fell for any woman who opened her arms to him, anyone who gave him affection," said Poupee Blanchard, Walsh's compañera between 1958 and 1963, "and that was very attractive in him, because he was very sweet, he had a very smooth body." Poupee called Rodolfo her "Irish orphan", a battered soul trapped by twin desires, solitude and solace.

Poupee, like Pirí after her, kept the home in Tigre habitable, as can be deduced from Rodolfo's diary entries in November 1962: "The island without P, the city without Laura, Sunday without football," wrote Rodolfo in his diary. "I don't know why she didn't come out [...] I popped my head out to check all the arriving boats and each time I felt betrayed [...] I know the importance of P, if I lost her it would be like losing a wall in the house" (Walsh, 1996 pp.36–37). Walsh's choice of simile is short on passion: "Shall I compare thee to a wall?" Zero points for romantic inspiration, yet in Walsh's mind, a wall was a damn useful thing to have around, like his women friends.

Puta's fever

Walsh had a quick sense of humour and a charming manner, twin strengths he used to maximum effect in the company of women. While friends and colleagues described him as a "timid, repressed Irishman", Rodolfo evidently harboured a secret world of erotic fantasy which emerged in diary entries, published posthumously: "I would like to go to Bahia and be a black man," he mused. It was 1962 and he was back in Buenos Aires after almost two years in Cuba. "I would like to work with black people, screw black women, learn to sing and dance" (ibid p.40). Walsh was fascinated by the sensuous rhythms of Afro-Caribbean life. He wrote up a number of encounters with black women into his personal diary in the manner of a forbidden fantasy.

Another Argentinian, Alfredo "El Chango" Muñoz, arrived in Cuba in 1962 to take up his post as stringer for *Agence France-Presse*. He described the amazing cultural differences between his native country and the tropical island: "In Buenos Aires it took months to get to know a woman, hold her hand, steal a kiss," he explained, "maybe years before sex." Muñoz, six foot five inches tall, stood out like a lighthouse in Havana, where people stopped and stared at him on the street. "One day", he recounted, "I turned a corner and noticed a group of women chatting. They stopped, looked me up and down and began to applaud." Muñoz was convinced that he had finally found paradise.

Likewise Rodolfo, who was educated by nuns and priests, married young and separated. He had plunged into life in revolutionary Cuba, working hard at *Prensa Latina,* then wandering the streets of old Havana. It was among these narrow streets and old bars where he met Cuban prostitutes in furtive encounters described in two diary entries published in 1996.

"People need to see Rodolfo as a flesh and blood character, not a superhero sanctified in marble," said his daughter Patricia, who authorised the publication of his diary (albeit omitting certain entries, vetted by her mother Elina), thus shedding light on Walsh's personal reflections in the 1960s. The incidents recorded by Walsh raised a question mark over his adherence to revolutionary discipline, as the elimination of prostitution was central to Castro's plan to end vices associated with the Batista dictatorship. The following stories owe a stylistic debt to the US writer Henry Miller, whose work he was reading at the time.

Diary entries

19/2/1961

Back in the terrible city, at [Calle] Montevideo 1009, the cats and the leaks. My last night in Havana was mysterious. I had 50 pesos left over and began to think of Ziomara with her fine slim waist, her dark, Asian face. Her body was splendid, long African legs and hips made to move all the time. There are no whores like Havana's whores, the last splendour of a disappearing world.

Almost all of them are smooth and silent and seem to understand, they are sad yet know how to smile on the inside. Ziomara knew, anyhow. They use colourful aliases: Ziomara, Estrella. (X has sat down opposite me along the round, glass table and she sews, making it almost impossible to write in her presence. But I have to.)

I went to the Music Box but didn't find her, just like the three times before that when I had to leave with María and with Reina. As we left, she chatted to a drunk but I heard her voice as I was going, *come here, why are you leaving*. I asked her about Ziomara, she said she might be next door. She wasn't. When I came back the drunk had gone but she was there and I invited her for a drink. Her name was Estrella, Zoila Estrella she said, sensing my doubts. She was sixteen years old and very beautiful. She asked for a vermouth. She had a cold, maybe sinusitis and needed operating on but she wouldn't do it as she was afraid of operations and she was taking god-knows-what. ("Me sewing and my husband working," X told someone she spoke to on the phone).

"Randolfo is taking care of his business affairs." It's R (they want to know if I am going to work in *Usted* or *Che*).

I don't like it, she said, but I have to do it because if I don't I'd have to live with my mother and I can't because she works as a maid. "And your brothers?" They don't give me anything, they just take. She had six brothers.

I have read about these things but it was still appalling and I really wanted to sleep with her. "The Music isn't the same since they changed it," she said. "I was in the Apache and then I came here, but it isn't the same." There was a smell of piss – I noticed it for the first time – and only two or three more women, one of them drunk.

"What a drunk," said Estrella and she laughed with Sergio. I asked her if she wanted to come with me and she said "If you like – I have to pay to leave." I gave her ten pesos. "Sergio, my handbag." Sergio whispered something in her ear. I didn't pay attention to the looks because it was always the same, one left and the rest turned around to look.

I took off my glasses as usual, I thought the same thing as I always did – that my baldness was unmistakable, for example. (This city stopped growing when it realised where it was, it stopped in horror: this climate, this bedevilled city; not like Paris, which stopped in the seventeenth century, out of self-satisfaction. I think it's the most dangerous city because it is populated by Buenos Aires demons. X looks like Colette, but lonely, not because she is solitary but because she ended up alone. Meanwhile she gains experience, she enjoys it – she says – being part of a couple.)

But what did I care about my baldness, I was leaving. J had seen me once but he didn't give me away. Grimly pure, J? (You don't know the pleasure it gives people to listen to you, said X. No, I don't. Everyone hates me, according to M, they judge me. Everyone loves me, says B. "Hey Walsh," he flicks his hand upwards, "maximum respect.")

Estrella said she preferred the Ariete, not the Rex, you get used to it, you know. The serene sleepyhead charged 15 for the two, for a while.

Then we were in the bedroom, what a beautiful face. Please, don't squeeze my waist, I'm seven months on. I hadn't noticed the leather jacket which she used to cover herself up. "You poor thing," I said, you are brave, but I must have changed my expression. She had a bump on her stomach. There are thoughts of pleasure in evil, to fuck a pregnant sixteen-year-old girl, push it in all the way, and feel a complete bastard, fuck it, fuck us all.

But "You are a man of conscience," she said, quite a while later when we were back on the street. I closed my eyes and didn't expect anything. I imagined I could have, in the beginning. Until I touched her between her legs (she rubbed my neck gently, rhythmically, her eyes closed) and I felt that dampness, that horror and the associations that went with it, the baby moving and kicking in the womb, everything behind. Then my prick, excuse me, shrivelled up like a small telescope and fell limply on its side, lifeless. But then afterwards I could have, because she smelt good, and had a shoulder profile so sharp and pure, such smooth fingers, her face asleep, not saying anything, not saying suck me Papa, oh give it to me, like Carmita would say, spread out over me, with that animal-like ecstasy. (Yes, I know but I'll correct it after.) So I said to her, "Are you sure it won't do you any harm?" She said, "No, I'm sure it won't" and it all ended there.

I cashed in my ten pesos, challenging her, smoothly, as befits a *señor*. I told her they could both die, her and the child. But, she said, I have to buy it a cradle. We got dressed so fast, me giving her advice, you have to go the Federation of Women, you have to get this seen to, you can't do this, you put yourself in danger, you compromise the man who sleeps with you – not so, she said proudly, and she was an object of horror.

At the corner I told her: "I would help you if I could, but I can only give you advice, don't do this anymore."

"You are a man of conscience," she said, putting her hand on my arm, and she went off, an object of horror.

Afterwards I played roulette and for the first time. I won 20 pesos – winning back the money spent in that last, strange night in Havana – and I gave them to X, my wife (flowers for your wife?) so she could buy a brooch.

I'll say more about this another day.

●◆ (Walsh, 1996, pp.23–7)

19/2/1961

...we went into the hotel, which was on a corner I think, we asked for a room for a while, it's the same the world over, you can ask for it "for a while" or "for the night". When I came out of the bathroom she was naked, big and black against the white sheet, I embraced her clumsily, she says "Do you want a kiss," and curls up in a ball, stroking my face with her stomach, I feel her lips on my prick, she sucks gently, like a kitten and the pleasure is so abominably good that I feel I'm going to go crazy and immediately I have to tell her to stop or I'll come in her mouth, which may well be what she's planning.

Then she came back up, she got on top of me, a great black feline creature, with powerful thighs, a great pleasure machine, moving rhythmically as she says things in a wild language, I pull on her tits as if they were made of soft rubber, I squeeze them like the top of a perfume bottle, she laughs and gyrates like she is rowing a canoe with her long, fine legs and I empty myself in one long semen spurt, like that magic smack of the wave, she screams and bites the pillow.

And I'm on her again straight after, I turn her onto her back, and beginning again without pulling out of her I stiffen up triumphantly, looking at my prick which goes in and out, in and out and in between her long African hairs, in that shady, damp cavity and I expel more of my tepid juices, almost painfully this time.

As we got dressed afterwards, because she has to keep working, I asked her how much it would be, and she said "Whatever you like," as they always say, but when I gave her five pesos she smiled a little and said "Is that all?" I made up any old excuse because I'm determined not to pay any more, I don't want to be tricked but the hounds of remorse and shame are closing in on me now so as soon as we left I got rid of her and at that point I started to wonder whether anyone might have seen me, or if she was beautiful or was she a monster and what would they say at the agency if they saw me with such a black woman.

Yes, I feel guilty about this great act of liberation and she did it without being asked, "as she will do it for others", I think, with something approaching repulsion, because *señor* was demanding. But it's the first time and little by little, I will catch on.

At first she said she came from Santiago de Cuba, but she had a foreign accent and she then admitted she was Haitian. I forgot her name and I'm not sure if that was the only time I slept with her, or if it happened another time. But I passed by her one night, on the opposite side of the road, she tried to catch my attention but I kept going. That's the way of the world. I thought I could at least have given her a cigarette.

Today November ends. I picked what must be the last of the blossoms. There are honeysuckles left, but few, the azaleas have disappeared, catfish begin to replace lobster, the air is filled with leaves, the shadow of a willow – a mossy emerald – was breathing in the river at sundown.

Rainy November, so different from last year. In September we had floods a metre deep, in October another 30 centimetres. The moon was 25 watts. December's coming, Catfish Month.

●◆ (Walsh, 1996, pp.37–8)

Susana 'Pirí' Lugones

In 1964, after his relationship with Poupee ended and he returned to Buenos Aires, Rodolfo took up with Pirí Lugones, another social animal who introduced Walsh to the radical left intellegentsia. Pirí accompanied Rodolfo on the last lap of his tortuous journey from right-wing nationalism to left-wing socialism. There was little of the "new man" about Rodolfo, who paid scant attention to household duties, even when he lived alone. Lugones would turn up at his home in Tigre each weekend with cigarettes, food and cleaning materials, arresting the impact of Walsh's slow descent into domestic ruin during the previous week. Pirí supported Rodolfo's writing but also wrote her own short stories. Part of her work was stolen and lost during the last period of military rule, when she was disappeared by a military unit along with her husband on Christmas Eve 1977.

"I am the daughter of the torturer."

Pirí Lugone's off-putting opening words to new acquaintances confirmed a family history indelibly marked by shame and tragedy. Pirí's grandfather, Leopoldo Lugones, was the nation's foremost poet, who took his own life in 1938, in a hotel room in Tigre. Pirí's father, a police chief, introduced the *picana*, an adapted electric cattle prod, into the nation's judicial system, making it a routine instrument of police torture. He too committed suicide. The cycle of suicide continued in Pirí's own family, claiming her son Alejandro. He was just nineteen.

Pirí was introduced to Rodolfo by her best friend Poupee Blanchard, first getting to know him in Cuba where she travelled on assignment for *Che* magazine in 1960. Pirí became a major influence in his life; she was employed as a literary scout for Jorge Alvarez, and helped publish Walsh's two short story collections, *Un Kilo de Oro* and *Los Oficios Terrestres*. She also included Walsh's stories and vignettes in at least five anthologies, published by Jorge Alvarez between 1964 and 1967. A well-known figure on the Buenos Aires social scene, Pirí introduced Walsh to people from all areas of artistic endeavour.

Lugones was a controversial figure in Argentina's vibrant cultural scene, a strong woman who was loved, feared and disliked in equal measure; several acquaintances who fell foul of her sharp tongue recalled her opening words in a new light. Above all Pirí was spontaneous, affectionate and passionate. "She had a fantastic sense of humour," recalled Horacio Verbitsky, who described the chemistry between Rodolfo and her. "There was an erotic charge between them, although she was also very maternal, very protective. She organised his work, cleaned his house, arriving at Tigre every Friday night with clean sheets, food, cigarettes and friends."

Lugones had a striking, beautiful face and was *renga*, with one leg longer than the other, like Rodolfo's wife Elina Tejerina. In later years Pirí suffered great pain in her feet, due to her refusal to wear orthopedic shoes. She was also outgoing and aggressive, "a feminist ahead of her time", as Ricardo Piglia, one of Argentina's leading novelists, has described her, maturing with the sexual revolution which took its time in reaching South America. "Rodolfo was like a priest in that respect," recalled Horacio: "he would get shy and embarrassed talking about sex."

Pirí secured a monthly advance for Rodolfo from Jorge Alvarez publishers against the promise of a future novel, a measure which allowed him to give up daily journalism between 1965 and 1967. She also introduced him to Horacio Verbitsky, a promising young journalist. Someone mentioned that Walsh would have to modify his short story "Esa mujer" if it was to be understood in French translation. "I'm not sure if I want it translated into French," responded Rodolfo, winking conspiratorially at Verbitsky. "That complicit wink brought us together," he recalled. "Both of us had our reservations about the literary circle." The two escaped and got something to eat, beginning a friendship which lasted until his death.

Horacio and his wife Laura became regular visitors to Rodolfo's Tigre home. The two couples held fishing tournaments and discussed politics, as Argentina slid toward serious social unrest in 1966.

Rodolfo lived simply, always in precarious financial circumstances. "He was remarkably austere," said Verbitsky. "He had two shirts, two pairs of trousers, one pair of shoes, one jacket, one tie; his chairs were falling apart, you always had to put something underneath them so as not to fall off; his tables were made with trestles, he used homemade lamps made with bottles, he drank the cheapest wine, ate *milanesas*[29] every day, he was a man without vanity, a man of essence. He didn't waste a second of his life, he was always doing what he considered important – this was very impressive to see." I asked Verbitsky if Walsh's asceticism wasn't excessive. "I didn't see it that way," he said. "It was a relief amongst so much frivolous stupidity in literature, politics and activism" (Author interview 1999).

---

[29] Breaded steak, made from 'poor' cuts of meat.

Secret lives

Rodolfo had secret love affairs which were kept as secret as his informants in the police force. It was rumoured that he had a fling with Norma Leandro,[30] the only Argentinian actress to win a Hollywood Oscar. "He acted like he was unattached, he was free and easy," recalled Leandro, speaking at her beautiful home in central Buenos Aires, where rambling bookshelves, a small swimming pool and large garden lend an air of rural tranquillity. Rodolfo met Norma through Francisco "Paco" Urondo and Noe Jitrik, two writers who participated in psychoanalytic sessions fuelled by LSD, the psychedelic drug which, still legal at that time, helped participants to unlock the doors of perception. "He was one of the most pleasant people I ever met," said Norma "very sweet, with a great sense of humour." At the time of her encounter with Walsh she was emerging from a failed long-term relationship and she dedicated her energies to her young child.

Halfway through the interview Norma cut to the chase: "Why are you here? What do you want to know?" I had to confess that I wanted to know if anything had happened between herself and Rodolfo. She hesitated. I waited for my marching orders. "Who gave you the hint?" she asked, as I began to regret my investigative zeal. I mumbled something about protecting my sources. "I didn't want it to be anything more than a fling," she said, putting me out of my agony. Once she began talking she continued without further prompting. "I had just separated, [...] our friendship was a more lasting thing but maybe he wanted more."

Rodolfo harboured hopes of a relationship but Norma knew it was not going to happen. Walsh would arrive unexpectedly at the house, carrying flowers and a bag of *masas*.[31] The two friends drank tea, discussed books and films, never straying too far into personal or political territory. Rodolfo rigorously compartmentalised his life, allowing little crossover between personal and political activities. These two worlds were only reconciled during his final relationship, with Lilia Ferreyra.

It was during one of the final afternoon chats when Walsh gave her what she called "the most beautiful piece of advice ever." Rodolfo liked Norma's writing and kept at her to publish her work. "Where is the writing that came before this?" he asked her. She confessed she had thrown it away. "Never throw any of your work away," he said, "because your old writing will help you spot the defects in your current work." The advice struck home.

---

[30] One of Argentina's best-known actresses, she won an Oscar for *La Historia Oficial*, a film about Argentina's disappeared.
[31] Pastries.

The last time Norma saw Rodolfo was in 1971 when he asked her to appear in the film version of *Operación Masacre*, filmed secretly in Buenos Aires. The country was under military rule at the time, turning the task into a potentially dangerous operation. Leandro played a minor part, spending one full day on the set. "He had lost the happiness and the shine which I'd seen before," said Norma. "He had always had something very youthful about him. That seemed to have gone."

Walsh's complicated love life occasionally blew up on him. On one occasion at least, Pirí Lugones made a noisy scene outside Rodolfo's flat in Calle Cangallo, while Walsh cowered inside with his lover Susana Iriarte. "He wasn't the saint that people make him out to be," commented Ricardo Piglia, who rented a room in Pirí's home during that period.

Lilia Ferreyra, 1967

"What has happened in these months? Lilia, the woman whose eyes grow the whole day long and are enormous by evening-time, filling up everything. I remember her one morning, sleeping face down, a smooth lioness, drinking *café con leche* as the sun came in through the window. Lilia, slow and even-tempered, I see her sitting beside a haystack watching the butterflies go by one summer" (Walsh, 1996 pp.80–81).

Lilia, just 20 years old, had left family and friends behind in Junín, convincing her employers at a chemical laboratory to transfer her to their city branch. The monthly salary was barely enough to get by on and most of it went on room and board at a modest hostel. On payday she allowed herself one special treat: a new book and a meal in a restaurant. Ferreyra was enjoying the personal freedom afforded by life in the big city after leaving small-town Junín, 200 km from the capital. "I wanted to be a revolutionary, a communist and to escape the conventional life plans awaiting me back in Junín," she said.

Several decades earlier, another Junín native, Eva Duarte, had fled to Buenos Aires to escape convention. "She hated the town and had only one fear: that Doña Juana would one day want to marry her off to one of the boring dinner guests." Eva Duarte became Eva Perón, altering the course of the nation's history.

The first time Lilia Ferreyra saw Rodolfo Walsh was in June 1967, in Café La Paz, a popular haunt for bohemians and intellectuals in Avenida Corrientes, the street that never sleeps, with theatres, cinemas and shops glittering in the heart of downtown Buenos Aires.

By coincidence or the invisible hand of destiny, Lilia had just bought Rodolfo's new collection of short stories *Un Kilo de Oro* that same day, and settled down to a feed and a read in Café La Paz. A friend of Lilia's joined her, saw what she was reading and pointed to a nearby table.

"That's Walsh," he said.

"I saw him from the side," recalled Lilia, "the spreading baldness like a monk's tonsure, the black frames of his glasses, the concentration of his reading, and the gesture of amused surprise when my friend asked for the autograph."

Walsh signed the book, smiled briefly at Lilia, then left the café in a hurry, as if he had forgotten something. Rodolfo Walsh was obliged to choose his cafés with care at that time, avoiding certain favourite haunts, including Café La Paz. His range of social places was dictated not by fear of State surveillance but because of the unique separation deal hammered out with his last partner, Pirí Lugones.

Lacking any worldly goods to divide between them, Rodolfo and Pirí divided up the city's cafés and bars; Pirí would enjoy exclusive rights to all on the left-hand side of Avenida Corrientes, looking down toward the river, while Rodolfo was master of all the cafés on the opposite side. Woe betide anyone who strayed into "enemy" territory.

"Rodolfo had sinned that evening," recalled Lilia, as Café La Paz was on the forbidden side of the street, hence his rapid exit.

A month later, Lilia once more received her monthly wages, stopped by a bookshop and entered another restaurant. Once more Rodolfo was there. "Not because of rituals like my own, but out of habits typical of a single man living in a small flat." Walsh invited Lilia to join him for dinner, curious to talk with one of his readers. Or perhaps he was simply looking for an excuse to chat her up. As Lilia discussed her life, they discovered common threads, as Walsh's mother Dora Gill had lived in Junín, where his uncle had worked on the railroads.

The conversation marked the beginning of Rodolfo's most important relationship, intact until the last goodbye ten years later, at a train station outside Buenos Aires, an hour before Walsh's death.

The first months together were tentative as Lilia, just out of her teens, was shy around Rodolfo, who was 20 years her senior, a successful writer and a man who rarely expressed his feelings in direct terms.

One evening in October of that year, Rodolfo arranged to meet her at the Politeama restaurant, located on the right side of Avenida Corrientes, this time on the safe side of Walsh's post-relationship agreement. I sat there with Lilia thirty years later, at the same table. Our conversation took place on a balmy summer evening, over coffee, food and wine. The Politeama has the same name and layout as it had in the 1960s, but the plastic seats, neon lights and touristy cuisine have sucked the place dry of its former atmosphere.

"I tremble inside thinking about those times," said Lilia, taking a deep breath, summoning up the intense memories evoked by this sudden revisiting of the past. A lengthy silence followed. Lilia has a fragile air about her, approaching each memory with the caution of someone entering a lion's cage, where the slightest false step could tear her apart. Rodolfo still casts a long shadow which accompanies her everywhere, watching over the past, an implacable guardian and a rhetorical question – could it have ended any other way?

The pain is evident in every phrase, every anecdote, every detail which emerges as Lilia's *churrasco*[32] and salad remain untouched. Lilia's life experiences enrich and breathe life into a figure who until then was a distant narrative of courage. Lilia guided me to the heart of Rodolfo.

On the evening that Walsh and Ferreyra first met here, Walsh had spent the previous two hours chatting with Paco Urondo in Walsh's flat around the corner, in what was Calle Cangallo, since renamed Calle Perón. Paco had returned from Cuba that day and filled Walsh in on the latest developments on the island. "It was the beginning of Rodolfo's return to Cuba," recalled Lilia. At the end of 1967 Rodolfo went to Cuba, spending six weeks there and arriving back in Buenos Aires in February 1968. He immediately fired off a brief telegram to Lilia, who was on holiday in her parents' home in Junín: "Back in Buenos Aires. Waiting for you. Rodolfo." Lilia packed her bags on the spot, took the next bus to the city, rang Rodolfo's doorbell and fell into his arms.

Walsh always seemed to be looking for something more from his relationships, a sense of inner calm which he finally found with Lilia. In her he found a loyal and brave compañera who assumed the risks of a committed militant, sharing the cause which eventually propelled Walsh into the armed resistance movement.

All this lay ahead for Rodolfo and Lilia as the reunited couple spent the night together, with Walsh full of tales from his Cuban trip. "Stay a while longer," pleaded Rodolfo as Lilia prepared to go home the next day. On Sunday, the same discussion took place, as Walsh invited her to a film and dinner. "What's the point in going home at this time?" he asked, delaying her departure by another day. By Wednesday the formalities were suspended and the happy couple began living together.

"There was no discussion about forming a relationship or getting married," said Lilia, "it didn't even cross our minds. We both believed that the truth was evident in the way you lived, not in symbols imposed from outside." The winds of change blew fast across the continent, bringing a whiff of sexual revolution and women's rights. "We were going to break with everything," smiled Lilia, "we were going to make a revolution."

Rodolfo and Lilia gradually fused their lives together, developing a deep, mutual understanding that passed through intuition, passion, trust

---

[32] An Argentinian cut of beef.

and enduring love. Rodolfo found it hard to express his feelings, raised in a family where his imposing, silent father and his dissatisfied, dominant mother played out the only roles they knew.

Rodolfo's daily routine began with a lengthy shave, during which he made a mental map of the day ahead. "He spent forever in front of the mirror," said Lilia. He'd be lost to the world, removing the tiny hairs which crept out of his nostrils, or trimming his moustache. "You could hear him laughing the whole time," she added.

Rodolfo clowned around, delighting in making others laugh, whether it was charades in Cuba or directing a phantom orchestra at home, his tone-deaf acrobatic gestures massacring Mozart's symphonies. On other occasions Rodolfo would stand on a chair and launch into a fiery speech to the "masses" who consisted of Lilia as observer, cheering wildly when Walsh scored a populist point. He raised and lowered his voice, testing his "crowd", searching for the right note.

On stifling summer afternoons the two lovers enjoyed a lazy siesta, napping between lunch and afternoon work. The soft thud of the afternoon paper through the letterbox signalled the end of their rest. Both of them pretended to be asleep before one of them made a sudden move and a vicious race began to see who could get to the paper first, leaping out of bed, grabbing and pulling at each other, to win first read of the all-important newspaper.

In the evenings Rodolfo would sip his vermouth before returning to his beloved Remington, while Lilia worked on domestic chores. One evening Lilia was dusting their home in Tigre when a sudden cry froze her in her tracks; Rodolfo caught her just as she went to clean a mirror on which Rodolfo had been encouraging dust spots for a fortnight, to monitor hourly changes in the reflected light.

Lilia played a support role in organising Rodolfo's work, adopting a role which obfuscated her own writing skills but left her with an inside understanding of Rodolfo's day-by-day evolution during the period.

Rodolfo did not find it easy to verbalise his feelings but he was hugely affectionate and expressed his love in many small ways. In the evenings, Lilia would approach Rodolfo from behind, put her arm around his neck and kiss his bald patch. Walsh responded by raising his head to meet Lilia's lips, before turning to her with his inevitable, rhetorical question:

"Why do you love me?"

chapter ten

The power of the word

The concern of the intellectual is by definition the conscience. An intellectual who fails to understand what is happening in his time and in his country is a walking contradiction, and those who understand but do nothing will have a place reserved in the anthology of tears but not in the living history of their land.

Semanario CGT, May 1st 1968

Cuba, second chance

Paco Urondo returned home from Cuba with an invitation for Rodolfo to join the jury for the annual Casa de las Americas literary prize in Havana, to be held in January 1968. The official invitation confirmed that any bad feeling left over from Walsh's previous trip had since been buried. Rodolfo's return to Cuba came nearly seven years after he left his job at *Prensa Latina*.

Walsh's visit to Cuba would also coincide with the Havana Cultural Congress, a gathering of intellectuals from around the world to debate the role and responsibility of the intellectual in society. The timing of the conference of intellectuals could not have been more poignant as it came just three months after Che Guevara was killed in Bolivia. The death of Guevara was a wake-up call to the world, the end of the dream of a lone superhero who would single-handedly bring about the revolution. The role of the intellectual in the transformation of society was under debate around the world, with Cuba an ideal setting in which to grapple with the issue.

Walsh had come a long way since his last visit to Cuba, radicalised by his own life experience and by his observations of the world around him. He returned to the Cuban revolution with a passion, sensing the strategic importance of the island's revolution for the whole region and with the personal need within him to match the commitment of those who had defended the revolution since 1959.

The second Cuba trip began with a 48-hour stopover in Mexico City, where Walsh marvelled at the Rivera and Siquieros murals and the imposing *zócalo*, the central square, writing to Lilia of the meagre remains of Zapata's revolution.

Rodolfo arrived in Cuba and wasted no time in getting a taste of campesino life. "In typical Walsh style Rodolfo put on a *guajiro* hat, picked up a machete and went to work," recalled Ricardo Piglia, who confessed to have been "horrified" at the prospect of voluntary work in the sugar harvest. "It seemed ridiculous, the symbolic work effort. I would have probably cut someone's head off if I had tried to do it," said Piglia.

Rodolfo's own rural background may have contributed to his enthusiasm, as he was genuinely interested in agricultural innovations on the island, which aimed at increased self-sufficiency. "Rodolfo worked hard, he was interested in coffee cultivation, cow-breeding techniques, he wanted to know about everything," noted Piglia, who laid low during the volunteer work period.

I found no mention of Walsh's volunteer labour effort, even in his personal diary, a noticeable oversight of an important if symbolic gesture. Rodolfo offered active solidarity rather than ideological backup to the men and women who sustained the revolution with the sweat of their brow.

The intellectual in his labyrinth

Intellectuals have played a disproportionate role in Latin American politics, frequently substituting for weak civil societies and unrepresentative political parties.

In the late 19th century Domingo Sarmiento participated in the establishment of Argentina's army, education and immigration policy, while Leopoldo Lugones, the poet, provided an ideological framework to the reactionary 1930 military coup, with his *'La hora de la espada'* (the time of the sword) speech. Cuban poet José Martí fought and died for independence while Ricardo Flores Magón and Valentin Gómez Farias, journalists cum historians cum politicians, helped forge national identity in Mexico.

Intellectuals occupied prominent roles in the development of universities and the mass media and drafted political platforms when parliamentary structures took hold. The explosion in the number of students attending university courses bolstered the status of intellectuals, who now had a much larger constituency as student campuses became centres of radical social unrest (Castañeda 1994, p.191).

The tradition of intellectual participation in political life still survives

today. The truth commission (CONADEP) set up to investigate disappearances during military rule in Argentina (1976–83) was chaired by a
leading writer, Ernesto Sábato. Argentinian poet Juan Gelman "defeated"
the Uruguayan military in April 2000, with the help of hundreds of
people from around the globe who lobbied Uruguayan President Jorge
Battle on his behalf. The Uruguayan government, which refused to even
acknowledge the existence of *desaparecidos* under military rule (1973–85),
finally traced Gelman's granddaughter, kidnapped and given away after
her mother gave birth in captivity in 1976.

"There is a curious relationship between intellectuals and political
power in Latin America. The State and the powers-that-be both need us
and fear us. They need us because we give them prestige they lack; they
fear us because our sentiments and views can damage them [...] No
wonder then that there was so much coddling of the intellectuals by the
State. Under these circumstances, one cannot always be completely
independent" Gabriel García Márquez (ibid p.196).

In the 1960s Latin American intellectuals constituted a left-wing
ideological bloc which coalesced around support for the Cuban revolution, largely substituting for governments and embassies. The revolution
initially enjoyed approval from intellectuals around the world, as David
vanquished Goliath and began building an egalitarian society. In a region
where US power made and broke governments at will, Cuba defied the
super-power and got away with it, becoming a symbol of Latin American
independence.

Castro's support for the 1968 invasion of Czechoslovakia and the
celebrated Padilla Case ended the consensus.

The Cuban revolution challenged intellectuals to set aside what
Uruguayan poet Mario Benedetti called the "succession of frustrations,
bitternesses, inferiority complexes, discussions until dawn, equal distribution of guilt..." which left them in permanent isolation (Benedetti
p.64). Benedetti threw his literary reputation behind the revolutionary
process: "It seems absolutely clear to me that if I fight for a more just
society, when that change occurs, even if a beginning, to try to subvert
that situation would be tantamount to demanding a return to injustice."
Not everyone agreed with this perspective. "The only support which a
writer can give his community is that of criticism, criticism as reason,
knowledge and options, and against irrationality and dogma," wrote
Mexican writer Carlos Fuentes (ibid p.138).

Before 1959, writers had the luxury of spilling ink on behalf of radical
change, safe in the knowledge that such change was unlikely to occur.
The Cuban revolution turned that notion upside down, inviting writers
and intellectuals to actively engage in constructing a new society.

"One of the paradoxes of our times – and not the least of them – is that we intellectuals and artists fight for a world in which perhaps we would find it impossible to live," wrote Juan Goytisolo.[33]

Benedetti argued that writers and intellectuals were evidently more comfortable with failure than with success. The frustrated May 1968 revolution in Paris caused just one death (an activist fell into the river Seine and drowned, as he escaped the pursuing police), yet provoked 300 books, while Latin America's frustrated assaults on power "produce far more deaths, far fewer books and inspire fresh attempts at liberation, every one more determined than the last".

Walsh recognised that the "cruellest blockade ever imposed on a country in the Americas" could end up "deforming certain aspects of the revolution". When he returned to Cuba in January 1968 he wondered aloud how writers were dealing with the notion of "writing to slogans". In July 1968 he wrote, "the most serious aspect of such a demand is that it formally separates writers from the revolution, stripping them of responsibility and participation in the process. Historic experience shows the uselessness of all art born of slogans rather than convictions. And if that sort of writing proved sterile, one was better off raising a rifle or driving a tractor and abandoning a literary style which was counter-productive in its insincerity" (Walsh, 1996 pp.73–74).

The Cultural Congress of January 1968 brought hundreds of writers to the island to discuss ways in which they might combine their craft with participation in the cataclysmic events occurring around them.

Did the writer have a social reponsibility that went beyond an occasional pamphlet, march or signed petition? In the year of 1968, from events in Paris in May to the repression in Prague and the Tlatelolco massacre in Mexico (where hundreds of students were massacred by government forces in October) that question became a matter of urgency.

In one round-table discussion, Walsh debated 20th-century Argentinian literature with fellow countrymen Juan Carlos Portantieri and Paco Urondo. The opening question was about the difference between the role of writers in the 19th and 20th centuries.

Walsh was the first to respond, noting that the "professional writer" didn't exist in the 19th century, as writing was a secondary activity. General Paz wrote his "excellent" memoirs about the life and times of Argentina between 1812 and 1845, noted Walsh, after he returned from the battlefield. "Writers were in the thick of events to the extent that they were terribly optimistic as the country grew and hopes were high for a prosperous future." The birth of the professional journalist, concluded Walsh, marked the end of unbridled optimism and the beginning of a more detached version of the day's events.

---

[33] "Exámen de conciencia", *Número*, Abril–Junio 1963, Uruguay.

In the late 1960s Rodolfo Walsh's attitude to the novel had become wrapped up in the continental debate on the role and responsibility of the writer/intellectual in the struggle for social justice. Walsh's shifting attitude to intellectual life was clear by 1971, when the Padilla Case hit the headlines. Heberto Padilla, a Cuban poet who once worked alongside Walsh in *Prensa Latina* and was a frequent breakfast guest at Rodolfo and Poupee's Havana apartment, was arrested by the Cuban government, held for 37 days and put on trial, eventually retracting criticism he had made of the revolution.

A group of 62 intellectuals demanded Padilla's release, signalling an historic rift with the revolution. The Club of 62, a group which included Jean-Paul Sartre, Juan Goytisolo, Octavio Paz and Carlos Fuentes, wrote an open letter to Fidel Castro, while PEN and other organisations took up the case, which received worldwide attention.

Shortly after the letter was published, a group of Argentinian writers met at Walsh's Buenos Aires apartment, planning their own letter to the Cuban government. Walsh's position was clear: if Padilla had been a campesino, no one would have made a fuss over him, but because he belonged to the sacred intellectual class, "tears and a tantrum" followed his detention.

"With great skill Walsh cut short any possibility of writing a critical letter to the Cuban authorities," said Ricardo Piglia, who recalled an "angry exchange" of words between Walsh and David Viñas. The issue marked a definite shift in Walsh's position on Cuba. "Rodolfo now took up the position of an *orgánico* [unconditional militant]," said Piglia. Walsh's loyalty to the Cuban revolution was reciprocated in later years, when Castro sent word to visiting Argentinian Montonero guerrillas, advising them to "take good care" of Walsh.

"Within the revolution everything, outside the revolution nothing," was how Fidel Castro defined the boundaries of free expression on the island. As time passed, and the US plotted invasion, assassination and economic embargo, the precise terms defining what lay "inside the revolution" were steadily whittled down to a dull chorus of praise on behalf of the embattled socialist paradise. The clampdown on critical writing forced more and more writers to abandon the island in order to continue their literary creation. Walsh disagreed with that position but his advice on abandoning writing for a more productive role in the revolution may well have been an acknowledgment that the revolution allowed little room for literary manoeuvre.

The right to unrestricted freedom of expression was now set alongside the right of the majority poor to eat and have a roof over their head.

When the first round of investigations into *Operación Masacre* had been published in the 1950s, Rodolfo was asked whether he thought all the effort and risk was worth the end result, given that the officials who gave the execution orders were still in their jobs. "It allowed me to put to use the press freedom which hasn't existed these past years," he told Juan Bautista Brun in an interview for *Mayoría* in December 1958 (Baschetti, 1994, p.148). By the time the Padilla Case had come to Walsh's notice, press freedom had lost its sacred value. "Press freedom is not the most important of freedoms," he said, in an interview published by *Primera Plana* in May 1972. "Besides, the only press freedom worth the name is that which expresses the interests of the people and in particular that of the working classes."

The Peruvian writer Mario Vargas Llosa claimed that the job of the writer is always to be the "critical conscience" of society, always subversive in the face of power and State institutions, even if the State has arisen from a process of popular struggle. Octavio Paz took that concept a step further, considering the role of the writer to be always a marginal, solitary figure. "As a writer my duty is to preserve my marginal status before the State, political parties, ideologies and society itself," wrote Paz (ibid p.139).

By the same logic, why shouldn't plumbers, bricklayers or accountants decide that they too had a duty to stay above parties, ideology and social activism? If each sector opts out of any involvement in social transformation, who is left to take up the banner of social justice? Gramsci maintained that "all men are intellectuals but not all men have the role of intellectuals in society" (ibid p.77).

Jean-Paul Sartre, Juan Goytisolo and other writers created fiction with a content which reflected a progressive social consciousness. Benedetti suggested that the writer come down from the self-imposed ideological solitude of the ivory tower "and immerse oneself in the bustle of the street, walking shoulder to shoulder with the people, throwing one's vanity carelessly into the gutter" (ibid p.121).

One of Rodolfo's greatest achievements was in resolving the dilemma of the intellectual before the challenge of revolutionary struggle; he experienced a more personal transformation, his literary creation transformed by his life experience in an organic, progressive way.

He would probably have sympathised with the words of Woody Guthrie, the radical 1960s folk singer who found himself thrust upon the intellectual stage: "I was pushed out of the main road pretty early and had to come up along the ditches and the mud and the weeds... Now I'm picked up out of this kind of life and find myself camped along the trail of the intellectuals... to put the matter mildly, I'm having a hard time. I hear their words that run like rainclouds and splatter a few drops across some hot pavement – and the sun and the wind turn the words to steam and they go up in the air like a fog" (ibid p.251).

Obfuscations, errors and fantasy in the badly named Padilla Case

Before I discuss the Padilla Case, I would like to limit the importance of the issue for Argentinians to within the already limited field of intellectual activity. In less than two years we have had the murder of a journalist in the street, the kidnap and murder of a lawyer, the imprisonment of the president of the University Federation and other student leaders, the closure of the workers' newspaper, the judicial sentencing of a novelist and a veto over the best film we've produced.

All this, I believe, should worry us more than the 37 days in prison and later humiliation of the Cuban poet.

Nonetheless the issue has been imposed from abroad with such anxiety that it cannot be avoided. Sixty-two intellectuals, mostly European, have discovered in the Padilla Case a reason to break with the Cuban revolution. Some are important artists, others aren't. Some have acted out of political conviction, for others politics is as alien as astrophysics. At least one of them has carried out political censorship over another: Carlos Franqui, editor of *Revolución*, in 1960 cut out of the transcription of *Hurricane over Sugar* the chapter dedicated to the urban guerrilla. In 1957 Sartre himself, director of *Les Temps Modernes*, was given 30 pages about executions in Argentina by a *France Presse* correspondent, but didn't publish anything on them.

After the Padilla arrest and a first ultimatum by the intellectuals, Fidel Castro delivered a stormy speech against the "half-left" intellectuals and Latin Americans who "live in the bourgeois salons, ten thousand miles from problems". The news agencies picked out the epithets: "intellectual rats", "bastards", "shameless".

Such language causes consternation in Europe, it seems Stalinist. It's Cuban in fact, almost a direct copy of Martí's tombstone written at a similar juncture in history: "Those who have no faith in their land are half-formed weaklings. Because they lack bravery, they deny it in others."

Fidel's speech precipitates the letter of rupture. Stalinism is no longer a theory: it's a certainty which grows with injured pride. Mario Vargas Llosa claims to have found the hand of the police in Padilla's syntax. He imagines that when Padilla says "I have been a cliché," the phrase is whispered in his ear by a security hack who may himself be disenchanted. In three weeks, an ocean apart, without proof, contradicting even the testimony of the French correspondent who physically examined Padilla, the 62 intellectuals concluded that his self-criticism could only have been obtained through torture. They cannot imagine that the self-criticism might be sincere; or even that it is insincere but written out of convenience like any prisoner would; and finally that Padilla, knowing the impact a text like that would have, might have chosen that path in order to be able to fight a fresh battle against the government of his country.

The whole procedure of the 62 intellectuals strikes me as remarkably shabby. They may be unaware of the significance of Stalinism in the construction of a nation, but they can't be unaware of what it meant in its repressive aspect: the physical liquidation of an entire revolutionary leadership, the execution of writers, the assassination of Trotsky and the extermination of hundreds of thousands of ordinary people. Where is the parallel? Impassioned by the external similarity of a procedure, they forget everything which until yesterday made them defenders of the Cuban Revolution, they mechanically transfer Russia in 1937 to Cuba in 1971. When heaven suddenly turns into hell, the method is overkill, the result a caricature.

There are still two things in the text which sound dishonest to me. The first is the recourse to Stalinism as a verbal crutch to exorcise from the European continent the demons of their own repression. The second, that pretence by which the Padilla Case "doesn't alarm us because a writer is involved but because any other Cuban compañero [...] might be the next victim of a similar violence and humiliation."

I think that in ten years of a relationship with the Revolution, if they haven't discovered "any other (humiliated) Cuban" it indicates either that they don't exist, or in fact they do have a preferential preoccupation with the fate of writers.

From France, where this letter reached us, Latin America has also received AMX-13 tanks, Mirage planes and anti-guerrilla helicopters. Who can assure us that words and weapons don't walk hand in hand; that a protest against alleged torture in Cuba may not contribute to legalise real torture in Brazil, Guatemala and Argentina? I am sure that this is not the intention of the 62 intellectuals, but if one of them reflected a little longer on the issue, we might get some fresh self-criticism, written this time from the banks of the Seine.

➥ (Published in Buenos Aires daily *La Opinión*, 26/5/71, reprinted in Walsh, 1995 p.369)

Cuba, 1970

In 1970 Walsh returned once more to Cuba, again invited by Casa de las Americas, who published their own edition of *Operación Masacre*. This time Lilia accompanied him, although she departed a week after him. She lugged a monstrously heavy suitcase which contained every daily paper published since Rodolfo's departure.

The man was an incorrigible newspaper junkie who craved information on events at home. Lilia carried the dead weight assisted by a strapping and sympathetic member of the *Fuerzas Armadas Peronistas*, FAP (Peronist Armed Forces), as far as the airport bus, where Vicki, Rodolfo's daughter, met her and accompanied her to the airport.

It was Lilia's first flight ever and she vividly recalls the point at which she had to change planes, causing a scandal by her insistence on taking the papers with her during the brief stopover. At moments like that Lilia must have recalled the words of Che Guevara's followers, who said that with people like Che "you had to love him for free."

The international boycott of Cuba meant that Lilia flew to Madrid en route to Havana, then back via Prague and Paris. On their return from Cuba, Lilia and Rodolfo spent ten days in Paris visiting a close friend, Milton Roberts, who was being treated for cancer in a French hospital.

On his return to Argentina Rodolfo reflected on the twin themes of exile and commitment: "All our writers are exiled in the face of the revolution," wrote Walsh, "the best of us send them [revolutionaries] off to fight, but we don't fight ourselves. Our place in the ranks of the people is the same as pregnant women, or the elderly, just helpers, accompanying the troops. This wouldn't be so bad if we were modest about it."

Exiles

Aztarain, be careful with the intellectuals, Dorticós told his minister for misappropriated assets. Guillermo Cabrera Infante smiled and they continued talking about books and revolution. The first article portrayed Dorticós as a liberal opposed to all forms of censorship and Cabrera Infante as the sort of jacobin who suggested banning certain novels from Cuba, "for being bad" and prompted official envy with phrases from Saint Just: "the revolutionary who does things by halves simply digs his own grave."

In those days, eight years ago, Cabrera Infante was the archetypal left intellectual. He accompanied Fidel Castro on his travels through the two Americas, he edited a beautiful weekly called *Revolution on Monday*, wrote best-selling guerrilla tales – no other writer had taken such a great leap in so short a time. What did the government need a cultural attaché in Brussels for? It's open to debate, but Cabrera Infante went anyway.

He got only the best from the revolution: a leading role in euphoric times when Havana devoured the last of its splendour; became an exile paid in dollars in the Europe he loved as French wines disappeared and broken cars were dumped on the roadside due to the lack of spare parts.

What could have happened to Guillermo, a Cuban bureaucrat in Europe, while Havana was deteriorating? He perfected his English and his taste for stylistic and linguistic detail but he lost, I fear, the bigger picture. As a visitor to Havana in 1965, he forgot what he knew when he was the cultural attaché in Brussels: that his country was at war with the biggest empire in the world and that one aspect of that war was the detergent for washing the walls of house fronts, which could no longer be found, and the antibiotics needed to save his mother, which suffered the same fate.

Alienated from a process in which he acted as a cheerleader, he discovered underdevelopment in 1965, and spoke out about it in 1968, but wasn't he aware of it in 1960?

In 1960 the city of Havana was to the rest of Cuba precisely what the centre of Buenos Aires, Calle Florida, is to Argentina, as he mentions, and what Tucumán sugar mills and atrocious shantytowns are, for example, to the city of Resistencia. When I spoke to the Urues in Misiones, who dry tea at 90 degrees and die old men before they reach 30 years of age, I recalled the Cuban coal-miners from the swamps who, when asked something about milk by *Revolution on Monday*, inquired as to what precisely milk was.

In the Corrientes countryside I met adult men who had never seen a city and didn't know what a film-maker was; I also remembered those guerrillas who came down from the mountains and mistook the first electric lights they ever saw for stars in the sky. A huge concentration of power and wealth on one hand, extreme poverty on the other. I have seen neither on my return to Cuba in 1968. The revolution didn't socialise misery, it organised a better distribution system for what we have. In the resulting swap, Havana lost what the rest of the island gained, the wealthy gained everything the poor had.

That's what bothers Cabrera. His vision is that of the sacred writer, stuck on the problems a man (Cabrera) can have in trying to find a cup of coffee. He doesn't ask himself where the coffee comes from or why it has run out, feigning ignorance of the fact that Havana province has its coffee rationed because it never produced it and will stop having it rationed when the 50 million coffee plants, recently sown, begin to yield. "Hungry faces," he says. The sacred writer can talk of hunger without worrying about statistics; his word is enough, an adjective. It doesn't matter that Cuba today produces 70 per cent more food than in 1959; that is wiped away in the description of a sandwich. It doesn't matter that the consumption of flour and wheat has risen from 180,000 tonnes to 570,000 tonnes; the ration system proves that people are hungry even though they eat more. It doesn't matter that the numbers of breeding cows have risen from four million to seven million; numbers are boring and the word breeding is ugly, just as the initials of the Cuban ministries are ugly and the "Rent a car" "Minimax" "Ten-Cent" and

"Two Twelve" signs were very beautiful.

I'm not happy, obviously, that Cabrera Infante had problems with his passport or his post, problems which many Latin American writers suffer every day in our countries, without considering ourselves particularly harassed. The revolution is an uprising of the weakest against the strongest and when the strongest blockade, marginalise and invade, the revolution turns ugly, it turns dirty and it becomes distrustful. The revolution on Monday becomes a hard life from Tuesday to Sunday. The revolution doesn't see him, or his beautiful literary supplement or the Rs in reverse in its beautiful typography.

It crudely watches over the land which must be defended in Playa Girón, the milk and bread which the miners won by fighting. It is quite likely that the revolution treats him, an artist, unjustly. But it's also certain that he doesn't see history and so says that history has died. I feel that history has never been as alive as it is today in Cuba. But I find even Cabrera's artistic vision flawed when it focuses on mysteries surrounding coffee distributors and bureaucrats and overlooks a beautiful people – his own – fighting today's nazism. Its victorious 20-year-old *campesinos* are becoming teachers and engineers and writers just like him, but also know how to plant coffee as well as drink it.

You cannot write in Cuba? I will not defend Lezama, or Carpentier, or Guillen, or Eliseo Diego. But his friends Fernández Retamar, his friend Pablo Armando, his friend Heberto, aren't they writers too? No, they are zombies. The people coming up through the ranks, aren't they writers? Those who don't suffer the incurable wound of not having been in the Sierra, or in the militia, or in the literacy campaigns? Aren't his books published in Havana and Paris at the same time? What Cuban books were published in Cuba before 1959?

I asked after him as soon as I arrived in Havana this year. The story about Cabrera Infante being an "underground" writer in Cuba is total fiction. All the writers I spoke to know about his tigers and several of them have already adopted his style. Heberto Padilla, quoted by Cabrera, told me that he hasn't given up hope of winning his argument in favour of publishing the book. Cabrera's fusillade in *Primera Plana* may have sabotaged these efforts. But it is useless and not very pure that Guillermo Cabrera Infante fears at a distance, "just as he fears for his family," for Heberto Padilla who addresses writers from within Cuba:

"Have you signed up to join
Those trembling hands,
which knew only how to write "I'm dead".

●◆ (Published as a letter to *Primera Plana* magazine, No. 295,
August 20th 1968)

Last fiction

Walsh completed his second and final short story collection, *Un Kilo de Oro*, which would be his last published book. By now Che Guevara had been executed in Bolivia, a loss which Walsh felt deeply, admiring the disappeared guerrilla's lifelong struggle for freedom.

Walsh finished "A Dark Day of Justice" just a month after Che's death in Nancahuazú. The story was the final part of the Irish Series, in which the defeat of the pupils' champion in Fahy boarding school offered a poignant parallel to the defeat of the guerrilla-hero, an end to the illusion that a single charismatic individual could save the country and lead a revolution, requiring of others only that they tag along and cheer the winners past the finishing line.

As Walsh said to Ricardo Piglia, who interviewed him in 1970, "The number of people who would say to you 'If only Che Guevara was here, then I'd be up for it and we'd all get on board and make the revolution happen'." It was, said Rodolfo, in a subsequent interview, "an utterly theoretical concept, you know, the myth, the figure, the hero, instead of the people making the revolution happen, the hero, as undoubtedly the most important expression of the people, in this case Che Guevara; but no one out there alone, however great, can do things on their own. When responsibility is handed over to one person and not taken up by all, then the process cannot take place, it doesn't happen" (Walsh, 1996 p.215).

It was clear to Walsh that only a well-organised popular movement could shake the system.

Guevara

For whom do the bells toll? They toll for us. I find it impossible to think of Guevara, in this lugubrious Buenos Aires spring, without thinking of Hemingway, of Camilo, of Masetti, of Fabricio Ojeda, all those marvellous people who were Havana or passed through Havana in '59 and '60. Nostalgia is encoded in a rosary of the dead and one feels slightly ashamed sitting here before a typewriter, even knowing that that too is a form of fatality, even if one could console oneself with the idea that it's a fatality which serves a purpose.

I see Camilo, one Sunday morning, flying low in a helicopter over the beach at Coney Island, poking his head out in fits of laughter and the crowd enjoying it below. I hear old Hemingway, at Rancho Boyeros airport, saying these next-to-last words: "We are going to win, us Cubans are going to win." And to my surprise: "I'm not a yankee you know."

Endlessly I see Masetti in the early hours in *Prensa Latina*, when *mate* was drunk and tangos were listened to, and the subject always turned to that necessary revolution, even though it seems so hard today, so dressed up in the blood of people one admired or simply loved.

We never knew when Che would appear in *Prensa Latina*, he would drop by unannounced, the only sign of his presence in the building was two *guajiritos*[34] wearing the glorious uniform of the Sierra,[35] one stationed by the lift, the other in front of Masetti's office, a machine gun in hand. I don't know exactly how they gave the impression that they would get themselves killed for Guevara and when that happened, they wouldn't go easily.

Many people were luckier than I, talking at length with Guevara. Although it wasn't impossible or even difficult, I just listened in, two or three times, when he was talking to Masetti. I had questions for him but didn't feel like interrupting him or maybe the questions were answered before they could be asked. I felt the same way he said he felt the only time he ever saw Frank País; all I can say now is that his eyes immediately revealed a man possessed by a cause and that the man was a superior being. I read his articles in *Verde Olivo*, I listened to him on television. That seemed enough because Che Guevara was a man without conflicts, his writings spoke with his voice and his voice was the same on paper or between two *mates* in that Retiro Medico office. I think the people of Havana took a while to get used to him, his cold, dry humour, so *porteño*, it must have been like a bucket of cold water. Once they understood him, he was one of the most beloved people in Cuba.

He was the first victim of his humour. If I remember correctly, no army chief, no general, no hero has written about himself fleeing on two occasions. Of the Bueycito battle, where his machine gun jammed in front of an enemy soldier who shot at him from close by, he would say: "My involvement in that battle was minimal and less than heroic, the few shots I faced with the back end of my body." And in reference to the surprise at Altos de Espinoso: "All I did was make a 'strategic retreat' at top speed in that encounter." He exaggerated these things, when everyone knew that Fidel had recalled how difficult it was to get him out of where the worst danger was. He controlled his vanity the same way as he controlled his asthma. In that denial of the ultimate passions, lay the seeds of the new man he spoke about.

Guevara didn't put himself forward as a hero; in any case he could be as much of a hero as anyone else. But this, of course was not true for others. His level was dumbfounding: it was easier to give up than follow him and the same was the case with Fidel and the people of the Sierra. This demand could be critical and that crisis has taken on its definite

---

[34] As people from the countryside are known in Cuba.
[35] The Sierra Maestra, the mountains where the revolution was forged.

shape, after the episodes in Bolivia.

To put it simply: it's hard not to feel ashamed, not of being alive – because it's not a death wish, it's the opposite, the strength of the revolution – but that Guevara died with so few around him. We didn't know, of course, officially we knew nothing, but we suspected something, we feared as much. We were slow, guilty? Pointless now to debate the issue, but that feeling is there, at least for me, and may be a new point of departure.

The CIA agent who, according to Reuter, elbowed and shoved one hundred journalists waiting to see the body in Valle Grande, said a phrase in English: "Awright, get the hell out of here."

That phrase with its stamp, its weight, its criminal mark, remains a challenge to history. And the necessary reply: someone sooner or later will get the hell out of this continent. It won't be Che's memory.

Now dispersed in one hundred cities
Devoted to the path of those who didn't know him.

Buenos Aires, October 1967
●✧ (Walsh, 1995 pp.270–75)

The novel that never was

The importance of the novel in establishing rank within literature's rigid caste system was never lost on Rodolfo, who grappled with the concept from the time of his earliest work. Walsh frequently regretted falling into what he called the 'intellectual trap', in which the novel acquired legendary status due to his bourgeois conditioning. On other occasions he dismissed the issue as an irrelevance: "Did anyone ever demand a novel from Borges?" he inquired of his diary.

In the late 1960s Rodolfo suffered writer's block as he grappled with the elusive novel, which appeared so important to his personal ambitions. If he could write a novel, and it was successful, he could then forget about literary achievements and focus on the most exciting adventure of all: life itself. The novel was a ticket away from the expectations arising from the quality of short stories like "Esa mujer" and the Irish trilogy.

The Irish stories were based inside the Fahy Institute but carried a universal message of faith and struggle. In "Irish Boys after a Cat", the first of the published trilogy, Walsh described the baptism of fire suffered by "the cat", a new pupil at Fahy, who must fight to establish his place in the pecking order. The rite of passage also hinted at the broader issue of how oppressed peoples compete for survival. In those circumstances, the prospect of collective action against the repressor was cancelled out, with the best possible outcome being a leadership role within the oppressed group, with access to minor privileges.

In "Earthly Responsibilities", the boys enjoyed the rewards of obedience to the system; an annual party and an outing to the zoo, one day of relative freedom in return for a whole year of obedience to the established order. In "A Dark Day of Justice", the boys' thoughts turn to rebellion and they place their hopes in the mythical strength of a conquering hero who, if triumphant, will free them from lockdown and corporal punishment.

Brilliant short stories kept appearing instead of the mythical novel, no matter how much he riled against it, a pattern which continued throughout his writing life. "I have worked out the outline for a novel which would take place in Paraguay or Bolivia and which might best respond to the requirement you mentioned, 'a colourful latin background'," Rodolfo told Donald Yates in May 1954, as he embarked on his literary career. He was only 27 years old.

The plot would involve international espionage, with a murder case resolved after "laborious investigation, like in Victor Canning's work [...] I think I have an original plot but I'm resisting the temptation to tell you about it, because if you know it in advance you may lose interest," wrote Walsh, once more confiding in Yates. "The action takes place in let's say Asunción, Paraguay, where the main character, a foreigner, will carry around plans for a military revolution for several days, without realising it."

The novel would involve "a crime, an investigation, a chief of police of the Latin American type, plenty of shootouts and substantial local colour." After several months of silence Rodolfo returned to the issue of the novel in September 1954. "The planned Paraguayan novel will have to wait. Personal issues made me put off my trip to Paraguay, I have the argument but not the atmosphere and I don't want to 'invent' places and people."

Rodolfo's novel was evolving from a short police story to a full-length book, while the author also had his eye on the closing date of an important literary competition, which had a first prize of US$2,000. Rodolfo missed the final entry date and abandoned the project. The novel was set aside once more as Walsh and Yates focused their energies on the planned launch of a Latin American crime fiction magazine.

In March 1955 Rodolfo suddenly returned to the novel which was still lodged in his mind, announcing now that it would be based on "prophetic dreams". The Paraguayan novel moved to Bolivia but before he had a chance to work on the plot, he had already converted it into a screenplay: "a North American, who is in La Paz by chance, wakes up one morning to discover that the overcoat he put away in his hotel room closet the night before has a bullet hole and a blood stain at the height of his heart [...] after a series of adventures (shots, chases, fists and women), he finds out that for the past month, without knowing it, he has been carrying around plans to overthrow the government..."

True to form Walsh located the film script in La Paz because there had been one hundred revolutions there in the previous 100 years and because "it is one of the few cities in Latin America where an overcoat would not be out of place."

In June 1956 Rodolfo clung to the novel as a means of distancing himself from the terrifying reality he discovered in the testimony of an *Operación Masacre* survivor. The frightened writer wondered aloud whether he could simply shut his eyes, close his ears and go back to "the novel I plan to write," an illusion shattered by subsequent events.

Pirí Lugones succeeded in persuading Rodolfo to drop everything and return to the novel in 1965. Walsh had already completed two non-fiction investigations, two plays, a crime fiction collection and several short stories. He retreated happily to his cottage in Tigre, enjoying ideal working conditions, but as soon as he set aside other distractions, he developed writer's block. Rodolfo would head off to Tigre for a week of intense work and come back with just half a page. "It would be an extraordinary half page," admitted Ricardo Piglia, "with that fluency which gave the impression it had been written in one go."

Walsh spoke to *Siete Días* magazine in June 1969, where he was asked why he had given up on the novel. "In a certain sense a novel is a representation of events and I prefer their simple presentation. Besides one doesn't write a novel, one is inside a novel, one more character living out the drama. I feel that the executions (*Operación Masacre*) and the death of Rosendo García (*Quien Mató a Rosendo?*) have greater literary merit when they are presented in a journalistic way than when they are translated into another form, which is the way of the novel."

Walsh spoke about the novel he had begun, acknowledging "a great nostalgia" and a desire to return to his work on it: "going back to it or not depends on the outside world. Right now I'm living out two realities, combining journalism of action, which requires me to be in the street, write at speed and finish a chapter or two in a day with the retreat into fiction where I produce, with some effort, five lines a day."

In September 1969 matters came to a head as Walsh managed just five pages in 30 hours of dedicated work. Walsh's fruitless efforts in front of a blank page and a Remington typewriter increased his doubts about the value of such an isolated craft in a world dominated by very concrete problems of State repression and social injustice.

Ricardo Piglia was also a close friend of novelist Haroldo Conti, and vividly recalled how Conti once showed him a book which Walsh had given him: "Haroldo", read the dedication, "you and me are going to make it happen" a reference to Walsh's novel in progress. "It was as if Walsh were saying Argentinian literature was an issue between them two," commented Piglia, who sensed an enormous literary ambition in Walsh.

On another occasion Walsh gave Pirí Lugones a present of Peruvian writer Mario Vargas Llosa's *Conversation in the Cathedral,* this time dedicating it with the phrase "I'm going to write a novel like this soon."

Years later Walsh criticised the Latin American literary boom, describing it as a boomerang which placed the writer and literary production itself on a pedestal, the potential for rebelliousness neutralised by ritual praise, financial reward and access to power. "The justification for the novelist is in the degree to which it can be proven that one's books can inspire and subvert," said Walsh, who hadn't thrown in the towel altogether on the issue. Walsh noted that a journalist had asked him why he hadn't written *Quien Mató a Rosendo?* in the form of a novel: "it would make a great novel," his interviewer commented, "a comment which carried the implicit opinion that a novelised version of the story would take it to a superior category [...] a typically bourgeois notion." Walsh expanded on his criticism: "Obviously the accusation [in *Quien Mató a Rosendo?*], once converted into the art of the novel becomes inoffensive, it doesn't disturb anyone, it is rendered sacred as art."

Walsh feared that *Operación Masacre, Caso Satanowsky* and *Quien Mató a Rosendo?* would have been diminished in their impact had they been consigned to the novel form: "The reader would take in the story like any other, at best indignant at the events [...] but the difficulty in understanding the social connections between the various events would still remain."

When asked about contemporary literature Walsh drew a blank, admitting he was "way behind" on current writing, reading up on political issues instead. He added that the bulk of the nation's literature, including his own (apart from his non-fiction books) was written from a bourgeois perspective, "reflecting the concerns of the middle class, not even the real economic conflicts, or power struggles, or spiritual dilemmas [...] in our literature no worker struggle has been represented, no short story, although there must be one, (he paused) which discusses a strike, a revolution or Resistance efforts, or what's happening now, nothing." If a martian came down and analysed Argentina on the basis of its literature, concluded Walsh, "they would leave with a totally exotic notion of reality [...] you can find out more from a newspaper, at least you have a photo to look at" (Baschetti, 1994 p.71).

Once more Walsh's evolution toward political militancy was clearly defined as a struggle between competing notions of the writer-activist.

The typewriter, said Walsh, is a weapon, the use of which depends on the person handling it: "it can be a fan or a pistol [...] with a typewriter and a sheet of paper you can move people in unbelievable ways, I have no doubt about that" (ibid).

Julio Cortázar pushed the novel toward Walsh's definition in his *Libro de Manuel* (1973) combining news clippings with a fictional tale of a guerrilla kidnapping. The impact was huge, as a confident fictional narrative was wedded with a non-fiction contextualisation. In one powerful scene the author reproduced the contents of a letter sent by the partner of a Tupamaro[36] rebel, tortured to death, to the partner of a man kidnapped by the rebels, but as yet alive: "I know, madam, that you are not in a position to understand my suffering, because each one's suffering is always greater than that of the rest. But you understand, I hope, that the conditions which brought about the kidnapping of your husband and the fatal torture of mine are the very same: that it is important to realise that hunger-violence, misery-violence, oppression-violence, underdevelopment-violence, torture-violence lead to kidnapping-violence, terrorism-violence, guerrilla-violence; and that it is very important to understand who puts the violence into practice, whether it is those who cause misery or those who fight against it [...] He (Mario Alves) died out of love for the oppressed, the victims of injustice, those who have no voice and no hope. He fought so that the immense material and human resources of our country could be used for the benefit of all" (Cortázar, 1978, pp.324–5).

In an interview published in *La Opinión* in 1972, Walsh outlined his political and personal evolution over the previous five years. He singled out the *Cordobazo* (1969) as a defining moment in his evolving conscious-ness, "from then on I had no doubts about whether to continue writing short stories, which I wrote with much effort and affection, or go with this burning, impetuous reality; whether to write the novel or live the novel, alongside the people, that was an easy decision."

Once Walsh had made up his mind he began campaigning against the novel, as Juan José Saer noticed when he next came across Rodolfo in Paris, in 1970. Saer, one of Argentina's most respected writers, had lunch with Walsh, who bluntly asked him why he continued to write fiction. "In the future world which we are all trying to make possible," answered Saer, "a world without literature would be a world in which I would never belong." Saer could think of no good reason for eliminating his craft in the name of a vague, future revolution.

Rodolfo had ceased to think about writing his novel, utterly absorbed by the task of organising for the struggle ahead. There was a final twist to

---

[36] The Tupamaros were one of the guerrilla groups in Uruguay.

the debate in the last months of his life, when he did return to the novel. Ricardo Piglia recalled his last meeting with Walsh, a chance encounter in Buenos Aires city centre in June 1976. Walsh sniffed and cursed the cold, drinking coffee in the bar of an old train station. He said he wanted to write a novel based on historical events in 1912, when a fisherman described how he crossed over to Uruguay on horseback along the dry riverbed after a great drought. It sounded like the River Plate's answer to Hemingway's *The Old Man and the Sea*. A short story would still win out over the novel: he wrote "Juan went down to the river" in the weeks before his death.

By then Walsh was living a clandestine life which paradoxically gave him the time he needed to write. He had resumed his fragmented autobiographical work, which began three decades before, as he pieced together aspects of his life in a race against time, as his implacable hunters narrowed the odds and closed in for the kill.

chapter eleven

Peronist politics

When I have to talk about Rodolfo I feel as though I lack the air to breathe, because it is a huge responsibility to recreate his personality as accurately as possible, from my own memory.

(Lilia Ferreyra in Camano and Bayer, 1998 p.235)

We could have been born into happier times, but we weren't. We can't listen to music, although we like to, we can't paint although we like to, we can't write, although we like to. We would like to be with our partners and our children, where our feelings lie. But they don't allow us to, they take everything away from us, everything is forbidden, forbidden, forbidden. So we say no, we won't obey.

(Paco Urondo quoting Raimundo Ongaro, ibid p.220)

Union politics

In February 1968, on a stop-off in Madrid, Rodolfo requested an interview with exiled former president Juan Perón, who was busy, as ever, plotting his return to Argentina. Visitors to Perón's Puerta de Hierro residence usually bowed and scraped to their host, seeking a favour or endorsement to advance their careers at home. When Walsh was ushered into Perón's private office, the caudillo's first words took him by surprise: "All Peronists owe you a debt of gratitude," he said, a compliment from the most influential Argentinian politician of the 20th century.

Rodolfo's *Operación Masacre* had skilfully exposed the brutality of the military junta which threw Perón out of power in 1955. The comment tickled Walsh's ego. The meeting was brief, with small talk exchanged and promises made to keep in touch. Perón, wily as ever, had a surprise for Walsh, introducing him to Raimundo Ongaro, a charismatic union leader, soon to become General Secretary of the breakaway Confederación General de Trabajadores de los Argentinos (CGTA) distinct from the government-controlled Confederación General de Trabajadores (CGT). Perón asked Ongaro if he knew who Walsh was: "What Peronist doesn't know who he is?" responded Ongaro, sounding almost offended.

Ongaro recalled Perón's exact words when the exiled leader introduced him to Walsh in Madrid, in 1968: "This is a man who will not give you a slap on the back to congratulate you or tell you that everything is fine, but this man will always be there wherever you are," (Camano and Bayer, 1998 pp.229–230).

The official CGT controlled the nation's largest unions, a conservative bureaucratic machine which expelled members on behalf of factory bosses, demoralised workers and dramatically reduced membership. It was in effect a union-bashing syndicate disguised as a workers' representative body. The discredited CGT was held together by corrupt leaders like Augusto Vandor who made his name during early Peronist resistance efforts, in the years which followed Perón's exile. "The treachery of a leader who has fought in their day and defected to the other side, thus provoking a terrible crisis of trust, is more difficult to overcome than the opposition of a recognised enemy," wrote Walsh, accounting for the drop in union membership and morale (Walsh, 1969 p.168).

The official CGT held a general assembly on March 28th 1968 in which the majority of union members rejected the collaborationist leadership and demanded a policy of resistance to military rule. The result was an historic victory for the independent union movement and paved the way for the immediate launch of the Confederación General de Trabajadores de los Argentinos, CGTA.

Walsh's Madrid encounter with Perón and Ongaro acted as a bridge linking Walsh's desire for more direct involvement in political militancy with his passion for the "violent profession" of the writer. Ongaro invited Walsh to edit the *Semanario CGT*, a new publication which would reflect the changes taking place within the union movement.

Rodolfo had grappled unsuccessfully with his planned novel for two years in his hideaway home in Tigre. Now he decided to abandon fiction and enter the world of radical politics at the centre of an independent media experiment. Walsh agreed to edit the weekly paper once he had persuaded two key allies to join him, Rogelio García Lupo and Horacio Verbitsky. The latter knew the ins and outs of layout, print and publishing, technical skills which Walsh never learned, as he had carved out a career as a freelancer, baulking at the restrictions of salaried newspaper work. García Lupo was a gifted journalist, with a capacity to drill holes in the enemy's argument, capturing the state of the nation's crisis in just a few lines.

Walsh walked into the CGTA building in downtown Buenos Aires for the first time in March 1968 and set about organising the launch of the paper. He was soon absorbed in the intense atmosphere, turning up every day, getting to know delegates and activists from all over the country, selecting the most important issues to cover. Walsh could easily have confined his duties to commissioning stories and overseeing the editorial process but true to form he ploughed every ounce of energy into the project. "When he began working with us," said Raimundo Ongaro, "he went to all the assemblies, meetings and congresses, with endless curiosity, he stood by the workers, not to pretend he was a worker while living a bourgeois life, or to talk from the left and live on the right [...] it was the workers themselves who confirmed him in his role as editor," said Ongaro.

"Rodolfo was particularly moved by this encounter with the world of political militancy, not so much out of guilt as out of a sense of discovering the role of the intellectual. While he was in the delta writing up short stories, there were people here organising for years, giving battle to the dictator in different ways," said Lilia Ferreyra, who lived with Rodolfo as he prepared the launch of the new paper.

Rodolfo stayed into the early hours of the morning at the CGTA office each week, holding on for some last-minute news item delivered by a breathless union delegate who arrived from some far-flung point around the country. "He would come home from the CGTA office talking passionately of the clarity and capacity of the union delegates in those years," Lilia recalled. One activist much admired by Walsh was John William Cooke, a radical Peronist who led resistance operations after Perón's exile in 1955, narrowly escaping a firing squad before moving to Cuba in the early 1960s. "In Cooke he found a revolutionary who had emerged from the Argentinian people's own history, through Peronism," said Lilia (Camano and Bayer, 1998 p.234). He also found in Cooke a left-wing pro-Castro perspective plugged into the broader Peronist movement, a position which coincided with Walsh's political convictions.

Semanario CGT

The first edition of the *Semanario CGT* was published on May Day 1968, launching a combative assault on union bureaucracy, transnational capital and corrupt politicians. The message of resistance dovetailed seamlessly with the growing social unrest which led up to the *Cordobazo* of May 1969, one of several worker uprisings which occurred that year.

The dictator of the day, General Juan Carlos Onganía, had seized power two years before, in 1966, launching an "Argentinian Revolution" which favoured foreign investment and lowered living standards for salaried workers and the rural bourgeoisie. The urban middle class felt the attack on universities, as traditional campus autonomy came to a violent end. On July 29th 1966, Onganía ordered an armed assault on the University of Buenos Aires, in an incident known as the "Night of the

Long Pencils", where hundreds of students were detained, seventy more hospitalised and one youth killed. There was a brain drain as hundreds of academics abandoned the country, their knowledge welcomed into top US, Mexican and European universities.

Right from the beginning Walsh set the combative tone that would characterise the popular publication and attract the attention of the Onganía regime, which shut it down less than a year later. The paper published 50 issues, the last copy produced in hiding, until the definitive shutdown in July 1969.

The first issue of the eight-page broadsheet was a rapid-fire run through recent labour history, alongside a broad socio-political analysis of the nation, from infant mortality rates in impoverished rural zones to the function of the IMF and the myth of "free enterprise". "The CGT de los Argentinos does not offer workers an easy road," read the opening manifesto, "it offers each one of you a place in the struggle."

The opening salvo established a seven-point plan of struggle and addressed a range of sectors, from the military to businesspeople, church representatives and students, calling on them to abandon an unjust government "elected by nobody". "Nothing can stop us," concluded the missive, with trademark Walsh optimism, "neither jail nor death. Because you can't jail or kill a whole people and because the vast majority of Argentinians, without electoral pacts, collaborationist or coup adventures, know that only the people will save the people."

The May Day message carried the signature of the CGTA's co-ordinating committee, eighteen names in all, but the style, language and tone belonged to Walsh. The sharp writing was complemented by the oratorial magic of Raimundo Ongaro, a popular national figure. The precarious legality of a radical paper publishing under military rule, the unsigned articles and the collective decision-making policy marked a new departure for Walsh. He left behind the intense personal experience of the frustrated novel and immersed himself in the day-by-day battle against the dictatorship. His individual identity as a writer was replaced by a collective identity: the people vs. the dictatorship.

Over the coming weeks and months, the office of the CGTA, located just around the corner from the official CGT headquarters, in downtown Buenos Aires, became a hotbed of activity, where workers turned up from all over Argentina to denounce labour repression and exploitation and draw up plans for national street protests. The CGTA picked out the regime's weak points, striking in Tucumán and Rosario, where two hundred demostrators were detained during disturbances following May Day 1968. In Buenos Aires province, San Justo was the scene of street battles, as hundreds of police tossed teargas at 10,000 protestors, who responded with stones. The wave of protests mobilised 30,000 people and

Circa 1949: 'I am an Irish descendant on all sides.' (Courtesy Carlos Walsh)

Circa 1930: carefree days in Choele-Choel. (Courtesy Carlos Walsh)

Circa 1931: at home in Choele-Choel. Left to right: Miguel, Carlos, Rodolfo and Héctor. (Courtesy Carlos Walsh)

1952: Rodolfo aged 25 with wife Elina and daughter Vicki. (Courtesy Carlos Walsh)

Circa 1956: Vicki and Patricia. (Courtesy Carlos Walsh)

1958: interviews and acclaim followed *Operación Masacre* (1957) and *Caso Satanowsky* (1958), earning Walsh a place in Argentina's Who's Who. (Courtesy Carlos Walsh)

In 'La Bodeguita del Medio,' Havana, with Orlando Contreras of *Prensa Latina*,
Castro-biographer Waldo Frank, *Prensa Latina* driver (furthest away) and
colleagues. (Courtesy Orlando Contreras)

EL NUEVO BAÑO CONTOUR

Montage by Poupee Blanchard, a
homage to Rudy's long bubble baths.
(Courtesy Poupee Blanchard)

Left to right: Rogelio García Lupo,
Rodolfo Walsh, Poupee Blanchard.
(Courtesy Poupee Blanchard)

1968: at the Cultural
Congress. Left to
right: Eduardo
Galeano, Rodolfo
Walsh, Lilia Ferreyra
and Ernesto Cardenal.
(Radar, *Página/12*)

1968: a rare glimpse
of the writer without
glasses.
(Radar, *Página/12*)

1970: Walsh loved to
clown about – here
he plays charades.
(Radar, *Página/12*)

A sombre Walsh, contemplating fresh horizons.
(Courtesy Lilia Ferreyra)

1969, left to right: Rodolfo Walsh, Raimundo Ongaro and colleagues of CGTA.
(Radar, *Página/12*)

The corner of Buenos Aires which is named after Walsh, Plazoleta Rodolfo Walsh. (Photo Derek Speirs/ Report)

Intrepid investigative reporter at work. (Radar, *Página/12*)

Rudy found a spiritual home and a refuge for his writing in Tigre, here in his house Lorerey, on the river Carapachay. (Courtesy Lilia Ferreyra)

resulted in 700 arrests.

The graphics and layout at the *Semanario CGT* were exceptional. "Here you had a subversive paper designed in a luxury hotel by workers from a PR firm, unbeknownst to their bosses," explained Verbitsky, complimenting the work of Jorge Saludiavsky and Oscar Smoje. "This was typical of the co-operation between people at the time, something unthinkable nowadays."

Rodolfo's younger daughter Patricia, then sixteen years of age, would travel from her mother's home in La Plata once a week and visit the CGTA offices, where she loaded copies of the *Semanario CGT* into bundles, sending off subscription copies around the country. "The first set of copies were sent to military barracks," recalled Patricia, a sign of her father's persistent attempts to win over members of the State security forces rather than simply brand them all as irreconcilable enemies of the people.

By issue two, dated May 9th 1968, the *Semanario CGT* was in full swing, lobbing finely tuned missiles at all the right targets. "Grenades and Guarantees" described the symbiotic relationship between torture and economic investment. "The attack dogs and gas grenades are the real investment guarantee for foreign capital, while the destruction of native industry is negotiated by electric prod on the torture table and national determination is disposed of in prison cells rather than the presidential palace."

The articles were unsigned but many bore the familiar Walsh imprint. There was no lack of confidence in the future of the outlawed worker's movement: "It has taken a month to get the workers' movement back on its feet," announced the weekly paper. "Thirty days more should be enough to wipe out the last traces of collaborationism and participationism."

The clock ticked away as the seeds were planted for the most significant union-led uprising of the decade, led by Agustín Tosco and other non-Peronist union leaders in Córdoba. The workers' rebellion showed that a class-based union movement had a crucial role to play in the growing climate of insurrection. The *Cordobazo* spread to Rosario and Santiago del Estero, a decisive factor in forcing the regime to replace General Onganía in 1970. The militant union action also inspired armed resistance to the regime which followed.

The *Semanario CGT* always gave space in the paper to non-union efforts, attempting to broaden the CGTA support base, on one occasion praising the efforts of a group of 360 of the *Movimiento para el Tercer Mundo* (Movement for the Third World) who sent representatives to a CGTA meeting and agreed to co-operate in areas of mutual interest.

Before May was out, the *Semanario CGT* published a "unique

testament" of the CGTA's moral solvency. One after another, the weekly paper listed properties, bank loans, savings, cars and any other relevant possessions belonging to all seventeen members of the CGTA steering committee. "Every worker can check, whenever they like, whether their leaders have grown wealthy, and if it is the case, then they have the right to remove those leaders."

Walsh worked flat out, didn't have a penny to his name but enjoyed the intense moments shared in the collective process. "One thing I never heard during all this time," commented Lilia Ferreyra, "neither from Rodolfo nor anyone else working on the *Semanario CGT*, was talk about money for their work, or the demand for public positions in return for the time they gave."

Walsh held weekly planning meetings in the couple's apartment, where the volunteers arrived to the usual Walsh work chaos, with newspapers strewn everywhere, waiting to be clipped and filed alongside books open for reference purposes.

Neighbourhood by neighbourhood: popular resistance

From an assessment of the June 28th events, the lessons learned and with the different groups now back on their feet, a new stage of mass struggle begins to emerge.

The unelected government has not resolved a single one of the problems which were around four months, four weeks or four days ago. Tens of thousands of students keep up their combative spirit.

By the end of the year, over 100,000 tenants will be evicted from their businesses or their homes. The set period for wage freezes steadily nears its end and the demand for a 40 per cent increase boosts morale in every factory and in every home.

The Argentinian CGT has become the greatest organised force in opposition to the government. We have a duty to establish a common strategy for the masses, to face every one of the real and inevitable conflicts that will arise before December 31st.

Experience shows that a regime lacking popular support can defeat each sector one at a time, simply by turning its repressive force on one sector then another during each isolated event. In that way one person can impose their will on one hundred, 10,000 police can paralyse a city of six million and the three commanders of the armed forces don't even need to send in their troops to impose their fast-track legislation on 22 million people.

The masses have fought their battles one by one, at times heroically, without securing a decisive victory. It's not enough to occupy a factory, if the neighbourhood surrounding the factory, the school or university department opposite, the parish hall half a block away, the co-operative around the corner, the political activist, tenant or small-business owner all stand watching as fifty armed guards evict one thousand unarmed compañeros.

The occupation of a university department isn't enough if the worker, the militant, or even a neighbour stand by as the students are taken prisoner.

It's pointless for a lodger facing eviction to resist if the active solidarity of the worker, the student, the neighbourhood, the entire town cannot be counted on.

Isolated in place and time, the workers will always be evicted from the factory they occupy, the students from the faculty they occupy, the lodgers from their own homes, the small-business owner from their own business.

But the same thing will not happen if a collective, united movement co-ordinates the popular acts of rebellion; if the suffering sectors learn the lesson of their defeats and learn to strike together at the same time in the same place.

The neighbourhood, the town, the district, with its everyday problems, is the most appropriate terrain for this common struggle. Without giving up on the mass protests which represent the sum total of each individual act of rebellion, we should concentrate our efforts on these basic community meeting points, organising our joint protests there.

The support of an entire neighbourhood for a strike in a factory can be more effective than a mass protest march, because that strike will not be defeated. The support of the workers for individual tenants evicted from a neighbourhood can force the government to make a battle out of each eviction. The presence of students in the shantytowns may be more effective than the occupation of a university faculty.

The CGT is not asking any sector to abandon its own forms of struggle; it is asking them to co-ordinate them with all the other resistances. From that common action will emerge, beyond the concrete results in each case, leaders, cadres and the organisations necessary to produce the revolutionary changes this country demands.

We know that this new form of struggle cannot be improvised. We are aware of the reluctance, the distrust, the lack of any tradition in this area.

Quietly however, the people have begun to move in that direction. In Santa Fe province, the action of two unions with both CGT backing and popular support have allowed the first ever workers' daily to be published in the interior of the country.

In Córdoba, the neighbourhood councils have begun to meet, called for by the CGT, to discuss together the problems in the neighbourhoods. The Bread for Struggle campaign run by our Solidarity Commission is bringing trucks with food and clothes to the furrows of Tucumán.

These initiatives must be multiplied. Every trade union office must become the centre not just of local, town or district labour demands, but also the place where the actions of workers, students, intellectuals, militants, politicians, priests and small-business owners are combined. The experience of the Santa Fe journalists and photographers must be repeated in the cities and towns of the countryside and in the neighbourhoods of the great capital cities: we need a popular and revolutionary press which brings to every corner of the country the truths which don't appear in the official media.

The regional offices must apply the Córdoba initiative, calling neighbourhood councils together, or helping create them where they don't exist.

The CGT calls on all Argentinians to form action and help commissions at neighbourhood level, which if united can become a mass popular resistance movement, capable of giving back the people what is rightfully theirs. A joint action by all sectors, in every place and opportunity where the dictatorship threatens the rights of one sector, is the way to get this movement underway.

The dictatorship can occupy a union, a factory, a university department, a town square, a building. But it can't occupy all the unions, all the factories, all the university departments, all the town squares, all the buildings.

If resistance finds a home in all people, neither the army nor the police can contain it. If national liberation takes off in the consciences of all Argentinians, there won't be enough teargas or batons to prevent it. If the social revolution takes root in the hearts of each one of us, there won't be enough tanks to stop it.

Isolated, we can expect only defeat. Together we have the right to trust in victory.

●◆ (Documentos/CGT/No 2, published by *Página 12*)

Who killed Rosendo?

Walsh contributed a lengthy series of articles to the *Semanario CGT* beginning on May 16th 1968 entitled *Quien Mató a Rosendo?* (Who killed Rosendo?) dealing with the killing of Rosendo García, a union leader shot dead in a pizza parlour in May 1966.

The official version of events maintained that one group of trade unionists sitting at a table in the pizzeria, led by official CGT leader Augusto Vandor, was attacked by a rival faction, with three men killed in the ensuing shoot-out. In the aftermath of the shooting, the media generously quoted Vandor and his allies, who fabricated the notion that the shoot-out was arranged for the purpose of eliminating Rosendo García, a myth blasted apart by Walsh.

Vandor represented the official CGT tendency which collaborated with the government and factory owners, fast losing support to the dissident CGTA. A former Peronist resistance leader, Vandor had now grown fat on corruption and was described by Walsh as "the main obstacle in the way of an independent, combative workers' policy."

While three men were killed in the shooting, attention focused on the death of Rosendo García, a Vandor associate who was about to run as a candidate for governor in upcoming elections, potentially eclipsing the ambitious Vandor. Walsh described Rosendo as a "decent thug and gambler" but quickly moved on to the unsung victims of the pizzeria massacre.

"In the so-called shoot-out in La Real of Avellaneda, in May 1966, someone far braver than Rosendo was killed," explained Walsh, in his prologue to the book version of *Quien Mató a Rosendo?* "That man, Blajaquis the Greek, was a true hero of his class. Another man was mercilessly gunned down, Zalazar, whose humility and desperation were so great that they acted as a mirror to the workers' misfortune. For the media, police, judges, these people have no history, only criminal records; neither poets nor writers know them, the justice and honour due to them doesn't fit in these lines; some day, however, the beauty of their deeds will shine through, like those of so many others, ignored, persecuted and rebellious to the end" (Walsh, 1969 p.7).

Walsh was off on another investigation which would unmask the betrayal of workers by union bosses cosy with factory owners and government bureaucrats, but he also offered an olive branch to the uncommitted reader. "If anyone wants to read this book as a straightforward detective story, that's up to them." A reminder that Walsh's crime fiction roots still played a fundamental role in his evolution as an investigative journalist (ibid p.9).

Walsh believed that the deaths of García, Blajaquis and Zalazar were the inevitable consequence of the power struggle carried on by Vandor, García and fellow CGT leaders at the expense of the struggle for improved working conditions for union members.

Walsh noted the chain of responsibility in the pizzeria killings: first came the gangsters (CGT leadership bodyguards) who carried out the killing, then the Macarthyite insinuations to lessen the impact of the crime ("they were only Trotskyists"), then the negotiation with each level of authority to ensure impunity. Finally, the opportunistic manipulation of the crime, as Vandor used the "attempt on his life" to crush a rival union tendency.

Walsh ran a fine-tooth comb through the events of May 1966, and with his forensic skills established the responsibility of Vandor in the death of the three men, throwing in a concise account of labour resistance since Perón's exile in 1955 for free.

On May 16th 1966, two groups of rival union activists found themselves sitting at different tables in a pizzeria, by utter chance. One of the groups numbered eleven men, centred around official CGT leaders Augusto Vandor, Rosendo García, their friends and bodyguards. Vandor was under pressure from the exiled Perón, who played each union faction off another, wary of a rival caudillo emerging in his absence. Perón suspected that Vandor had ambitions to replace him as the leader of Argentina's opposition movement. "In politics, wounding isn't enough," wrote Perón, in his euphemistic style, "you have to kill, because someone wandering around with an injured foot can do a lot of damage," (ibid p.42).

Vandor and his bodyguards occupied separate tables, guns at the ready, anticipating trouble from the disgruntled activists at the table across the room, incorrectly assuming that they too were armed.

José Petrarca, one of Vandor's henchmen, took objection to the looks directed his way by Raimundo Villaflor. "What's your fucking problem?" snarled Petrarca, who lunged at Villaflor. The two men grappled with each other, Villaflor recalling, with irony, how he used to distribute leaflets demanding the release of Petrarca from prison, back in the days when the union leaders were activists rather than collaborators with the regime.

Everyone now stood up, and as confusion reigned, chairs were smashed over heads, bullets flew and three men lay dead, all in a matter of seconds.

Walsh reconstructed the pizzeria crime scene in his apartment, as Lilia helped out, unrolling pieces of string to establish the trajectory of the bullets. In comparison with Walsh, the State forensic team were beginners, making elementary errors, hardly accidental, so that the scientific evidence would fit the official story, that Rosendo was killed by shots which came from the rival faction's table. In addition, Rosendo's last words, "This had to happen just now," left a whiff of betrayal in the air, as Walsh suspected that he was referring to his imminent opportunity to oust Vandor as leader.

By studying the path of a dozen bullets fired in the fracas, Walsh proved that García, who stood up and placed himself between the rival groups, was killed by "friendly fire" from his own table, probably by Vandor, who unloaded six bullets during the incident.

Walsh also demonstrated that no one at Zalazar's table had fired a gun, for the simple reason that they were unarmed. Witnesses backed up Walsh's version of the events, but court testimony was falsified to protect Vandor and material evidence disappeared.

Walsh also built up a picture of the union dissidents, notably the murdered Domingo Blajaquis and Juan Zalazar, Peronists who actively opposed the CGT policy of collaboration with the military regime.

Blajaquis

"Domingo Blajaquis was in prison from the moment he was born," wrote Walsh, "the first person to suffer the *picana* [...] the police always came looking for him and he always talked back at them and answered back all the exploiters of the world with bombs that destroyed bridges and factories. Thus the legend grew."

Blajaquis became a living example of dignified resistance, "always hunted, never defeated," someone who "never had anything nor became anything in the bourgeois sense [...] because a true revolutionary achieves nothing until the corrupt, parasitic regime is destroyed and a new society is in place."

Blajaquis was a tireless propagandist who lectured youths hanging around his neighbourhood, telling them to stand up for themselves and fight for their rights.

Zalazar

Zalazar was another well-known militant, a mediocre boxer turned bodyguard for unionists "who were destined to become leaders and forget about him." He had five children and struggled desperately to find work, blacklisted in factories across the city.

Walsh visited Zalazar's widow and children, read the notebook where the murdered man had jotted down his changing moods and came up with a moving conclusion to his brief, intense life. "He boxed when he could, against anyone. They tore him to shreds but he went home happy with a few pesos to feed the kids. On one of the many occasions when there was nothing left to eat in the house, he brought home fish which he found along the coast. The whole family got food poisoning. He cycled around selling flowers and dreamed of inventing a sausage machine with himself as the motor. And the night they killed him he had just worked 36 straight hours in Shell, because finally he found a job and didn't want to let it go, yet still he was anxious to meet up with his compañeros and see if something could be done for the sugarcane workers in Tucumán."

Walsh immediately contrasted the selflessness of Zalazar with the cynicism of his killer: "Armando Cabo, sitting beside Vandor, finished up his whisky, took aim and shot him dead."

Crime fiction

When it came to the evidence, wilful negligence knew no bounds. The crime scene was dismantled before forensic experts arrived, after a nervous waiter, himself a former policeman, rang the police to check if he should clean up the restaurant or leave it as it was. The police gave him the go-ahead to clean up the crime scene as new tables replaced damaged ones and glasses were wiped free of fingerprints. "The only thing they couldn't get rid of was the bullet holes," wrote Walsh.

The forensic team got round that by altering the scant remaining scientific evidence, "inventing" four bullet holes out of cracked plaster-work behind Vandor's seat, to give the impression that both parties had fired shots during the incident.

In the aftermath of the crime, the pliant media quoted only Vandor's allies while the victims went into hiding, fearing that Vandor's thugs might track then down to eliminate witnesses. Days after the killing, Vandor delivered the final oration at Rosendo García's funeral, warning of "rivers of blood" should the crime not be clarified.

When it came to giving his testimony however, Vandor suddenly suffered a bout of amnesia, unable to remember any of the people who were with him at the scene of the shooting, including his own bodyguards. Yet Vandor's minimal testimony was enough to demonstrate that the official version was incorrect. As logic and science defeated Vandor, he clutched at one final straw, suggesting that "a third group" of police officers from Buenos Aires province had suddenly arrived on the scene, tried to intervene in the punch-up and ended up shooting at the people involved.

Vandor's lawyer tried to convince defence lawyer Norberto Liffschitz to accept that version of events, but Liffschitz refused. On August 22nd 1966, Vandor perfected his story before the presiding judge: in the latest version of the events, the shooting began and Vandor announced that he "dived to the floor and only got up when the whole incident was over."

In February 1968 Vandor's legal team made another attempt to muddy the waters, coming up with the fabulous version of the "jumping, spinning" García, who, it was now acknowledged, had indeed been shot in the back, but only after he had jumped up and spun around to meet his attackers – from behind!

The final court declaration was as confusing as the case itself, defining the testimony to date as "semi-full proof" of the participants' involvement in the events. Needless to say no one was ever detained or punished for the three deaths.

Once Walsh was on the case he quickly managed to find the "missing link" in the Rosendo investigation, in the form of Norberto Imbelloni, one of Vandor's men, who in the lapse between the pizzeria crime, the legal inquiry and the Walsh investigation (May 1968) had fallen out with Vandor.

Rolando Villaflor, off to a flying start

Rolando Villaflor, who was at the pizzeria with the CGTA contingent on the fateful night, was a successful small-time thief and pimp, a streetwise operator who, by his own admission, picked out the most elegant foreign exchange centres in Buenos Aires, relieving them of their dollars. His father was a respected man in the Avellaneda district, a combative working-class neighbourhood where Villaflor senior was appointed local mayor by Perón himself. It was also the birthplace of Jorge Masetti, Walsh's friend from *Prensa Latina* days, who was baptised at the church in the main square. A year after Che Guevara's death, the national flag flew at half mast and an image of the murdered guerrilla was flown at the top of the mast, left there by John William Cooke and a group of local Peronist activists.

The Villaflor home, a comfortable, modest one-storey house at Pasteur 607 in Avellaneda, became a meeting point for Peronist plotters and union dissidents, searching for ways to defeat the collaborationist leadership which had turned the General Confederation of Workers into a State appendage.

John William Cooke was a frequent visitor to Pasteur 607, where he held long discussions with Villaflor senior, who noticed the Peronist resistance hero's growing influence over his own children: "What are you going to do with my sons?" Villaflor asked Cooke, sensing his son Raimundo's deepening commitment to revolutionary struggle.

The other son, Rolando, was more fond of booze and violence, quick to start a fight and more than likely to finish it, with scant respect for his own wellbeing. His father installed the first telephone in the neighbourhood around 1950, but subsequently took an axe to it, fed up with late-night calls from prostitutes looking for favours from Rolando.

The wayward Rolando admired his brother Raimundo, but felt that he was wasting his evenings planning union strategy with his friends Blajaquis the Greek, the Vázquez boys, Juan Zalazar and others. Rolando would arrive in after midnight, pausing at the dinner table on the patio, imparting his traditional greeting: "Still trying to change the world?" as an ironic grin creased his hard features. "Ah, it's the beast," was Blajaquis' inevitable response.

Rolando marvelled at the innocence of his brother, who he called "*hermanito*" (little brother). Raimundo didn't have career or money ambitions, didn't seem to want to make anything of himself. "He accepted beatings for free," explained Rolando, sitting at the same kitchen table in February 2000, reflecting at length on his life: "at least if I copped a beating I had something to show for it."

One night in 1964, Rolando quietly entered the house where he overheard a conversation about plans to sabotage a nearby chemical factory in support of a strike. A bag of explosives lay next to the table, in the darkness. Rolando picked up the bag of explosives and left the house.

No one heard him go.

He went up to the factory, climbed a fence and laid out the dynamite, then lit the fuse and casually left at walking pace. Within seconds he was airborne, lifted by the force of the deafening explosion he had just detonated. "I'm flying", he thought, as his body travelled through the air, landing several metres away, covered in black ash and his own blood. He managed to stagger away from the building, picking up his step when he heard sirens signalling the arrival of fire engines and police. Back at the house his brother was shocked to see the state of Rolando, dishevelled and bloodstained, imagining a beating due to some botched criminal escapade.

"Make the fuse longer next time," gasped Rolando, before collapsing into the nearest chair.

It took some time to convince the incredulous union activists of his remarkable feat. It was two weeks before Rolando dared to head out on his bicycle and pass by the scene of the explosion. "The entire building had disappeared," said Rolando, still proud of his achievement. He had done it for the sake of his brother, fearing that their attempt to inflict a blow on the factory would surely backfire, leaving his *hermanito* facing a lengthy stay in prison.

"We have to talk," said Blajaquis, the ideologue of the group.

"Yes," agreed Rolando, still in shock, "make the fuse longer next time."

The event was a turning point in Rolando's life, as he realised that his life as a thief had been a pointless distraction, an individual, selfish solution to poverty. "It's about class concepts," Rolando said, a phrase he often repeated during a conversation which began at 6 p.m. and ended in the early hours of the morning, his wife Marisa and his three children listening in throughout.

Rolando's growing class-consciousness changed his life. He read Lenin and Dostoevsky, scribbling furiously between the margins, cursing the writer when a character in the book betrayed the struggle, or failed to connect his personal circumstances with the broader theme of capitalist exploitation. Walsh summed up Villaflor's conversion to revolutionary politics: "Rolando Villaflor wanted to save himself alone but there is no such thing as individual salvation, only collective effort."

Rolando was deeply involved in union struggle by the time of the pizzeria shoot out in June 1966. "If we had had guns, none of those bastards would have left the place alive," said Rolando, who, like his compañeros, was unarmed that night. Vandor's thugs killed two of Rolando's friends, Blajaquis and Zalazar, and one of their own, Rosendo García. It was a pivotal moment, when the enormity of enemy deceit acquired a face and an identity. In the years that followed, the Villaflor brothers became involved in the *Fuerzas Armadas Peronistas*, FAP, considering armed struggle and mass popular mobilisation the only possible way to defeat the dictatorship.

Two years after the pizzeria killings Rodolfo Walsh crossed the threshold of Pasteur 607, anxious to hear Rolando's testimony on the events surrounding the pizzeria murders. Walsh quickly gained the trust of the Villaflor brothers, who were struck by Rodolfo's coherence, the harmony between what he preached and what he did. "A friendship was born," said Rolando, as Walsh talked at length about revolutionary Cuba, Peronist politics and the pizzeria killings, a crime which had yet to be resolved.

Walsh had pieced the story together but lacked one crucial testimony, that of Norberto Imbelloni, one of Vandor's men who had attacked Rolando on the night of the killings. In the two years since the pizzeria shooting, Imbelloni had broken with Vandor, giving Walsh the opening he needed.

One evening Rodolfo turned up at the Villaflor home, carrying his heavy tape recorder, en route to interview Imbelloni, who had cautiously agreed to see him. "I told him Perón had ordered me to talk directly to him, to get the full version of what had happened in La Real," Walsh told Rolando, chuckling at the ease with which Imbelloni fell for the ruse. "*Che*, Rolando," said Walsh, in his ironic tone, "why don't you come with me?" Rolando Villaflor headed off with Rodolfo, travelling the short distance to Imbelloni's door. The door opened a crack, revealing a suspicious bodyguard who cautiously allowed them to proceed. The passageway into the kitchen was littered with heavies who kept their hands over bulky, suggestive lumps inside their coats. "As if we would have called him ahead of time if we planned to kill him," said Rolando.

"Is there a socket in the house?" asked Walsh, his question defusing the deafening tension in the room. The bewildered hosts pointed at a wall, where Rodolfo immediately plugged in his tape recorder.

"Walsh had balls," Rolando Villaflor recalled approvingly.

Walsh and Villaflor were also wearing long and bulky winter coats, unnerving Imbelloni, who greeted them with silence. "Are you Imbelloni?" asked Walsh, struggling to mask his own fear.

"Contrary to our fantasies Imbelloni didn't greet us with a machine gun but with *mate*," wrote Walsh afterwards, sounding relieved. "The mystery that stayed secret for two years was suddenly unravelled in just fifteen minutes," he recalled.

"I'm going to ask you some questions," said Walsh, slipping into detective mode, "I need you to answer with the truth." Imbelloni told the whole story, from beginning to end, naming all the Vandor people at the pizzeria. Walsh then demanded their current addresses.

Every so often Walsh turned the tape off, took a long look at Imbelloni: "this is for the General [Perón] so you have to tell me the truth." Imbelloni continued with greater detail than ever, incriminating Vandor's henchmen. The interview lasted several hours.

They got up to leave, feigning calm, waiting for Imbelloni to come to his senses and order them to leave the testimony behind at gunpoint. They made it to the door, exchanged pleasantries then walked slowly to the gate. "Don't say anything," hissed Walsh, "just keep walking and stay calm." They rounded the next corner, then fled. Rodolfo removed the tapes and threw the tape machine into the nearest ditch, to lighten his step. "Run like fuck," said Rodolfo, as they took off through side streets, losing themselves in the Buenos Aires suburb before happening upon a bus, expecting an angry Imbelloni to appear any second.

The *Semanario CGT* revealed the information in several instalments, baiting Vandor: "If you have something to say, say it," challenged Walsh from the pages of his paper, before disclosing another detail, letting them know he knew as much as they did about the pizzeria killings.

Thirty years later, Rolando Villaflor's body is a road map through Argentina's painful history; his arms, legs and testicles have white blotches, the indelible mark of the *picana*. Villaflor, aged 63, is built like steel and derives a perverse pleasure from his ability to withstand pain, testing himself when the opportunity arises. He has two bullet wounds, his windpipe is gone, his knee cap opens and shuts like a ventriloquist's dummy, he has more surgical pins than flesh in his right leg, even his eyebrows have been stitched together in the past.

Villaflor prides himself on his ability to maintain his dignity, never making a cent from the struggle, never handing over a compañero, never selling his story. "Selling?" he asked contemptuously, "that's for Coca-Cola, and the like, no?"

Union resistance

Walsh's investigation into the pizzeria killings gave him the key to unravelling the history of labour resistance since Perón was ousted. Raimundo Villaflor told him of his growing involvement in radical union politics, beginning with a metal workers' union congress, in 1956, interrupted by the arrival of truckloads of police and soldiers. "As usual the army commander acted as though he was in his barracks, threatening to disperse us with bullets, detention and dismemberment," explained Villaflor, "until one person spoke up, 'Why don't you go fuck yourself?'"

Walsh marvelled at the story, revealing once more the power of people who stand and fight together. He searched for the crucial instant when the voice of the people finally challenged the guns and bullets, calling the bluff of the outnumbered security forces. It took just one person to break the spell of army omnipotence and open the floodgates. "Yeah, get lost, you butcher," said another, emboldened by the anonymous opening gambit. "He had to leave or kill us all," added Villaflor. The army troops sullenly retreated.

At the end of *Quien Mato a Rosendo?*, Walsh analysed the state of the official CGT under Vandor's leadership, revealing a disastrous drop in union affiliation. In 1953 the CGT had six million members, a figure which had dropped to 2.4 million in 1963 and 1.9 million in October 1966, a small percentage of the nation's nine million workers.

As Walsh concluded, "barely one in five workers trusted their union with the defence of their rights." The right to collective bargaining and the right to strike had been lost, while one million people were unemployed and half a millon more workers had their unions "intervened" by the State, that is, declared illegal.

Talk vs. action

Walsh was still caught between his passion for literature and his growing involvement in political activism. "It must be possible to regain the revolution from the artistic perspective [...], to recapture that creative happiness, to feel and to be a writer but to leap off the fence, to denounce, shake things up, stir up unrest."

After four months "entirely devoted" to the *Semanario CGT*, noted

Walsh in his diary (12/8/68) the "working class appreciates it to the tune of 200,000 copies a month, which is nothing when you consider how good the paper looks" (Walsh, 1996 p.80).

There was a certain level of risk involved in his work but Walsh kept it in perspective. "On some nights I carry a revolver when I go out, just in case, never really believing that anyone would have a go at me, just as I probably wouldn't have a go at anyone" (ibid).

Rodolfo felt insecure as he walked the long road from conscientious writer to committed activist and every challenge to his integrity felt like a dagger blow to his heart. "I don't get it," asked Raimundo Ongaro in November 1968, "does he write for the bourgeoisie?" The words rankled with Walsh, who heard them back through another source. "That got to me because I know he's right," reflected Walsh: "the issue has always bothered me, even though it never came into the open." Rodolfo wondered what novels weren't written for the bourgeoisie and what stories might be written "for" the workers. Walsh made a note in his diary to discuss the issue with Ongaro, while owning up to "a mysterious compulsion to go to the toilet" every time his thoughts became complicated!

Walsh had set aside his personal projects and felt some weariness, as union activity occupied all his energy. "I haven't answered letters, I haven't visited relatives, I haven't even seen my mother," he wrote, also expressing frustration at leaving aside his writing work. "The most beautiful ideas pop into my head just when I can't write, then they disappear when I sit down in front of the typewriter, like now." The death by illness of Peronist resistance hero John William Cooke, in September 1968, gave Walsh the opportunity to reflect once more on the role of the intellectual in society, taking Cooke's life as an example of what could be achieved. "Cooke was undoubtedly an intellectual, but one who understood and defined the role of intelligence in the contemporary world," wrote Walsh. He quoted Cooke: "The intellectual revolutionary is that person who cannot conceive of access to culture as an end in itself or as a personal attribute but as an advantage that an unjust regime places within the reach of a few and as such can only be justified when that knowledge is shared with the masses and adds to their awareness of reality insofar as such knowledge can be transformed into revolutionary action" (*Página/12*, Documentos Semanario CGT p.66).

Cooke was imprisoned for participating in Peronist resistance actions but successfully faced down a firing squad, convincing his captors that they had no right to execute him. He turned up at the Bay of Pigs in his revolutionary militia uniform, prepared to sacrifice his life in defence of the Cuban revolution. At home in Argentina he bitterly opposed the CGT union bureaucracy; he preached revolution but rejected isolated acts of violence as the pointless activity of "an illuminated sect", divorced from collective struggle. "There can be no nationalist strategy without a working-class leadership which mobilises public opinion behind a revolutionary enterprise aimed at changing the existing social order and assuring its material needs through independent development."

Cooke's words probably reflected Walsh's thinking after nine months of immersion in union activism, a period which left him exhilarated, exhausted and broke. It also marked a continuation of the consciousness forged through his previous experiences. In *Calle Amargura 303*, Walsh quoted a disappeared journalist whose personal possessions fell into his hands in the *Prensa Latina* office: "I believe in journalism, a noble profession which, if practised with generosity, allows us to give back to society some small part of what we have received from it."

1969

At the end of 1968 Walsh was still devoted to the *Semanario CGT* but time ticked away and it was obvious the regime's tolerance for the paper would soon wear thin. Rodolfo was also in a permanent state of financial ruin, which he pondered in a diary entry on December 31st 1968. "I finished the year with the left shoe visibly broken, 1,500 pesos in my pocket [just under US$8] unable to buy presents, unwilling to receive them, a thousand things to be done, all postponed or half-completed and in an almost permanent bad, apathetic mood" (Walsh, 1996 pp.92–3).

Walsh continued to meditate on his lack of revolutionary discipline, particularly in his work methods. "I have been trying for years to eliminate things which are part of an 'erroneous infrastructure', alcohol, cigarettes, unsuitable work hours, laziness and resulting postponements, self-pity, disorder, lack of discipline; the subsequent lack of happiness and confidence. All this locked inside a mental structure which is still bourgeois" (ibid).

The tension between his conflicting passions, between the overdue novel, requiring solitude and concentration, and the *Semanario* which tied him to meetings, deadlines and poverty, had a greater impact on his morale than has been publicly acknowledged. "I sleep up to twelve hours a day, I go through industrial quantities of newspapers and magazines, I also read too many books, I write less than half a page per day. I am tired and defeated, I need to recover a certain happiness, need to see that my book serves a purpose too, I need to break the dissociation that revolutionary ideas have produced in all of us, the tearing-apart and perplexity between action and thought."

Walsh knew by then that his own role had to be greater than that of a revolutionary cheerleader musing over his novel as the barricades went up. "It may be that at the end of the day I become a revolutionary," wrote Walsh to himself, "but the beginning is far from noble, it's almost offensive. It's easy to draw up an agitprop project, virulent, making no concessions, but it's damned hard to carry it out. It demands a work capacity which I still don't possess."

Walsh claimed two advances: he gave up alcohol, "which has improved my health, or at least reversed the decline," and he began studying Marxism, improving his theoretical knowledge. "I am far more committed," he wrote, adding that he would never make concessions on the packaging of a book or accept a grant to visit the USA[37] (ibid).

These two examples bear witness to an evolving awareness, a writer consciously preparing to abandon the easy road to success, veering into uncertain territory. In his own words, Walsh had moved "to the people's side" even though he didn't foresee a revolution soon. "Not in my lifetime!" he exclaimed to his diary (ibid p.94), once more catching himself out on a bourgeois vision of the revolutionary process, by which participation was conditional to the prospect of triumph within a reasonable time period.

Walsh had just watched the inspiring *La Hora de los Hornos* (The Hour of the Furnaces) an underground film by Pino Solanas which recounted popular resistance efforts since Perón's exile. The film was watched by some 300,000 people in five years of clandestine screenings around the country.

"The revolution must first be made within the minds of the people," noted Walsh, "so that the oppressed want to fight and love the revolution, and the oppressors detest themselves and lose the will to fight" (ibid).

Walsh returned to his novel in January 1969 but by the end of the month his difficulties lay not just in a lack of time but also in the subject matter of the novel, which involved his brother Carlos the navy captain and his own friends. "To the degree which the novel questions my life, the life of my brother and of my friends, certain psychoanalytical obstacles have surfaced [...] a clear example is when I tried to tell the captain's story – and as I have managed to write just two pages in two weeks" (ibid p.101).

As a child Rodolfo admired his older brother Carlos, envying his effortless entry into the naval academy, a career path he desired for himself. Rodolfo remained close to Carlos, in spite of their differing political views. Carlos was an anti-Peronist who piloted a plane during the September 1955 coup which deposed Perón. Three months after the

---

[37] Before Walsh left for Cuba in 1959 he had applied for a job as a UN interpreter in the US.

events Walsh wrote a glowing homage to navy pilot Eduardo Estivariz, who fell in combat: '2-0-12 Never Returned' described the decisive days which concluded on September 18th 1955, as warplanes dropped bombs on troops loyal to Perón and civilians. The planes rained death, while bridges and roads were destroyed, to isolate loyalist troops. The daring Captain Estivariz flew mission after mission in low-altitude strikes that offered an easy target to the artillery fire below. Walsh noted how an observer had asked Estivariz some months before how he managed to hold his nerve in such precarious planes: "They're old," he agreed, "but they're faithful." Rodolfo then added, "I have seen the twisted, burned wreckage of 2-0-12, and the remains bear witness to the pilot's words. The plane took him to his death, but it too died alongside him" (Walsh, 1995 p.27).

Rodolfo reluctantly faced up to the necessity of working for *Panorama* news magazine to reverse his financial decline. "I am fed up with my poverty," he wrote, "and would like to change the situation even for a few months." Walsh felt guilty about taking up work with a magazine which accepted the restrictions dictated by military rule. "I have already begun to justify myself in company, to make excuses for myself," lamented Walsh: "this is a sign of insecurity." Walsh acknowledged that he arrived at *Panorama* "a defeated man," due to reasons "beyond my will and because that will is not strong enough to search for other options" (Walsh, 1996 p.102).

Rodolfo's diary entries revealed his inner turmoil but his articles in the *Semanario CGT* (unsigned but identified as his own) were implacable, sharp and clear. In his "Vuelve la secta del gatillo y de la picana" (The return of the sect of the trigger and the *picana, CGT* 2, 27/3/69) Walsh provided a detailed list of police atrocities which left no doubt that the security forces were engaged in a systematic policy of assassination against "undesirables". Walsh noted how police in Buenos Aires province killed fifteen "delinquents" between January 1st and March 20th 1969, without suffering a single death or injury among their own ranks.

Walsh also kept his eye on the exceptions within the force, describing police officer Antonio Lara as a "working-class hero". Lara had refused to accept the orders of his superiors to repress a peaceful protest inside a factory in Tucumán. He committed suicide soon after. Rodolfo was unable to resist the final twist in the tale: "there are even compañeros inside the police force who have helped us in this paper," he wrote, hinting at the origin of stories on police corruption.

In April 1969 Walsh paid his one and only visit to Lilia Ferreyra's parents in Junín, spending the last weekend of that month there. "Rodolfo derived great amusement from my obvious discomfort and relished analysing my family, soaking up the atmosphere," recalled Lilia.

Her parents added to the awkwardness by kindly giving up their double bed to the couple. "That felt strange," noted Lilia.

In his diary Rodolfo wrote about the visit, thoughts on the sights and smells of the rural bourgeoisie: "Quaint incidents, a storm, a blackout, aunts, the double bed," he began, "if I had the patience I would return to the towns, to the petit bourgeois mentality, their doctors and lawyers, tearing their souls out to make money, betraying youthful rebelliousness, settling down as cogs, working out their analysis of the underclass, concluding that they are lazy, drunk, ignorant etc and that's why they never triumph" (Walsh, 1996 p.114).

Walsh travelled to Tucumán province, north-west Argentina, in April, to make contact with the region's combative workers. One of his contacts was Roberto Perdía, a lawyer and militant with the burgeoning Montonero armed organisation, which would soon become a household name. Walsh was sent to help organise an exhibition to pay homage to the struggle of sugarcane workers, involved in a bitter struggle over work conditions. Perdía, defending striking and imprisoned workers, discovered in Walsh someone who was far more than a writer-journalist: "He was the complete militant," recalled Perdía, "certain of the path chosen, obsessed by detail, critical and upright."

The worker uprising in Córdoba struck a month later, inspiring Walsh. "Now we no longer have to look back to the year 1919 but to what has happened in the past few days, involving people we know [...] when 40,000 men and women take to the streets, as in Córdoba, everyone is a hero" (ibid pp.144–45).

In June 1969, Walsh gave a lengthy interview to the magazine *Siete Días*, running through the main events in his life, outlining his position on the role of the intellectual and the place of literature in the contemporary world.

"I have to say that I am a Marxist," Walsh told his interviewer, "but a poor Marxist because I don't read much, I don't have time for ideological formation. My political culture is empirical rather than abstract. I prefer to draw my inferences from daily life. I throw myself into life on the street, into reality, and then I join that information to an ideological basis which is fairly clear in my mind" (ibid p. 117).

Death in the afternoon

Walsh's world was turned upside down when unknown assassins killed Augusto Vandor. The corrupt union leader denounced by Walsh in his *Quien Mató a Rosendo?* series was gunned down on June 30th, the very day in which Rodolfo published a new chapter in his exposé of the union leader, forcing him into hiding and marking the end of the dictatorship's tolerance of the CGTA's *Semanario*. "I felt glad," Walsh confessed to himself, on hearing the news of Vandor's death. "I said I felt glad, I still feel glad. But then I knew I had to run away, till things settled a bit. It took almost two hours, arranging my things, shaving even. Shaving!" (ibid p.122).

"Do you know who this is?" asked the caller.

"Yes, I was expecting to hear from you," said the woman at the end of the phone line. "Do you want to come over?"

"OK."

Rodolfo went into hiding that afternoon, starting his lengthy peregrinations at the house of Elba Izarduy, a doctor involved with the *Fuerzas Armadas Peronistas*. Rodolfo and Lilia moved into Elba's home while Vandor's henchmen sought revenge for the killing of their boss.

The union paper was swiftly shut down, its equipment confiscated, its leaders imprisoned, including Raimundo Ongaro. The *Semanario* continued to be published clandestinely for several weeks, but its impact was minimal.

Walsh and Ferreyra moved on from Elba Izarduy's home, as friends and contacts shifted them from safe house to safe house, always at the mercy of unforeseen circumstances, aware that every welcome came with a 'best by' date. They had a limited number of hours and days which ticked away until it was time to move on.

"We didn't have many places to go," wrote Walsh in a diary entry dated August 10th 1969. "We had already exhausted the three friends who had no problem in putting us up, and now we depended on the three who did have a problem in sheltering us. They didn't say anything but you could see it in the worried frown, in the questions they asked" (ibid p.123).

As the crackdown continued in the wake of the Vandor killing, Walsh and Ferreyra had no alternative but to remain in hiding. "Are you thinking of staying the weekend?" asked the wife of one of Walsh's contacts, in what amounted to a veiled request for self-eviction. "That was the time to say no, that we were planning to leave on the Friday," said Walsh, who was then forced onward to test the loyalty of yet another sympathiser called into active service (ibid).

A trace of bitterness surfaced as Walsh weighed up the rush to get Lilia and himself out of another home, this time someone's holiday home, whose occupants mentioned something about visitors arriving the following weekend. "They didn't really need the weekend home, they could have let a weekend go by without the house which for us, in these circumstances, was our home. But that's the way it is. She didn't stick her nose in our affairs, it was us who poked our noses into her life and her weekend."

October 1969 found Walsh and Ferreyra tapping the walls and testing the decibel level of Rodolfo's typewriter, as personal security became their first priority. "I understood that I had to abandon writing, or at least writing the way I was accustomed to," mused Walsh, installing himself in his fourth home since disappearing from public view.

Over a period of 42 days, Walsh was shunted in and out of eleven homes. "In three months," predicted Walsh, in one of his more prophetic moments, "they will all be fed up with us." Yet there were demonstrations of kindness too, as friends collected 60,000 pesos for the fugitives and someone gave Rodolfo a suit.

Despite the imminent risk of arrest Walsh finished a feature article for *Georama* magazine, "Claroscuro del Delta", published in September 1969. Walsh explored the Paraná river delta, accompanied by accomplished photographer Pablo Alonso. It was in a small boarding house in Cívico, Villa Paranacito, where Rodolfo and Lilia, along with a motley collection of "bored travellers and lost journalists" watched the first man walk on the moon.

"For five months I have held together the remains of the *Semanario*; I haven't written a line for myself, I haven't earned a cent; I have wandered all over the place, I have let my health go, I haven't had a weekend off, in brief, I began to live like an animal, alienated within the struggle. But I have held up, now I have to slack off a little" (ibid).

Walsh also wondered how he could keep up such a rate for 10 or 20 years, or until death, or whatever it took to change the country. He concluded that it was wise to use his head, his best talent: "I must think, without retreating, think some more and above all, use some of my intelligence and affection."

In one final and lucid reflection on the year gone by Walsh pondered the different faces of Peronism, concluding that he had erred in denouncing Vandor and his crowd as traitors: "We were the traitors," Walsh realised, in a curious intuition of future days, "because Perón always supported them."

chapter twelve

No turning back: 1970–74

Events are what matter these days, but rather than write about them we should be making them happen.[38]

(Walsh, 1996 p.115)

From Peronism to revolution

Armed resistance efforts began soon after Perón was ousted from power in 1955, an exile which lasted 18 years. Small groups formed and dispersed over time but the struggle was constant, with 5,000 attacks on the State recorded between 1958 and 1960 alone. The Uturuncos (tiger-men in Quechua), a rural Peronist armed resistance group, emerged in 1960 as part of a general campaign "to link worker resistance in the cities, dissident army units and the first Peronist guerrillas in the north." Inspired by the Cuban *foco* guerrilla model, the Uturuncos attacked isolated police posts but never managed to spark a broader insurrection and the group was quickly dismantled by security forces.

Jorge Masetti's Ejercito Guerrillero del Pueblo, EGP (People's Guerrilla Army), launched in the wake of the Cuban revolution, hoped to create the conditions for Che Guevara's return to Argentina. The effort ended in failure when Masetti died in combat in the hills surrounding Salta, northern Argentina, in April 1964.

The Peronist Destacamento 17 de Octubre cell attacked a hospital for bank employees on August 29th 1963, escaping with US$100,000. The Destacamento grew into the Fuerzas Armadas Peronistas, FAP, in 1968, which followed the traditional "war of guerrillas" path into the hills of northern Argentina, but was flushed out in just 13 days. The FAP made a successful transition to urban warfare but ground to a virtual halt due to endless ideological disagreements.

---

[38] Diary entry, June 6th 1969.

The death of Che Guevara in October 1967 did nothing to dim rebel hopes – on the contrary, it increased the anger and militancy of Argentina's dissidents. In the city of Rosario, a small Guevarista guerrilla unit formed on the very night that the news of Guevara's death was heard. Even the cautious Perón spared no praise when he spoke of Guevara's untimely end. "His death tears my soul apart," said the caudillo, "because he was one of us, maybe the best." Perón could well afford to be generous in his estimation of the dead martyr; it cost him nothing to heap praise on someone who would never have accepted his shallow populist posturing (Bonasso, 1984 p.134).

One of the significant debates at the time was on the nature of armed resistance. Should Guevara's *foquista* model be followed, or did Mao's prolonged popular warfare offer a better hope for victory? The *foquistas* believed that a small group of professional rebels could spark a national insurrection from the hills. The Maoists believed that the revolution could only be won in distinct phases, as the masses were drawn progressively into the developing struggle, which grew over a longer period of time and ended with direct engagement of enemy troops.

By 1970 a number of guerrilla groups had established a presence in Argentina: the Marxist/Guevarista/Peronist Fuerzas Armadas Revolucionarias, FAR (Revolutionary Armed Forces); the Marxist-Leninist Fuerzas Armadas de Liberación, FAL (Argentinian Liberation Forces); the Trotskyist/Guevarista Partido Revolucionario de los Trabajadores/Ejercito Revolucionario del Pueblo, PRT/ERP (Workers' Revolutionary Party/People's Revolutionary Army); three left-wing Peronist groups, Fuerzas Armadas Peronistas, FAP (Peronist Armed Forces), Descamisados[39] and Montoneros.

The Fuerzas Armadas Revolucionarias, FAR, made its public appearance on July 30th 1970, occupying the village of Garin, just outside Buenos Aires. In a prior unclaimed action during Nelson Rockefeller's visit to Argentina in June 1969, the FAR destroyed thirteen Minimax super-markets with remarkable precision and with no loss of or injury to life; Rockefeller owned the Minimax chain. Several of Walsh's friends told me that they suspected he had planned the operation. Walsh was friends with many of the historic FAR leaders but had yet to engage directly in armed struggle himself. The principal FAR leaders received military instruction in Cuba and launched dozens of operations between 1970 and 1973, when they fused with the Montonero organisation.

The Fuerzas Armadas Peronistas, FAP, consolidated its position as the main Peronist armed group, composed of activists who began their

---

[39] Literally "Shirtless Ones", the name given by Juan and Eva Perón to the workers who supported them.

militancy in right-wing nationalism but were swayed by the Algerian and Cuban revolutions. The FAP also attracted radical elements from the Juventud Peronista, JP, (Peronist Youth) movement, who graffittied the walls with their slogan *"Ni votos ni botas: fusiles y pelotas"*, neither votes nor boots but guns and balls (ibid p.147). The FAP carried out an audacious raid on the army's Campo de Mayo base and also held up food lorries, distributing food in shantytowns. They suffered a split in the run-up to the 1973 elections, one part fusing with the Montoneros.

The Descamisados were drawn from the youth wing of the Christian Democratic party and Catholic nationalist circles. They were active in unions and shantytowns in Buenos Aires and opted for armed struggle in 1970, appearing in public at a showing of the film *La Hora de los Hornos* at the moment when Perón speaks out in favour of armed resistance. The Descamisados kidnapped the head of General Electric-ITT, demanding a million dollar ransom; they also blew up a navy recreation centre, before fusing with the Montoneros in early 1973.

In 1968 a group of activists met in the hills of Córdoba to discuss the launch of a politico-military organisation. Mario Firmenich, future Montonero leader, came from a militant Catholic student movement while Fernando Luis Abal Medina had been associated with Tacuara, a violent, right-wing organisation, active in the 1960s and modelled on the Spanish fascists. As social unrest grew in Argentina, progressive christian beliefs met left nationalist tendencies and produced the largest urban guerrilla group in Latin America. The Montonero organisation gave up on Guevara's doomed *foco* strategy and established themselves in the cities, where 75 per cent of the population now lived.

Meanwhile, Roberto Santucho and 40 members of the Partido Revolucionario de los Trabajadores, PRT, broke with the party nucleus and formed the most effective of the non-Peronist armed groups, the Ejercito Revolucionario del Pueblo, ERP. The ERP believed it impossible for the struggling working-class to seize power "without previously building, through armed struggle, the revolutionary party formed by its vanguard, which will lead it in their struggle against the bourgeois State and its armed forces. Only a Marxist-Leninist party can lead and direct the working class in an authentic struggle for national liberation." The ERP staged dozens of armed operations, kidnappings and bank robberies before the leadership died fighting the dictatorship in 1976.

In May 1970 the Juan José Valle commando of the Montoneros publicly launched the movement with the daring kidnap of former dictator General Pedro Aramburu. He was interrogated about his role in the *Operación Masacre* executions, which he had ordered in 1956. His captors also demanded to know the whereabouts of Evita's kidnapped corpse.

Aramburu was executed at dawn on June 1st 1970 by Abal Medina while Firmenich hammered nails into the floor of their safe house to drown out the sound of the bullets. The nation was shaken by the events and ruling dictator General Onganía was dismissed a week later. He was replaced by General Roberto Marcelo Levingston who in turn was ousted by General Alejandro Lanusse in March 1971 (Gillespie, 1998 p.115).

The Montoneros' action was initially dismissed as a one-off until they struck again exactly one month later, occupying La Calera, a small town ten miles from Córdoba city. Twenty-five guerrillas, with armbands and walkie-talkies, took over the local bank, police station and mayor's office after destroying the post and telegraph office. The police were forced to sing the Peronist anthem, and US$26,000 was stolen, along with weapons and equipment, although a disastrous retreat led to losses among the rebel ranks. The Montoneros had arrived.

The organisation's top leaders, Mario Firmenich, Norma Arrostito and Fernando Luis Abal Medina drew inspiration from Carlos Mugica, a young Catholic priest from a wealthy background who converted to radical politics. Mugica built a chapel in a shantytown known as Villa 31 and helped organise families into neighbourhood networks; he led a grassroots movement for social reform. Mugica stopped short of endorsing armed struggle, yet he was shot dead by a government extra-judicial death squad in May 1974.

Perón recognised the strength of the Montoneros, notably the Juventud Peronista (JP) movement, blessing them on his first return to Argentina in November 1972. "Either the youth take charge of this, by force if necessary, or no one will sort it out," said Perón. "The world is changing and the *muchachos* (young men) are right. And if they are right then they deserve to be recognised and they must take over the government." Perón also said that if he was 50 years younger he would be "out throwing bombs" himself. The *jefe* had given the organisation his stamp of approval. The Montoneros didn't need any further encouragement.

A month later Perón returned to Madrid where Montonero leaders visited him, taking him at his word on the issue of youth leadership. The cocky visitors brought with them a list of 300 people who they believed worthy of posts in the next government (Gasparini, 1999 p.50).

Perón had no intention of allowing the radical Montonero wing to determine the political direction of the next government and quietly searched for ways to dismantle the "special formations," or armed sectors linked to the Peronist movement. Perón's wife Isabel Martínez and their special advisor José López Rega, a sinister thug, began to plan the Triple A death squads, the Anti-Communist Alliance which first appeared in late 1972.

Over time it became clear that the Triple A consisted almost entirely of Federal Police officers and official union thugs who hunted down and assassinated left-wing Peronists. Amnesty International linked López Rega and his extra-judicial squads to 1,500 deaths over 18 months in 1973–4 (ibid p.71).

After 18 years of military rule, (1955–73), interrupted twice by elections in which Perón was not allowed to run, the army announced that elections would be held in 1973, a move welcomed by most Argentinians. The announcement was the result of a shrewd calculation by the military, who recognised that the unstoppable process of popular mobilisation had spread throughout the country. If elections were denied then revolution appeared a real possibility. The decision to hold democratic elections would undermine the legitimacy of armed struggle, which had enjoyed substantial support in preceding years, precisely because all other avenues of opposition were blocked.

Closer to the struggle

"Rodolfo had a great ability to allow himself be guided by events rather than ideology," recalled Horacio Verbitsky, accounting for his friend's gradual shift toward armed Peronist resistance. After the exhausting but rewarding months editing the *Semanario CGT*, Rodolfo swallowed his pride and began working with *Panorama, Siete Días* and other magazines. He wrote a memorable feature on the supply and consumption of electricity in Buenos Aires, "La luz nuestra de cada noche" (Our light each night), which was packed with technical details about the way energy was extracted, stored and pumped into the city. Walsh visited the central electricity control system in January 1970, still watching his step since the killing of Vandor had forced him into hiding. He was fascinated by the power of the workers in the energy sector. "Four words from one of them and a neighbourhood is plunged into darkness," he wrote. "A lever moved within the grid can wipe San Martin's electricity off the map." Rodolfo's detailed study highlighted the fragility of the city's supply network and probably gave him some helpful hints for future sabotage, (*Siete Días*, 9/3/70).

Walsh had two constant companions – his compañera Lilia and his old Remington typewriter. He became fed up with their nomadic existence and longed to resolve his severe financial shortfall. In a bitter and self-deprecating diary entry, he analysed his work output in terms of labour and capital. "THINK," he wrote, in bold capital letters, in a commentary dated February 4th 1970, "for the article on electricity I invested 60 pages of notes and transcriptions, 30 draft pages and 20 pages of the original, 110 typed pages in total. I recorded six hours of tapes. I invested 87 work hours, spread out over 13 days, i.e. 7 hours a day" (Walsh, 1996 pp.152–3).

Walsh handed over the article to his editor at *Siete Días* magazine, where a payment of 30,000 pesos had been agreed: "in other words 2,300 pesos per day, or 345 per hour" (less than one US dollar) noted Walsh, with more than a hint of irony. The article took 16 days to complete, including three bank holidays. Walsh told his editor how much time and energy had been invested in the article, hinting that his work deserved better payment.

"Let's not start a conversation that will be annoying for both of us," responded his (unnamed) editor. "I had to stay quiet," said Walsh; "in the early days I was capable of fighting these assholes." Walsh came to another capital-letter conclusion at the end of his meditations: "I CAN'T GO BACK TO WRITING STORIES FOR SIETE DIAS OR PANORAMA BEYOND OCCASIONAL WORK [...] PREFERABLY WHEN I DON'T REALLY NEED IT [...]. WHEN THEY NEED ME. THE NEEDY FACE IS THE FIRST THING THEY SEE" (ibid).

Walsh's book *Quien mató a Rosendo?* was on the year-end bestseller lists for 1969, with 5,000 copies sold in just six months. Walsh recognised that the financial return of book-length work compared favourably against journalistic efforts, with the additional advantage of allowing him time to devote to other projects. As he looked back on the year Walsh expressed dissatisfaction with past literary efforts, some of which he destroyed, while *Adios a la Habana*, a piece of erotica, was declared "in quarantine" until further notice.

In early 1970 Rodolfo and Lilia found time to take a break, sharing a *quinta*, a holiday home, with four other couples. At weekends the guests included psychoanalyst Claudia Barrera, cartoonist Quino, Paco Urondo and others who spent time there between November and February, Argentina's summer months. Sometimes Rodolfo stayed on during the week to write. When the couples were there, they divided up domestic tasks, taking turns to cook and clean, buy groceries and wash clothes. "Rodolfo refused to do anything like that," recalled Elba Izarduy, a doctor and FAP militant. Rodolfo took care of administrative duties, totting up the daily accounts, working out what was spent by each visitor on food and other expenses, dividing up the costs and managing each person's contribution. While it was understood that Rodolfo didn't have the resources to pay his way, members of the holiday group resented his non-involvement in daily chores. "We gave him an ultimatum," said Claudia, "and he chose the task of cleaning out the swimming pool each morning." Rodolfo was up at 5 a.m., draining and refilling the pool each day.

By June 1970 Walsh was out of hiding and attending literary events again but his attitude to such social circles had shifted from bemused tolerance to outright derision: "It seems that literary circles are the same shit everywhere, an unbearable mixture of vanity, poor conscience and ignorance."

As the atmosphere in Buenos Aires eased up, Rodolfo and Lilia risked a night out with friends, enjoying dinner and wine and chatting until the early hours of the morning. If Rodolfo had his way they would catch a late film, choosing a spy movie or a thriller.

One regular outing was the celebration of the birthday of Pirí Lugones, Walsh's former compañera, still a close friend, on April 30th each year. In 1970 her birthday coincided with Salvador Allende's success in winning sufficient collegiate votes to take up the presidency of Chile, marking an historic victory for democratic socialism.

As the inebriated birthday revellers stumbled out of a café on Avenida Corrientes, the early-morning headline caught Rodolfo's eye: "Christ," said Walsh, "now that is imagination seizing power." Walsh was sceptical about the limits of parliamentary democracy, anticipating that Chile's democratic socialist experiment would come to a bitter end. "He was right," reflected Horacio Verbitsky, speaking 30 years later, as Allende's ouster, General Augusto Pinochet, was detained in London on charges of crimes against humanity.

In that year Rodolfo joined the FAP's surface organisation, Peronismo de base, which applied Marxist analyses to Argentina's Peronist movement. Walsh got to know FAP members through his *Quien Mató a Rosendo?* investigation, becoming friends with Raimundo Villaflor and other members.

Horacio Verbitsky, also a FAP militant, remembers with incredulity the organisation's preferential option for talk over action. Most of 1971 and 1972 was taken up by discussions which were known as the "Compulsory Political Homogenisation Process". "The discussions were positive," said Verbitsky, as the FAP reached a consensus on the need for their own alternative political structures. They favoured efforts aimed at insertion into the popular movement and rejected any excessive reliance on militarism and any questionable deals with opportunistic politicians. "The problem was that the group never made it beyond discussion," said Verbitsky.

In 1971 Lilia and Rodolfo moved into a new apartment in Calle Tucumán in Buenos Aires, between Reconquista and San Martin, ushering in a period of relative prosperity and a less secret existence, after a year spent living out of a suitcase, dependent on the goodwill of others. Rodolfo enjoyed the luxury of a long desk in the couple's new home, allowing him to look out on the street and work with his back to the wall, his books and papers stored close to hand, precisely the way he liked to organise his space. Lilia now worked as an archivist at *La Opinión*, a newspaper set up by Jacobo Timmerman in May 1971, its offices half a block from their home. The cream of the nation's journalists passed through Timmerman's paper, which was known as "leftist in culture, centrist in politics and right-wing in economics" (Anguita and Caparrós, 1997 pp.449).

The newspaper also employed Vicki Walsh, who followed her father into journalism. Vicki launched her writing career two years earlier, with a feature on the Irish in Argentina, published in *Primera Plana* magazine, (1/4/69). Lilia recalled the difficulty Vicki had in writing her first article: "She asked Rodolfo for ideas," explained Lilia. He advised her to write something that drew on her own experience, so she researched her family roots. It seemed fitting that Vicki's first venture into journalism resulted in controversy, as Irish descendants took offence at her depiction of their community. Vicki resurrected buried tales of legendary drinking and gambling bouts on festive days while William Brown, an Irishman and founder of the Argentinian navy, was described as "a privateer and paranoid". Vicki also revealed how the poorer Irish retained their identity while the wealthier immigrants began calling themselves "English", anxious to ingratiate themselves with the oligarchy.

Yet Vicki was more interested in union activism than daily journalism and dedicated most of her time to labour issues. Lilia took over Vicki's union tasks at *La Opinión* when she left, after a bitter dispute with Timmerman.

Rodolfo contributed a handful of articles to *La Opinión* but worked more frequently on feature stories for *Panorama* magazine, where poet Juan Gelman was in charge of international news. Walsh was a marked man in the small world of Argentinian newspapers, his name "provoked a certain unease" in editorial circles, according to Lilia Ferreyra, who acted as his "straw man", signing her name on Rodolfo's *Panorama* pay cheque. The general opinion was that you could assign an article or two to Walsh, preferably on foreign issues, but he was too hot to handle on the payroll. Lilia was Rodolfo's *de facto* minder, sorting out papers, analysing his work, debating each new challenge presented by Argentina's turbulent political scene, her presence a peaceful, harmonious refuge from the stormy world. Rodolfo had finally found a compañera, lover and partner in struggle, all in one person.

In October 1970 Rodolfo travelled to Bolivia to write a feature story about president Juan José Torres,[40] the "proletarian general" who led a popular nationalist reform movement until his democratic mandate was cut short by Hugo Banzer in 1971 (Walsh, 1995, p. 353–61).

---

[40] Torres was assassinated in an Operation Condor action, by Argentinian State security forces. It was late 1999 before the Argentinian State acknowledged its guilt, paying compensation to Torres' family.

Walsh then travelled to Chile in December 1970, writing "La Muerte de Anaconda" for *Panorama* in December 1970 about President Salvador Allende's efforts to nationalise the country's copper mines, Chile's single greatest source of revenue (Baschetti, 1994 p.288). He travelled once more to Chile in March 1971, publishing an article called "The Race against the Electoral Clock." Walsh focused on the imminent threat to Salvador Allende's rule, as economic sabotage increased, a draining process which paved the way for the savage "stability coup" led by General Pinochet in September 1973. Walsh's faith in parliamentary democracy was rapidly crumbling.

Radio Free Walsh

One of the fruits of Walsh and Ferreyra's prosperity was a second-hand black and white television set with a dodgy aerial. In the evenings, Rodolfo and Lilia would unwind to *Planet of the Apes, Superagent 86* and the occasional documentary. The TV aerial kept coming loose, blurring the screen, and had to be constantly twiddled with, until one night it broke off altogether.

The voice on the television disappeared but another voice could now be heard: "QP, QP, command over..." By a stroke of luck it turned out that the loose aerial was now tuned into police radio frequencies.

"That was the end of *Planet of the Apes* and *Superagent 86*," said Lilia, as Rodolfo, crime buff turned political activist, launched his most ambitious move yet: a home-based counter-intelligence operation. Walsh maintained files on police promotions and other internal aspects of the force, listening in to police radios through short-wave frequencies, applying his code-breaking skills with discipline and rigour, enlisting the help of a small group of friends to maintain round-the-clock vigilance and build up a more complete vision of police activities. The counter-intelligence initiative came after a lifelong interest in the activities of the police force.

A new era of political involvement was beginning. "A group of close friends came together, heavily preoccupied with political events," recalled Verbitsky, describing the origins of Walsh's incursion into counter-intelligence activities. The informal team began investigating police abuses, helped by Walsh's contacts in La Plata (a sympathetic judge passed on case files and contacts) and by police chief Vitanni, still the romantic partner of Poupee Blanchard's mother.

Walsh was convinced that a substantial section of the police force was dissatisfied with the role thrust upon them by unscrupulous politicians. As early as 1958, after investigating the Satanowsky murder, Rodolfo wrote: "I am convinced that a great number of career officers feel that the failure of their mission in this case (Satanowsky) and other investigations is an insult to them and they attribute that failure to the fact that in recent years the force has been in the hands of outsiders and people whose hands are tied by political interests" (Walsh, 1996 pp.149–50). Among the people who were dissatisfied was Vitanni, a talented chief who spoke out against corruption in the police force.

Rodolfo organised extensive files, cross-referencing information. "He divided up the newspapers, everybody had a different one to study and cut," recalled Verbitsky. Walsh's police file grew over the years, providing him with a unique database on relationships inside the force, training, promotions, policy and internal scandals. Before long, the files proved inadequate and he launched a more sophisticated network of "radio-listeners" who quietly gathered intelligence for operational purposes.

One of Walsh's "listening soldiers" was Tununa Mercado, now a successful writer and newspaper columnist. Then she was recently returned from exile after the fall of the Onganía dictatorship in 1970. Tununa worked at *La Opinión* and was a regular visitor to Tucumán 456, Rodolfo and Lilia's home, where she enjoyed "exquisite" meatball lunches served by a housekeeper. She connected with Walsh's sense of humour and was invited to join the listening team, taking her turn late at night, when her two small children were asleep.

The listening team included Rodolfo's close friend Horacio Verbitsky and his second wife Mónica, Pirí Lugones and her partner Carlos, and Milton Roberts, a FAP militant. Together they gained a substantial insight into the tactics, strategy and internal workings of the police.

The listeners intercepted police plans to transfer prisoners; they listened in on tactical discussions with army officers, plans to raid homes, upcoming court cases or details of security measures in place to protect high-ranking officials planning a break in the countryside. "It was an important glimpse into the future," recalled Mercado, "a sneak preview into the way the State security apparatus was coming together, co-ordinating police, army and judicial action."

Tununa copied the information from her late-night radio sessions onto tiny pieces of paper which were rolled into cigarette papers and dropped off at Rodolfo's house on the way to work each day. "I enjoyed it immensely, it was a small but significant way to fuck with the system; its value lay in its simplicity, of being a tiny part of a tiny detail which was part of a bigger story."

Rodolfo picked Tununa out of the *La Opinión* crowd as someone trustworthy and disciplined enough to complete the task. "We used to call him *el capitán*," recalled Tununa, who noted in Rodolfo a charisma which dragged others along with him in his intelligence schemes, "he was a natural leader."

Walsh regretted his inability to act on much of the information he received through the radio interception work, as there was no organisation in place to exploit the inside tips. Walsh received advance notice of house searches, sometimes minutes ahead of their execution. Occasionally one of the listening soldiers would have time to race to a house targeted for a search, leave a note under the door, ring the bell and run away, hoping the people within would act on the anonymous tip.

"Rodolfo got enormous pleasure out of attacking the enemy in this way," said Tununa, "it was a positive, life-affirming action." When Rodolfo moved closer to the Montonero guerrilla organisation, Tununa parted ways, anticipating a dark future ahead. By 1974 she was in exile once more, remaining outside the country for a decade.

Walsh dreamed of applying his counter-information service to other parts of the country, and once dispatched Mercado to Córdoba city, an industrial province in northern Argentina, bearing the codes to the police radio network. She waited in vain, three days in all, for a contact who never appeared. "He was disappointed that other militants didn't understand the importance of this type of work," added Tununa.

Gregorio "Goyo" Levenson, a Peronist activist, was one direct beneficiary of the Walsh intelligence team. The radio interceptors learned that a team of police planned to kidnap Goyo's two grandchildren, born to his son Miguel Alejo, a FAR guerrilla who died fighting in the hills of northern Argentina. The boys, aged six and eight, were due to be snatched from their primary school. Walsh got word to Goyo who managed to get the children safely out of the country, to Venezuela.

Capitán Delirio

Milton Roberts baptised Rodolfo *Capitán Delirio*. "Once he got an idea into his head, there was no stopping him," said Lilia, explaining the concept. Walsh's charismatic style inspired others to follow him, a word of encouragement or praise was enough to send an activist into orbit. A man of few words, the initial impression caused by Rodolfo was that of a serious, aloof type, not given to shows of emotion. His reputation preceded him in every new endeavour, thus raising expectations another notch. Activist and writer Miguel Bonasso recalled one of the first times he met Walsh, shortly after Bonasso had published a lengthy article on political prisoners in *La Opinión* in 1972.

"It was more like a phone directory than an article," laughed Bonasso, as the story simply listed the names of 483 political prisoners held throughout the country, shortly after General Alejandro Lanusse's government announced that there were no political prisoners in Argentina's jails. "What you did there was very important," Walsh told

Bonasso, when they next crossed paths, "both journalistically and politically." Bonasso was ready to levitate: "I felt like I had just been awarded a medal," he recalled.

The downside of such admiration lay in the fear of letting Rodolfo down. Marion, a friend from *Semanario CGT* days, remembered the honour she felt when Rodolfo entrusted her with a letter for personal delivery to Raimundo Ongaro in late 1969, when the latter was in prison, and Walsh was unable to visit him.

Marion held, or rather clutched the letter close to her chest, all through the long bus ride. She got off at her destination, walked a couple of streets and realised with horror that the unthinkable had happened – she had left the letter on the bus. "Sometimes when you pay absolute attention to something it just vanishes on you," she said, still shaken, 30 years after the events. She traced the bus back to the terminus, several hours later. The letter was sitting on the same seat, opened but in one piece. "The relief was tremendous, I couldn't possibly have faced Rodolfo if it had gone," said Marion, who reckoned that someone opened the envelope, read the contents and quickly left it well alone.

Rodolfo also hatched plans to find a safe spot for gun practice in the countryside and turned to an old friend who had just acquired a ramshackle farm. Lilian Hezler, a 30-year-old Frenchwoman, moved to Argentina in 1960 and eventually married Rodolfo's friend Rogelio García Lupo. She became involved in radical politics, editing a successful Spanish-language version of US magazine *The Nation*.

In 1970 she inherited a beat-up farm in Chascomus, two hours from Buenos Aires. Her wealthy father, who left US$30 million to the State of Israel in his will, refused to speak to her for eight years after she married Rogelio. Her father regarded him as a subversive and left her only the dilapidated farm, considering it punishment rather than patrimony.

Hezler's farm, La Emma, was unsuitable for Walsh's plans though. In addition Lilian disapproved of armed struggle although she agreed to help out the movement in other ways, contributing money and running errands.

"One weekend Rodolfo came out and we took a horse ride around the land," explained Hezler. "He got excited when he saw the untilled land, he went up and down, analysed the soil, made a long list of things to do," she added, surprised at Rodolfo's knowledge and interest in the land. "We were out there with Rodolfo for six hours looking at every square metre," said Lilian, "he knew everything and asked the foreman all the questions I wouldn't have known to ask." The lengthy ride was followed by a three-hour meeting indoors, in which Rodolfo outlined Hezler's strengths and weaknesses in relation to taking on the farm.

"You know how to listen to other people, you don't underestimate them," said Rodolfo, "but you're not good at negotiating." Rodolfo's tutorial gave Lilian the confidence to begin work on the farm and protected her against the barbs of her left-wing friends, who equated all land ownership with aristocratic wealth and privilege.

"Rodolfo was great," she recalled. "He believed that everyone should do what they felt they had a talent for." The reservations expressed by her Marxist friends, notably Walsh's daughter Vicki, didn't prevent the same revolutionaries from enjoying idle weekends at Lilian's farm, at her expense. Lilian recalled driving Vicki and her boyfriend Andres Alsina to the ranch one Friday evening. The customary wind-up began, with sharp words directed at bourgeois property owners. "That's enough," snapped Lilian, "you two can get out here if you find this place too much for your sensibilities." The young couple spent the weekend curled up in a Paraguayan hammock, expressing no further discomfort at their surroundings. Rarely did any of the guests raise a finger to help her out with farm work.

Lilian travelled twice a year to Europe on business but also acted as a messenger for Rodolfo, bringing letters and information to human rights organisations. One of the errands she ran for Rodolfo, in 1973, was to contact Julio Cortázar, president of the Latin American Committee for the Chilean People, based in Paris. She smuggled out photos secretly taken in the Santiago stadium chronicling the mass executions carried out by Chilean dictator General Pinochet. The photos were sent to the UN offices and published in *Paris-Match*, the proceeds returned to Rodolfo and passed on to Chileans still in hiding.

When Chilean President Salvador Allende was overthrown by Augusto Pinochet in September 1973, there was a mass exodus of political activists to neighbouring countries. Hezler secured 72 work permits for exiles on the run, accrediting them as workers on her farm. President Perón soon clamped down on the new arrivals, briefly imprisoning Hezler. She got out only because her lawyer had establishment connections.

Walsh's transition from liberal conscience to implacable revolutionary passed through several stages, from the isolated campaign against a corrupt police chief (*Operación Masacre*, 1957) to the excitement of post-revolutionary Cuba (1959–61), the editorial direction of the gritty *Semanario CGT* (1968–69) to the deadly union feud (*Quien Mató a Rosendo?*, 1969), a trail of experiences which led to a broader structural analysis of social injustice, laid out in the Epilogue to the 1972 edition of *Operación Masacre*.

Operación Masacre was still in demand when Rodolfo republished it, adding a fresh afterword: "Aramburu and the Historic Trial". Walsh dismissed Aramburu's apologists who claimed the executed general was "a champion of democracy, a soldier of freedom, a simple ruler whose temperament was incompatible with excesses of authority". Once Walsh had explained the viewpoint of Aramburu's apologists he methodically demolished their arguments. "The Aramburu government was obliged to execute and outlaw in the same way that his successors to date have been forced to torture and kill: for the simple reason that they represent a criminal minority who can only hold on to power through trickery and violence" (Walsh, 1972 p.196).

In the first edition of *Operación Masacre*, Walsh had still believed in the system, in its ability to correct injustices and punish the guilty. His outrage and indignation were first aimed at Lt Col Fernández Suárez, the police chief who ordered the executions. In the 15 years that followed these events Walsh shifted and took aim at a more powerful enemy, as evidenced by his economic analysis in the revised edition: "The Argentine Republic, one of the countries with the lowest rate of foreign investment (5 per cent of all investment) which only remitted one dollar abroad, per person, per year, began to seek those loans which benefit only the lender [...] One decree alone, number 13.125, removed two billion dollars in national deposits and put them in the hands of international banking who now control credit, strangle small industry and prepare the way for the mass influx of big monopolies" (ibid p.198).

Official statistics backed up Rodolfo's claim. In 1970 Argentina's agrarian bourgeoisie owned 74 per cent of all fertile land; just 1,800 individuals and companies controlled an area the size of Italy, Belgium, Holland and Denmark combined (Gillespie, 1998 p.51). Land distribution had changed little in a century.

In addition, the Argentinian armed forces had consolidated their role as business partners with foreign companies, principally from the US. In 1970 a total of 260 high-ranking army officers sat on foreign company managerial boards, while by 1971 the army had taken control of 66 of the country's one hundred biggest companies (Gasparini, 1999 p.38).

The Aramburu administration left behind "a dependent, stalled country, a depressed labour force, rebellion blowing up everywhere." Walsh's conclusion left no doubt as to his feelings about the justness of the execution. "The rebelliousness finally reached Aramburu, confronted him with his actions, stopped the hand that signed away loans, proscriptions and execution orders" (Walsh, 1972 p.197).

Walsh's appraisal was in line with popular sentiment. A remarkable opinion poll, commissioned by the regime in early 1971, showed that in Buenos Aires, Rosario and Córdoba, the country's three largest cities, public approval for the guerrillas ran to 49 per cent (M.E. Anderson, 1993 p.73). One of the key reasons for the support was the guerrillas' care in causing the least possible loss of life during their operations, which focused more on "armed propaganda" than on inflicting enemy losses.

The writing goes on

Walsh still came and went from his home in Tigre, outside Buenos Aires, preparing the first book-length version of the "Satanowsky Case", having finished a fourth edition of *Operación Masacre* (De la Flor, 1972). The film version got underway in 1971, directed by Jorge Cedrón, with the greatest possible secrecy and on an infinitesimal budget. It would later be screened to groups in 1973, publicised by word of mouth, from town to town throughout the country.

Walsh immersed himself in writing projects, but also devoured books, particularly on the subject of Argentinian history. He also found time to translate crime fiction classics for a series edited by Ricardo Piglia called *Tiempo Contemporáneo*. He tackled Horace McCoy (*Luces de Hollywood*, 1970) and Raymond Chandler (*Viento Rojo*, 1972). The last recorded translation by Rodolfo was a curiously apt choice: Dalton Trumbo's implacable anti-war novel *Johnny Got His Gun*. Lilia recalled that Walsh was fascinated by Trumbo's eerie novel, which takes place inside the head of a soldier whose entire body has been reduced to a breathing apparatus after a battlefield injury.

"Today in Argentina," Walsh told fellow writer Ricardo Piglia, "it is impossible to conceive of literary work which is disconnected from politics." Walsh grappled with his inner doubts, as evidenced by diary entries at the time, but by 1971 he was committed to the sacrifices which he knew lay ahead along his chosen path. The debate among intellectual circles focused on how best to express a revolutionary consciousness while remaining true to oneself. There was a rush toward "becoming proletarian", as writers and artists felt guilty about exalting the masses and their struggle while living comfortable lives.

Nicolas Casullo, a young Peronist and aspiring writer, was going through the same process of self-doubt and asked Walsh whether he should just give up writing and go off and live in a working-class neighbourhood.

"What you need, before you even start talking, is to become a Peronist, in all seriousness," began Walsh. "I was also quite a *gorila* (anti-Peronist) in 1955 but life improves you a bit sometimes and this way you save yourself a Trotskyist outburst where they send you off to be made proletarian in Quilmes. Peronism doesn't need test tube workers: it has all the workers it needs. Nor does it have a tradition of working out everyone's place in the struggle, a place for the intellectual, the politician over there and the tango singer here. Everyone is who they are, does what they know best, as best they can and if possible, at the right time. It may be that as a writer, or a journalist, you may have skills that could be of use, but you have to have things clear in your head."

Walsh's heartfelt advice struck Casullo, who was caught in his piercing gaze.

"The fight that is coming is going to be very tough, Nicolas. Sometimes I think people aren't aware of that. This activism asks for your life, and one of these days, it will demand your death too. It's something that requires rigour, great discipline, sobriety and seriousness. And the festivities begin when it's over, not at the beginning or halfway through" (Anguita and Caparrós, 1997, p.469).

Casullo responded by telling Walsh that it was easy for him to talk about giving up on literature, with a successful career behind him, whereas Casullo was an aspiring and as yet unpublished writer.

"These are different times, Nicolas, and this is a time for a bigger undertaking. When you're trying to change important things, then you realise that a short story, a novel, aren't worth it and won't satisfy you. Beautiful bourgeois art! They taught us that it was the supreme spiritual value. But when you have people who gave their lives, and continue to, literature is no longer your loyal and sweet lover – it's a cheap whore. There are times when, as they say in *La Hora de los Hornos*, every spectator is a coward or a traitor. This might be a pain for the more intimate questions of the soul but that's the time we're living in," (ibid).

Rodolfo continued this debate in his correspondence with Cuban poet Roberto Fernández Retamar. Dated April 27th 1972, he wrote, "This painful exchange is extraordinary nonetheless. For some, life is now full of meaning, although literature cannot exist. The silence of the intellectuals, the collapse of the literary boom, the end of the salons, are the greatest proof that even those who don't participate in the popular revolution now underway – in its own slow way – can no longer be accomplices to the culture of the oppressor, can no longer accept privilege without guilt, nor disconnect themselves from the suffering and struggles of the people, who are showing themselves to be, as usual, the main protagonists" (Fernández Retamar, 1993).

Villa days, 1972

In 1972 Walsh began working in Villa 31, Retiro, a *villa miseria* (shantytown) behind Buenos Aires' central train station, in the heart of the city's docklands. It offered Walsh an opportunity to test his organising skills among the working class, making direct contact with the expanding popular movement, another step on his revolutionary path. Rodolfo's contact for working there was Jorge Cedrón, an architect who worked with the Municipal Housing Commission.

The Retiro shantytown consisted of six neighbourhoods: Saldias, Laprida, Comunicaciones, YPF, Martin Guemes and Inmigrantes, spread out along a 3 km strip running from the port to Mitre railway yard, with a population of about 50,000 people.

Most of the inhabitants were displaced rural families, who came to the capital city in search of work, while 30 per cent were foreigners, mainly Paraguayans and Bolivians. Tucumán province, in northern Argentina, had suffered an economic collapse when sugar prices dropped, scattering 100,000 people, many of whom ended up in the cardboard shacks behind Retiro train station.

The first Retiro neighbourhood was established by Italian immigrants, who arrived in 1946, but quickly moved to more permanent homes when their economic situation improved. Two years later the first homes went up in Saldias, as families of railway workers occupied train carriages along abandoned tracks. When water taps were installed, the population grew. More solid homes went up in the 1960s, with *villeros* (shantytown residents) organising for the first time to demand basic services: more piped water and electricity.

The streets were dark and filled with potholes, dank pools of water which served as transmitters of diseases fatal to small children; health services were minimal. The area boasted one sturdy police station, and the newly built Sheraton hotel (at political rallies the locals chanted 'We'll turn the Sheraton into a hospital') and a small primary school.

State security forces had spies posted to keep an eye on all organising activity, while Paraguayan dictator Alfredo Stroessner also sent agents to monitor Paraguayan exiles living there, fearing they might plan a rebellious return to their country.

The men found employment as dockers in the nearby port, leaving their homes when it was still dark, drinking *mate* in the first light of dawn, before beginning the heavy loading and unloading work among transport ships which carried the city's wealth in and out of the country.

When Rodolfo first arrived in Villa 31, in June 1972, he spent ten days in the home of community leader José Valenzuela, from where he began reconnaissance work, learning about the *villa* and how it worked, hoping to apply his organisational and intelligence skills to advancing existing activism.

In turn, Valenzuela adopted Walsh's obsession with personal security. "I didn't lose a single militant back then," boasted the elderly activist, still organising for change 30 years later. "The guns, the security was about protecting our families and each other," clarified Valenzuela, who never engaged in armed operations. "*El Capitán* [Walsh] was very happy when he saw the care we took in all this," smiled Valenzuela, "because we had learned it from him."

"*El Capitán* walked around, talked to people, listened to what was going on, watching life in the *villa*," explained Valenzuela, whose wife cooked meals for Walsh and Jorge Cedrón, who often stayed in the house also. "All the *compas*[41] liked Rodolfo," said Valenzuela. Locals slowly got used to the presence of outside agitators, overcoming their initial suspicions. Rodolfo's aloof manner gave way to a respectful curiosity and a genuine empathy which helped him connect with the local people.

In the minds of the government and State security forces, the *villa* inhabitants lived like animals and worked as thieves, an eyesore to be fenced off out of sight of the tourists. Those who worked in the *villa* had another vision however, one of admiration and respect for the solidarity, unity and generosity of the dispossessed, who, like the rest of the country, were waking up to the possibilities of popular struggle.

Walsh found documents on the history of the *villa* and spoke to its older inhabitants, tracing a rough history of local organising efforts. As early as 1962 Belgrano Railways had attempted to evict families from the YPF and Comunicaciones neighbourhoods. A group of one thousand protestors marched to the Interior Ministry and the plan was scrapped. Street lights and water taps were installed in 1965, along with a medical dispensary, but a new period of military rule cut short the organising efforts.

The residents formed the first inter-settlement committee in 1968, realising that their best chance of obtaining concessions lay in collective struggle. The repeated efforts to evict them were invariably accompanied by search and arrest operations by police.

Something had shifted, though, in the social climate. People stood firm together, determined to pursue their demands for social justice. By 1968 the combative sectors of the CGTA had rallied to their cause, making it more difficult for the regime to catch them unawares.

The residents told Walsh how Welfare Minister Francisco Manrique and city Mayor Montero Ruiz made a surprise visit in late 1971 "to soften us up" according to locals. "In less than ten minutes we had a crowd of three thousand to greet them." The protest forced the hapless delegation to sign a nine-point neighbourhood development plan.

"If these promises are not carried out within two months," announced minister Manrique, "call me Manrique the liar and spit in my face." Jocular residents chanted "Manrique the liar" and spat on the floor on their way into polling booths in March 1973, as they queued up to vote for Perón's presidential nominee, Héctor Cámpora.

For the first time ever a Peronist candidate carried the day in Buenos Aires voting districts 19 and 20, where working-class locals voted alongside the wealthy oligarchs living in posh Barrio Norte. By early 1973 Retiro's delegates were refusing to deal with the outgoing government at all, announcing their plan to discuss future development only with the

---

[41] Short for compañeros/as

newly elected "popular government" led by Cámpora.

The new president lasted just 49 days in office, replaced by a conservative stand-in who kept the seat warm for Perón until fresh elections were held. The early mood of optimism faded as Perón relied on the reactionary elements within his movement to regain his position as undisputed leader of the nation.

Fast forward

When I first wandered into the Retiro neighbourhood in 1999, the barren waste ground, abandoned chapel and unused storage containers made it difficult to imagine a thriving community there in Walsh's time. The beating heart of the city's docklands has been privatised and dismantled.

It was only when I stood on the higher ground above Carlos Mugica's chapel, looking across the city along the new six-lane highway, that the strategic importance of Retiro district became clear. The Retiro shantytown consisted of six connected neighbourhoods which controlled vital access points to the city.

The area backed on to the city port, where thousands of locals worked, loading and unloading the boats that served as entry and exit points for much of the city's trade. Back in 1972 a dockers' strike would have paralysed the city; the militant workers could have occupied the city streets, erected barricades or engaged in hit-and-run operations against local power points. Retiro was a strategic enclave should a Buenos Aires version of the *Cordobazo* occur.

There was initial resistance to radical organising efforts, particularly when strangers turned up, their intentions unclear. A slow process of unity between neighbourhoods led to the establishment of the Frente Villero Peronista in 1972, establishing an alliance across 33 *villas*.

Villa activists recruited new militants and analysed strategy at monthly co-ordinating meetings. Walsh stayed quiet when local organisers talked to local people about local issues, saving his analysis for the fortnightly neighbourhood meetings and the monthly assembly of delegates. "We have to strengthen the organisational process to be ready for the final triumph," Walsh told activists, urging them to greater sacrifice. Meanwhile he helped put together a local publication, *Semanario Villero*, and trained activists in journalism skills.

"The armed struggle was rarely discussed," explained my elderly guide José Valenzuela. The inhabitants of the *villa*, with jobs, homes and families to take care of, developed an open, legal movement which grew from within the masses, enjoying the margin of protection afforded by their united, collective stance.

The first challenge to the residents was a proposed relocation plan for dozens of families living in the Cava area where a road-building plan required taking 30 metres of land which already had houses built on it. A group of one hundred Retiro residents, including Rodolfo, took the city train and visited Cava early one morning.

The result was an impromptu visit to the office of the mayor of San Isidro, where the large group demanded the highway project be rethought. The situation was tense, but the mayor spotted what looked like a television camera, in the hands of Walsh and Cedrón, who were filming different meetings and events in the *villas*. "Please, no cameras," said the embarrassed mayor, "we can sort this out between ourselves."

Walsh spoke for the first time, camera in hand. "*Che*," he said, in his tone of mock apology, "look, if there's no agreement we'll have to record this." The mayor cancelled the plan for the highway. "That was a triumph for the people," said Valenzuela, who was the movement's spokesman at the time. Walsh admitted later that the camera had no film in it.

The organising efforts focused on community mobilisation but Walsh also anticipated a brutal State response to their efforts and provided weapons training to a handful of militants.

Walsh paid close attention to his own personal security, a habit acquired during the *Operación Masacre* investigation. "The use of torture, the kidnapping and murder of activists has become weekly or daily. Some friends have died, others are in jail, others you can't see as frequently as one would like. You get used to keeping the house clean, you never carry a personal diary around or an address book," Rodolfo wrote in a letter in 1972, "you burn letters from Havana, you have no choice, you always look up and down both sides of the street, presume that every telephone is bugged, don't go out at night and have someone call up regularly to see if we still exist" (Fernández Retamar, 1993 pp.221–4).

The authorities waited for the right moment to move on Retiro, aware of its strategic importance. A final "compulsory eradication" plan was announced, whereby they were legally obliged to move into homes provided elsewhere. By then Perón was president of Argentina and despite pledges to respect the plans for community development, he ordered troops to "help" with the relocation process, which began in early 1974.

By then Walsh had taken on other responsibilities within the popular movement but he stayed in touch with his friends in Retiro.

José Valenzuela looked back on an era when everything seemed possible, when young people joined student, church and neighbourhood groups, demanding a more humane system. "I still ask myself whether we might have got further if our ideas were clearer and we hadn't lost so many of our people," he concluded, sipping *mate* as he watched the busy Buenos Aires traffic and fanned himself in the implacable midday heat.

The return of Perón, 1973

In 1973 Argentina's popular movement had never looked healthier or better focused, putting all its energy into securing the election of Héctor Cámpora, Perón's chosen candidate in the presidential elections scheduled for March 1973 (Argentina's residency laws prevented Perón himself from running for office). After a brief, intense and exhilarating election campaign, run largely by the progressive Peronismo de Base, (Peronist Support Bases), Cámpora strolled to victory, winning 49 per cent of votes cast. The result was predictable, as Perón's influence was always sufficient to ensure national support for his chosen delegate. Unlike previous elections, however, Perón was coming home and he planned to take greater control of the political process.

In May 1973 Héctor Cámpora was sworn into power, flanked by Chilean President Salvador Allende and Cuban President Osvaldo Dorticos. The mood was decidedly militant as boisterous crowds prevented US Secretary of State William Rogers from leaving his car to witness the ceremony. Security for the event was organised by members of Juventud Peronista, identified by red and black shirtbands, while army band members were jeered and turned back by the crowds.

After 18 years of proscription, Peronism was in power, creating a huge sense of expectation. Cámpora, an avuncular former president of the Chamber of Deputies, was a loyal Peronist who promised industrial reactivation, wage increases and the release of prisoners. It was always understood that his true role was that of facilitating Perón's return to power.

The sense of hope was such that in the evening a spontaneous march took place on prisons around the country as Peronists demanded the immediate release of all political prisoners, an important pledge made on the campaign trail. Thousands of people gathered outside Villa Devoto prison in Buenos Aires where 180 prisoners anxiously awaited liberation. By 8 p.m., the scene bordered on chaos, as 30,000 festive but determined militants waited outside the prison, where the order was passed on from mouth to mouth, "No one leaves until the last compañero is out!"

Walsh got out of a taxi and marvelled at the scene before him. "It looked like the fucking Bastille," said Miguel Bonasso, who accompanied him. Prisoners set fire to their bedclothes, holding them out of their cells, flames shooting up toward a black sky, throwing fantastic shapes into the night air. Walsh hoped to see his friend Paco Urondo walk free that evening.

President Cámpora quickly signed an amnesty law to legalise the mass release of political prisoners while beleagured prison authorities began to type up release forms at 10 p.m. The inmates now had control of the prison and the telephone system. The first 20 prisoners walked free at 11 p.m., carried shoulder-high by the ecstatic crowd, including relatives and friends.

Paco Urondo emerged, a small bag of possessions in his hands, overcome with emotion, as Walsh hugged him. "We needed to be among the people," said Paco, all hugs and smiles in the jubilant crowd, "to chat to each other, with people we didn't know, because they were there, shaking our hands."

In La Plata, Julio Troxler, a survivor of the *Operación Masacre* executions, led a huge crowd to Olmos prison, releasing imprisoned guerrillas. Troxler had come a long way – that day he celebrated his promotion to assistant police chief inside the very force which had tried to kill him in 1956.

Outside Villa Devoto prison a thousand people were still gathered in the early hours of the morning. The small crowd sought cover when shots rang out from inside the prison. A small group of militants attempted to storm the building, mistakenly thinking there were more political prisoners inside. The area around the prison was suddenly occupied by police, who tossed tear-gas grenades, while machine-gun fire came from inside the building.

"Walsh looked calm, his hair tousled, his eyes big as saucers behind those thick glasses and that disparaging smile which hid his feelings," recalled Bonasso. Walsh, Ferreyra and Bonasso left with one of the injured people, taking him to a nearby hospital.

The euphoria of the night, a tantalisingly brief moment in which the passion of the people overran the caution of their leaders, offered Walsh one more glimpse into the possibilities available to the Peronist left when allied to the greater Peronist mass movement. "When everyday life takes on magical qualities, you know you're in the middle of a revolution," wrote Che Guevara, (Urondo, 1999 p.147). Argentina came alive to the possibility of radical change and the Montoneros occupied political centre-stage after a generation of military rule.

It was around this time that Aníbal Ford, a novelist, academic and friend of Walsh's, invited Rodolfo to address his students. "That man Walsh," said Ford, trying to recall the Rodolfo who visited his students during those tempestuous days, "always walking up the street against the traffic, not wanting to be shot or surprised from behind. He is a character from that novel we call Reality. But he doesn't believe in it. In 1973 we took him to the university, where a student asked a question: 'Tell me Walsh… what principles led you to write *Operación Masacre*?' 'Principles?' responded Walsh, feigning surprise, 'I wanted to be famous, win a Pulitzer… make money…'" (Ford, 1987 p.11).

Never one to miss an opportunity, Walsh took Aníbal to one side and asked him to write a manual of industrial sabotage for a planned campaign in Córdoba, taking advantage of his background in systems technology.

The election victory of Peronist presidential candidate Héctor Cámpora, the liberation of political prisoners and the general perception that the armed groups played a key role in securing Perón's return from exile had placed the Montoneros at the heart of the nation's vibrant political scene. When Cámpora assumed office in May 1973, the Montoneros effectively controlled two governorships, the main universities, the streets, the shantytowns and the football stadiums. The Cámpora administration appointed Ricardo Vitanni, the police chief known to Walsh, as deputy director of the Federal Police. General Iniguez, a progressive army general, dined with Montonero leader Mario Firmenich and even made him a present of a gun.

Cámpora's presidency was only a prelude to the return of the caudillo, in line with the popular slogan: *Cámpora Presidente, Perón al Poder* (Cámpora for president, Perón to power). Cámpora resigned 49 days after taking office, to make way for fresh elections in which Perón would be eligible to participate.

Senate President Alejandro Díaz Bialet should have assumed office as fresh elections were organised, but with Perón's connivance José López Rega forced Díaz Bialet to take an unplanned trip abroad, allowing him to appoint his own brother-in-law Raul Lastiri to the post. López Rega, popularly known as *el brujo*, the sorcerer, was a former police officer and a fan of the occult. He was close to Isabel Martínez, and together they met Perón in 1956; eventually she would become Perón's wife, and López Rega his trusted personal secretary.

When Perón's health suffered a radical decline between December 1972 and March 1973, López Rega attended every political meeting in the general's house, advising Isabel on strategy and tactics. President Cámpora placed López Rega in charge of the Social Welfare Ministry, responsible for handling the arrangements for Perón's return. López Rega in turn named Lt Col Jorge Osinde Secretary for Sports and Tourism. Osinde had been counter-intelligence chief for the army intelligence service, as well as acquiring fame as a torture addict with the notorious Special Section of the Federal Police. López Rega and Osinde planned to displace the police from their task of providing security for Perón's return. They organized a private army of 3,000 men and filled Perón's podium with members of the official CGT, the far-right Concentración Nacional Universitaria, CNU (National University Centre) and the Alianza Libertadora Nacionalista, ALN (Nationalist Liberating Alliance).

On a political level, interim-President Raul Lastiri immediately moved to seize control of the State machinery, determined to exclude Montonero sympathizers from his temporary administration.

Massacre in Ezeiza

Juan Domingo Perón's long-awaited return to Argentina raised such high expectations that it was bound to fail to meet at least some of them, if not most. Before his plane touched down on Argentinian soil on June 20th 1973, upwards of two million people (some say as many as three million) had gathered at Ezeiza airport in Buenos Aires to welcome the leader home.

There was a stage constructed on a motorway flyover where Perón would greet the people and re-establish the mythical direct dialogue first seen in October 1945, on the night which confirmed Perón's working-class support. As the crowds swelled and heaved, the stage was occupied by dozens of armed guards, determined to prevent columns of Montonero supporters from finding a place anywhere near the stage. In the run-up to the big day, union bureaucrats forcibly expelled Montonero supporters from public positions within unions, universities and radio stations. On June 9th, the anniversary of the *Operación Masacre* executions, rival factions clashed on the city streets, resulting in the death of one union leader.

Lt Col Jorge Manuel Osinde was put in charge of security at Ezeiza, despite (or because of) his proven record as a torturer during Perón's first government. Weapons were distributed to hundreds of thugs who occupied the stage or positioned themselves in nearby trees, behind the crowd.

While in exile Perón was everyone's man, pulling the strings of rival tendencies with Machiavellian genius. "We must plan ahead, convincing (the people) that with all the legal doors closed to us, we have only the path of violence left in order to solve our problems," said Perón back in 1958. "The dictatorship which whips our country will only give up on its violence when faced with a greater, alternative violence," Perón told the Fuerzas Armadas Peronistas in February 1970 (Gasparini, 1999 p.39).

Perón's armed left-wing followers considered his arrival at Ezeiza a crucial test of their public support and planned a show of strength to impress their leader, albeit without weapons. Crowds of people began filling the area on the night before his return, joined by children and locals the next day. The gunmen on stage were arrogant and threatening, rehearsing security manoeuvres which involved throwing themselves to the ground and aiming their weapons at the crowd. As the time of Perón's return drew close the space in front of the stage was a mass of people, with thousands more pressing against wavering human security cordons.

Rodolfo Walsh had gathered his intelligence team to monitor police radios and uncover the strategy used by Perón's heavies to control the crowd. His team operated from the seventeenth-floor home of a sympathiser, tuning into police frequencies, noting the positioning and movements of the security forces and the conversations between superior officers and patrols on the beat. When gunfire rang out around Ezeiza, Walsh quickly established from the radio communication that the crossfire was taking place between armed groups on the same side, the thugs onstage and the thugs in the trees, who mistakenly believed they were under attack.

Perón opted to divert his arrival to another airport while "the explosion of 30 years of contradictions," led to a massacre among the crowd at Ezeiza (Verbitsky, 1998 p.13). The assumption on all sides was that a battle had erupted between the left and right-wing factions of Peronism.

The official death toll was 13 dead and 355 injured, marking the launch of open warfare on the popular movement, which would in turn re-activate its armed movement and begin the deterioration toward the 1976 coup.

The events at Ezeiza ought to have alerted the Montoneros to the risks involved in tying their fortunes to Perón's populism. Perón wanted the support of Argentina's working class, but social struggle would stay strictly within the limits of Evita's mattresses and Christmas hampers. The left-wing armed tendencies naïvely believed that Perón was on their side, quietly galvanising forces before launching his bid for a socialist revolution.

Perón was returned by a landslide vote in elections held in September 1973, winning 62 per cent of the votes, over seven million preferences. Perón's vice-president was his wife, Isabel, a combination which harked back to the enduring memory of the beloved Evita. Isabel never succeeded in matching the charisma and determination which defined Evita's ascent to national prominence.

The presidential inauguration took place on October 12th 1973, shortly before Perón turned 78 years of age. The loyal Cámpora was not even invited to Perón's inauguration ceremony.

José Rucci had succeeded Walsh's old nemesis Augusto Vandor as CGT leader in 1970, clamping down on left-wing influences within the organisation. He flaunted his considerable wealth, owning several cars and luxury apartments, lived the life of a playboy and always travelled with a dozen armed bodyguards. In 1973, he was murdered. As Perón's unconditional CGT union ally, his death deepened Perón's resolve to deal with the Montoneros without mercy. The Federal Police initially blamed the Ejercito Revolucionario del Pueblo for the death of Rucci, but that group generally claimed responsibility for their attacks and rarely targeted union leaders, regardless of how conservative or anti-worker. The Montoneros first denounced the killing of Rucci then belatedly took responsibility for it a year later, on the orders of Mario Firmenich. Army intelligence apparently told US officials that Rucci had been killed by "orthodox" (right-wing) Peronists anxious to carve up his business empire. The FBI traced the weapon used in the killing of Rucci to a gun dealer in New York, who had sold it to an Aerolíneas Argentinas air hostess who in turn bought the weapon for a friend in the military. The die was cast though, and Perón declared war on the Montoneros.

On October 1st, provisional President Lastiri called provincial governors to a conference at which he released a "reserved document" signed by Perón. It was an "order" for the rank-and-file of the movement: "Marxist terrorist and subversive groups have declared war against our organisation and our leadership," read the document, which called on all Peronists to fight back, in order to foil the enemy's plans and punish them to the fullest extent.

The *New York Times* captured the mood of Perón as he assumed power: "Last year when his return to power [...] was not at all certain, [Perón] justified guerrilla action by saying that if he were fifty years younger he too would probably be a bomb thrower [...] But now that he is only a step away from formal as well as effective power, his views appear to have changed. He scoffed at the young lawyer who was Interior Minister during the short-lived government of Dr Héctor Cámpora, his stand-in. The minister told police that he wanted them to be more humane and less repressive. Mr Perón observed, 'that's what the police are for: to repress'." (NYT, 30/9/73)

Perón quickly delegated clandestine repressive tasks to López Rega, who from the Ministry of Social Welfare organised commandos of right-wing thugs for 'special tasks' which included gun-running, drug-trafficking and extortion as well as murder. The killers also hunted left-wing dissidents, signing off as the Triple A, or Anti-Communist Alliance.

Perón formally expelled the radical youth wing of his movement in a humiliating public address on May Day 1974. The Montonero supporters left the square in protest, leaving a sizeable hole in the crowd; their leadership decided to go it alone, convinced they could outsmart Perón and inherit his mantle as the ailing leader approached death.

Noticias – armed journalism

The progressive sectors within the movement sought to "preserve the banners of struggle" and set up a daily newspaper. A plethora of Peronist publications already existed in 1973, the best-known being *El Descamisado* (The Shirtless), which acted as the official organ of the armed movement. "It was rhetorical, dull and unbearable," said Horacio

Verbitsky, "just a vehicle to pass down the party line." It was enlivened by the superb photographs taken by Venezuelan Jaime Colmenares, who was later disappeared.

The ambitious *Noticias* was launched in November 1973, its start-up capital obtained through bank robbery and kidnappings, according to Goyo Levenson, the paper's accountant. The 24-page broadsheet launched its first issue on November 20th 1973, covering politics, economics, social issues and sport. "The paper should be a space to bring together different sectors which may coincide with our [Montonero] proposals [...] setting up alliances, expanding spaces," said Miguel Bonasso, *Noticias*'s editor.

"Listen to the reformist Russian-Peronist populist," Rodolfo would joke at editorial meetings, giving Bonasso a hard time for his populist style. "*Noticias* achieved something which is unthinkable today," recalled Bonasso. "It brought together journalists with great technical and individual ability, but who also had a profound personal and political commitment."

Bonasso was chosen as the paper's director due to his track record inside the Peronist movement, where he was campaign press secretary during Cámpora's successful presidential bid. The real editor behind the scenes was Paco Urondo, a political appointment approved by the Montonero leadership.

Francisco "Paco" Urondo (1930–1976)

Poet, novelist and revolutionary, Paco was a close friend of Rodolfo's, who first visited him at Poupee's antique business in the early 1960s. They shared the long march from intellectual realisation to clandestine guerrilla service. Both were inspired by their own daughters, who were early recruits to Argentina's emerging armed groups.

While Rodolfo's character was cool and terse, Paco was chatty and sociable, a drinker and conversationalist, relaxed and carefree.

In his novel *Los Pasos Previos* (1972) Paco anticipated the terrible days ahead, the agonising options between prudent activism, "doing the right thing" and *entrega*, the sacrifice of the individual to a larger enterprise, to the dream of revolution. In one memorable episode, similar to Christ's biblical encounter with the decent rich man, who wants to join the church but can't renounce his worldly possessions, Paco's character Simon discusses his commitment with Che Guevara: "Che listened carefully as Simon explained that he wrote in favour of the revolutionary process, within the modest limits at his disposal." Che told him that he too once thought the same way, that "by working on popular medicine at all levels, he was advancing the cause. That one merely had to do things as best as one could." The scales finally fell from his eyes, explained Che, as he realised that "the only way to make a real contribution to the revolution was in making the revolution happen" (ibid p.140).

When it came to the issue of armed struggle, Paco traced a chronological path through recent union history, leading to the only possible conclusion: "The issue of violence or non-violence is not a philosophical one but rather it is the anguished response chosen by the poor majority today" (ibid p. 327). Paco was imprisoned by the military junta in 1973 at the tail end of army rule and regained his freedom on the night Cámpora assumed presidential office.

Urondo ran *Noticias*, keeping an eye on the political line of the paper, acting as a link to the Montonero leadership. His irreverent style irked the movement's leadership but the paper's success vindicated his strategy.

Walsh belonged to Urondo's Montonero unit and was a senior editor at the paper, in charge of crime news: "Rodolfo didn't just report crime cases," said Bonasso, "he investigated them himself."

In addition Walsh continued his intelligence work, drawing up an x-ray of the State security forces which would provide crucial help to the Montonero movement. At that point the Montoneros planned their return to armed struggle. All armed activities had been suspended in the wake of the Cámpora election victory and the return of Perón, but the ceasefire cracked under the pressure of Triple A terror and the realisation that Perón had no interest in radical social reform.

Walsh put his formidable police and judicial contacts at the service of the paper and also monitored the work of his reporting team: Alicia Barrios, Leandro Gil Ibarra, Martin Caparrós and his daughter Patricia Walsh, who worked on crime stories and general news. Rodolfo had a tiny office of his own, where he spent most of the day working on his articles. One of the most important moments of each week was the arrival of the Federal Police weekly bulletin and the daily news brief of the Buenos Aires provincial police. Walsh spent hours scouring the bulletins, dwelling not on the news section but on the "social" pages, which no one else bothered to read. It was on those pages that promotions, transfers and weddings were recorded, revealing useful tips on friendships within the force, inter-marriage between prominent families and security force chiefs, and by extension, the possible falling-outs and emerging power circles. His thoughts came together out loud in his office, directed at no one in particular.

"He carried an encyclopedia of police history in his head," recalled Martin Caparrós, who was sent to work at Rodolfo's desk at sixteen years of age. Caparrós was active in the Juventud Peronista but entered the paper as a "cadet", serving coffee and sorting agency cables as they came out of the telex machine. "I was hopelessly clumsy," explained Caparrós, who was sent to Walsh's department after spilling coffee once too often.

"Rodolfo had a strange presence," recalled Caparrós in early 2000, speaking in his new apartment close to Buenos Aires' beautiful botanic gardens. Caparrós is a writer and documentary maker, editor of the epic *La Voluntad*, a three-volume history of activism between 1966 and 1976. "Rodolfo spent the whole day working away in his small office, we didn't have much contact with him, I think he was very shy," said Caparrós. On one occasion Walsh's cub reporters discovered that Rodolfo's birthday was coming up the following day, January 9th 1974. Patricia Walsh supplied the details but even she didn't know how old her father was. No one dared to organise a cake, let alone sing happy birthday. "He was *el capitán* and you didn't mess around with him," laughed Caparrós.

Caparrós was impressed by Walsh's extensive police contacts and his obsession for crime news. "He seemed to have the police going round and round in his head," said Caparrós, and the contacts paid off. "The police used to call us up and tell us that a corpse had been found in such-and-such a place, giving us half an hour to take pictures before their own detectives had even got there." Rodolfo spoke little to his colleagues at the crime desk, beyond an occasional comment on the day's news. "I learned from him by reading his work, not from working with him at the paper," concluded Caparrós.

Rodolfo once asked him to write up brief biographical notes on all the Peronist resistance martyrs since 1955, a series called "When the Dead Still had a Name". Shortly before the paper was closed down Walsh suggested he write a story which compared the figures for "delinquents" killed in alleged confrontations with the police and the number of police killed in action.

Caparrós spent three days digging through archives to find the numbers, then published a banner story, "Federal Police Kill Thirty-Three to One". The style was identical to Walsh's own reports on "the trigger-happy sect" published several years previously. Caparrós's research revealed that armed confrontations with the police left one injured person for every person killed, an impossibly high kill rate compared to wartime, when the average rate was six people injured for every fatality. "The police were killing like crazy," concluded Caparrós.

The young reporter was satisfied with his work, which appeared in the final editions of *Noticias*, just before it was closed down in August 1974. Caparrós waited for a word of praise from Walsh, which never came. "That was a great story Rodolfo did," commented several of his colleagues as he gritted his teeth and kept a firm grip on his ego. Walsh finally acknowledged the story several days after it appeared in the paper: "That story went well," was all he said.

Rodolfo would occasionally wander over to his charges on the crime desk and say, "Hey, you know that on boats and in the newsroom there should be no women on board." Everyone smiled politely, not knowing whether to take him seriously or not. "He was smiling too," said Caparrós, "as if he dusted down the phrase so that it wouldn't be forgotten." Walsh's crime desk had two men and two women on board. Caparrós once made the mistake of asking Rodolfo if he thought a spell in journalism school might be of use. "Forget it," said Walsh, "a journalist can be a thief or a dimwit but he can never be that stupid."

Outside the paper Walsh remained in contact with Retiro and also organised the Montoneros' intelligence apparatus, leaving him with constant work overload. "He used to complain that he had lost the pleasure of reading," recalled Bonasso, "that he'd really love to spend time sitting under a lamp, indulging his passion for literature."

Horacio Verbitsky found himself working at *Noticias* despite his reservations about the project. At the time of the paper's launch he was working in the nation's widest-circulating national newspaper, *El Clarín*, where he had carved out an important space as news editor. One day he got a call from his Montonero commanding officer, advising him to meet someone in a city café. "Who is it?" asked Verbitsky.

"Don't worry, you'll recognise him," came the response.

The next day he sat face to face with Montonero chief Mario Firmenich.

"You have to work at *Noticias*," he said, "it's an order."

Verbitsky reluctantly abandoned *Clarín* but was soon caught up in the excitement of producing the new paper, which began competing with sensationalist tabloid *Crónica*, while maintaining a left-wing perspective. The news section discussed poverty and police corruption, while international news covered Nixon, Northern Ireland and Vietnam. Walsh was sent to Palestine to cover the conflict there in May 1974, producing a memorable seven-part series, the only time he signed his name to his work in the paper. The Israeli Embassy in Buenos Aires took offence at his articles, sparking a lively exchange of letters.

Verbitsky and Walsh were joined at *Noticias* by Juan Gelman (home desk editor), and exiled colleagues from Chile and Uruguay, along with a team of photographers and sports reporters who quickly established a reputation for excellence. Walsh's police section kept a count of victims of police violence, correlating corpses marked NN (John Doe) with killings carried out by the Triple A (Anti-Communist Alliance). The accuracy of Walsh's analysis angered Federal Police chief Alberto Villar, who suspected inside informers. Walsh combined details gleaned from his radio scanning operation with tips provided by disgruntled officers who resented Villar's brutal leadership style.

The paper sold respectably well from the outset but Bonasso tracked sales which revealed gaping holes in working-class neighbourhoods and rural areas, two areas in significant need of alternative information to counteract tabloid propaganda.

Bonasso decided that the sports page needed improving and hired writers to analyse upcoming races and soccer games. The paper's circulation climbed steadily, then took off when the turf correspondent predicted six winners out of eight races in one weekend. The paper still focused on political, social and economic issues, but the audacity of Urondo, who allowed sports news to occupy the front headlines, brought him into conflict with the Montonero leadership, who frowned on the apparent incitement to gambling and vice made by revolutionary compañeros.

"There were political differences between the leadership and the compañeros at *Noticias*," acknowledged Roberto Perdía, one of the Montonero leaders at the time. "The newspaper staff were aspiring members of the organisation, I was part of the leadership," said Perdía. The former Montonero recalled heated words when the journalists refused to follow his advice. "I told them to stop messing around or get the fuck out of there." Perdía attributed the lawlessness and lack of discipline at *Noticias* to the leadership of Paco Urondo, who was considered soft on the staff, many of whom were close friends.

Manufacturing militancy

The Montonero leadership expected members to turn their hand to any skill required for the organisation's activities. "The criteria for militancy were insane," recalled Bonasso. "You had to be capable of shooting a policeman, stealing a car, addressing a crowd, running a newspaper, robbing a bank, it was too much."

Every Montonero member belonged to an *ambito*, an organic cell structure shared by five or six people. The *ambito* was the militant's everyday connection to the movement, where political strategy, family problems and personal security issues were resolved.

An *ambito* could share a common profession, for example media workers, whose immediate task might be to win union representation in their place of work. Montoneros held "double militancy", participating in surface organisations (such as the Peronist Youth) while also acquiring rank as a clandestine combatant, training for future operations.

Rodolfo Walsh also criticised the movement's exaggerated expectations of its members, arguing that it was the *organisation* which had to be comprehensive, not each one of its members. The Montoneros had a remarkable pool of talent at their fingertips but over-stretched their members with excessive demands on each individual.

Urondo's compañeros at *Noticias* would troop off to Tigre at weekends, where they held target practice at Rodolfo and Lilia's home. "It was a complete circus," recalled Bonasso, as Walsh, Lilia, Gelman, Verbitsky, Alicia Raboy and Gregorio "Goyo" Levenson, the oldest of the group, huffed and puffed in the back garden, learning how to break ranks and retreat under fire. "I used to crack up laughing," recalled Levenson, speaking in 1999, aged 87, still active in left-wing politics. "Paco would get mad and send me into the house to wash dishes."

The weapons were pistols and hunting rifles, but one day Paco turned up with an Uzi, impressing his charges. "We were bowled over by the Uzi," said Bonasso, relishing the memory.

The Tigre delta was an important hunting spot and the shots went unnoticed. Moreover, Walsh and Ferreyra's next-door neighbours were Pirí Lugones and her partner Carlos. On the other side of their house lived a family linked to the ERP guerrillas.

Rodolfo attended *Noticias* editorial meetings but stayed out of the controversy over the paper's political direction. His experience of destructive sectarianism at *Prensa Latina* in Cuba had given him a clear idea of the pitfalls involved in reconciling ideological discipline with good reporting.

On December 11th 1973 Rodolfo arrived at *Noticias* and took his daughter Patricia aside.

"*Mamá* has died," he said.

"That won't affect you much, will it," said Patricia, an off-the-cuff remark as she thought of her own relationship with Dora, her tradition-bound grandmother.

"He just looked at me, saying nothing," recalled Patricia.

A couple of hours later Patricia ran into Rodolfo once more, at the house of his brother Carlos Washington, where the wake was due to take place. "He looked terrible," said Patricia, "he wasn't crying but he was very upset."

Rodolfo didn't go to the funeral, mindful as ever of his security.

On the eve of May Day 1974 Rodolfo set up a listening post in a city centre building, monitoring both police communications and the advancing convoy of buses bringing militants into the city from around the country. He used a dozen phone lines tapped from the empty offices around him.

Roberto Perdía accompanied him on the 24-hour watch. Walsh soon discovered that the police had set up roadblocks to prevent Montonero sympathisers from reaching the city. A combination of secondary roads and intercepted radio messages kept Walsh a step ahead of the security forces, while Perdía kept in contact with the bus drivers, advising them on how to avoid the trouble ahead.

The interception mission turned to farce when Walsh discovered a second radio surveillance operation, organised by disgruntled former police officers who had taken equipment with them after being sacked by chief Villar. The former cops jammed the airwaves with expletives directed at their former bosses but they also taunted them with snippets of information on illicit love affairs and corruption in the ranks, the details gleefully scribbled down by a giddy Walsh.

A radio detection van trawled the streets, looking for the transmitter used by the sacked cops while Walsh and Perdía sat tight, planning their escape route through the empty offices they had occupied for the day. When the Montoneros arrived in the city, Walsh guided them through the streets, advising them of the precise location of police positions. When the day arrived the authorities were dismayed to find the Montoneros had quietly "occupied" the city, creating a festive atmosphere and demanding Perón shake off his repressive allies. The authorities tried detaining activists but Walsh had a group of "notables" on stand-by, sympathetic legislators and journalists who would immediately turn up at the flashpoints, warned in advance through the radio messaging system.

"I think most of us held out hopes that the General would rectify his position," wrote Perdía in his memoir of that era, *La Otra Historia* (Perdía, 1997 p.226). The Montoneros made a disastrous miscalculation, as a furious Perón now publicly disowned the Montoneros. He called them *imberbes*, callow youth, inexperienced. In exile Perón had showered them with praise, "our marvellous youth", acknowledging the heroic struggle which forced the army to accept his return after eighteen years.

The Montoneros thought they had been promised a privileged role in the new government, some acknowledgment of the sacrifice along the way, the martyrs left behind and the outstanding capacity of idealistic young activists. That dream was now over.

"One minute we were the 'marvellous youth', then we became 'infiltrators'," explained Perdía, who recalled the silence in the room as they listened to Perón's words on that May Day 1974. Rodolfo had anticipated the rupture, criticising the Montoneros for "provoking" Perón, when a wiser strategy would have been to bide their time, increase their representation inside the popular movement and hold out for Perón's death.

Death of Perón

On July 2nd 1974 Juan Domingo Perón died, throwing the country into turmoil, even though his death had been anticipated for more than a year. His wife Isabel assumed office, a post she held onto until the March 1976 coup.

"Populovich has to edit the paper for the next few days," said Rodolfo Walsh at a special meeting convened to plan coverage of the funeral and mourning period. "I was surprised when he proposed my name," said Bonasso, alias Populovich. "He will best interpret the feelings of the nation," said Walsh. Bonasso lived up to Walsh's hopes, piecing together a 24-page homage to Perón, with photo essay, analysis and vox pops. One front page simply bore the word *Dolor* (pain) in bold letters, another carried a black banner headline, 'A CRY FROM THE HEART' (*Noticias* 4/7/74), beside a large photo of tearful women gathered in a house around an altar dedicated to the dead caudillo.

Noticias produced several special supplements on the historic event, with staff working days and nights to cover the period of national mourning. When the frenzy died down an assembly was held at the paper to evaluate the coverage. Caparrós almost fell off his chair when Walsh named every one of his colleagues at the crime desk, praising them for their hard work and commitment. In finest Walsh style he told the workers' assembly that his department had worked precisely 138 hours and 14 minutes in the previous week. "I was chuffed that he noticed the work and mentioned it," said Caparrós.

Circulation soared to 150,000 copies a day, creating a fresh set of problems, as the paper now required nightly delivery to three separate printers to keep up with demand.

Noticias outsold their tabloid rivals, predicted winners at the races and faced down stuffy political superiors yet they still faced another serious obstacle to running a newspaper – the distribution mafia. "These guys killed a paper if they wanted to," said Goyo Levenson, explaining how entire delivery batches of *Noticias* would simply disappear, stolen or abandoned by powerful distributors.

The distribution issue was resolved by Walsh, Bonasso and Levenson, who paid a visit to the director of the company in charge of the job. Each day the freshly printed paper would be stacked outside the company doors for loading and distribution at about 3 a.m. "You know who owns this paper?" asked Bonasso, referring to the poorly concealed links between *Noticias* and the Montonero rebels. "The *muchachos* are getting restless," he added. The company chief, a former navy captain, was apologetic but non-committal.

Bonasso suddenly banged the director's desk for effect, while Walsh was tight-lipped and acted coolly, modelling himself on a hard man from a Chandler novel. Levenson wondered if they would get out of the building alive, their guns deliberately showing every time they "arranged" their overcoats.

The visit did the trick and distribution problems ceased.

In March 1974 a bomb exploded outside the offices of *Noticias*, miraculously failing to cause deaths or injury, but the incident suggested that the paper's days were numbered. The office atmosphere became increasingly tense as the production of the paper each day turned into a military operation, with the newspaper vehicles shot at by Triple A gunmen.

The three print runs required to publish the paper tripled the risks of attack; armed escorts accompanied the paper to the printer, with occasional shootouts along the way.

The Montonero escort left the paper in a Catch-22 situation. If they travelled unarmed they risked a Triple A ambush, but if they went armed they ran an equal chance of being stopped by the Triple A in uniform (Federal Police) and facing charges of weapons possession.

The *Noticias* staff were warned to take precautions when leaving the office, travelling in groups and changing their routines. If anyone wanted a drink they took it with them into the office. When the paper was finished Rodolfo would leave the building with Gelman, Urondo and Bonasso.

One night they squeezed into a small car, backing out of the street as a colleague's vehicle blocked the oncoming traffic to prevent an ambush. "It was a stupid thing to do," said Bonasso, "if they had ambushed us they would have killed the entire editorial staff in one go." In the event of attack the group was too cramped to even draw their guns, let alone shoot. The situation was nerve-wracking yet comic, as the over-enthusiastic driver took off with a screech of rubber only to find he was racing the wrong way up a one-way street, almost running over a police officer standing outside a police station.

The Renault 4 stopped at the police checkpoint, but the registration papers couldn't be found. "Machine guns poked in through the windows," said Bonasso, who didn't know whether to laugh or cry. Every one of the car occupants had a weapon on him. Walsh used to carry his pistol in an unusual position, tucked into the front of his trousers.

"I told him he was going to blow his balls off one day," said Bonasso.

The search for a driver's licence produced only a pair of old socks and a stale sandwich.

The ordeal ended when Bonasso pulled out his journalist ID, apologising for the bad driving, muttering something about a rush to an impending interview, praying the officer wouldn't know what type of newspaper *Noticias* was. The ruse worked but the car broke down shortly afterwards. The weary group waited in a nearby café, more vulnerable than they could ever have imagined.

"Those Triple A people must be a bunch of complete losers," commented Bonasso: "they could have beaten us to death with a pair of high-heeled shoes, never mind blowing us away with bullets."

On August 2nd 1974, *Noticias* published a letter written by disgruntled Federal Police officers. It highlighted internal dissent over Alberto Villar's leadership. "As police officers and patriots," began the letter, "we feel obliged to point out that the current police leadership, in its illegal use of the police apparatus, is fomenting an atmosphere of chaos and instability in the country, undermining confidence in Perón's government and paving the way for a coup." The letter described how officers were ordered to destroy evidence and release killers on direct orders from Villar. "Such illegality offends, contradicts and ridicules our purpose, which is not determined by one boss but by the laws of the country." Many of Villar's own officers despised him, blaming his reign of terror for the backlash against the men in uniform. The average officer lived in permanent fear, never knowing when he might become a target of those seeking revenge for the torture or assassination of an activist (*Noticias* 9/8/74).

Shortly afterwards a second bomb exploded outside *Noticias* injuring a woman who lived next door.

On August 28th Villar led a convoy of patrol cars and stormed into the *Noticias* office, guns and grenades at the ready: "I have the pleasure to inform you that I bear orders to close down this nest of subversives," said the police chief, unable to conceal his joy. "Where is Rodolfo Walsh's desk, WHERE IS IT?" Villar demanded, scattering papers but finding nothing of interest. "I know you have a coffin prepared for me," he said, looking at Walsh's empty chair, as if talking to him. "Well, I have a coffin for you too."

It took just 35 days for Walsh to fulfil the first half of Villar's prophecy. The police raid put an end to a remarkable experiment in committed, quality journalism. The line-up was a journalistic dream team, the survivors now occupying central roles in Argentinian letters: Bonasso is a best-selling author, Verbitsky is one of Argentina's leading investigative journalists, Juan Gelman was named Poet of the Year in 1998, and other staff are scattered throughout prestigious European magazines.

The police arrived and cordoned off the *Noticias* building, waiting for further orders. The newspaper filed a court order to reopen the paper, which took weeks to process. In the meantime, a month's wages were sitting in a safe inside the office, which was guarded by police, while a police station was located within sight of the building.

The *Noticias* office was a two-storey building with a skylight and a rooftop terrace. A few days after the paper was closed down, a Montonero unit climbed over neighbouring roofs and landed on the terrace. They removed the skylight, dropped into the office, opened the safe with their keys and escaped the same way they had come in.

A week later, as the judicial system dragged its heels, the judge agreed to send a delegation to make an inventory of the *Noticias* office. The night before the judge visited the building, the Montonero furniture removal team went into action. First they stripped down a prefab building which squatted on the roof, then they removed 50 desks, 100 chairs and about 100 typewriters; the contents were hauled back up through the skylight and away. The next day the judge responsible for the case broke the seal on the police tape and entered the office, finding nothing but empty floor space. The *Noticias* archive had been safely delivered to Walsh who anticipated the coup ahead and began working on his next media venture – an underground news agency.

In September 1974 Isabel Martínez de Perón introduced a new anti-subversive law which established prison sentences of five years for any journalist or newspaper owner who published information that "disturbed or eliminated the institutional order". Soon after that it became illegal to even mention the guerrilla groups by name, making it difficult for the Montoneros to explain or justify their actions to the public. *La Causa Peronista*, the remaining radical paper, was shut down in September 1974. The situation deteriorated further when the Interior Minister announced that the state of siege would continue for an indeterminate period of time, clearing the way for all-out confrontation.

Armed groups would briefly seize radio stations and publish communiqués but the results failed to counteract the impact of official propaganda. A year later *El Auténtico* appeared every fortnight, its Montonero sympathies partially disguised by verbal caution. It lasted just eight issues. At the beginning of 1975 *Evita Montonera* was launched, a clandestine weekly outlining armed actions and political strategy. The paper was distributed by word of mouth, circulating only within activist circles, thus limiting its usefulness. Eight issues were published that year, with an estimated circulation of 70,000, in total.

The absence of communication channels meant that the guerrilla actions had to "explain themselves" or risk backfiring on the organisation. The care required to ensure that each armed operation was understood by the public flew in the face of the planned upsurge in military action which turned the organisation into a war machine, fighting now to take power, rather than merely open up democratic spaces. The Montoneros established themselves as the most powerful urban guerrilla movement in Latin America but the seeds of their downfall had already been sown (Gillespie, 1998 pp. 234–6).

chapter thirteen

Walsh and the Montoneros, 1975–77

"Give up," suggested Laurenzi.
   "Not yet."
   "It's over."
   "In theory," I shot back. "But the important thing is to find out if you can beat me. Let's face it, I'm not playing against theory, I'm playing against you."
                 ("Trasposición de Jugadas", Walsh, 1992 p.75)

Endgame

The political stakes were high in Argentina by the time *Noticias* was shut down in August 1974. Rodolfo increased his security measures, reduced his public outings, abandoned routines, perfected his disguises and avoided meeting people at home. He lived between Carapachay 459 along the Tigre riverbank and the apartment he rented with Lilia in the centre of Buenos Aires. Perón was dead, his wife Isabel was president but real power lay with José López Rega and his Triple A death squads.

The *Noticias* archive was delivered to Walsh, who took charge of a treasure trove of files, clippings and intelligence work which would soon be put to use in a novel type of news agency. Rodolfo focused his energy and intelligence on strategies which would aid the Montoneros's armed resistance efforts, as legal avenues for political expression were brutally shut down while dissidents were kidnapped, tortured and shot dead.

The streets of Buenos Aires had become death traps for militants. Montonero combatant Nicolas Casullo opted for exile after thugs entered his home and scrawled death threats on the walls of his living room. Casullo was lucky to get a warning. The decision to go into exile was an agonising one which left a whiff of betrayal in its wake. Casullo recalled a hurried, awkward goodbye from fellow militants, among them Vicki Walsh. "I suppose you realise this is desertion," said one member of his *ambito* or revolutionary cell, "if you go you're abandoning all your convictions, your compañeros, your life" (Anguita and Caparrós, 1998a p.468).

"Argentina seemed to have gone completely mad," recalled Tununa Mercado, who had begun a second period of exile in 1974, as the country suffered rampant inflation, a political killing every five hours and a bomb blast every three hours (Gillespie, 1998 p.272).

Rodolfo had no interest in leaving the country, determined to resist shoulder to shoulder with the common people, despite the growing security risks. From his early involvement with the Fuerzas Armadas Peronistas, Walsh was aware of the extreme anxiety suffered by activists involved in armed actions. The organisation held internal discussions on the issue, in which Walsh argued strongly for the availability of counselling to activists. Walsh recommended the work of Laura Bonaparte, one of Argentina's leading psychoanalysts and a committed revolutionary. She believed that certain compañeros should be withdrawn from positions of combat to less exposed positions in an effort to safeguard their mental health.

Every time a militant left his or her home, they were unsure as to whether they would ever see their partner or child again. Bonaparte, a member of the FAP, felt that the decision to give one's life on behalf of others and the reality of taking another's life had potentially devastating consequences. "In the case of some combatants," explained Laura, "something came unhinged after an armed confrontation, something which had its source in the individual life story of each person."

One evening Raimundo Villaflor arrived at her house with a stranger, who she later discovered was Rodolfo Walsh. "He was a great listener," she recalled, "he didn't say much, he just wanted me to talk through my ideas." Bonaparte had been receiving FAP combatants who showed signs of psychological disturbance and she proposed relocating them away from the battlefield.

"Rodolfo was obsessive about the details," recalled Laura, "that made me feel much better, as the opinion I gave was a difficult one, which went against accepted wisdom." The FAP leadership accepted her idea, yet it was her own colleagues in the psychoanalytic profession who proved more difficult to convince. "At that time psychoanalysts believed that the revolution could be won from the couch, such arrogance!" added Laura, who finally prevailed within her profession. The army got wind of the role played by psychiatrists in counselling combatants and added them to their list of "subversives".

Rodolfo reacted to the increasing tension and terror by combining his information and intelligence work with special attention to what he called the Frente Armónico Interno, or Harmonious Internal Front. Walsh placed great emphasis on core relationships that provided support and sustenance in times of great tension.

Walsh was thinking principally about his most intimate relationship, the love he shared with Lilia Ferreyra. "When the outside world is crashing down around you," said Lilia, expanding on the concept, "when all certainties are undermined, then, Rodolfo believed, personal relations took particular priority."

On the practical issue of self-protection, Rodolfo's network of police contacts helped him stay abreast of unfolding events, occasioning a certain cockiness. "I'm a day ahead of them," snapped Walsh to his brother Carlos during a rare family gathering in 1974. It was the last time they would meet.

Many of Rodolfo's friends told me that their last meeting with him occurred around 1975, as social gatherings were restricted to an intimate circle: Lilia, his two daughters, Horacio Verbitsky and his Montonero cell companions. Some sharp-eyed friends still spotted him in the city centre but knew better than to approach him, as he clearly didn't want to be recognised or greeted.

Death of a police chief

Walsh's patient intelligence-gathering work, cultivated over the previous two decades, began to pay handsome dividends. In November 1974, acting on inside information, a Montonero commando set off in a dinghy and silently approached a motor boat docked in Tigre. Máximo Nicoletti,[42] an expert diver, submerged himself in the water and resurfaced beside the motor boat, where he planted a huge bomb, unnoticed. Nicoletti and the team retreated to a safe distance and waited for Alberto Villar, Buenos Aires Federal Police chief, to return to his boat.

The automatic detonator failed the first time, then failed again but connected at the third attempt, shattering the silence of the delta, instantly killing Villar and his wife. The blast could be heard at the Olivos presidential residence several miles away. Villar's death was widely celebrated; in the months before his assassination, thousands of people at public demonstrations called for Villar's head, chanting "Montonero, listen to the people/we want the head of Villar and Margaride."

The operation demonstrated technical skill and answered a popular call for justice, but also precipitated the suspension of constitutional guarantees, on November 6th 1974. Rodolfo was now on active service for the Montoneros, co-ordinating police and army informers to gather

---

[42] Nicoletti was subsequently detained by the army and collaborated with navy intelligence, turning in former comrades. In the 1990s he led a "super-gang" of armed robbers, was caught and given a lengthy prison sentence.

information and prepare further armed operations. The long, twisting path from right-wing nationalism to left-wing revolutionary action was complete: "Total inflexibility is justified by the difficulty of the road ahead," wrote Walsh in his diary in September 1968 (Walsh, 1996, p.83). Back then he struggled to reconcile ideas with actions. The dilemma had been resolved by the dramatic pace of events, as he joined first the FAP and then the Montoneros in October 1973.

As the nation's democratic institutions began to crumble, undermined by State terror and economic downturn, the CGT union bureaucrats faced rebellion from the grassroots. The rebellion manifested itself in Villa Constitución, a sprawling working-class neighbourhood, home to one of the country's most important metallurgical plants. Three companies dominated the town, including Acindar, a subsidiary of US Steel. The workers had long tried to wrest union control away from official CGT bureaucrats and in 1974 a centre-left coalition swept to victory in a local union election, with 64 per cent of votes.

In March 1975, Acindar's chief shareholder José A. Martínez de Hoz, a large landowner and close friend of the Rockefeller dynasty, warned Isabel of the climate of insurrection which reigned in Villa Constitución. The scaremongering came at a time when production had increased under the new union leadership and not a single hour's worth of strikes was recorded. On March 20th 1975 a convoy of Ford Falcons silently converged on Villa Constitución, launching an occupation of the town which resulted in a rampage of anti-labour terror. The operation was ordered by Federal Police chief Margaride, with López Rega contributing firepower.

The workers struck back, holding out for 59 days on strike. By the end of the struggle one worker in eight was fired and blacklisted by factories in the area; one out of every 100 people in Constitución was jailed; one out of every 1,000 was murdered; one out of every 2,200 remains *desaparecido*, missing (M.E. Anderson, 1993 pp.146–8).

The US connection

One of the prominent people who courted the favour of José López Rega was US businessman-diplomat Robert Hill, appointed to the Board of Directors of United Fruit Co. as a reward for his role in promoting the CIA coup in Guatemala in 1954.

He was also a Trustee of the American Institute for Free Labour Development, which actively infiltrated and divided Latin American labour movements. In December 1973 President Nixon appointed Hill as US ambassador to Argentina. The appointment was considered a clear sign that the US viewed growing class conflict in Argentina as a threat to

US interests.

Ambassador Hill immediately signed an anti-narcotics agreement with López Rega, signalling the green light for covert political action. "Drugs are an essential aspect of the guerrilla struggle," said López Rega, who claimed that captured rebels were invariably discovered to be high on drugs. When they sobered up, said López Rega, they begged for their mothers (*Noticias* 29/5/74).

In a subsequent press conference López Rega confirmed that the "war on drugs" was part of a broader political plan, namely "the war on subversion". US technical and financial aid was now used to assemble the Triple A death squads, in an imitation of Plan Phoenix, used to eliminate thousands of political opponents in Vietnam.

The rise of Argentina's popular movement had alarmed US companies and local representatives of US national security agencies, as illegal kidnappings became weekly occurrences. Classified documents later revealed that many of the kidnappings attributed to guerrillas were actually carried out by State security forces, taking advantage of the reigning confusion to reap financial benefits for themselves.

The guerrillas did manage to pull off dozens of high-profile kidnappings, notably of the Born brothers, business magnates with Bunge and Born, released after a US$60 million ransom was paid, a huge heist in 1974. The money from the ransom added up to the equivalent of one third of the entire defence budget for that year.

In a revealing insight into US thinking on Argentina, the US State Department's handbook on Argentina (1974) dedicated an important section to "Subversive Activity". The report gave a description of the four principal guerrilla groups, before contemplating "two opposite points of view" on how to eliminate the threat. According to US analysts, the Federal Police advocated "combing" operations in Buenos Aires, with dawn raids and surprise roadblocks. This strategy however, had been tried before, proving "extremely irritating to innocent people" and "costly in men and resources".

The second approach, which "had the endorsement of top military circles" consisted of "letting the urban guerrilla movement develop and unify itself, making it possible for the authorities to infiltrate a particular level of the organisation". Argentina's army leadership was heavily influenced by counter-insurgency methods imported from Algeria and Indochina through French army instructors.

"There are difficult days ahead," warned ambassador Hill in his "Country Analysis and Stategy paper", published the day before the March 1976 coup. "The strategy is essentially one of protecting our people and property from terrorism, and our trade and investment from economic nationalism during this trying period."

In the months after the coup, ambassador Hill's enthusiasm for the rampaging generals was dampened by the case of an embassy employee whose son, a student, was disappeared by the regime. By then Nobel Peace prizewinner Henry Kissinger had met the junta's foreign minister Admiral César Guzzetti. "How long will it take to clean up the problem?" asked Kissinger. Guzzetti assured him that political subversion would be wiped out by the end of the year. Kissinger gave the green light for State terror to continue, if the "problem" was resolved by January 1977, when the US Congress reconvened.

Changes afoot

On June 27th 1975 the CGT organised a work stoppage and a rally at the Plaza de Mayo, in what looked like a show of support for President Isabel Martínez but also allowed workers to loudly denounce Celestino Rodríguez, the Economy Minister, and his political mentor José López Rega. "The ship is sinking and we're not going down with it," said one union leader. The besieged president was forced to sacrifice López Rega, who retreated to the presidential residence in Olivos; matters did not improve, as he then controlled access to Isabel. Pressure mounted to get rid of López Rega after a group of cabinet ministers told her that the military demanded an end to his presence. The "minister of death", as he was called, packed his bags and left for Europe, still claiming the title of "extraordinary and plenipotentiary ambassador" as appointed by the late President Perón. The armed forces quickly took over López Rega's paramilitary terror squads, anxious to retake control of State repression ahead of their planned coup.

Meanwhile Walsh received a copy of the armed forces' "Battle Order", containing the plans for the upcoming coup. The document fell into Rodolfo's hands in mid-1975 thanks to the son of a general who secretly worked for Walsh's intelligence network. The contact was sent out to copy the document, the ink still fresh on the pages, where he made an extra one for Rodolfo.

Just as Walsh decoded cables in 1960 indicating the secret preparations for the Bay of Pigs landing, allowing Cuba time to prepare its defences, so too did Walsh inform the Montonero leadership that the coup was on its way. The advance warning period should have been sufficient to prepare defences, particularly safe hideouts, evacuation into exile and procedures to follow in case of arrest and torture. Instead, the Montonero leadership believed that the coup would favour their armed strategy and spark a civil insurrection, precipitating the speedy downfall of the military junta.

Walsh's importance to the Montonero movement did not go

unnoticed among the Cubans who advised the organisation to protect cadres like Rodolfo and Paco Urondo. "I want to be straight with you," said a Cuban military instructor, a Sierra Maestra veteran, during a five-day combat exercise with Montonero militants in Cuba. "We don't know of any better cadres than the Argentinians, they have exceptional intellect and morale, as combatants [...] you talk to Rodolfo Walsh, Paco Urondo or Santucho [...] they have 20 years' experience [...] do you understand what I'm getting at? You can't replace people like that overnight [...] when we lost a compañero like that, we felt it was the worst thing that could happen, worse than losing a battle [...] take care of them, none of them should die unnecessarily."

The advice was directed at Montonero militant Nicolas Casullo during a training trip to Cuba in June 1974. The origin of the advice came not from the instructor, but from a higher source: "that's what Fidel says, when he talks about you lot" (Anguita and Caparrós, 1998b p. 350).

Walsh studied the odds with the vast information at his disposal and came to the same conclusions, but limited his activity to passing on the information, failing to spark a debate ahead of the defeat. He also ignored the warning signals he saw inside the organisation, the arrogance and authoritarianism of the movement's leadership. Despite Walsh's immense experience, his late entry to the organisation left him operating at the rank of "second officer", several rungs away from the leadership; yet his track record and position as intelligence chief ensured him direct access to the leadership, who paid close attention to his comments, even if they were slow to act on them. A contemporary of Fidel Castro and Che Guevara, it was strangely anomalous that he did not occupy a top leadership post. His daughter Vicki, who joined the movement before him, had already achieved a higher rank, rising to the position of captain.

"If I had known how Rodolfo felt back then," lamented Miguel Bonasso, "it would have given me the confidence to challenge the leadership far earlier." Walsh stayed loyal to organisation discipline, refusing to break publicly with the leadership. Nicolas Casullo recalled the difficulty in raising internal issues with Rodolfo, his immediate superior in the organisation. "Walsh would let slip a phrase which let you know he was thinking along the same lines as you," explained Casullo, "but he refused to be drawn into a debate, simply arguing that all organisations had virtues and vices, and that the role of the combatant was to focus on the practical issue of defeating the enemy."

"Any unit which questions the leadership is to be dissolved," warned a Montonero policy document from that period. Members critical of movement policy were to be dispersed among other units, a move which backfired on the organisation. "Dissidence simply multiplied," said Horacio Verbitsky, who was assigned an "observer" after he expressed discrepancies with the direction of the movement. The "observer" was quickly won over to Verbitsky's critical perspective.

The Montonero leadership appealed to an abstract mystique surrounding the armed struggle but Walsh, Verbitsky and others brought a scientific rigour to the battlefield, insisting that the organisation's job was to know the enemy in order to defeat it.

Argentina's Clandestine News Agency

Walsh planned a mobile, low-tech response to State censorship and repression, which would abandon sloganeering rhetoric and focus instead on exposing the difficulties imposed on ordinary citizens in their daily lives. Rodolfo instructed a team of four trusted volunteers who began assembling information and files, combing the newspapers for fresh data, swapping snippets with Walsh's intelligence unit, which itself fed into a network of army and police informers. Walsh called his endeavour the Agencia Clandestina de Noticias, ANCLA (Clandestine News Agency).

"It was amazing the information to be had on the army and police in the mainstream papers if you knew where to look," recalled Lila Pastoriza, one of Walsh's recruits. Lila Pastoriza was a Communist Party member until the Che Guevara debacle in Bolivia, when that country's communist leadership effectively sabotaged Che's efforts to launch a guerrilla *foco* there (1967). Her criticism of party policy led to her expulsion.

Pastoriza worked briefly in the *Semanario CGT*, where she met Walsh, a friend of her partner Eduardo Jozami, who by late 1974 was a high-ranking Montonero leader. The Montoneros worked on a parallel media project, with Eduardo Jozami preparing the launch of a new paper, *Información*, which would act as the official organ of the armed group. "I had my differences with the Montoneros," said Pastoriza, smiling, as the term "differences" clearly failed to convey the contempt in which she held the Peronist true believers. Pastoriza volunteered as an activist in a shantytown but her paid employment was wrapping gifts for a shop. "I was a good wrapper," she told me.

Rodolfo and Lilia now lived a "hyper-clandestine" existence, antici-pating the imminent coup. The couple's last home in the city was in Calle Malavia, where they spent much of their time "plugged-in" to listening devices, feeding scraps of information to the Montoneros's intelligence network.

In different safe houses in the city Walsh would spend hours with his news volunteers, wandering from one person to the next, jotting down everything of interest in his long spiral notebooks. He sorted information into patterns which allowed him decipher the methodology of the Triple A death squads, using the same methods once applied to his crime fiction stories. His handwriting was meticulous, as tiny but impeccable letters grew into compact paragraphs which allowed him to squeeze copious quantities of notes into each page.

Walsh's underground news agency needed a name and an identity separate from the Montoneros's publishing ventures, one which would keep the security forces guessing over the nature of its origins. ANCLA took shape gradually, involving a small group of journalists who listened to international radio broadcasts and scoured the national media for information. The news was then collated and sent by post to foreign embassies, news agency correspondents, national media and international human rights organisations. The ANCLA team also collected information from neighbours, prisoners, army and police troops, anyone who exposed the State's murderous policy long before the extent of its terror operation was fully understood.

The first (and last) issue of the official Montonero propaganda organ *Información* was published on March 24th 1976, the day of the coup, an apt symbol of the organisation's poor interpretation of the rapidly unfolding events. The launch of a Montonero newspaper with fixed assets, offices, machinery and a printing press was a catastrophe at that time, a gift to the junta which shut down the unwieldy experiment overnight.

On that same night Rodolfo and Lilia were plugged in to army and police communications the whole evening, another ear to BBC World Service broadcasts, anxious to secure as much information as possible about the likely direction of events over the coming weeks and months. "If these guys win, this country is finished," said Rodolfo, who couldn't have imagined the scale of terror about to be unleashed. Repression increased with every fresh coup in Argentina yet Walsh and other combatants imagined an increase in deaths due to armed confrontations rather than the systematic elimination of all opponents to the regime.

When the military seized power they moved quickly to shut down all access to independent information, issuing Edict 19, which established a ten-year prison sentence for "any media which spreads, divulges or propagates news, communiqués or images with the intention of disturbing, prejudicing or discrediting the armed forces or police". In addition the junta ordered the media to promote "the correct use of the national language," prohibiting "double entendre" and "subliminal propaganda".

ANCLA's time had come: the military had banned the publication of all information relevant to their repressive regime but news still circulated throughout the country. In factories and law firms, in schools and on the streets, millions of eyes and ears saw and heard what was happening each day, even inside military barracks and police stations, where dissident officers took note of the unfolding horror. Walsh wanted ANCLA to report daily events but he also saw the importance of tying each loose end together, to build up a broader analysis of military misrule.

ANCLA newswire copy

... According to locals, the youth, who wore a blue suit and stood one metre and eighty-five centimetres tall, was intercepted by a light blue Ford Falcon. Four men in civilian clothes quickly got out of the vehicle. They attacked him without saying a single word, then tried to handcuff him and get him into the car. The youth tried desperately to resist and called out to the many passers-by in the area. During the fracas he received a blow in the head which knocked him to the ground, where his attackers savagely assaulted him once more. They tried vainly to control him. One of the stunned neighbours watched as one of the group, the fattest of them, took out a revolver and tried to hit the youth. The victim's strong physique made him difficult to subdue and he took a swipe at the gun which went off, landing a bullet in a nearby wall. He then managed to grab the weapon itself, take a shot and lightly injure his assailant. The rest of the group went into a rage, took out their weapons and executed the unlucky youth. Over twenty bullets hit his body, which lay face down, lifeless.

●◆ (December 21st 1976)

The ANCLA newswire pumped out a steady diet of eyewitness accounts from the terror zone, denouncing the intensity and magnitude of the regime's violence. The junta planned to create, in the minds of citizens, a climate of permanent conflict between "right-wing and left-wing extremists" with the State portrayed as a beleaguered power broker, striving to maintain order against all odds.

The State's propaganda department fabricated nightly gun battles between non-existent guerrillas and the security forces; the resulting corpses were found at dawn, all too real. They were prisoners who had been executed before they were taken to the scene of the "armed confrontation". Most citizens were prisoners in their homes, terrified they might be caught in the crossfire. The "subversives" who "died" in the fictitious battles were the unarmed civilians abducted during the day, tortured for information, then discarded. The stage management of the war against subversion paved the way for the spread of the "two demons" theory used by the regime to justify the repression, claiming that two implacable extremes were destroying the country.[43]

The snatch-squads who trawled the city for rebel sympathisers or collaborators, or their relatives and friends, were the front-line troops in the effort to instil fear in the common citizen. Kidnappings were witnessed by anything from five to five hundred people, as terrifying scenes occurred in bakeries, shops and other public places.

The chilling phrases *"por algo será"*, "there must be a reason", and *"algo habrán hecho"*, "they must have done something", became the mantras of a terrified population, as fear turned to relief when police and security forces picked up someone else, until the someone else became a relative or friend. By then it was too late.

In hundreds of similar cases, a death squad made up of six to twelve people, in three vehicles, arrived in a neighbourhood and demanded entry to a house, leaving women and children locked in a room while they searched the house for valuables. They would then lie in wait, for hours, or overnight on occasion, creating a *ratonera* or rat trap, waiting for an unlucky relative, friend or casual visitor to turn up. The new arrivals would be tied up and taken away, to face unspeakable torture and likely death. How many neighbours watched from behind their curtains, too petrified to warn anyone they recognised coming home?

Rodolfo Walsh wanted to break the isolation surrounding these incidents, name the assassins, identify their modus operandi. It was an essential reconstruction of the crime scene, just as in a murder case, except that this was a national crimewave in which all citizens were potential victims or unwitting accomplices and the killer was the State itself.

The State committed thousands of "perfect crimes", 30,000 dead, no witnesses, all evidence destroyed and the guilty pardoned before the investigation began. If they had paused to read Rodolfo's crime fiction work, which survived the general purge of his work, they would have realised that their crimes were witnessed by an entire nation, which slept with one eye wide open.

The success of the underground news agency can be measured by the response. On March 19th 1977, General Carlos Alberto Martínez, army intelligence chief, blamed ANCLA for what he called "the international vilification campaign against Argentina." The military junta opened up a press office in Paris to counteract the vivid descriptions offered by eyewitnesses of State terror. Army task groups periodically raided non-existent

---

[43] The two demons theory was written into the nation's history books on March 23rd 1998, when President Menem approved Decree 314/98, requiring the nation's educators "to remember the victims of the irrational violence unleashed by the armed groups and by the illegal repression." The decree spoke of "institutional rupture" rather than a military coup and never mentioned the estimated 30,000 *desaparecidos*.

printing presses and agency offices, puzzled at their inability to uncover any evidence of a functioning news agency.

The ANCLA team paid a high price for their bravery. Eduardo Suárez and Luis Guagnini were killed, along with Sergio Tarnopolsky, an army recruit and past assistant to navy torturer Jorge "Tigre" Acosta. The army not only killed Tarnopolsky, but also assassinated his parents, his wife and a 16-year-old sister. The price for informing from within army ranks was high: Mario Galli, a member of the coastguard, was also disappeared, along with his mother and pregnant wife. The testimony of the two army recruits provided the basis for ANCLA's 'History of the Dirty War in Argentina,' a timely exposé of terror inside the Escuela de Mecánica de la Armada, ESMA, where 5,000 prisoners were killed.

ANCLA news copy

... Security forces continued their constant operations in search of subversives, focusing on popular meeting places: bars, restaurants, squares, cinemas and even the circus. The self-styled "pedestrian control and sweep operations" consist of a tight, inescapable encirclement of a chosen location. The action usually takes place during the busiest time of the day. If a bakery is chosen for the search, then the entire block is sealed off beforehand, with side streets blocked by army trucks or police patrols. A platoon of soldiers led by an officer then enters the place, warning the surprised neighbours as to what is taking place. One by one, without exception, everyone must show their ID and have their cases or handbags searched. Then they check the bathrooms – in case anyone hides out there – and the basement of the business.

Sometimes the operation involves forcing everyone in a building to board a bus which has been emptied of its passengers. The detainees are taken to the nearest police station, where the identification procedure takes place.

Some of the businesses which have suffered this type of search are: the bakery between Heras and Azcuénaga; La Biela in the Recoleta neighbourhood; La Fragata in San Martin and Corrientes; De las Artes in Figueroa Alcorta and Pueyrredon; Café Tabac, on Figueroa Alcorta and others in the capital.

Another objective of Argentina's forces of repression are parks and squares. Anything up to two hundred men are involved in these cases, due to the huge area being searched. Not long ago one of these operations occurred in Circuit KDT – a typical Buenos Aires spot where every sport is practised, cycling in particular – a security operation in which two hundred people were searched and ten detained.

Lands which once belonged to the National Penitentiary system were also searched, in Las Heras between Salguero and Coronel Díaz, in the capital. A circus is based there and had to be evacuated during one search, provoking protests from the crowd. Two youths who were in attendance were beaten in full view of hundreds of children, including their own. At all times the army attitude is arrogant and aloof, according to witnesses.

Several youths who meet there to play football every Sunday were detained for not carrying their ID with them while a group of elderly women out sewing and chatting in the sun were surrounded for an hour and a half. The officer in charge told them that they should learn to carry ID with them when they leave their homes, provoking protests from the women and their husbands, who on hearing what was happening, had arrived on the scene.

In several cinemas and theatres troops have interrupted the show and repeated the behaviour described above. In one of those operations a youth was stopped for not having ID. When he was about to be transported to a police station he asked to speak to the commanding officer and told him he had "A Jockey Club ID",[44] a development which immediately changed his situation and saw him released.

Witnesses to the new operation techniques told this news agency that "the population repudiates these forms of persecution, as no one is spared the discomfort and fear they inspire, more so when they take place in moments of peace and relaxation."

●◆ (October 7th 1976)

Disguised lives

Walsh now lived on tenterhooks, a marked man, high on the junta's hit-list, protected only by his age and appearance, as a balding 50-year-old man was untypical of the guerrilla profile. Rodolfo was an enthusiastic combatant who evolved slowly toward a decisive revolutionary position. Once there he left all doubts behind and handed himself over to the struggle with unnerving certainty. Rodolfo also enjoyed the cloak-and-dagger aspects surrounding combat operations; before the coup occurred he often volunteered for *mimetización* tasks, which involved staking out a building or home which would be used for an operation. The challenge was to find a disguise which would allow him to spend sufficient time watching the street in question without drawing undue attention to himself.

One of his favourite disguises was as an ice-cream seller; he had a three-wheel bicycle cart with a basket in front, which he pedalled to the

---

[44] An exclusive country club.

required destination, then set up shop. True to his rigorous obsession with detail Walsh had a selection of ice creams for sale, change for the customers and even two different signs, "Noel" and "Ponela" which were used at different times to visit different neighbourhoods.

On other occasions Walsh would be dressed in priestly garb, complete with a cassock, a large cross, his solemn thick glasses, a bible and sandals. The cassock served to hide weapons while Walsh's Latin lessons in the Fahy school were sufficient for occasional blessings. One fellow militant, who recognised Walsh despite the disguise, received a wink and a blessing in return: "In the name of the father, the son and the holy ghost," intoned Walsh, blessing his surprised witness, before continuing in a whisper, "now fuck off home and leave me alone."

His other disguise was that of a newspaper-seller; he carried a range of daily papers, wore a vendor's cap and worked the streets. Rodolfo would buy up a dozen or more papers in town, then head to the area requiring surveillance duty. On the streets of Buenos Aires, an ice-cream seller, a priest and a newspaper-seller were unlikely to attract immediate suspicion. Other activists wore suits and ties and arranged contact meetings in fashionable hotels, another way to pass relatively unnoticed in the city.

Rodolfo had no qualms about participating in combat operations yet his most vital role in the armed organisation was his contribution to intelligence services, which fed into both the ANCLA project and the Montoneros's military apparatus. Rodolfo virtually slept with a pair of headphones clamped on his ears, eagerly lapping up all available scraps of information.

The information chain

Walsh recognised the "internal exile" forced upon Argentinians of conscience as citizens spent their time within the private realm of home and family, as fear paralysed the silent majority. Walsh believed that a prophetic voice would find fertile ground to plant seeds of dissent.

The Cadena Informativa (Information Chain, 1976–78) was a co-ordinated attempt to gather and distribute details about military misrule. "You too can be the Information Chain," announced Walsh and his network of informants, "a tool to free yourself and others from the terror. Make copies of this information by all the means at your disposal: by hand, typed, mimeographed. Send copies to your friends, nine out of ten will be waiting for it. Millions of people want information. Terror is based on incommunication. Break the isolation. Feel once more the moral satisfaction of an act of freedom" (Walsh, 1995 p.411).

Walsh viewed the information chain as a word-of-mouth

complement to ANCLA, whereby any individual could become a source of counter-information simply by writing up a story and leaving it somewhere public. The mechanism eliminated the need for risky meetings with fellow activists. The twin instruments of information dissemination recalled the principle upheld by Che Guevara, who, in a conference given on January 27th 1959, told a Havana audience that in the early days of the war against Batista, the presence of a journalist, "preferably North American", was more important than a military triumph (Winocur, 1963 p.13).

chapter fourteen

Critical retreat

We have to resist the dictatorship together with the people, organising ourselves in the struggle without delusions of grandeur and thinking a long way ahead.
(Walsh, 1994 p.212)

Lost patrol

"The Montonero leadership was always afraid of Rodolfo and his intelligence work," said Miguel Bonasso. Walsh's insight and experience into the world of radical politics was a threat to the organisation's control over policy. A similar case was Horacio Verbitsky, who was accused of being a "technocrat" for basing his projections about the fate of the struggle on the ample information at his fingertips. The Walsh team had privileged access to a wide range of data, combining the stories of ordinary people with media reports and the testimony of police and army dissidents or infiltrators. "They held him down at the rank of captain then ordered him to leave the country when it was too late," concluded Bonasso.

Montonero combatants numbered 5,000 in 1975, while active support was calculated at 100,000 people (Gillespie, 1998 p. 221). The crackdown on the media, even before direct military rule, was a key factor in isolating the movement from the masses. Once cut off, they could no longer explain their actions to the people in whose name they struggled.

The Triple A killed hundreds of militants before military rule began, enjoying total impunity. When their creator, López Rega, fell out of favour, the Triple A went into decline, as the army and police took control of State terror. "From the moment the armed forces assumed operational control over all security organs, every armed, uniformed man – independently of his social extraction and his ideas – contributes to the anti-popular repression and is co-responsible for the atrocities and killings committed by the repressors," announced the Montoneros in March 1976, justifying attacks on any officer in uniform.

The open season declared on every level of police activity was counterproductive, forcing Montonero combatants to carry out actions which mirrored the operations of the death squads. On March 13th 1976, eleven days before the coup, Montonero guerrillas mounted "police patrols" in a city suburb in reprisal for the death of a compañero. The guerrillas stopped passers-by, demanding ID, until they found a police officer, who was immediately executed.

The Montonero's Third National Military Campaign strategy called on activists to "multiply small operations" causing enemy casualties without direct engagement. "This means indiscriminate attack against all representatives of repressive institutions," explained the document. In the week before the coup, eight police officers were killed in Buenos Aires province, with ten more injured.

The Montonero reprisals demonstrated the military capacity of the guerrillas but failed to advance their political objectives. The relentless cycle of military action and clandestine existence isolated the movement from the masses, whose support was vital if the armed group was to have any hope of ending the dictatorship. The average Peronist sympathiser continued to go to work each day and risked his or her life by simply reading a Montonero newspaper, let alone engaging in some form of "productive" sabotage, as the organisation demanded.

"The policy of infiltration is incompatible with the military line which the party has followed since March," wrote Rodolfo on August 27th 1976, at the beginning of a series of documents offering constructive criticism to the leadership.

Before the order to kill police officers had been issued, the Montoneros had called for members to infiltrate the police, while disillusioned agents within police ranks were already passing on information to the organisation. "On the one hand we kill any police officer we can but at the same time we aspire to having compañeros on the inside," wrote Walsh, revealing a fundamental contradiction in Montonero policy.

Walsh had cultivated contacts within the police force since the 1950s and the resulting tipoffs and collaboration far outweighed the temporary satisfaction derived from a successful "kill" against rank-and-file police. During Héctor Cámpora's brief presidency in 1973, there was a hint of détente between security forces and the popular movement, notably during Operation Dorrego when army troops and Montonero militants teamed up to help victims of a flood. The short-lived Cámpora administration also appointed Ricardo Vitanni, Rodolfo's old friend, as deputy-chief of the Federal Police.

The Montonero battle order sounded the death knell for Walsh's meticulous rapprochement with disgruntled police, forcing him to rely on more vulnerable infiltrated agents. Argentina's police force was the first line in the "legal" repressive apparatus but in the early 1970s the force still contained hundreds of members who had Peronist sympathies and quietly tried to help the movement.

By the time military rule began in March 1976 many progressive officers within the police had been hounded out of the institution while the leadership openly backed terror tactics against political suspects. The Montoneros responded to the terror by planning a revenge attack on the Federal Police HQ. Walsh's inside agent, José María Salgado, carried an identical empty package into the police dining room every day for a week, before arriving with a powerful bomb on the appointed day, July 2nd 1976. The agent left the table seven minutes before the bomb exploded. The massive charge ripped through the room, killed everyone inside and triggered gas leaks which led to further explosions (Anguita and Caparrós, 1998, p.89). Walsh's most ambitious military operation left 42 police dead and 100 more injured.

Salgado was eventually captured and after several days of savage torture he gave away the information which led to Walsh's death. As the rate of capture increased, it became evident that many of the tortured militants were giving information to the enemy, permitting the security forces to piece together the internal structure of the Montoneros, its modus operandi and chain of command.

In September 1976 the Montonero leaders issued a communiqué in which they broached the subject of torture and talk: "A few have collaborated [...] those people belong to the ranks of infamy [...] the majority however gave us an example of bravery in death." "It isn't a crime to talk," countered Walsh, "getting arrested is the crime." Walsh had no illusions about the capacity of the enemy to extract information on the torture table. On his visit to Palestine in 1974, Walsh studied the tactics of Palestinian rebels, who instructed captured militants to hold out for 24 or 48 hours, before giving information away. Under that system the organisation had a window of opportunity to clear out of a building while giving the captured militant a small chance of survival by "informing" on a prearranged asset.

"If they capture me," Walsh warned his ANCLA colleagues, "pack up everything and start running." Walsh believed that the organisation had to help the captured combatant, giving them a margin of manoeuvre with which to save their lives. The Montonero leaders offered only suicide, ordering members to carry a cyanide pill which they should swallow before being captured.

On October 2nd 1976 the organisation almost killed the three junta leaders at a public ceremony, a blow which, if successful, would have had serious consequences for the regime. The failed bombing attempt highlighted the organisation's operational limits, now restricted to one-off spectaculars, while Montonero members died every day, a chronic bloodletting which was never reversed.

Less than two weeks later, the security forces kidnapped Marisa Murgier, who was carrying the list of all the organisation's contact points around the country. Two hundred Montonero militants were killed as a result, losses which would have been far greater were it not for inter-service rivalry, with the navy opting not to hand on the information to the army, which had better operating capacity. Two events, an unexploded bomb and a chance capture, shifted the balance of terror against the Montonero's resistance efforts.

In January 1977, despite all the evidence at hand, the Montonero leadership expressed optimism at the prospects of success in the coming year. The regime was losing political space, the working class repudiated their rule; the middle class no longer supported them; the grassroots church was in rebellion. In spite of all the evidence, the leadership claimed that the "definitive crisis of dependent capitalism" would permit the Montoneros "to lead the counter-attack of the popular forces".

Walsh delivered another set of criticisms, debunking the Montonero viewpoint in a manner normally reserved for the hated junta. Walsh began to realise that the organisation's leadership was deaf to all reason.

Between August 1976 and January 1977 Walsh wrote analyses which were not for publication, but to increase internal discussion within the Montonero movement. They were entitled, "A contribution to a resistance attempt", "The course of the war, according to the enemy" and "The state of the military enemy" (Baschetti, 1994 pp.206–40).

In his habitual style Rodolfo first cautioned against alarmism over the catastrophic developments that had occurred since the army seized power in March 1976. "If we correct our mistakes we can once more become a real alternative to those in power," wrote Rodolfo. "We have all the necessary time, if we know how to use it." The opening salvo was classic Walsh: a log book of catastrophes prefaced by an optimistic comment on the future. Walsh politely rubbished the Montonero leadership's analysis, citing "the retreat of the working class, the defeat of the middle sectors and the desertion of the intellectuals and professionals" (ibid). Walsh explained how the Peronist movement had created the Montonero guerrilla vanguard, and that the latter had grown through taking up its role as the force which would guide the mass movement toward democratic socialism with an emphasis on national economic development.

The army coup, wrote Walsh, had presented ideal conditions for the vanguard to shift the struggle decisively in their favour, had they remained in dialogue with their superior structure: the mass Peronist movement. "We didn't do it," admitted Walsh, "we decided that the principal fronts of confrontation were military ones and so we concentrated our attention on reaching ideological agreement with the ultra-left" (ibid).

The "ultra-left" was the Ejercito Revolucionario del Pueblo, ERP, which carried out armed actions even after the return of democracy in 1973, considering Perón a capitalist puppet. The return to military rule in March 1976 led to a reappraisal of Montonero–ERP relations and the move toward a federation of armed groups called the Organización para la Liberación de Argentina, emulating the Palestine Liberation Organisation. Talks broke down after the ERP leader Roberto Santucho was killed in June 1976.

Walsh had observed with growing alarm that the guerrilla vanguard had been cut off from the masses and now acted virtually alone, a "lost patrol" foundering in enemy territory, unable to reconnect with its home base. Isolated militants carried out sporadic acts of sabotage but nothing which could alter the army's programme of government.

Walsh proceeded to question the "triumphalist" tone of the Montonero leaders, even when events proved that the movement was up against the wall, facing an enemy far superior in resources and prepared to act with limitless brutality. "We decided that the enemy plans had failed utterly," complained Walsh, a grave error arising from "a lack of understanding of our own history".

The spectacular rise and rise of the movement, between 1970 and 1974, was attributed to the "genius" of the leadership, instead of a more mundane yet significant reason – "proposals which were understood and accepted by the people" (ibid).

The Montonero leadership had become intoxicated by its own success: "Our propaganda has to reach four million people," quoted Walsh with irony, urging the organisation to reduce its plans to the real dimensions of its operating capacity. Walsh didn't hesitate to give credit to the enemy where credit was due. "One of the greatest successes of the enemy was waging war against us instead of the broad mass of people" (ibid).

The armed forces were isolated in their role as an army of occupation but by playing to their rules, the Montoneros had plunged into a futile exchange between their military "apparatus" and that of the army, a battle they were always destined to lose. Walsh warned the movement leadership that the organisation was not ready for all-out war against the State. "What we have is a class struggle, with growing levels of violence, which we must intensify, but it's not a war yet" (ibid). The struggle to earn the right to represent the Argentinian people was a far more pressing task, Walsh believed, than the prosecution of a doomed war.

In spite of the claims of the movement, the military still maintained significant institutional support, including part of the bureaucratic union structure, the Catholic church hierarchy, and sectors within traditional political parties. The nation's second most powerful party, the Unión Cívica Radical, UCR, accepted political posts in the military government.

"We must be more self-critical and realistic. Of course there is a class struggle, there always has been and always will be, but one of the big successes of the government has been to wage war on us, not on the people as a whole. And this is largely due to our own mistakes, we isolated ourselves with ideology and our lack of political proposals for ordinary people" (ibid).

The consequence of isolation could be seen in every neighbourhood as "the masses ceased to be a safe space for us", permitting the detection of militants by the security forces. "We can presume that the masses are condemned to use their common sense," wrote Walsh, with a familiar touch of irony. "To assume as we sometimes do that the masses can retreat toward the Montoneros is to deny the basic element of a retreat which is to move from the most exposed positions to the least exposed" (ibid).

The Montonero leadership completed their annual report by predicting the imminent demise of capitalism. "We all wish this were the case," wrote Walsh, "but in practice our theory has galloped way ahead of reality. When this happens, the vanguard runs the risk of turning into a lost patrol" (ibid).

The lost patrol was speedily dismembered on the torture table, sealing the fate of each remaining member at large. The loss of each activist heightened the sense of isolation and danger, inducing a "state of defeat" which paralysed the organisation: "Very often, when an activist had someone close to them die, the resulting depression and weakness hurried up their inevitable end, couples often died within a short period of each other, not because one betrayed another, but out of sheer sadness" (Anguita and Caparrós, 1998a p.127).

Vicki Walsh

Vicki Walsh first came to live in Buenos Aires in 1965, aged 15, a teenager attending Guido Di Tella's renowned school of arts. In 1967 Vicki was selected to participate in a language exchange programme, spending a month with a family in Michigan, USA. Vicki fled her host family and the authoritarian father after one day, before finding a more congenial home.

Vicki admired her father but resented the lack of contact she had with him, which he put down to his erratic lifestyle. Always a star pupil, Rodolfo and Elina would joke over which of the two parents Vicki most resembled: "she gets it all from me," Rodolfo would say, before Elina cut him short.

Lilia Ferreyra had just moved into Rodolfo's apartment in 1968 when Vicki paid a surprise visit to her father. "I heard a voice calling *'Papá,'*" recalled Lilia. Rodolfo had left earlier that morning for a conference in La Plata. Lilia pretended to be asleep as Vicki peeked in, saw Lilia and left. Vicki soon left her mother's home and moved to Buenos Aires, where she demanded a share in Rodolfo's life. She developed a close relationship with Lilia and suggested the three of them share a home together. Vicki looked around for an apartment but just as the move was about to happen she fell in love, altering her accommodation plans. The object of her affection was Andres Alsina, a young Uruguayan who moved to Argentina in the late 1960s, his father a friend of Horacio Verbitsky's. Vicki had just turned 21, a carefree woman savouring the joys of passion while also nurturing her growing commitment to social justice. "She used to drop into my house, she borrowed make-up, what I saw back then was a young woman tasting real romance," said Lilian Hezler, a friend of the Walsh family.

Vicki's life changed dramatically when she met Emiliano Costa in 1972 at a meeting of the Agrupación de Prensa 26 de Enero, a Peronist press union. The two activists fell in love even as Vicki was still going out with Alsina. In the early months of the relationship Vicki's militancy in the FAP clashed with Emiliano's loyalty to the FAR even though the two groups eventually fused. In November 1972 Vicki joined the FAR, resolving that particular conflict. Emiliano was a member of the national committee of the Juventud Peronista but was also a FAR leader, involved in negotiations to fuse that organisation with the Montoneros, a move finalised in October 1973.

The FAR paid the rent of his small apartment and gave him 100 pesos a month to live on, an austere existence complemented by Vicki's salary in *La Opinión* newspaper. Emiliano's leadership post occupied most of his time, annoying Vicki, who was unaware of the extent of his role, such was the need for secrecy at the time. Vicki complained that she ended up doing the domestic chores and that they rarely got to spend much time with each other. "You're becoming more and more like other compañeros," she said, "when it comes to everyday things, let the women take care of it [...] as the organisation grows I see more and more machismo."

Women and the Montoneros

The role of women in the armed movement was a constant topic of discussion. In Argentina, the two main armed groups, Montoneros and ERP, published strict internal guidelines which regulated the formation and separation of couples. Unions with non-combatants were strongly discouraged. Guerrilla chiefs were also separated from their posts for so-called "skirt scandals" when they began affairs with compañeras behind the back of their own partner, who was also frequently a member of the organisation.

The Montoneros encouraged women to have children, accepted them as combatants but kept them away from positions of leadership. Osvaldo Bayer recalled a conversation he had with Walsh in which Bayer recounted the attitude of militant anarchists in the 1920s, who argued that women should remain away from the front line. Walsh felt their struggle had a different approach. "Our women combatants deserve better, they believe in the revolution, like us, they demand equality, they debate ideas, they bring new ideas, they are firm, brave and work hard. Why deny them a prominent role? Despite motherhood, despite the burden of child-rearing, despite knowing that only in exceptional cases will they get to occupy an important role at the hour of victory, despite their awareness that men will always use them, they continue to struggle [...] Women participate in the danger, out of pure idealism, without calculation."

Vicki earned the respect of fellow activists, and the organisation sent her on a delegation to Cuba, where she saw first-hand the successes and contradictions of Castro's revolution. Vicki played guitar and sang for her hosts, a slender but strong presence. In April 1974 Vicki split up briefly with Emiliano and moved into an apartment with Rodolfo and Lilia. She left Emiliano with the task of deciding whether he was committed or not to their relationship. It would be six months before Emiliano resolved his doubts and told her he was ready to be with her: "My dream is to be with you, I would love to have a child with you," he said, melting any resentment at the temporary split (Anguita and Caparrós, 1998a p.463).

Within a few months Vicki was pregnant. Such was the pressure of the times that it fell to Emiliano to take the urine sample to the doctor and collect the test that confirmed Vicki's pregnancy. Vicki sensed the impermanence that marked their relationship and the need to enjoy the times they had together, "when you feel death around each corner, that's when you most appreciate life," she told him.

Vicki rose quickly through the ranks of the Montoneros, displaying bravery and determination. Old friends recalled a growing inflexibility, a hardening of the heart which reflected her all-or-nothing gamble on armed revolution. Vicki and Emiliano were married on January 3rd 1975 in a brief ceremony in a civil registry office in Calle Uruguay, downtown Buenos Aires. A tense moment occurred when Walsh was introduced to Miguel Costa, Vicki's father-in-law, a retired air force commander.

"Nice to meet you," said Costa.

"My pleasure," answered Walsh.

"Well, now we're all family," replied Costa, winning a smile from Walsh.

Emiliano's parents found them an apartment in a neighbourhood associated with the military, as Vicki's pregnancy advanced toward the big day, while armed training continued. It was to be a short-lived period of family unity. The couple took off to Rodolfo and Lilia's home in Tigre, where Vicki shot herself in the foot during shooting practice. A few days' rest followed, in which the couple read and chatted together. It was a fortuitous period away from their hectic activity.

In a moment of carelessness Emiliano dropped his wedding ring between the wooden slats of the cottage floor, helplessly watching it swirl away in the river below. Vicki scolded him while he took the loss as a bad omen: "Maybe the end is near," he said, unable to sleep, staring into the darkness beyond.

Emiliano was detained and imprisoned on April 17th 1975, accused of involvement in the kidnap of industrialist Jorge Born. He spent the next eight years behind bars. On August 1st 1975 a telegram reached Emiliano in prison: "Congratulations! Our daughter Victoria María Costa Walsh was born today. She weighed 3.1 kilos. I love you. Vicki."

Vicki's clandestine life made it impossible for her to visit him and contact was limited to occasional letters signed in the name of her cousin. They never saw each other again.

Letter to Vicki

Dear Vicki,

News of your death reached me today at three in the afternoon. We were in a meeting when the communiqué came through. I heard your name pronounced wrong and it took me a second to take it in. I crossed myself automatically, like I did as a child, but didn't finish the gesture. The world suddenly came to a halt.

"She was my daughter," I said to Mariana and Pablo. I ended the meeting.

I am disoriented. I often feared it would happen, I thought it was too lucky, avoiding such a blow, when so many others had suffered. Yes, I feared for you, as you feared for me, although we never used to say it. Now fear has become affliction. I know all too well what you lived and fought for. I am proud of those things. You loved me, I loved you. You turned 26 the day they killed you. The last few years were very hard for you.

I would like to see you smile again.

I won't say goodbye, you know why. We die hunted and in darkness. Your final resting place is in my memory. That's where I keep you, I cradle you, I celebrate you and maybe I envy you, pet.

I spoke to your mother. She is proud in her pain, secure in having understood your short, tough, marvellous life.

Last night I had a monstrous nightmare: there was a cloud of fire, powerful but contained around the edges, which burst up from the deepest of depths.

Today on the train a man said: "I'm truly suffering. I would like to go to sleep and wake up in a year's time." He spoke for himself but he also spoke on my behalf.

Letter to my friends

It is three months to the day since my daughter María Victoria died after a gun battle with army troops. I know that most of you who knew her mourned her and others; my own friends or those acquainted with me, wanted to console me in some way. I am writing to thank you all and also to explain how and why Vicki died.

The army communiqué, published in the papers, doesn't differ that much from the truth on this occasion. Vicki was a second officer of the Montonero organisation, in charge of the press union, and her *nom de guerre* was Hilda. She was at a meeting that day with four members of the political secretariat who fought and died alongside her.

I don't know exactly when she joined the Montoneros. At twenty-two years of age, when she probably joined up, she was known for her firm and clear decisions. At that time she began working in the daily *La Opinión* and quickly became a journalist, although that work didn't interest her overmuch. Her colleagues elected her union representative, a role in which she had to face a difficult showdown with the editor of the paper, Jacobo Timmerman, whom she disliked intensely. She lost the battle and when Timmerman began to denounce his own journalists as guerrillas she asked for time off and never went back.

She went to work in a *villa*, her first contact with the absolute poverty in whose name she struggled. She emerged from this experience with an impressive asceticism.

Her husband, Emiliano Costa, was arrested at the beginning of 1975 and she never saw him again. Their daughter was born shortly after. The last year of my daughter's life was very tough. Her sense of duty led her to put off all individual pleasure and work way beyond her physical capacity. Like so many youths who suddenly turn into adults, she was all over the place, fleeing from house to house. She never complained but her smile was a bit more forced.

In the final weeks many of her compañeros were killed but there was no time to mourn them. She was burdened by the urgent need to set up outside communication on the media front, which was her responsibility. We saw each other once a week, or every fortnight, brief meetings while walking along the street, or ten minutes on a park bench. We made plans to live together, to have a place where we could talk, or remember, or just be silent together. We sensed however that this wasn't going to happen, that any one of these furtive meetings would be the last and we said goodbye feigning bravery, consoling ourselves before the anticipated loss.

My daughter was prepared to fight to the death. It was a mature decision. She knew, through endless testimony, the treatment dispensed by the army to anyone unlucky enough to fall prisoner. The skinning alive, the mutilation, the torture without limits in time or in cruelty, while also achieving a moral humiliation, that of betrayal. She knew perfectly well that in a war of such proportions, the issue was not about talking but about being taken prisoner in the first place. She always carried a cyanide pill on her – just like the one with which our friend Paco Urondo killed himself – just as many others have obtained a final victory over barbarity.

On September 28th (1976), when she entered the house on Calle Corro, she turned 26 years of age and was carrying her daughter in her arms, as she had been unable to find anyone to leave her with. She lay down with her, in her nightdress. She wore these absurd white nightdresses which were always too big for her.

At 7 a.m. the next day she was woken by army loudspeakers and the first shots. Following a pre-arranged defence plan she went up on the roof with political secretary Molina while Colonel, Salame and Beltran returned fire from the ground floor. I have witnessed the scene through her eyes, the roof overlooking the houses, the brightening sky and the encirclement. One hundred and fifty men dug in, with a tank. I received the testimony of one of these men, a conscript.

"The battle lasted over an hour and a half, a man and a woman firing from up above. The woman stood out because every time she fired a machine gun burst and we took cover, she laughed."

I have tried to understand this laughter. The machine gun was a Halcon and my daughter had never fired one, although she knew how to use it from previous training. New and surprising things always made her laugh and this latest novelty was both those things: to discover that a simple pressure of the finger brought forth a burst which made one hundred and fifty men run for cover on the cobblestones, beginning with Colonel Roualdes, the operation chief.

In addition to the trucks and tanks there was a helicopter hovering above the roof, protecting itself from the fire. "Suddenly", said the soldier, "there was a silence. The woman put the machine gun down, she stood over the parapet and opened her arms. We stopped shooting without even being told and we took a good look at her. She was thin, with short hair and wore a nightdress. She began speaking to us in a loud but calm voice. I don't remember everything she said but I remember the last phrase: it keeps me awake at night. 'You can't kill us,' she said, 'we choose to die.' Then she and the guy with her put guns to their heads and killed themselves in front of us."

There was no more resistance down below. The Colonel opened the door and threw a grenade in. Then the officers went in, finding a one-year-old girl, sitting on a bed, and five dead bodies.

Over time I have thought about this death, I have asked myself if all those who die like her had another option. The answer comes from the depth of my heart and I want my friends to know it. Vicki could have chosen other paths which were different but no less honourable, but the one she chose was the most just path, the most generous path, the most thought-through path. Her lucid death is the synthesis of her short, happy life. She didn't live for herself, she lived for others, and those others can be counted in their millions.

Her death, yes her death, was gloriously hers and in that pride I steady myself and it is I who am reborn in it. That is what I wanted to say to my friends and what I would like them to pass on to others by whatever means decency dictates.

●◆ (Walsh, 1996)

We choose to die

When Rodolfo heard the news of Vicki's death, he went home to Lilia, where he lay down on a bed and collapsed, inconsolable with grief and infinite sadness. They held each other. Words were unnecessary. Weeks later, when Lilia borrowed her parents' car and moved their possessions to their new home in San Vicente, a photo of Vicki appeared. "Rodolfo recoiled, as if struck by a physical object," recalled Lilia. He would never recover from the blow, his morale and his will to live suffering irreparable damage.

Rodolfo knew all too well that his example had played a major role in Vicki's decision to follow his political path, even if she formally joined the Montoneros ahead of him. Rodolfo was fiercely proud of her. Now he was devastated. Something in him died with her.

The prospect of exile was again a permanent topic of discussion among organisation members. Rodolfo was bitterly opposed to leaving the country but when conditions became intolerable he mentioned Cuba as a possible refuge, the only country where he could exercise his militancy in a revolutionary setting. "Can you imagine Vicki's face if she could see us in Paris," mused Rodolfo, after someone suggested leaving for exile to France. Vicki's commitment, her noble death in battle, held Rodolfo in its grip. He owed it to her to fight on to the bitter end.

Rodolfo was now "on the other side" where death was a daily presence, its final certainty coming almost as a relief from the asphyxiation of the unequal struggle against a genocidal regime. It was around this time, September and October 1976, when the Montonero leadership took the unprecedented step of taking a vote on the direction of the movement, spurred by the open dissidence of the movement's Northern Battalion in Buenos Aires Province. The dissidents proposed that the Montoneros abandon Peronism as a political identity and launch a National Liberation Movement to broaden their political support base. The movement leadership rejected the proposal, a position ratified in the subsequent ballot.

Meanwhile Walsh prepared a critical analysis of the movement but situated it within "an internal dialogue" rather than framing it as a challenge to the movement's leadership.

Strategic retreat

By December 13th 1976, with the death of his daughter Vicki still weighing heavily upon him, Walsh drew up a plan of defence and reconstruction of the Montonero organisation.

The seven-point plan included recognition by the Organización Político Militar, OPM, that it had suffered a military defeat which "threatened to turn into extermination," and a call to define the next stage as one of strategic retreat, "without fixing time limits." Peronism and the working class would be the main engines of resistance, with the reformed Montonero movement a crucial factor in the new strategy. The leadership and "historic" figures would be spirited out of the country, thus "denying the enemy the possibility of inflicting decisive defeats by their capture or death" (Baschetti, 1994 p.314).

The organisation would maintain the existing party structure, leaving the resistance plan to the "tactical" leadership, still inside the country. "Individual and collective security would be declared the principal criteria for resistance, terms which would now be linked to policies which involved the masses, with an emphasis on information, communication and propaganda" (ibid p.315).

Walsh's plan of retreat included active resistance, beginning with one hundred members spread throughout the country "with sufficient resources in money, documentation, propaganda and explosives" to hold out indefinitely. The initial advantage to this strategy would be "the preservation of the popular forces until a new opportunity to seize power occurred" (ibid p.316). In what initially appeared a terrible paradox, the first step toward winning the war would be declaring it over for the time being.

The first advantage of acknowledging defeat would be leaving the enemy with no one to fight. If peace was not achieved, then at least the tactic would demonstrate who was responsible for the violence. If violence continued during this interim period then future resistance would be easier to justify, now with a broader popular consensus, inviting forms of action within the people's reach, linked to their own survival.

The political and historic leaders would continue to criticise the government from abroad, beginning with the defence of human rights.

The organisation would launch a fresh political offensive, opening up spaces where the mass movement could recover its voice, despite the repression. The recognition that the political destiny of the country should be decided through peaceful, democratic means would be accompanied by a call for the list of detained people to be made public, for torture and executions to end and the right to use *habeas corpus* restored in order to track down missing suspects believed to be in the hands of the army or police.

While the enemy might ignore the peace offer, the slogan "peace is possible in 48 hours" (ibid p. 229) would impress political parties, the church, professionals, businesspeople and international opinion, the elite sectors crucial to the survival of the dictatorship.

The Montoneros would begin a unilateral 30- or 60-day ceasefire, during which they would monitor and denounce State violence, laying bare the real perpetrators of terror in Argentina. The ceasefire would allow the organisation to devote energy to the "relocation" of militants, finding them "clean" houses, fresh documents and a cover for their new identity.

The Production Team would then dedicate itself to acquiring the weapons required for the next stage of resistance, primarily "explosives, home-made grenades and incendiary devices." The rules of engagement with the enemy would be strict and followed the logic of the "retreat into the masses." There would be no military action that could steal "the human rights banner" from the movement or prevent it from engaging in political activity "in the heart of the enemy" (ibid p.316).

The Montonero resistance strategy would focus its energy on the dictatorship's productive apparatus, with assassination sanctioned only in exceptional circumstances, requiring a propaganda effort far superior to the efforts involved in the attack itself.

At last the organisation would have a chance of reconnecting with the everyday life and possibilities of struggle open to the masses. "A thousand small victories" were preferable to "spectacular operations which drew massive reprisals." The organisation, said Walsh, now needed "the mimeograph and the pipe bomb" (ibid p.234).

On the streets

The army and police "task groups" continued to prowl, the death count continued to rise, as 320 clandestine torture centres held thousands of people throughout the country. Private enterprise lent an enthusiastic hand to the security forces, with at least half a dozen companies, including Ford Motors, establishing holding and torture centres inside their factories. The Ford plant managers not only knew about the torture centre, they even selected dissident workers for punishment (*Página/12*, 21/3/98).

Many army commanders followed the example of General Luciano Benjamín Menéndez, commander of the army's Third Corps, who organised a 'blood pact' among his officers in La Perla concentration camp, where each man was obliged to kill at least one prisoner each, resulting in an estimated 2,000 deaths. The obligatory murder, akin to a gang "blooding" ritual, ensured complicit silence, for the time being.

In 1976, said Walsh, "the enemy fulfilled all its Phase Two objectives" ahead of schedule, and was about to implement Phase Three. He now expected the army to target the Montoneros' national leadership, their national support network and focus on preventing reconstruction efforts. The army had sufficient intelligence information to guarantee a 60 to 90 per cent success rate. The final months of 1976 saw 200 to 300 deaths per month while the ERP leadership was wiped out in July, leaving the regime free to focus on Montonero targets. "Their knowledge of the [organisation's] structure allowed the regime to be selective in its targets, while the volume of captures and confessions obtained through torture facilitated the constant renewal of intelligence sources."

Walsh also noted that the beefed-up defence budget, over a billion dollars per year, had allowed the Federal Police to radically improve its communication network, shifting to DIGICOM, a system of computerised finger-printing, which speeded up the identification process.

Walsh explained to his superiors that putting his thoughts and analyses on paper "should not be understood as a form of questioning but part of an internal dialogue." The principal weakness in Montonero thinking, concluded Walsh, was "a deficit of history." The current party documents had no historical references beyond 1945. "The average Montonero knows how Lenin and Trotsky took control of St Petersburg in 1917," concluded Walsh, "but doesn't know how Martín Rodríguez and Rosas took control of Buenos Aires in 1821" (ibid pp. 316–17).

Montonero leader Roberto Perdía responded to the criticism of Walsh and others with a 20-page communiqué, in February 1977, denying all evidence of the organisation's collapse: "it must be understood that the enemy has no hope of triumphing over the people [...] alone, politically trapped, militarily spread out over the whole country."

It sounded like he was describing the state of his own organisation. Perdía had no facts to back up his case, not a shred of evidence to suggest that the forces of repression were at the end of their offensive and that the advantage would soon fall to the resistance. Worse still, he did have the information required for an accurate analysis of the situation, painstakingly collected by Walsh, ANCLA and hundreds of contributors, at great personal risk. That information was ignored. In his memoirs, published in 1997, Perdía acknowledged the value of Walsh's analyses, describing the disappeared writer as: "one of those few voices, who at the time, properly understood the tangled web of erroneous paths we were taking." In his lengthy *mea culpa*, Perdía recognised the leadership's "insufficient self-criticism and realism," but also pointed out that Walsh's "internal dialogue" did not set out to break with the movement.

The young leadership proved as stubborn as their mentor Juan Perón. "Discussion was tantamount to betrayal, criticism was taken as hostility," recalled one activist. The criticism and comments made by Walsh were kept hidden from movement members until 1979, when dissident leaders publicly broke with the movement.

It was not until late in 1977 that the leadership seemed to act on some of Walsh's recommendations; many in leadership positions left the country and began to operate from abroad. Yet in 1978–79, still maintaining that there was a "popular counter-offensive", militants were sent back into Argentina, to almost certain death. Internal splits multiplied within the Montoneros and Walsh's harshest predictions were tragically fulfilled.

The Montoneros in perspective

The dominant historical explanation of Argentina's "years of lead", as they are known, has told the story of uncontainable violence between two competing extremes, left and right, which left ordinary citizens "banging on the doors of the army barracks" begging them to restore order.

A close look at the statistics for pre-coup violence reveals that between 1973 and 1974, there were four members of the popular movement killed for every member of the security forces, and two members of the popular movement for every security force member killed in the 1974–76 period.

The "subversive" armed attacks inflicted material damage rather than murder (81 per cent of cases) while the "antisubversive" State-sponsored terror caused death in 80 per cent of attacks. The number of "injured" or imprisoned steadily dropped to zero, as the security forces ceased to take prisoners.

The guerrillas accepted exaggerated State tallies of the numbers of dead and injured as they suggested that the Montonero organisation posed a real threat to the survival of the State and its beleaguered security forces. The theory was then advanced that the masses, inspired by rebel attacks on the repressive State, would rise up and put an end to autocratic rule.

The pattern of State terror had been firmly established long before the military formally seized power in March 1976, but from then on the kidnappings, disappearances, torture and killings became State policy, in the hands of a ruthless military invested with absolute power. "As many people as is necessary will die in Argentina [...] to protect the hemisphere from the international communist conspiracy," said General Jorge Videla, speaking at the Ninth Conference of American Army Commanders in Montevideo in 1975, months before the brutal coup which would install him as "president" of Argentina.

One month after Walsh's death, Gabriel García Márquez interviewed Mario Firmenich, maximum leader of the Montonero organisation. The Colombian writer met the exiled leader and got straight to the point, suggesting that after a year of military rule, the Montoneros had been "liquidated". Firmenich disagreed with Gabo, insisting that the organisation knew the coup was coming since October 1975 but did nothing to prevent it. Instead the organisation worked out its "war calculations", anticipating "a number of human losses of not less than 1,500." If losses were kept to that level, said Firmenich, "sooner or later we would win."

What if the dictatorship had also calculated the losses and decided *they* had won, asked Gabo, but Firmenich insisted, "the dictatorship was deflated, with no way out, while we enjoy ever greater prestige among the masses." The interview ebbed and flowed with Firmenich rejecting all evidence that his organisation was on the ropes, close to outright annihilation. Gabo signed off by describing Firmenich as "the oddest fellow I have ever met in my life."

The history of the era is still fresh and evidence is constantly uncovered, revealing fragments of the overall picture.

In his *Dossier Secreto*, published in 1993, Martin Anderson, a US journalist with extensive US intelligence contacts, suggested that Montonero leader Mario Firmenich was an army intelligence operative since 1973, citing a US diplomat who was given the task of "monitoring the guerrilla threat" during Robert Hill's tenure as US ambassador in Buenos Aires. Anderson's book linked Firmenich to Argentina's infamous 601 army battalion, suggesting that all was lost long before the army coup. Alberto Valin, a colonel working in Battalion 601, allegedly confirmed Firmenich's role to the US agent, claiming Firmenich worked with him since the Montonero movement shifted to the left in the early 1970s. His help was "ideological at first, then done for the thrill."

According to Anderson's US intelligence contact, Firmenich had the organisation take credit for a series of spectacular but politically costly murders which they may not have even committed. The first case was the death of official CGT leader José Rucci, in September 1973, who died after 23 bullets were pumped into his body. It was an inexplicable act against Perón's hand-picked union leader just two days after a landslide election returned Perón to power.

In August 1976 Firmenich's pregnant wife, María Elpidia Martínez Aguero, aged 27, was arrested by Federal Police, not long after a powerful bomb destroyed their HQ, killing and injuring dozens of agents. She claimed she was tortured, a version disputed by a US intelligence agent who said he saw her in captivity. Martínez Aguero gave birth in a legal jail in Buenos Aires and held onto her infant. She was released from prison in 1981, given legal documents and allowed to go into exile abroad. Her fate contrasted sharply with that of other pregnant captive women who gave birth and had their infants stolen by their captors, before facing execution themselves. Firmenich's parents were never bothered during the dictatorship, a remarkable exception to the rule, as relatives and friends of rank-and-file activists were harassed and abused.

Firmenich lives in Barcelona, Spain, where I contacted him repeatedly by phone and email, anxious to hear his response to such serious allegations. He finally wrote back with a brief note which said no comment.

Many observers of the Montoneros point to the remarkable arrogance of the leadership, and Firmenich in particular, who compounded bad decisions with utter self-belief. His terrible misjudgements were partly rooted in an inflated sense of importance, while his contact with the security forces, the source of doubt concerning his loyalty, may well have been due to his belief that as the man who would replace Perón, he was entitled to negotiate the transition toward a revolutionary regime.

San Vicente

In December 1976 Rodolfo and Lilia decided to leave Buenos Aires and journey southward, away from occupied territory. "I need to live close to the water," said Rodolfo. The first place that came to mind was his beloved Tigre but that area had fallen into enemy hands, an extension of the occupied city. Months before the military coup, a State-sponsored death squad visited Rodolfo and Lilia's home in the river delta; the house was "marked" and Lilia had bravely made one last trip to remove the couple's most important belongings. He hung a map of the province of Buenos Aires on the wall of their cramped city centre apartment and stared at San Vicente lake, the starting point for the journey toward freedom.

The couple took a train to San Vicente, a sleepy village on the outskirts of Buenos Aires, where they discovered an empty lake, as "the tall reeds had reduced it to the size of a puddle." They sat down on some nearby stones and Rodolfo imagined the lake suddenly refilled with water. The trees, the silence and the prospect of a more peaceful existence were decisive factors in determining the move, which took place over the following three months.

The couple rose early each day, pottering about the house and garden. Rodolfo suddenly found himself with the free time he had craved since joining the Montonero organisation. "Scattered papers were put into order, files on different themes began to occupy shelf space. The threads of past investigations criss-crossed into fresh lines of inquiry," recalled Lilia. Rodolfo's period of reflection was interrupted by his constant worries about fellow combatants and their families, who lived in even more precarious circumstances, confined to the city streets.

Rodolfo spent his days in the quiet surroundings of San Vicente, which had a village-like atmosphere; a dirt track, washed out in winter, led to their unassuming home. Walsh bought a "DIY manual for beginner farmers" at a local newsagent's and began to turn over the land for crops. Lilia and he began growing vegetables for subsistence. In addition, Walsh talked about the intensive production of saffron, as he heard it would give the best yield for a cash crop. There was even wild talk of buying a new Japanese wonder-tractor, purposely designed for small-scale agriculture. "The house had brick floors and a hand-operated water pump," recalled Horacio Verbitsky. "It didn't have gas or electricity but Rodolfo was enthusiastic. He'd chase anthills with a stick and mow the grass with a scythe."

On New Year's Eve 1976, Rodolfo and Lilia left their home in San Vicente and travelled by train to the centre of Buenos Aires, hoping to meet up with a couple of friends for a rare social outing. Such furtive encounters were risked on occasion as busy train stations offered minimal cover for the hunted militants.

There could be no visit to a restaurant or a late-night film now, just a chat on a bench in a crowded station. You couldn't ask anyone over to your house, as one more person with knowledge of your address was akin to adding another bullet to the loaded chamber for a game of Russian roulette. "The less you knew the better off you were," a former Montonero intelligence official told me. Rodolfo and Lilia sat on the bench and watched the crowds pass by, young and old on their way to end-of-year parties, blissfully unaware of the tension flowing through the unremarkable couple. He looked like a retired teacher, she might have been his young wife. They might have been waiting for their children to arrive off a train, greeting them as summer holidays began.

Rodolfo mused over how far the life of the revolutionary had been removed from the life of the ordinary citizen, once their co-conspirator in the struggle for social justice.

Two hours passed and no one appeared, another typical missed encounter. The absent couple may have opted to stay home at the last minute, to avoid the danger of a public meeting, or they may have been arrested. If they were detained, it may have been an hour or a day before, indeed that very meeting place may have been "poisoned" or revealed on the torture table.

"Let's buy something nice to eat," said Rodolfo, in an effort to revive flagging spirits. Lilia bought chicken and wine, which they took home with them. They played Scrabble and Go, a Japanese game. Shortly before midnight Rodolfo cleared the table and sat down in front of his Olympia typewriter, writing about the evening just passed, describing the sense of desolation and loneliness among the crowds, in that sad defeated city, sagging under the weight of so much fear.

When midnight rang in the new year, Rodolfo leapt to his feet, hugged Lilia and sat down again. "That's how I want to begin the year," said Rodolfo, tapping the keys. "I want to let those fuckers know that I'm still here, still alive and still writing."

The loss of his daughter was compounded by the recent death of two compañeros, Pablo and Mariana, a young separated couple, both under Rodolfo's command, who disappeared in December of that year. "The boy was like a son to Rodolfo," according to one of Walsh's friends.

Rodolfo turned up at the regular meetings with Montonero compañeros, always heavily disguised. He listened to the tales of sacrifice and suffering, piecing together his critique of military rule. At home he wrote at night, then corrected each new page by day. On one bus journey from the city to San Vicente, in January 1977, a newspaper seller brought news of seven more deaths, including the historic Peronist combatant Dardo Cabo. "The atmosphere suddenly turned even more suffocating than before," noted Lilia.

Walsh was angry at the complicit silence or outright endorsement of the junta by Argentina's well-heeled intellectuals. "I personally thanked him [General Videla] for the coup which saved the country from ignominy," said Jorge Luis Borges, Argentina's most famous writer, after attending a luncheon given by Jorge Videla and other coup leaders. "General Videla made an excellent impression on me," added Ernesto Sábato, another writer who attended the luncheon, "he is a cultured, modest and intelligent man."

Rodolfo planned his "Open Letter" as a challenge to the resignation and cowardice of Borges, Sábato and others. After a decade of collective, unsigned work it was time for Rodolfo to reassume his identity, as expressed in the title of his work-in-progress: "An Open Letter from a

Writer to the Military Junta". Walsh was a revolutionary combatant, but his status as a writer would lend greater urgency to his denunciation. He understood that entire sectors of the population had to bow their heads and wait for the worst of this oppressive storm to pass, but noted intellectuals like Jorge Luis Borges and Ernesto Sábato still enjoyed a level of protection which afforded them space to pressure the regime. It was an opening they ignored until it was far too late.

One crucial source of information for Rodolfo was the daily newspaper *La Prensa* which published lists of *habeas corpus* writs served to judges, an indication of the number of people reported missing by relatives. There were 7,000 in a single year, all of them rejected by the State. Such figures indicated the extent of the massacre underway. In addition, Walsh's listening devices continued to yield useful information: one night, after hours of painstaking work, he deciphered an army communiqué which forbade all units from reporting the discovery of corpses.

Being captured was now only a matter of time and chance, Walsh told his ANCLA colleagues, as even the tightest security precautions were insufficient to guarantee protection. ANCLA journalists bravely continued to write up cables and distribute them to local and international media. "I dreaded it each time I saw Lilia arrive," confessed José Bodis, a Cuban friend of the couple, then working as Prensa Latina correspondent in Buenos Aires.

Ferreyra would occasionally bring articles to the agency offices, located inside a building known as the *ciudadela*, a city centre press bunker where local and European news agencies kept their offices. "I wondered each time I saw her if it would be the last or if it would be my last if I was seen talking to her." Bodis said that out of every three people who walked into the building, at least one of them was a police or army spy.

Around this time Carlos Bares, a therapist and friend of Walsh's, spotted Rodolfo in a park. "He was staring up at a tree, looking at a flock of birds," said Carlos. "He seemed oblivious to everything else." Bares, like so many other friends and colleagues, resisted the initial urge to greet Walsh, turning away instead, knowing the potential price to be paid for associating with "subversives".

Walsh thought long and hard about his commitment to the Montonero organisation in the final weeks of 1976, his sense of loyalty delaying an inevitable split with the organisation's leadership. All through Walsh's life, he had moved at the speed of the masses, evolving in his own slow way toward revolutionary action. He had formally joined the Montonero organisation in October 1973, at the height of their representative power, when their political delegates won governorships, controlled the universities, the streets, the football stadiums, the shantytowns and the popular imagination.

By 1976, though, the organisation had lost touch with its roots, as people stopped talking to each other about politics, retreating into their private world instead, only feeling secure inside their own home. The street was no longer a space to celebrate change, it had become a no-warning death trap. The organisation did not have the wisdom nor imagination to react to this new reality, retreating into an exaggerated militarism which isolated them from their support base.

"In the early days you could knock on any door, tell people the police were after you and be almost certain of a refuge," said one former Montonero combatant. "By the time of the military coup your own people wouldn't allow you past the door."

In early January 1977 Walsh put the finishing touches to the batch of comments aimed at the Montonero leadership, a detailed critique which evolved from discussion and debate with dozens of activists over the previous months. It was a document which rejected the organisation's "strategic plan" to absorb losses and launch a counter-offensive in the months ahead. As matters stood Walsh believed the movement was defeated and the first task was to recognise that reality, then regroup and organise a resistance strategy more in tune with the organisation's real capacities.

While Walsh prepared his "Open Letter" to the junta he also worked on a new short story, "Juan Went Down to the River", betting with Lilia that they would both be finished by March 24th 1977, the first anniversary of the coup. Rodolfo paced the floors, reciting latin verse, *Quosque tandem*, Videla, *abutere patientia nostra*! He based his accusation on Cicero's 'In Catilinam', slowly finding his own voice again, after a decade of collective, anonymous work, settling on the Latin invective as a narrative style. After a series of working drafts, Walsh began to find the right tone, rhythm and tension for his letter. Over his morning coffee or his evening gin Rodolfo returned to Cicero's phrases, verses he had painstakingly copied into his small Avon ring-binder notebook. He hammered away at the letter by the light of a paraffin lamp, determined that his public accusation against the State would combine "the written word with the roundness of the spoken word" (Ferreyra, *Página/12* Sunday supplement *Radar*, 23/3/97).

Back in 1957 Rodolfo had published a trivia column of vox pops in *Leoplán* magazine, entitled "What Would You Do if You Had Five Minutes to Live?" The question was put to a journalist, a trapeze artist, a cinema usher, a politician, a writer, a journalist, a crime fiction writer, an ambulance driver, an actress, a bullfighter and a comic author. The journalist was Ignacio Covarrubias, the writer was Jorge Luis Borges and the crime fiction writer was Rodolfo. Borges gave a complex, philosophical treatise on mortality while Rodolfo responded with just one word –

testamento, a will.

As time ticked away Rodolfo worked on his "five minute" contingency plan which would haunt the regime beyond his death and leave a permanent record of their crimes. But Rodolfo's last will and testament was not limited to his critique of the dictatorship. He also worked on his internal criticism of the Montonero movement and grappled with a new short story, about his childhood days. The body of work in progress finally pulled together the various threads of a remarkable life and fulfilled Walsh's pledge to "bear witness in difficult times."

In January 1977 Rodolfo celebrated his fiftieth birthday, a remarkable feat in a country which devoured its bravest and brightest long before maturity.

He planned only as far ahead as March 24th 1977, the first anniversary of military rule. His final short story, "Juan Went Down to the River", was a composite vision of past, present and future. "At the end of the story," explained Lilia, who read the work in progress, "Juan, remembering his past, his history and the history of his country, sitting on a low stool by the river, begins to get rid of the burden of the past. He looks toward Colonia, on the other side of the river, where he would like to go. One afternoon the waters subside and the river dries up. Juan gets on his horse and starts to cross it. When he can see the tiny white houses of Colonia on the horizon, the waters come back. The river swells, using all its might to halt the progress of man and horse."

For Lilia, the closest witness to Rodolfo's last decade, the story of Juan's search for new direction was a parable for Walsh's escape from the clutches of terror: "he too wanted to let go, to reach for something new." The move to San Vicente was the start of a longer journey south, away from enemy territory, to triumph over death and live to fight another battle. But Walsh refused to disconnect himself from the armed movement, which, discounting exile, was the only possible way to save his life at that point.

Rodolfo was also suffering from feeling burnt out, something common to militants at this time, hunted down like dogs, sensing the futility of the dying resistance effort and the imminent and apparent certainty of capture. Rodolfo's surviving daughter Patricia compared the downcast Rodolfo with his defeated father before him, who suffered "spiritual and financial bankruptcy" in 1947 when he died after he came off his horse. Rodolfo, the intelligence expert famed for his exaggerated security measures, made careless mistakes, ignoring signs that his police agent had been captured.

Rodolfo and Lilia kept a very low profile in San Vicente, making contact with only a handful of neighbours, Rodolfo posing as a retired English teacher. In the first week of March 1977 a delegation of neighbours got together to demand water from the local authorities. Rodolfo was selected to join the delegation, a respectable, retired teacher representing all things civilised. How could a man of his status be expected to live without a steady supply of water? The protest was an absurd act of madness in the midst of the war being waged by the State against all forms of dissidence. Walsh naturally agreed to take part and headed off with a group of locals, who entered the town hall, leaving the women to chat in the sunshine outside. Within minutes the protestors watched as military trucks pulled up, unloading dozens of soldiers, weapons at the ready. One group of soldiers took up battle positions on the street corners, while others cautiously edged their way into the council offices. There was nowhere to run and no chance of escape. Half an hour later Rodolfo emerged, smiling, with the delegation. His disguise had held. The soldiers let them off with a warning, ordering them to return to their homes.

Just before midnight on the night of the coup anniversary, Rodolfo put the finishing touches to the last version of his "Open Letter", massaging his fingers, which had developed a painful cramp. "Arthritis," he said, looking at Lilia, "but I can still bang the keys." Walsh won the bet he made against himself, finishing the letter and his new short story on the day of the coup anniversary. In celebration the couple planned an *asado* at the house on Saturday 26th, inviting Patricia, his surviving daughter, along with her partner Jorge and their children, María, aged three and Mariano, an infant.

The couple laughed and joked as they put all ten copies of the letter into envelopes, the result of three months' work. They planned a trip into the city centre the next day, where Rodolfo had set up three different meetings.

chapter fifteen

Rodolfo's last bullet

When, General, when? [45]   (Walsh, 1996)

A matter of chance

In a prophetic letter written in December 1976, Walsh described the events leading up to the death of Paco Urondo: "A chain of arrests, houses which had to be evacuated, betrayal and finally, the poisoned meeting," he wrote, little knowing that the script for his last day would be terribly similar. A week before his death Rodolfo met Lila Pastoriza, one of the surviving members of the ANCLA team, and discussed the deteriorating situation.

"It's not a question of sufficient security measures anymore," said Rodolfo, "being caught is now only a matter of chance." The repressors had pieced together the entire working structure of the guerrilla organisation and every fresh catch added a new detail, leading to further captures. Rodolfo interrupted the conversation to call his "control phone", the operator service used to co-ordinate clandestine meetings. A week had passed since Salgado, the infiltrated police agent, had checked in with Walsh. There was still no response; Walsh should have known to cut off all contact then. Walsh said his last goodbye to Lila; two months later she too was captured.

Walsh's police agent Salgado had carried out the single most audacious attack on the security forces, leaving a bomb in Federal Police HQ, which killed dozens of officers and injured over one hundred more. The army responded by executing 30 prisoners that night, a reprisal which left a bitter aftertaste to the guerrilla attack. Walsh later acknowledged the error of carrying out the bomb attack without calculating the

---

[45] Title of a piece recounting Walsh's meeting with Perón in Madrid.

savage reprisals likely to be taken by the regime.

Walsh had no way of knowing that Salgado lay in final agony, destroyed by savage torture inside the *Escuela de Mecánica de la Armada*, ESMA. He died hours after revealing the telephone codes that would confirm a future meeting with Rodolfo, who was anxious to re-establish communication with one of his most important operatives. Salgado withstood torture for at least two days before giving anything away. The captured agent had good reason to believe that Walsh would smell a rat and avoid any further meetings with him. In previous conversations on the issue, Rodolfo warned that no one could be expected to hold out for more than 24 hours in the hands of torturers.

On the same day he posted copies of the letter to the junta, Rodolfo arranged to meet the wife of a compañero who was living in the home of Salgado at great risk to her two children. She wrote a heartbreaking letter to Walsh, complaining that the organisation had failed to help her, despite promises of financial support.

A tortured comrade, a desperate woman with two children and nowhere to go, a fatal combination of circumstances which led Walsh to compromise his legendary security measures. The plan was to invite the woman and her children to move into their home in San Vicente. The third meeting planned for that day was with his superior officer Ricardo Haidar.

"The last time I saw Rodolfo alive he was crossing the street in the city centre. He saw me, lowered his head and kept on walking. He obviously didn't want me to greet him. I presumed he was being followed," said Daniel Divinsky, his editor at De la Flor.

Poupee Blanchard remembers, "The last time I saw Rodolfo was in the botanic gardens, sitting with his daughter Patricia and her baby boy. He saw me and looked down at the ground. I assumed he was being followed. I walked around a bit, then he got up and left by another exit. Just as he left he made eye contact, as if to say 'I know it's you'."

The testimony of friends and colleagues who glimpsed Rodolfo Walsh in the final weeks and months of his life all bear a striking resemblance, reflecting a clandestine existence where a careless nod or wink could cost a life. Buenos Aires was occupied territory where State kidnappers waited around every corner, promising a fate worse than death.

Friday March 25th 1977

On the last Friday, bright sunlight streamed in through the windows of the small kitchen in Rodolfo's home in San Vicente, as he prepared to go into town. Lilia prepared coffee and chatted as she packed up the letters due to be sent that day.

The couple left their house and walked along the muddy dirt track which led to the nearby train station. They bumped into the former owner of the home, who had agreed a sale that same week. The couple signed the papers with a false name and the house was purchased with money from the organisation. Rodolfo took the papers with him, a security lapse which allowed the army to find their way there later that day.

12 noon

A Task Group comprising ten men left the ESMA, the main concentration camp in Buenos Aires, and took up positions along Avenida San Juan, close to Calle Sarandí. Each had a specific duty: Alfredo Astiz, known as "the angel of death" was delegated the job of the "rugby tackle" to immobilise his prey. The Buenos Aires assistant police chief Ernesto Webber was present to smooth over operational difficulties, while sharp-shooter and torture addict Jorge "Tigre" Acosta would be on hand to deliver a fatal shot, if plans went awry. Retired Army Major Julio César Colonel participated in the operation, along with Roberto Francisco González, a Federal Police inspector.

"I asked for him alive," confirmed junta leader Admiral Emilio Massera. Walsh carried more knowledge in his head about infiltrators in the army and police than anyone else, making him a prize catch. The Task Force had asked for a "free zone" that day, a common maneouvre whereby the State's "clandestine" repressors notified the legal security forces to stay away from a certain area, giving them a clear field of action for their "disappearing" missions.

Walsh's future prospects would likely have included extended torture by electric prod and medical instruments, followed by the traditional "transfer" where prisoners deemed "unrecoverable" were taken from their cells, drugged and dragged aboard a helicopter. They were then tossed over the River Plate from a height of several thousand feet. A Catholic army chaplain would be on hand to hear the confession of the helicopter pilots on their return to base, comforting them in their hour of guilt, reminding them of God's call to "separate the wheat from the chaff" (*Página/12*, 2/7/97).

Rodolfo and Lilia got off the train at Constitución station, where Rodolfo called his "control phone" one last time. "It's on," said Walsh, smiling at Lilia, confirming the meeting with Salgado. The couple parted ways in the market thoroughfare outside, where crowds of people bought cheap goods at stalls or hauled bags toward the nearby bus station.

"Don't forget to water the lettuces," said Rodolfo, waving to Lilia as he turned away and disappeared into the crowd. It was her last glimpse of Walsh. He went on his way, depositing copies of the "Open Letter" in postboxes. Somewhere else in the city, Lilia Ferreyra was posting several more copies of the letter.

He got on a bus which took him closer to the meeting point, then walked the last few blocks. When he reached the corner of Calle Calvo and Avenida Entre Rios, the trap was set, the assassins at the ready. The orders had been emphatic: "Bring that fucking bastard back alive, he's mine," Admiral Massera told his death squad.

Miguel Bonasso, *el Sobreviviente* (the survivor), had spent the previous fortnight fruitlessly trying to track down Walsh, a plane ticket in his hand. The Montonero leadership planned to relaunch the movement the following month in Rome, Italy, by bringing historic and youth figures together in a single, broad-based resistance strategy.

Walsh's formidable reputation would have been a crucial factor in achieving that unity. Ironically Walsh's cover proved too good for his own organisation but not good enough to fool the State terror apparatus. Walsh walked past the assassins, sensing something out of place. No one knows for sure what happened next; someone apparently shouted "Stop, Police!" giving Rodolfo several crucial seconds to take out the pistol he kept hidden in his waistband, his last birthday present to Lilia Ferreyra, in May 1976. The gun would have little effect in a shootout but would provoke his kidnappers into shooting him dead, a more desirable alternative to the suicidal certainty of the cyanide capsule.

The assassins opened fire but the first shots went wide of the mark. Walsh ran into the street and hid behind a parked car, emptying his small Walther PKK calibre pistol at his assailants. He managed to injure one of the killers who was subsequently awarded a medal for bravery on the battlefield.

Seconds later Rodolfo lay dying, mortally wounded, while onlookers hurriedly left the scene, obeying the first law of survival under military rule: see nothing.

"I fired at him, I fired again and again but he didn't fall," said one of the killers, testifying in court, years later. "He didn't fall, he still didn't fall. Blood poured out of him, more blood and I kept shooting and blood flowed, more blood and the guy didn't fall."

The bullet-ridden body was dragged to a waiting car and dumped in the boot. The killers returned to their offices, preparing a credible story to justify the botched operation. The corpse was left in a corridor in ESMA for 24 hours, according to the testimony of Sara Osatinsky and María Pirles, before it was set on fire and dumped in a nearby river. The Task Group found the property deeds and made their way to Lilia and Rodolfo's home, which was raided, looted and wrecked. The army spoke to neighbours, telling them that the house was booby-trapped, justifying the armed assault on the empty home. A month later, the house had a new owner, a police chief who eliminated all traces of the previous occupants.

Many thought Rodolfo had become another *desaparecido*, and his death was not fully confirmed until 1979 when the women who saw his body in ESMA were released. In Argentina and abroad, campaigns were organised calling on the junta to guarantee his life. An open letter to the junta on Walsh's behalf was published in *La Nación* on November 25th 1977, signed by, among others, Roland Barthes, Eugene Ionesco, Michel Foucault and Italo Calvino.

Life after death

At great personal risk Lilia lodged a *habeas corpus* writ, waited a week and then took an even greater risk by returning to the court clerk, in case there might be an official response to Walsh's disappearance. Lilia came face to face with the same young bureaucrat who had collected the form from her a week previously. He looked more frightened of the procedure than she did.

"Señora", he said, "he is dead, there is no news, there will be no news." Lilia turned to go and as she left the office she heard the tremulous final words, barely audible: "I am a relative of Rodolfo Walsh's." The court clerk turned out to be the husband of Carlos Walsh's daughter.

In the weeks after Rodolfo's capture, Lilia Ferreyra wandered around Buenos Aires, frantically seeking a safe place to stay and advising friends of Walsh's capture and possible death. In July 1978 she escaped to Mexico City, where she first published Walsh's criticism of the Montoneros, and confirmed his death. "It was a relief to know they had killed him," said Poupee Blanchard. "The idea that they might be torturing him was enough to take away all my will to live."

The papers which Lilia Ferreyra managed to smuggle out of Argentina and into Mexico were first published in a Mexican magazine edited by Nicolas Casullo. The exiled Montonero leadership published the letter but omitted a crucial section where Walsh claimed that the most severe face of repression was not the attack on militants, ferocious as it was, but the long-term implications of the junta's economic policies, which affected millions of people.

The "Open Letter" circulated from person to person in exile haunts, from London to Mexico City, quickly establishing its place as the historical record of the junta's social, economic, political and cultural performance.

In the weeks after Rodolfo's death and the capture of his files, ESMA intelligence officials and guerrilla *quebrados* (lit. "the broken", collaborators) pored over Rodolfo's kidnapped work, trying to decipher maps, charts and scribbled notes found in his home. There was one mysterious map which caught the eye of army investigators as they searched for hints of upcoming operations or coded information on spies within the security forces. The subject of their intrigue was a detailed chart with a disc placed on top, which moved through certain marked points, as if identifying locations or targets. This chart, the authorities hoped, might shed light on future guerrilla plans, but no one could figure it out.

Years later, sitting in our regular meeting place, the Varela Varelita café, Rodolfo's daughter Patricia solved the mystery of the map. In the early 1960s Patricia and Vicki, barely in their teens, would visit their father on weekends, taking the train from their home in La Plata to Buenos Aires, switching trains to reach Tigre, then taking the ferry to Rodolfo's riverside retreat.

When the two girls got to their father's home they would sit beside the river on a makeshift bridge, fishing for their supper. Whatever they caught would be cooked up on a kerosene stove, the leftovers then dumped in a bin which the girls carried outside, where one last treat awaited them. Rodolfo sat with them in the darkness, looking at the stars, spreading out a map he had made for them.

In his passion for knowledge and his desire to pass it on, Rodolfo had drawn up a map of the sky, complete with stars and constellations, outlining their passage through the universe. The disc in the centre allowed Rodolfo to show Patricia and Vicki the changing course of the planets as they made their way round the sun.

Open Letter from a Writer to the Military Junta

1. Press censorship, the persecution of intellectuals, a recent police raid on my house, the murder of dear friends and the loss of a daughter who died fighting the dictatorship, are some of the circumstances which oblige me to adopt this form of clandestine expression after working openly as a writer and journalist for almost 30 years.

The first anniversary of the latest military junta has been marked by many official documents and speeches evaluating the government's activities over the past year; what you call successes are failures, the failures you recognise are crimes and the disasters you have committed are omitted altogether.

On March 24th 1976 you overthrew a government, to whose downfall you had contributed as the executors of its repressive policies, its lifespan already defined by the elections due to be held nine months later. From this perspective it can be seen that what you put an end to was not the temporary mandate of Isabel Martínez but the very possibility of a democratic process in which the people could have set right the evils which you have perpetuated and aggravated.

Illegal in its origins, your government could have legitimized itself by returning to the kind of programme which 80 per cent of Argentinians voted for in 1973 and which continues to represent the will of the people, the only possible interpretation of the "national spirit" to which you so often appeal.

By turning that notion on its head you have restored a current of ideas upheld by a defeated minority who block the development of productive potential, exploit people and tears our country apart. Such a policy can only be imposed temporarily, by banning political parties, taking over trades unions, muzzling the press and implementing the most savage reign of terror Argentina has ever known.

2. Fifteen thousand disappeared, ten thousand prisoners, four thousand dead, hundreds of thousands uprooted; these are the raw statistics of terror. With normal prisons filled to overflowing, you created virtual concentration camps in the main barracks around the country, where no judge, lawyer, journalist or international observer ever sets foot. The military secrecy of the procedures, cited as an investigative necessity, transforms most arrests into kidnappings which permit torture without limits and execution without trial.

Over 7,000 *habeas corpus* writs have been denied by you this year. In thousands more cases of disappearance the legal recourse wasn't even made, because people understood the futility of the gesture or because people couldn't find a lawyer who would dare to present it after the 50 or 60 colleagues who did so were kidnapped in turn. This is how you have stripped torture of all time limits. As the prisoner doesn't exist there is no possibility of presenting them to a judge within ten days, as demanded by the law, a measure respected even at the height of repression during past dictatorships.

The lack of any time limit has been accompanied by a lack of any limit to the methods applied, taking us back to epochs in which victim's joints and insides were directly operated upon, except that today you enjoy the benefits of surgical assistants and chemists whose services were unavailable to the ancient executioners. The rack, the clamp, skinning alive, the saw of the medieval Inquisition have reappeared in testimonies alongside the "submarine" and the blowtorch, taking us to the present day.

One after another the supposed concessions to the goal of wiping out the guerrilla are used to justify maximum torture, unending and metaphysical. In the degree to which the original goal of extracting information has got lost within the sick minds operating the process, this has given way to the impulse to crush human substance to breaking point and steal its dignity, the dignity which you yourselves, the executioners, have lost.

3. The junta's refusal to publish the names of its prisoners is a cover for the systematic execution of hostages in quiet locations in the early hours of the morning, under the pretext of non-existent combat and imaginary "escape attempts".

"Extremists" who head into the countryside, leaflets in hand, who paint canals or pile ten to a vehicle which bursts into flame are the clichés of a script designed not to be believed but to ridicule international reaction to the systematic killings. Inside the country these reports underscore the nature of reprisals unleashed in the same places and dates as guerrilla actions.

Seventy executed after the Federal Security bomb, 55 in reprisal for the blowing up of the La Plata Police Department, 30 for the attack on the Ministry of Defence, 40 in the New Year massacre which followed the death of Colonel Castellanos, 19 after the explosion which destroyed the Ciudadela police station, are all part of the 1,200 executions in 300 alleged "battles" where the enemy had no injured and the troops under their command suffered no losses.

The repository of a collective guilt abolished in the civilised norms of justice, unable to exert any influence over the policies which determine the actions for which they will be punished, many of those hostages are union representatives, intellectuals, relatives of guerrillas, unarmed opposition or suspects killed to balance the losses, in line with the foreign "body count" doctrine used by the Nazi SS in occupied territory and by the invaders of Vietnam.

The execution of guerrillas wounded or captured in real battles is demonstrated by the army's own communiqués, which spoke of 600 deaths in one year but only 10 or 15 injured, a proportion unheard of in the bloodiest of conflicts. This impression is confirmed by a clandestine press source which revealed that between December 18th 1976 and February 3rd 1977, out of 40 real battles the security forces suffered 23 deaths and 40 injured, with guerrilla losses at 63 dead. Over 100 convicted prisoners have been shot dead in "escape attempts", which are publicised not to be believed by anyone but to warn guerrillas and political parties that even recognised political prisoners are a strategic reserve for reprisals, their destiny in the hands of Corps Commanders waiting for news of progress in combat, convenience or the whim of the moment.

That is how General Benjamín Menéndez, chief of the army Third Corps earned his medals before March 24th 1976, first by killing Marcos Osatinsky, detained in Córdoba, then with the death of Hugo Vaca

Narvaja and another 50 prisoners in different applications of the attempted escape law, executed without pity, the episode recounted without shame.

The murder of Dardo Cabo, arrested in April 1975, executed on January 6th 1977 with seven other prisoners in the First Corps army jurisdiction under the command of General Suárez Masson, shows that these episodes are not the excesses of some insane centurion but the policy planned by yourselves among the general staff, discussed at cabinet meetings, imposed by the commanders-in-chief of the three branches of the armed forces and approved as members of the ruling junta.

4. Between 1,500 and 3,000 more people have been massacred in secret since you suppressed the right to publish information on the discovery of corpses, which in some cases have gone beyond these shores, as they affect other countries, because of their genocidal magnitude or because of the horror provoked among your own forces.

Twenty-five mutilated bodies surfaced between March and October 1976 along the coast of Uruguay, a fraction of the torture load from the Escuela de Mecánica de la Armada (ESMA), sunk in the River Plate by navy boats, including the 15-year-old youth, Floreal Avellaneda, hands and feet bound, "with wounds in the anal region and visible fractures," according to his autopsy.

A veritable lakeside cemetery was discovered in August 1976 by a local man out snorkelling in Lake San Roque, Córdoba. He went to the local police station where they refused to register his report, he wrote to the newspapers but they never published it.

Thirty-four bodies were found in Buenos Aires between the 3rd and 9th of April 1976, eight more in San Telmo on July 4th, ten in Rio Luján on October 9th. In the build-up to the August 20th massacres, 30 bodies were piled high at a distance of 15 km from the Campo de Mayo army base, with 17 more killed in Lomas de Zamora.

These details put an end to the fairytale of right-wing gangs, the alleged successors to López Rega's Triple A, who could pass through the biggest barracks in the country in military vehicles, carpet the River Plate with corpses or toss prisoners into the sea from First Brigade transports, all achieved without the knowledge of General Videla, Admiral Massera and Brigadier Agosti. The Triple A are now the three branches of the army and the military junta over which you preside is not the referee between "two terrorisms" but the very source of the terror, which has lost its way and can only babble its discourse on death.

The same historic continuity ties the murder of General Prats during the last government with the kidnap and murder of General Juan José Torres, Zelmar Michelini, Héctor Gutierrez and dozens of exiles whose deaths were carried out to kill off any possibility of a democratic opening in Chile, Bolivia and Uruguay.

The confirmed participation of the Federal Police's department of Foreign Affairs in these crimes, carried out by officers on CIA grants, courtesy of (US)AID, such as police chiefs Juan Gaiter and Antonio Gettor, themselves under orders from Gardener Hathaway, CIA station chief in Argentina, is the seed of future revelations such as those which now shake international opinion, revelations which will not be exhausted even by the clarification of the Agency role and that of top-ranking army chiefs, led by General Menéndez in the creation of the 'Lodge of American Liberators,' which replaced the 'Triple A' until its overall mission was taken on by the junta in the name of the Three Armed forces.

This extermination map doesn't exclude personal account-settling, such as the killing of Captain Horacio Gándara, who spent the past decade investigating the investments of the top navy chiefs, or the case of Horacio Novillo, a *Prensa Libre* journalist, stabbed and burned alive after his paper denounced the links between Minister Martínez de Hoz and international business monopolies.

The definition of the war made by one of its leading figures takes on its full significance in the light of these events: "The battle we are waging has no moral or natural limits, it takes place beyond good and evil."

5. These events, which stir the conscience of the civilised world, are not however the greatest suffering inflicted on the Argentinian people, nor the worst violation of human rights which you have committed. It is in the economic policy of this government where one discovers not only the explanation for the crimes, but a greater atrocity which punishes millions of human beings through planned misery.

In one year you have reduced the real value of salaries by 40 per cent, diminished their participation in national income by 30 per cent, extended the number of work hours required to afford basic necessities from six to eighteen hours, thus reviving forced labour practices which no longer exist in even the farthest-flung colonial outposts.

Freezing wages with rifles butts while prices rise at bayonet point, abolishing all forms of collective bargaining, prohibiting assemblies and internal commissions, extending working days, raising unemployment to a record 9 per cent, promising greater heights with 300,000 fresh layoffs, have taken the relations of production back to the beginning of the industrial era; and when workers complain they are branded "subversives", with entire union delegations kidnapped, some of whom reappear as corpses, the others disappeared.

The results of this policy have been devastating. In the first year of government, food consumption dropped by 40 per cent, clothes purchases by over 50 per cent, while medicines have practically disappeared among the poorest sectors. There are parts of Buenos Aires where infant mortality exceeds 30 per cent, a figure which puts us on the same level as Rhodesia, Dahomey or the Guyanas; illnesses like diarrhoea, parasites and even rabies, which climb toward world record figures and beyond. It is as if such figures were desirable goals to be pursued, seeing as you have reduced the Public Health budget to less than a third of military spending, abolishing even the free hospitals as hundreds of doctors, professionals and technicians join the exodus sparked by the terror, the low wages or "rationalisation".

You only have to walk around greater Buenos Aires for a few hours to check the speed with which such a policy transforms the city into a "shantytown" of ten million people.

Cities in semi-darkness, whole neighbourhoods without water because big business loots the underground aquifers, thousands of streets turned into a single pothole because you only pave military neighbourhoods and dress up the Plaza de Mayo; the world's biggest river contaminated along all its beaches because Minister Martínez de Hoz's partners dump industrial waste there and the only government measure taken is to prohibit bathing.

You have fared no better on your abstract economic targets, a term freely interchanged with "the country". A decrease of almost 3 per cent in gross national product, an external debt worth 600 US dollars per person, annual inflation of 400 per cent, a currency hike of 9 per cent in just one week in December, a 13 per cent drop in internal investment, all add up to world records, the strange fruit of cold deliberation and raw ineptitude.

While all the creative and protective functions of the State seize up until they dissolve in true anaemia, just one sector grows and gains autonomy. One thousand eight hundred million dollars, a sum equal to half our total exports, have been budgeted for Security and Defence in 1977; four thousand new jobs for Federal Police agents; twelve thousand in the province of Buenos Aires with wages worth twice the salary of an industrial worker, three times that of a school head, while military wages are secretly raised by 120 per cent from February, proof that there are no freezes or layoffs in the kingdom of torture and death, the only field of activity in Argentina where the demand grows and where the price of each assassinated guerrilla rises faster than the dollar.

6. An economic policy dictated by the International Monetary Fund, following a recipe applied indiscriminately in Zaire or Chile, in Uruguay or Indonesia, the junta accepts as its beneficiaries only the old cattle oligarchy, the new speculative oligarchy and a select group of transnational businesses led by ITT, Esso, the car industry, US Steel and Siemens, all linked personally to Minister Martínez de Hoz and members of his cabinet.

A 722 per cent rise in the price of animal production in 1976 highlights the magnitude of the oligarchic restoration undertaken by Martínez de Hoz in harmony with the Rural Society credo as expressed by its president Celedonio Pereda, who pronounced himself "utterly surprised to hear that certain small but active groups continue to insist that food should be cheap."

The spectacle of a Stock Exchange where in one week people can earn 100 or 200 per cent profit without working, where firms double their capital overnight without producing any more than before, the crazy wheel of dollar speculation, bills, adjustable values, plain usury which calculates interest by the hour, are very strange events under a government which seized power to put an end to "the corruption spree."

By privatising the banks you have placed savings and national credit in the hands of foreign banking, by indemnifying ITT and Siemens you reward firms which cheated the State, by giving back the filling stations you increase the profits of Shell and Esso, by lowering tariffs you create jobs in Hong Kong or Singapore and unemployment in Argentina.

Taking all these facts into account you have to ask yourself who are the real traitors of the official communiqués, where are the mercenaries at the service of foreign interests and what is the ideology which threatens our national identity.

If the overwhelming propaganda, a twisted reflection of half-truths, wasn't claiming that the junta is trying to bring peace, that General Videla defends human rights and that Admiral Massera loves life, it might still be worth asking the heads of the three armed forces to think about the abyss to which they are taking the country, with the illusion of winning a war which even if every last guerrilla was killed, would simply start up again in different ways, because the causes that inspired the resistance of the Argentinian people 20 years ago wouldn't have disappeared. Indeed they have been worsened by the memory of the destruction caused and the revelation of the atrocities committed.

These are the thoughts I wanted to send the Junta members on the first anniversary of your ill-fated government, without hope of being listened to, with the certainty of being persecuted, true to the commitment I took up a long time ago, to bear witness in difficult times.

●◆ Rodolfo Walsh, ID 2845022
Buenos Aires, March 24th 1977

chapter sixteen

Walsh – alive again

My life isn't in there, no one's life is contained in a written piece of paper, not in a million scraps of paper.

(*La Granada*, Walsh, 1965 p.61)

Sometimes I wonder what would have happened if I had stayed. I would probably have a ranch or at least a plot of land and a horse.

(*Trasposición de Jugadas*, Walsh, 1992 p.75)

The killing team

Astiz, the rugby tackler in the Walsh kidnap attempt, is a social pariah, in and out of detention for unresolved cases of child theft. He cannot leave the country, as an international arrest warrant awaits him around the world. Inside Argentina he has been declared Persona Non Grata by several local authorities, further limiting his freedom of movement.

The HIJOS[46] activists treated Astiz to a vibrant *escrache* party: a home visit with banners, drums, leaflets and paint, where several hundred youths let the neighbourhood know who is hiding out in their midst, all in an atmosphere of celebration rather than vengeance.

Sharp-shooter and torture addict Jorge "Tigre" Acosta handed himself in to the law in December 1998, another criminal with an outstanding warrant for child theft. After the first *escrache* by HIJOS activists, Acosta moved home in the dead of night but the removal truck was spotted by keen-eyed revellers on their way home from a party. The second Acosta *escrache* occurred a day before he was due to testify in court on charges of child theft, when a journalist tracked him down to a holiday home in Pinamar beach resort. The next day Acosta had disappeared, not at the

---

[46] HIJOS, Children of the disappeared: "for identity and justice, against silence and forgetting".

hands of a death squad but in a last-gasp effort to evade the justice system. The nation's courts, unable to match Walsh's investigative skills, were likewise unable to match the skills of writer Miguel Bonasso, a pupil of Walsh's, who caught up with Acosta by combining phone taps with a network of neighbourhood volunteers.

When Bonasso confronted Acosta in a popular Pinamar restaurant, he pressed him on the issue of his violent past:

"Do you remember Rodolfo Walsh?" asked Bonasso, tape recorder in hand. "Let us eat," said the woman who was with Acosta. "You dumped more than 4,000 Argentinians into the sea, you killed Rodolfo Walsh," responded Bonasso.

"Go away," said Acosta.

"Rodolfo Walsh can't eat anymore," responded Bonasso.

Acosta hurried out of the restaurant, where he found a vehicle blocking his escape. He flagged down a taxi and raced away, the indignant cries of the locals ringing in his ears.

The repressors enjoyed power of life and death over Argentinians during military rule, roaming Buenos Aires day and night, picking up citizens at will, disposing of them as they desired. At the turn of the century Argentina's repressors now live a virtually clandestine existence, as walking the dog, going shopping or on holiday have become risky adventures.

On the night of my interview with Bonasso, which stretched into the following morning, we went for a walk at 3 a.m. looking for cigarettes. A lone painter on the night shift spotted Bonasso, stepped down from his ladder and approached us: "Thank you for representing all Argentinians in Pinamar," he said, shaking Bonasso's hand. The hearty handshake turned into a hug, rewarding Bonasso with flecks of yellow paint on his jacket.

Massera

A day before former junta leader Emilio Massera was due in court, Alicia Oliveira, an activist lawyer since appointed the nation's ombudswoman, signed a document legalising my "instant" marriage to María Inés Roque, daughter of Jorge "Lino" Roque, a Montonero leader at the time of his death, in August 1976. Roque fought a fierce gunbattle with dozens of soldiers sent to detain him, until he ran out of ammunition and burned down the house he was holed up in, to prevent documentation falling into enemy hands.

I met his daughter, a film student, in a Zapatista village in south-east Mexico, in March 1994, where she was making a documentary about insurgent Zapatista women. María Inés interviewed Subcomandante

Marcos. "It was like meeting my father again," she said. She offered him a copy of Lino's celebrated "Manual for Cadres", but he declined. "I already have a copy," he said.

Four years later, María Inés queued up to enter a court and face Emilio Massera, the navy admiral and junta leader who issued the order to kill her father and the order to kidnap Rodolfo Walsh. My "marriage" to María Inés lasted just 24 hours, sufficient time for me to witness the private hearings between Massera and relatives of the disappeared, access to which was restricted to relatives and spouses of the victims.

For the first time since the trial of the generals, in 1985, Massera came face to face, or as it turned out, back to face with relatives of his victims. María Inés wanted to ask Massera where her father's remains had been taken.

The Walsh family was represented by Rodolfo's surviving daughter Patricia, her two children María and Mariano, and Lilia Ferreyra, Rodolfo's partner during the last ten years of his life. The Walsh family wanted to know what Massera had done with both Rodolfo's body and with the work stolen from his home in San Vicente.

Massera was already sitting in court when we filed in. He sat stiffly in a red velvet chair, surrounded by thick volumes of legal resolutions which sat on dusty bookshelves stacked almost to the ceiling.

Massera looked straight at the judge, never risking even a sideways glance at the relatives seated in rows behind him. The tension was palpable. The security detail was focused outside the building, where protesters gathered to repudiate the genocide.

None of Massera's bodyguards were permitted inside the room. I had a burning desire to take down one of the thick volumes of legal history and beat Massera to death with it. I imagined my future defence: your honour, this man stamped out the rule of law and by the same rule of law has honour been restored.

The presiding judge, María Luisa Servini, reminded Massera that the sole function of the inquiry was to help relatives complete their search for information about their lost loved ones, a token gesture after decades of uncertainty and suffering. The hearing could have no legal consequence, as Massera was covered by amnesty laws.[47]

Massera sank further into his seat. "I have nothing to say," he said, a phrase he repeated 132 times that day, as one relative after another confronted him with a detailed account of his crimes, before requesting some missing scrap of information which would allow them to reconstruct the last days and final resting place of their loved ones. "I

---

[47] Only months later, Massera was put under house arrest and tried for child theft, a charge which is not covered by the amnesty.

have nothing to say," the mantra of a coward.

There were tears, hugs and a sense of catharsis among the relatives gathered there, even though no one expected Massera to confess to his murders. In breaks between the questions, I chatted to the Walsh family, beginning a relationship which made this book possible.

Rodolfo Walsh, an historian of the present

by Osvaldo Bayer

I always remember a meeting in Callao and Corrientes. If my memory doesn't deceive me it was late summer in 1972. The second volume of my book on Patagonia had just come out. Someone tapped me on the shoulder in the street and said, half serious, half smiling: "You're going to have to watch yourself from now on, they won't forgive you for that." It was Rodolfo. I answered without hesitation, "Look who's talking." And I added something that I wanted to express in a few words, "You're the only one at risk, you're an historian of the present."

And that was essentially Rodolfo Walsh: a committed historian of Argentina's present.

Even though I was born the same month and year as Rodolfo, I always looked on him as an older brother, an example to follow. I passionately read and still read his pages like someone who learns things which mature over time, like someone who needs to feed himself to avoid resignation or shameful compromises.

My conscience had developed increments of respect toward him. The times we met I harboured a permanent feeling of shyness and a desire to listen to him in silence, not wanting to miss a single word of his. Rodolfo Walsh was killed in the time of shame. They selected the best. And the killers made no mistake. They silenced his reporter's voice which uncovered, one by one, the crimes of a selfish and unscrupulous bourgeoisie, the betrayal of their own country and of the human condition. He was essentially a reporter who stirred everything up to find the truth but he was also a chronicler who – in his penetrating and rigorous style – made his investigation into chronicles for the people. And he was, at the same time, the editorial writer who could draw conclusions which showed the path ahead. Everything was direct, clear, quick and divested of any empty erudition.

The bourgeoisie killed Rodolfo Walsh because he knew too much about their sins, their baseness, their egoism and principally, about their methods. The system's intellectuals didn't waste a single word on his fall. Those were the times when Ernesto Sábato considered Videla a cultured general and for Borges, Pinochet's Chile was a country in the shape of a sword. Today they take up the role of a society without memory. With enviable skill they form a society of weakling democrats. The governments and multi-national corporations who collaborated with the ferocious dictatorship take them round the world today, showering them with prizes.

West Germany just gave Sábato the same Order of Merit that was awarded to Colonel Masi, the official censor at the Ministry of Public Information during the terrible years. History contains sarcastic ironies. The bourgeoisie, at times, commits some *faux pas*, which is immediately corrected with medals, speeches and *honoris causa* titles.

Rodolfo Walsh was the intellectual without medals, without prizes, without titles. He was a writer for the ones who come last, for the humblest, for those who want the sun to shine for them once in a while.

In my long years of exile I searched Germany for an intellectual of the anti-nazi resistance who would most resemble Rodolfo. I found him in three people, in different aspects which together added up to his personality: Karl Von Ossietzky, who died after a long time spent in captivity in Oranienburg concentration camp, a man who dedicated his unstinting reporter's soul to uncovering the businesses, dirty dealings and shameful deals of big capital, the military and politicians; Kurt Eisner, kicked to death by right-wing commandos in Bavaria, the intellectual turned politician who highlighted strategies by which the people could seize power; and Erich Mühsan, the poet and refined stylist whose pleasure, vocation and duty were to accompany the people, but showing them the dangers ahead, warning them to be ready to take to the streets and defend for themselves their rights through the vote or the barricade. Erich Mühsan was captured and hanged by the nazis in the prison toilet. Beautiful, strong souls who like Rodolfo wanted to use the lives given to them by nature to struggle for the only transcendental theology: solidarity.

I have to name three in nazi Germany to represent thousands. I name Rodolfo in representation of all those who gave their lives in our land against unjust privilege.

Today those intellectuals who first greeted the dictatorship and then alighted in 1982, so they could happily jump on the bandwagon of the new government, formed commissions for the disappeared whose fate they ignored at the time, and now they want to teach us that humankind is evil by nature.

How different to Rodolfo Walsh, the eternal optimist, who believed in the word because he believed in the human being.

When he wrote his "Letter from a Writer to the Military Junta", those intellectuals performed cartwheels using brilliant, vacuous literary turns of phrase in search of forms to distract the awareness of collective guilt at the crime being carried out.

Those were the years of "it is nothing to do with me", of looking the other way, the years of staying silent. Our bourgeoisie isn't going to sweep away its guilt by creating commissions of notables or through spectacular trials which take two or three scapegoats; seeking to avoid the bigger discussion of how the Argentinian holocaust was made possible, how the cruellest of cruel methods of repression were possible: the disappearance of people, in this country which calls itself christian.

Or did the shame arise only from the military hierarchy? If so what was the role of those who have economic power, what was the role of political parties, the church, the intelligentsia, what of the role of the chiefs of union bureaucracy?

Did all these forces just sit back and say "it is nothing to do with me", stay silent or look the other way?

What was the role of our bourgeoisie, who travelled to Europe, Miami and South Africa to escape their moral doubts while their own children were raped, tortured and burned here?

Rodolfo Walsh would be saying it today: it's not just a problem of the Masseras and Videlas. The problem is the behaviour of a whole section of society which always held the strings of power and still does so today, fresh as ever, their sins barely washed clean.

I am sure that tonight, Rodolfo Walsh, on the eve of a general strike, would have sat down to write a letter to Dr Alfonsín, as he did on March 24th 1977 to the military junta. He would tell him, in succinct terms, what he had failed to do within this space which was reluctantly given to the bourgeoisie: he would remind him of the ignominy of the existence of political prisoners, the shame of the frustrated trial of the criminals of the dictatorship, the lack of response to the Madres de la Plaza de Mayo about the fate of their children, the Latin American solidarity turned into rhetoric, the external debt further legalising dependency and Argentinians debased by ever-growing misery.

But he would also be very critical of the progressive forces, of their lack of unity, their short-sighted thinking and their sectarian egoism.

Nine years after his kidnapping, we have a lot to learn from Walsh. In the face of past defeat and the question of what is to be done, he would be very concrete: we must begin again.

➼ Baschetti, 1994 pp.332–36

Heirs and graces

Uruguayan writer Eduardo Galeano described Rodolfo Walsh as "the best Argentinian narrator of his time" who restored faith in a profession beset by "imposters and salesmen." Who does he compare with today?

Hundreds of journalists and intellectuals continue to bear witness in difficult times, facing censorship, harassment, imprisonment and death. As I searched for comparisons many names flashed through my mind; yet my thoughts kept returning to Subcomandante Marcos, the "Sup", the Zapatista military leader based in south-east Mexico.

The Ejercito Zapatista de Liberación Nacional, EZLN (Zapatista National Liberation Army), launched an armed uprising in January 1994, the first rebel army to declare war on an international trade agreement, NAFTA,[48] anticipating the emerging global citizens' movement by several years. The chief weapon of the Zapatistas is their word, transmitted through the poetic communiqués penned by Marcos. The "Sup" has become an international symbol of dignity, rebellion and humour in the face of global corporate greed. Marcos is not alone. The Zapatista words are delivered by an army of supporters, a low-tech courier service rapidly connecting with cyberspace at the click of a keyboard command.

Rodolfo Walsh created similar information networks in the pre-computer age. It's easy to imagine Walsh today, hunched over a computer screen, hacking into corporate databases and networking with multiple resistance efforts around the globe. Marcos and Walsh both sacrificed personal ambitions for the challenge of creating a more just society. Rosario Ibarra embraced Marcos at the Zapatistas' National Democratic Convention in August 1994, discovering in him the resurrected spirit of her own disappeared son who died fighting Mexico's repressive State. So too is Rodolfo Walsh resurrected in the figure of Subcomandante Marcos, who happens to be a crime fiction addict, an accomplished writer, a cryptologist and a revolutionary. Several publishers have reportedly offered him tempting advances to write a novel but the 'Sup' has turned them down, as he lives out a different novel, called Reality, alongside the indigenous people of Chiapas.

Walsh in the 21st century

A thriving "Walsh industry" has spilled forth hundreds of newspaper articles, essays, analyses, theses, documentaries and books, along with films adapted from his work, breaking the decade of silence after military rule (1976–83).

Rodolfo Walsh has returned to the front pages of Argentina's newspapers, his books have been reprinted and continue to sell, his name is still a source of controversy, as he would have wanted. There are monuments, plazas and streets named after him, including the Faculty of Social

---

[48] The North American Free Trade Agreement, linking Canada, the US and Mexico into a common market.

Sciences at the University of Buenos Aires.

In the city of La Plata, where Walsh's adventures first began, the Journalism Department at the local university carries his name, along with its annual prize for investigative journalism.

In July 1997 the Ministry of Education named a new school St Exupery after the author of *The Little Prince*. Pupils, teachers and parents protested, saying they had already named the school after Rodolfo Walsh. The dispute turned to a ballot in which Walsh supporters outvoted St Exupery adherents by 180 votes, ensuring the name will forever accompany the chalk and the playground, so that children might know and remember.

Walsh, compañero

Rodolfo was reserved and detached with others, yet he was also passionate and engaged, leaving contradictory recollections in his wake.

"He was very sober, you wouldn't exactly call him the king of sympathy, he was a quiet type, observant and prudent. But his personality drew people to him and even though he didn't seek it out, he ended up surrounded by people [...] he was austere, but didn't miss out on the fun [...] he liked to mimic people, but usually in private. He played charades, he liked to mess around, but spontaneously. Nowadays you hear people say that you have to be an activist with a sense of fun, which has become a cliché. We had happiness in our life, but it was the way we were, it wasn't cultivated" (Ferreyra quoted in Camano and Bayer, 1998 pp.230–231).

"I think it's a disgrace that they honoured someone who planted bombs and tried to destroy the country," said Carlos Walsh, referring to the memorial square dedicated to his brother near his home. Yet his voice cracked as he recalled Rodolfo's tragic end. "He ended up dead, his daughter dead, without fulfilling any of the goals he had set for himself. I often wonder if I could have done anything, if I was too indifferent in those years..."

"I don't think Walsh was a heroic figure," said Andrew Graham-Yooll, former editor of Argentina's *Buenos Aires Herald*. "Heroes are large and imposing but Walsh was thin and not very tall." Graham-Yooll met Walsh through Pirí Lugones, moving in the same literary circles. He compared Walsh to Irish independence hero Michael Collins: their ruthless strategy of war, their betrayal and final ambush. "On the last day of his life he tells Lilia, it's time to leave, this has failed, the cause has been betrayed by its leaders – those are words you could put into the mouth of Collins."

Walsh's thoughts on armed struggle remain the subject of intense debate. On the 20th anniversary of Walsh's death in 1997, Horacio

Verbitsky suggested that in his final writings Walsh had rejected violence as a tool for change. Verbitsky turned to Walsh's own words to back up his opinion: "A thousand small victories," wrote Walsh, were preferable to "spectacular operations which draw massive reprisals." He acknowledged that the organisation needed to replace its FAL rifles with "the mimeograph" (Baschetti 1994, p.234). From his prison cell in Villa Devoto, Argentina's best-known political prisoner, Enrique Gorriarán Merlo, challenged Verbitsky's assertions about Walsh. Gorriarán wrote a letter to progressive daily *Página 12* on the coup anniversary in 1997, in which he completed the phrase cited by Verbitsky. Walsh had indeed called for the replacement of the FAL rifle, wrote Gorriarán, but with "the mimeograph *and the pipe bomb,*" lending an entirely different emphasis to the analysis. The letter was never published.

For his daughter Patricia, Walsh only found his true vocation toward the end of his life as a guerrilla combatant. For his muse and unrealised love Enriqueta Muñiz, Rodolfo's death was "a stupidity".

In the time I spent researching Rodolfo's life, I met sons and daughters of the disappeared, their childhood cut short by the brutal clash between their parents' idealism and the terror inflicted at the behest of the ruling elite. The children grew up with photos and anecdotes and struggled with competing emotions, as pride in their parents' struggle clashed with searing anger at the tremendous absence and sense of loss.

It was one thing to discuss the painful past with Walsh's peers, quite another to face someone who had neither voice nor vote in the events of the time, yet lived with the consequences. In her first year on earth Victoria María Costa Walsh, daughter of Vicki (born August 1st 1975) was to all intents and purposes a Montonero combatant, like her mother, carried from meeting to meeting, sharing the tension inside her mother's breast.

On September 29th 1976 she almost shared her mother's death, as she sat on a bed, her mother on the roof, facing down tanks and troops with a machine gun. The soldiers found Vicki on the bed. They kidnapped her and gave her away to a police officer in Buenos Aires province, to be added to the junta adoption list of "subversive children".

Fortunately for Vicki, her paternal grandfather, Miguel Costa, a retired navy commodore, moved quickly and was able to recover the child within days. They left for Uruguay, where she was joined by her father Emiliano, when he was released from prison in 1983.

Vicki greeted me with a broad grin on board a scooter which had seen better days. She treasures her mother's memory but is not tied down by it, wisely letting go in order to move ahead, but never forgetting her mother's extraordinary sacrifice.

On September 29th 1998, Vicki, her father Emiliano, Lilia, and other friends went to the house on Calle Corro, where the fatal gunbattle had occurred. The house was rebuilt and sold on by the army. Some neighbours quietly joined the group. Vicki began reading Rodolfo's "Letter to My Friends", managing just one sentence before she broke down. She passed the letter on to her father, who struggled through a paragraph before he too choked. Lilia Ferreyra took up the reading and finished it, fighting back the tears.

Rodolfo's friends recalled a man who listened patiently to other people's problems, while one woman said he was the only man with whom she could really discuss issues of the heart without misinterpretation. In his public life he was a bridge between intellectual reflection and revolutionary commitment.

On January 9th 1999, at a barbeque held in Walsh's old home in Tigre, two dozen guests gathered to celebrate what would have been Rodolfo's 72nd birthday. Talk turned inevitably to the past, as we wondered what might have been, until Lilia Ferreyra broke the spell.

"If Rodolfo were here now," she said, "he'd say, ok, so what we are going to do now?"

Walsh's legacy lies in the idea of "living for others". When Che Guevara is a t-shirt and Revolution a corporate brand strategy, Walsh's example is an implicit challenge to stand up, wherever one is, and fight for a better world whatever the personal cost. "Death no longer holds so much fear, it's like going to a country where we have a friend," wrote Vicente Zito Lema, about Walsh. "Every time I say your name I say the name of every one of the thousands of faceless, nameless men and women, disappeared for the same crime that you so passionately committed – to live for others."

Epilogue

If these guys win this country will be asphyxiating [irrespirable].

(Walsh, 1977)

The "Open Letter" provided a framework for understanding the nature and extent of state terror in Argentina and its overwhelming impact on civil society. It was a revelation at the time and it remains vitally relevant today. Walsh estimated that it would take "twenty to thirty years" for the effects of the dictatorship to wear off, allowing civil society to regain confidence and try once more to overhaul the nation's unjust social and economic order. Recent developments in Argentina sustain his claim.

The return of constitutional rule in 1983 signified the retreat rather than the defeat of the state terror apparatus. The National Commission for the Investigation of Disappeared Persons (CONADEP) was an important mechanism but the grisly findings were simply filed away as it lacked any faculty for punishing the willing executioners and their civilian collaborators. Nor could the guilty be dislodged from public positions. The survivors of state terror, their families and friends, were expected to return to daily life as if nothing had happened. The tortured bumped into their tormentors on the beach, in the cinema, or walking in the park.

The trial of the generals in 1985 offered a brief moment of justice which was neutered in 1989–90 with the laws of Due Obedience and Full Stop. The state decreed the end of remembering but memory proved more resilient; the sense of collective shame inhibited discussion but not remembrance. Argentina was paralysed by fear throughout the junta years, yet the example of the Mothers of the Plaza de Mayo showed that dissent was possible, notwithstanding the enormous risks attached. The Mothers stood up to the dictatorship, beginning their weekly rounds in February 1977, at the height of the killings. They still march every week, joined now by the Abuelas (Grandmothers) and HIJOS. Repressors are pursued through the courts on crimes against humanity which cannot be covered by any amnesty, notably child theft.

In Ireland, in the 1840s, a terrible famine swept the land, killing an estimated one million people and forcing two million more people to emigrate. Among the emigrants was Rodolfo Walsh's grandfather, Miguel Walsh y Kelly. The famine was sparked by the failure of the potato crop but the massive death toll was driven by British economic policy, as liberal or "laissez-faire" concepts provided the colonial power with an ideological pretext for ignoring the Irish as they starved to death. The legacy of the famine remains today, just two lifetimes away, buried within the Irish psyche, even as successive upbeat Irish governments strive to put the "unfortunate" episode behind us. "All nations which have suffered traumas similar to our own have come, sooner or later, to the realisation that they must return to the past one last time in truth and reverence before they can make the first real steps into the future," wrote John Waters, an Irish journalist, commenting on the long-term impact of the famine years.

The legacy of the Argentinian dictatorship, its long-term "victory", has been its "success" in manufacturing consent and indifference to social inequality. Or so they thought. Under the free-market model your work colleagues are competitors, your grandparents are an unproductive burden, your children an expensive accessory. Combative trade unions are troublesome institutions holding back foreign investment. Labour must be "flexible", meaning submissive, under-paid and overworked. With official unemployment figures at 24 per cent (April 2002) it would take a brave soul to face down the blackmail of reduced pay or face unemployment. Argentina is a model nation for the latest trends in global capitalism, as profits are privatized and losses socialized. National budgets are drawn up with external debt repayments in mind, even as families queue for soup kitchens or sleep outside foreign embassies to secure a visa out of hell.

Since December 2001, when the nation's economy formally collapsed, Argentinian citizens have shaken themselves out of their lethargy, giving a collective Enough! to politicians. The new challenge to state authority first made headlines in April 1997 when 15,000 people led a spontaneous citizen uprising in Cutral-Co and Plaza Huincol, in southwest Argentina. The protests were short-lived experiments in grassroots democracy, where decisions were made at citizen assemblies, spokespeople rotated, "to avoid them being bought off" with access refused to traditional union and church leaders. It lacked the organisational flair demonstrated during the *Cordobazo* of 1969 but put the government on notice that people were not willing to sit back and watch their children starve.

Then President Menem immediately denounced the "return of subversion" and warned that he would not tolerate the disruption of transport and industry. The savage disruption of livelihoods by planned misery (28,000 small and medium-size industries shut down in 1998, unable to compete with cheap imports) didn't merit a mention at all. The

Cutral-Co/Plaza Huincol protest reached crisis point when police shot dead a 25-year-old woman, Teresa Rodríguez, as she walked to work around the huge protest. Citizen outrage and dramatic live television footage forced a government climbdown. Menem quickly cobbled together an aid package which included 800 work subsidies at $200 a month, for four hours' work a day. The petroleum giant YPF added 500 jobs and one thousand low-cost houses. Finally, the authorities agreed to abandon legal action taken against the rebellious citizens. Dissent did pay after all.

In Cutral-Co the repression was led by Comandante Mayor Eduardo Jorge, who was in charge of the first secret detention centre in Tucumán, 25 years previous. Jorge personally helped out in the execution of prisoners, who were shot in the head, their bodies thrown down wells, or doused in petrol and set alight. Jorge had been formally denounced by CONADEP.

The failure of successive civilian governments to act on the findings of CONADEP and similar inquiries has been highlighted on many occasions, as impunity breeds fascism. The state security forces have seen no major change in training and procedures since the dictatorship years. The police shoot to kill, targeting poor youths in marginal neighbourhoods or peaceful protestors in the Plaza de Mayo (December 2001).

Poverty levels rose rapidly during the Menem years (1989–1999) with 400,000 "new poor" declared in Buenos Aires province in 1996 alone, bringing the total number of poor to 3.2 million, more than 30 per cent of the population. The figures came from the government's own National Census and Statistics Institute, (INDEC), an office of the Economics Ministry. Back in 1973, INDEC registered 3.7 per cent unemployment in the capital city and what they described as an "explosive" 11.3 per cent in the impoverished province of Tucumán. Such figures seem utopian in the privatised, "new" Argentina, basking in an alleged economic miracle (*Noticias* 24/7/74).

One million Argentinians dropped beneath the poverty line between January and April 2002, while unemployment now affects 30 per cent of the population, according to economic consultancy group Equis. The institute announced the result of an economic survey which revealed that 60 per cent of children under 14 years of age survive in poverty, with 2.5 million classified as indigents. The average monthly income before the December 2001 devaluation of the peso was $623 dollars per month, a figure which dropped to just $207 per month, in a country where the cost of living is comparable to European nations.

The street mobilizations that led to five presidents in two weeks could easily have been dismissed as temporary rage, were it not for the organizational initiatives that followed. In the early months of 2002, hundreds of neighbourhoods began organizing weekly assemblies, where local people discussed all aspects of the ongoing economic and political meltdown. They also set up barter clubs operating outside the official economy, providing both material resources and a sense of solidarity. There were no leaders and no political parties allowed, no bureaucratic structures set up. This was an autonomous space for launching a solidarity movement which challenged the notion that only "experts" and "professionals" could rescue the nation from its moribund state.

A powerful symbol of that expert-obsessed culture was Domingo Cavallo, architect of Argentina's economic "miracle", or catastrophe, depending on your place in the economy. Cavallo was an accountant for the military under junta rule, then reinvented himself as a neoliberal statesman in the Menem era. Cavallo ran for president in December 1999, putting his popularity to the test. He won just 10 per cent of votes. President De La Rua (1999–2001) subsequently made him "super-minister" in 2000 under pressure from international financial institutions, eager to have one of their own at the helm. Cavallo is now virtually a prisoner in his own home, unable to appear anywhere in public as citizens heckle and threaten him.

Argentina cannot prosper while repressors and their collaborators are allowed to hold on to positions of public influence which were acquired and consolidated even as the systematic extermination of social activists was taking place. The shadow of the State terror apparatus has inhibited popular mobilization, while disgraced repressors have moved into the private security industry, whose ranks now outnumber the police force.

"This is Chiapas," said a frightened police chief in April 1997, as he ordered security forces to withdraw from Cutral-Co and Plaza Huincol. The comparison is more apt than at first may appear. Since the armed indigenous uprising in January 1994 the Zapatistas have consolidated autonomous self-rule in areas under their influence, while also channelling international aid through sympathetic non-governmental organisations.

Argentina must abandon her dependence on global capital to look within at national resources and wealth. The global economy rests on a high-risk bluff whereby wealthy nations and corporations accumulate imaginary fortunes based on speculation and dazzling profit margins. Argentina, as a nation, must withdraw its consent and short-circuit the wheel of misery. The task is huge, energy is low. Yet the realisation of our potential to run our own lives is a powerful motivating factor, which can spur us on to work with friends, neighbours, allies and even our opponents. Street by street, neighbourhood by neighbourhood, as Rodolfo suggested.

Argentina: key dates

1516: Juan Díaz de Solís explores Río de la Plata estuary
1536: First founding of Buenos Aires by Pedro de Mendoza; settlement destroyed by indigenous peoples
1580: Second founding of Buenos Aires by Juan de Garay
1778: Birth of José de San Martín (independence leader)
1806–7: Unsuccessful attempts by the British army to take Buenos Aires
1810: Buenos Aires *cabildo* or revolutionary council declares freedom from Spain
1816: Formal declaration of Argentine independence
1817–19: San Martín fights for independence in Chile and Peru
1835–52: Rule by military caudillo Juan Manuel de Rosas
1853–61: First unified national constitution followed by struggle between Federalists (provinces) and Unitarians (Buenos Aires)
1868–74: Domingo F. Sarmiento president
1880: Buenos Aires replaces Rosario as national capital
1890: Founding of Unión Cívica Radical or Radical Party, UCR
1914–28: Presidential rule of Hipólito Yrigoyen, a democratic reformist who belonged to the Unión Cívica Radical, UCR
1916: Universal male suffrage introduced
1930: Yrigoyen deposed by the military; start of period of military rule known as the "infamous decade"
1931: Nationalists apply "patriotic fraud" to ensure victory for their candidate, General Agustín P Justo
1943: National revolution led by nationalist military officers, among them Colonel Juan Domingo Perón
1945: Perón arrested, freed after massive popular protest
1946: Perón elected president for first term
1947: Perón signs the Chapultepec Acts which brought Argentina into line with US foreign policy objectives
1951: Perón's second term as president
1952: Eva Duarte de Perón (Evita) dies of cancer
1955: Perón ousted in military coup known as "liberating revolution"
1960s: Struggle for power between different military factions
1966: General Juan Carlos Onganía comes to power; Congress closed; repression against Peronist and other political parties increased
1967: Death of Ernesto "Che" Guevara
May 1969: Thousands of citizens take control of Argentina's second city, Córdoba, for two days, routing the army and police

1970: Onganía ousted by fellow officers; General Alejandro Lanusse eventually takes over as president

1973: Peronists allowed to stand in elections; their candidate Héctor Cámpora wins

1973: Fresh elections; Perón elected president for the third time, dies a few months later, leaving his widow Estela "Isabelita" Martínez as president

March 1976: Military coup

1976–1983: Period of the *proceso militar*; up to 30,000 people disappear at the hands of the State

1982: Junta leader General Leopoldo Fortunato Galtieri sends troops in April to the Falklands/Malvinas islands; British task force retakes them by mid-June

1983–84: Collapse of military regime; UCR leader Raúl Alfonsín elected president

1989: Radicals lose presidential elections; amid growing economic chaos, Alfonsín hands over power to elected President, Carlos Saúl Menem of the Peronist party

1991: Start of economic policy with *peso* at parity with US dollar

1994: New constitution approved, allowing the president to serve two consecutive terms in office

1994: New party, Frente Pais Solidario (FREPASO) is formed

1995: Menem wins second term

1996: Fernando de la Rua elected as first mayor of the city of Buenos Aires

1996: Broad coalition of unions organises two general strikes against proposed law of labour flexibility and government's economic policies

1997: Teachers' union sets up teacher hunger strikes in front of national congress

1997: Alianza, an electoral alliance of UCR and FREPASO, formally established

1999: Fernando de la Rua wins the presidential election for the UCR/FREPASO coalition

November 2001: Government responds to a run on banks by freezing all bank deposits

December 2001: Large segments of the middle class take to the Buenos Aires streets in protest. Supermarket ransacking occurs in poorer neighbourhoods and violent protests in the Plaza de Mayo.

December 2001: Fernando de la Rua forced to abandon presidential residence, signalling the collapse of his government and an ensuing power vacuum

December 2001: Argentina temporarily ceases payment on its foreign debt

January 2002: Eduardo Duhalde selected by Congress to serve as president, after three interim presidents step down.

Bibliographies

General bibliography

Amar Sánchez, A.M. (1992) *El Relato de los Hechos*, Beatriz Viterbo: Rosario
Anderson, J.L. (1997) *Che Guevara, A Revolutionary Life*, Grove Press: New York
Anderson, M.E. (1993) *Dossier Secreto*, Sudamericana: Argentina
Anguita, E., Caparrós, M.(1997) *La Voluntad*, Norma: Buenos Aires
Anguita, E., Caparrós, M.(1998a) *La Voluntad, Tomo II*, Norma: Buenos Aires
Anguita, E., Caparrós, M.(1998b) *La Voluntad, Tomo III*, Norma: Buenos Aires
Arlt, R. (1997) *Los Siete Locos*, Altamira: La Plata
Asociación Madres de la Plaza de Mayo, (1999) *Massera, el genocida*, Editorial
    La Página: Argentina
Baschetti, R. (1994) *Rodolfo Walsh, Vivo*, Ediciones de la Flor: Argentina
Bechara, M.A. (1998) *Periodismo y Literatura*, Universidad Nacional de Entre Rios:
    Argentina
Benedetti, M. (1986) *El Desexilio*, Nueva Imagen: México
Benedetti, M. (1986) *El escritor latinoamericano y la revolución posible*, Nueva
    Imagen: México
Blixen, S. (1997) *Conversaciones con Gorriarán Merlo*, Ediciones de la Campana:
    La Plata
Bonasso, M. (1984) *Recuerdo de la Muerte*, Bruguera: Buenos Aires
Borges, J.L. (1986) *Labyrinths*, Penguin: England
Calveiro, P. (1998) *Poder y desaparición*, Ediciones Colihue: Argentina
Camano, J.C., Bayer, O. (1998) *Los periodistas desaparecidos*, Grupo Editorial
    Norma: Argentina
Castañeda, J.G. (1994) *Utopia Unarmed*, Vintage: New York
Castillo E. C. (1999) *Un día de octubre en Santiago*, Lom: Chile
Cohen, J.M. (1967) *Writers in the New Cuba*, Penguin: England
CONADEP, (1984) *Nunca Más*, EUDEBA: Argentina
Conti, H. (1971) *En Vida*, Barral: Barcelona
Conti, H. (1976) *Cuentos y Relatos*, Editorial Kapelusz: Buenos Aires
Conti, H. (1985) *Sudeste*, Alfaguara: Madrid
Corradi, J. E. et al. (1992) *Fear at the Edge: State Terror and Resistance in Latin
    America*, University of California Press: Berkeley
Cortázar, J. (1978) *A Manual for Manuel*, Pantheon: New York
De Biase, M. (1998) *Entre dos fuegos*, Ediciones de la Flor: Argentina
Diana, M. (1997) *Mujeres Guerrilleras*, Planeta: Argentina
Dorfman, A. (1998) *Rumbo al Sur, deseando el Norte*, Planeta: Spain
Duhalde, E.L. (1983) *El estado terrorista argentino*, El Caballito: Argentina
Dujovne Ortiz, A. (1997) *Eva Perón*, Time Warner Books: UK
Eloy Martínez, T. (1996) *Santa Evita*, Planeta: Argentina
Evans, M. (1997) *The Memory of Resistance*, Berg: England
Feitlowitz, M. (1998) *A Lexicon of Terror*, Oxford University Press: New York

Fernández Retamar, R. (1993) *Fervor de la Argentina*, Ediciones del Sol: Argentina
Fisher, J. (1989) *Mothers of the Disappeared*, South End Press: Boston
Ford, A. (1987) *Desde la orilla de la ciencia*, Puntosur: Argentina
France, M. (1999) *Bad Times in Buenos Aires*, Phoenix: England.
Gabetta, C. (1983) *Todos somos subversivos*, Bruguera: Buenos Aires.
Galeano, E. (1997) *Open Veins of Latin America*, Latin America Bureau: London
García, A., Fernández Vidal, M. (1995) *Pirí*, Ediciones de la Flor: Buenos Aires
García Lupo, R. (1975) *Contra la ocupación extranjera*, EFECE: Buenos Aires
Gasparini, J. (1999) *Montoneros, final de cuentas*, Ediciones de la Campana: La Plata
Gelman J., La Madrid, M., (1997) *Ni el flaco perdón de dios*, Planeta: Argentina
Gillespie, R. (1998) *Soldados de Perón*, Grijalbo: Argentina
Goñi, U. (2002) *The Real Odessa*, Granta: London
Gonzalez Janzen, I. (1986), *La Triple A*, Contrapunto: Buenos Aires
Gourevitch, P. (1999) *We Wish to Inform You that Tomorrow We Will Be Killed with Our Families*, Picador: New York
Graham-Yooll, A. (1989) *De Perón a Videla*, Legasa: Argentina
Guevara, Ernesto. (1986) *Guerrilla Warfare*, Manchester University Press: Manchester
Hayden, T. (1997) *Irish Hunger*, Wolfhound: Dublin
Hemingway, E. (1995) *A Farewell to Arms*, Scribner: New York
Hiney, T., MacShane, F. (2001) *The Raymond Chandler Papers*, Penguin: England
Index On Censorship (1997) 1972–1997, *An Embarrassment of Tyrannies*, Victor Gollancz: London.
Katzenberger, Elaine (1995) (ed) *First World, Ha! Ha! Ha! The Zapatista Challenge*, City Lights: San Francisco
Kimel, E. (1995) *La masacre de San Patricio*, Ediciones Lohle-Lumen: Buenos Aires
Klein, J. (1980) *Woody Guthrie: A Life*, Faber and Faber: London
Lafforgue, J. (2000) *Textos de y sobre Rodolfo Walsh*, Alianza: Buenos Aires
Leante, C. (1999) *Revive, historia. Anatomía del castrismo*, Biblioteca Nueva: Spain
Masetti, J. (1999) *El furor y el delirio*, Tusquets: Mexico
Matthews, H.L. (1961) *The Cuban Story*, George Braziller: New York
Mendoza A. P. (2000) *Aquellos tiempos con Gabo*, Plaza Y Janes: Barcelona
Naipaul, V.S. (1988) *The Return of Eva Perón*, Penguin: England
Nosiglia, J.E. (1997) *Botín de Guerra*, Editorial La Página: Argentina
Oesterheld, H.G. (1994) *El Eternauta*, Ediciones Record: Buenos Aires
Olguín, S. (ed) (1999) *Los mejores cuentos argentinos: los cuentos más votados por escritores y críticos*, Alfaguara: Buenos Aires
Ousby, I. (1997) *The Crime and Mystery Book*, Thames and Hudson: London
Paino, H. (1984) *Historia de la Triple A*, Platense: Uruguay
Paz Durruti, A. (1976) *The People Armed*, Black Rose Books: Montreal
Perdía, R.C. (1997) *La otra historia*, Grupo Agora: Argentina
Piglia, R. (1997) *Plata Quemada*, Planeta: Buenos Aires
Poe, E.A. (1962) *Selected Stories and Poems*, Airmont: New York
Potash, R.A. (1985) *El ejercito y la política en Argentina*, Hyspamerica: Argentina
Romero, J.L. (1998) *Breve historia de la Argentina*, Fondo de Cultura Economica: Argentina
Rosell Vera, P.I. (1995) *Himno y Requiem*, Arlequín de San Telmo: Argentina
Rosenberg, T. (1991) *Children of Cain*, William Morrow: New York
Sebastian, A. (1982) *Rodolfo Walsh o la desacralización de la literatura*, Argenguay: Amsterdam
Seisdedos, G. (1996) *El honor de dios*, San Pablo: Argentina
Timmerman, J. (1982) *Preso sin nombre, celda sin número*, El Cid Editor: Buenos Aires
Tosco A. (1985) *Escritos y Discursos*, Contrapunto: Argentina
Urondo, F. (1999) *Los pasos previos*, Adriana Hidalgo: Buenos Aires

Verbitsky, H. (1985) *La posguerra sucia*, Legasa: Argentina
Verbitsky, H. (1985) *Rodolfo Walsh y la prensa clandestina*, Colección El Periodista: Buenos Aires
Verbitsky, H. (1987) *Medio siglo de proclamas militares*, Editora/12: Argentina
Verbitsky, H. (1998) *Ezeiza*, Planeta: Argentina
Viñas, D. (1982) *Los dueños de la tierra*, Folios Ediciones: Mexico
Waugh, E. (1943) *Scoop*, Penguin: London
Wilson, J. (1999) *Buenos Aires*, Latin America Bureau: London
Winocur, M. (1963) *Cuba a la hora de América*, Ediciones Procyon: Argentina
Woodward, B. (1987) *Veil: The Secret Wars of the CIA, 1981–87*, Simon and Schuster: New York
Woolrich, C. (1998) *The Cornell Woolrich Omnibus*, Penguin: New York
Yates, D. (1972) *Latin Blood: The Best Crime and Detective Stories of South America*, Herder and Herder: New York

Musicography

Music has been a huge influence in my life so it seems only fair to mention some of the sounds that inspired this book. I include just a few names as the complete list would fill a book of its own. I avoided naming particular songs as virtually everything recorded by these artists is heavily rotated on the turntable so Hail Hail to Pearl Jam, Manu Chao, Fugazi, Mike Scott and the Waterboys, Shane MacGowan, Sinead O'Connor, Silvio Rodriguez, Rage Against the Machine, Current 93, The Clash, Kila and Jackie Leven.

Rodolfo Walsh bibliography

Walsh books

Walsh (1953) *Variaciones en Rojo*. Hachette, Serie Naranja
Walsh (1957) *Operación Masacre*, Sigla
    (1964) Continental Service, (1969) Jorge Alvarez, (1972) Ediciones de la Flor
Walsh (1958) *Caso Satanowsky*, Editorial Verdad
Walsh (1965a) *Los Oficios Terrestres*, Jorge Alvarez
Walsh (1965b) *La Granada, La Batalla*, Jorge Alvarez.
Walsh (1967) *Un Kilo de Oro*, Jorge Alvarez
Walsh (1969) *Quien Mató a Rosendo?* Tiempo Contemporáneo
Walsh (1973) *Un Oscuro Día De Justicia*, Siglo XXI: Argentina

Posthumous collections

Walsh (1981) *Obra Literaria Completa*, Siglo XXI: Mexico
Walsh (1985) *Rodolfo Walsh y la prensa clandestina*, Ediciones de la Urraca
Walsh (1987) *Cuento para tahures y otros relatos policiales*, Puntosur
Walsh (1990) *Yo también fui fusilado, Vuelve la secta del gatillo y la picana y otros textos*, Los Libros de Gente Sur, (comp) Roberto Ferro.
Walsh (1992) *La máquina del bien y del mal*, Clarín/Aguilar
Walsh (1993) *Cuentos*, (1993) Biblioteca *Página/12*
Walsh (1994) *Rodolfo Walsh, Vivo*, anthology and prologue by R. Baschetti, Ediciones de la Flor
Walsh (1995) *El Violento Oficio de Escribir: Obra periodistica 1953–77*, (comp) Daniel Link, Espejo de la Argentina/Planeta
Walsh (1996) *Ese Hombre y otros escritos personales*, Seix Barral/Biblioteca Breve
Walsh, *Semanario CGT. Página 12*/Universidad Nacional de Quilmes

Anthologies compiled by Walsh

Walsh, (1953) *Diez cuentos policiales argentinos*, Librería Hachette
Walsh, (1956) *Antología del cuento extraño*, Librería Hachette
Walsh, (1969) *Crónicas de Cuba*, Jorge Alvarez

Short stories published in magazines

1 Las tres noches de Isaias Bloom, *Vea y Lea* 17/8/1950
2 Los Nutrieros, *Leoplan* 20/6/1951
3 Los ojos del traidor, *Vea y Lea* 20/3/1952
4 El viaje circular, *Vea y Lea* 18/12/1952
5 El santo, *Fenix*, La Plata,1953
6 El ajedrez y los dioses, *Fenix*, La Plata, 1953
7 Crimen a la distancia, *Leoplan* 21/9/1953
8 La sombra de un pájaro, *Leoplan* 20/10/1954
9 Tres portugueses bajo un paraguas (sin contar el muerto), *Leoplan* 16/3/1955
10 Simbiosis, *Vea y Lea* 15/11/1956
11 La trampa, *Vea y Lea* 3/10/1957
12 Zugzwang, *Vea y Lea* 12/12/1957
13 Los dos montones de tierra, *Vea y Lea* 25/5/1961
14 *Transposición* de jugadas, *Vea y Lea* 14/9/1961
15 Cosa juzgada, *Vea y Lea* 12/4/1962
16 Los oficios terrestres, *Adan* 6/12/1966
17 Un oscuro día de justicia, *Adan* 18/12/1967

Walsh, journalism

1 La misteriosa desaparición de un creador de misterios, *Leoplan* 4/3/1953
2 Vuelve Sherlock Holmes! *Leoplan* 20/5/1953
3 El genio del anónimo, *Leoplan* 3/12/1954
4 Dos mil quinientos años de literatura policial, *La Nación* 14/12/1954
5 Giovanni Papini y la lucha contra el demonio, *Leoplan* 19/5/1954
6 Un estrecimiento por favor, *Leoplan* 18/5/1955
7 Cierra la puerta, *Leoplan* 20/7/1955
8 [ ] 2-0-12 no vuelve, *Leoplan* 21/12/1955
9 Los peores desastres de este siglo, *Leoplan* 15/9/1956.
10 Aqui cerraron sus ojos, *Leoplan* 1/10/1956
11 De Copenhague a Tokio a traves del Polo, *Leoplan* 15/2/1957
12 [ ] 3120-5699-1184 (lenguaje universal cifrado) *Leoplan* 1/3/1957
13 El fin de los dirigibles *Leoplan* 15/3/1957
14 El automovil del futuro, *Leoplan* 15/8/1957
15 Adios al "Pamir" *Leoplan* 15/10/1957
16 Los métodos del F.B.I. *Leoplan* 15/10/1957
17 Kapitza, el enemigo publico No. 1 de occidente, *Leoplan* 1/11/1957
18 General Mosconi, el gran visionario, *Leoplan* 15/12/1957
19 Se hace la represa del Chocón, *Leoplan* 1/2/1958
20 Veinte preguntas al presidente electo (entrevista a Arturo Frondizi),
   Leoplan 1/3/1958
21 El equipo del doctor Frondizi, *Leoplan* 15/3/1958
22 Aplausos, Teniente Coronel *Azul y Blanco* 18/3/1958
23 Un niño secreto que no se dirá, *Leoplan* 15/4/1958.
24 Y ahora... Coronel? *Azul y Blanco* 29/4/1958
25 Caso Satanowsky, [28 articles published weekly from June 9], *Mayoría* 1958
26 El mundo de los grandes en boca de los chicos, *Leoplan* 1/3/1959

27   Tibor Gordon, profeta de la tierra prometida, *Leoplan* 15/3/1959
26   Llegaron los Comet, *Leoplan* 1/4/1959
27   El hombre del guardapolvo gris, *Leoplan* 15/4/1959
28   Un año de gobierno, qué piensa la gente, *Leoplan* 1/2/1959
29   Argentina en el ojo del mundo, [Series of articles, published from 15/5 to 10/11 in *Leoplan*, as a Special Service of Prensa Latina]
30   Fidel renuncia, Fidel se queda, *Leoplan* 5/8/1959
31   No te fies de un enviado especial, *Che* 15/11/1960
32   Guatemala, una diplomacia de rodillas, *Che* 9/3/1961
33   Walsh sobre el tapete, *Che* 17/5/1961
34   El extraño caso de las dos confesiones, *Usted* 23/5/1961
35   La última pirueta de Allen Dulles en Argentina, *Voz Popular* 2/10/1961
36   "Olvidanza" y "La Noticia" Gregorio, *Leoplan* supplement 5/2/1964
37   Claroscuro del subibaja, Gregorio, *Leoplan* supplement 5/1964
38   La cólera de un particular, Gregorio, *Leoplan* supplement 3/6/1964
39   Carnaval Cate, *Panorama*, April 1966
40   La isla de los resucitados, *Panorama*, June 1966
41   El expreso de la siesta, *Panorama*, July 1966
42   San la Muerte, *Panorama*, November 1966
43   Viaje al fondo de los fantasmas, *Adan*, November 1966
44   La Argentina ya no toma mate, *Panorama*, December 1966
45   Kimonos en tierra roja, *Panorama*, February 1966
46   El país de Quiroga, *Panorama*, August 1967
47   Vida y muerte del último servicio secreto de Perón, *Todo es Historia*, August 1967
48   El matadero, *Panorama*, September 1967
49   Las carnes que salen del frio, *Panorama,* October 1967
50   Magos de agua dulce, *Panorama*, December 1967
51   Una literatura de la incomodidad, *Primera Plana*, 19/12/1967
52   Guevara, *Casa de las Americas*, Jan–Feb 1968
53   La secta del gatillo alegre, *CGT* 9/5/1968.
54   Quien mató a Rosendo García? *CGT* [series of seven articles, between 16/5 and 27/6] 1968
55   La secta de la picana, *CGT* [series of four articles between October and November] 1968
56   Vuelve la secta del gatillo y la picana, *CGT* 27/3/1969
57   Qué es el vandorismo? *CGT* 22/5/1969
58   Las ciudades fantasmas, *Georama* August 1969
59   Claroscuro del Delta, *Georama* September 1969
60   La luz nuestra de cada noche, *Siete Días* 9–15/3/1970
61   Bolivia: el general proletario, *Panorama* 20–26 December 1970
62   Chile: La muerte de Anaconda, *Panorama* 29/12/70
63   Chile: la carrera contra el reloj electoral, *Panorama* 23/3/1971
64   Ofuscaciones, equívocos y fantasias en el mal llamado caso Padilla, *La Opinión* 26/5/1971
65   40 tigres de papel, *Panorama* 29/6 to 5/7 1971
66   Rodolfo Walsh: el delito de opinar, *Primera Plana* 10/5/1972
67   El drama de Bolivia visto y analizado por uno de sus principales protagonistas, *La Opinión* 14/7/1972
68   Apología del capitalismo norteamericano: una curiosa investigación sobre el humanismo del 12 por ciento, *La Opinión* 25/7/1972
69   Vigoroso testimonio sobre el infierno de los reformatorios, *La Opinión* 8/8/1972
70   Quien proscribe a Perón? *Antropología del Tercer Mundo*, Aug–Sep 1972

71 Tres retratos, *Crisis* 3/7/1973
72 El sionismo, el Estado Israelí y la lucha del pueblo palestino, *Noticias*, 13/6–19/6, 1974
73 Respuesta a la embajada Israelí, *Noticias* 17/7/1974
74 El común oficio del periodismo, *Crisis* 15/7/1974
75 Calle de la Amargura número 303, *El Periodista de Buenos Aires* 17/3/1989
76 Rodolfo Walsh: dar testimonio. *Página/12*, 25/3/1990. Includes Claroscuro del subibaja; Epilogue to 1964 version of *Operación Masacre* and *Una serie de TV*, about prominent personalities.

Clandestine political documents

Reflexiones sobre la situación partidaria. Sin Lugar, Cuadernos del Peronismo Montonero Auténtico, 8/10/1979
Discusión en el ámbito partidario 27/8/1976
Observaciones sobre el documento del Consejo de 11/11/1976
Diciembre 29 [on Paco Urondo's death]. *El Porteño*, April 1976
Aporte a la discusión del informe del Consejo 13/12/1976
Aporte a una hipótesis de resistencia 2/1/1977
Curso de la Guerra en enero-junio de 77 según la hipótesis enemiga [unfinished, 2/1/1977]
Cuadro de situación del enemigo militar a comienzos de 1977, (5/1/1977)
Carta a mis amigos. Cuadernos de Marcha, July–August 1979, Mexico
Carta Abierta de un Escritor a la Junta Militar, 24/3/1977
Los papeles de Walsh. Cuadernos de Jotape, 10/3/1988
Textos Políticos de Rodolfo Walsh. Mexico, *Controversia*, 4/2/1980
Los partes de la Cadena Informativa, los cables de la Agencia de Noticias Clandestina (ANCLA), compiled by Verbitsky, H. (see general bibliography)

Prologues by Rodolfo Walsh

"Noticia" *Diez cuentos policiales argentinos*, Libreria Hachette, 1953
"Cuba escribe" *Crónicas de Cuba*, Jorge Alvarez, 1969
"Prologo" *Los que luchan y los que lloran*, Jorge Ricardo Masetti, Jorge Alvarez 1969

Translations by Rodolfo Walsh

In Biblioteca de Bolsillo, Serie Naranja:
    Irish, William *Lo que la noche revela*, Hachette, 1946
    Queen, Ellery *El asesino es un zorro*, Hachette, 1947
    Irish, William *Si muriera antes de despertarme*, Hachette 1947
    Woolrich, Cornell *El angel negro*, Hachette, 1948
    Irish, William *Siete cantos funebres*, Hachette, 1948
    Woolrich, Cornell *La novia vestía de negro*, Hachette, 1948
    Irish, William *El perro de la pata de palo*, Hachette, 1950
Canning, Victor *Luna de las panteras*, Hachette, 1951
Piper, Evelyn *El motivo es todo*, Hachette, 1951
Canning, Victor *Un bosque de ojos*, Hachette, 1951
Loomis, Andrew *Ilustración creadora*, Hachette, 1951
Piper, Evelyn *La trama usurpadora*, Hachette, 1952
Berrow, Norman *Peligro en la noche*, Emece, 1952
Queen, Ellery *Tras la puerta cerrada*, Hachette, 1952
Irish William *Alguien al teléfono*, Hachette, 1952
Young, Cliff *El dibujo del vestido de pies a cabeza*, Hachette, 1952
Young, Charlotte H. *Fundamentos de la ilustración de modas*, Hachette, 1952
Marshall, Daniel *El dibujo de la cabeza en el arte commercial*, Hachette, 1952

Loomis, Andrew *Dibujo de éxito*, Hachette, 1952

Bierce, Ambrose "Un hijo de los dioses", *Leoplan*, 4/3/1953

Queen, Ellery *El cuatro de corazones*, Hachette, 1953

Dickson Carr, John and Conan Doyle, Adrian "La aventura de los jugadores de cera", *Leoplan*, 16/6/1954

Beresford, J.D. 'El misántropo' and Russell, John, "El precio de la cabeza", *Leoplan*, 15/1/1955

Irish, William "La ventana indiscreta", *Leoplan*, 16/3/1955

Simenon, George "El cliente mas obstinado del mundo". *Leoplan*, 20/4/1955

Cuentos de Edgar Allan Poe, H.G Wells, Jack London, Anthony Boucher, *Leoplan* 18/5/1955

Hauser, Gayelord "El régimen lo hace todo", Sopena, 1955

Bierce, A., Dahl, R. Sullivan J.F. et al: short story anthology, selected and translated by Walsh, *Leoplan* 5/10/1955

Caldwell, Erskine "De rodillas ante el sol naciente", *Leoplan* 1/2/1956

Dinneen, Joseph F. "El robo del siglo", *Leoplan* 4/4/1956

Cooper, Duff "Operación desengaño", *Leoplan* 15/7/1956

Wouk, Herman "El cuaderno de bitácora del primer viaje a la Luna!" *Leoplan* 15/7/1956

Chessman, Caryl "La ley me quiere muerto", *Leoplan* 15/10/1956

Dahl, Roald "La vida a sus espaldas", *Leoplan*, 1/3/1957

Dickson, Carter "El escenario del crimen", *Leoplan* 1/5/1957

Dahl, Roald "La pata del cordero", *Leoplan* 1/10/1957

Whitehead, Don *La historia del F.B.I.* Sopena Argentina, 1958

Bierce, Ambrose *Diccionario del Diablo* Jorge Alvarez, 1965

Maia Netto, Joao Candido *La crisis brasileña* Jorge Alvarez, 1965

McCoy, Horace *Luces de Hollywood* Tiempo Contemporaneo, 1970

Labrousse, Alain *Los tupamaros. Guerrilla urbana en el Uruguay*. Tiempo Contemporaneo, 1971

Chandler, Raymond *Viento Rojo*, Tiempo Contemporaneo, 1972

Trumbo, Dalton *Johnny fue a la Guerra*. Ediciones de la Flor, 1972

Interviews with Rodolfo Walsh

Brun, Juan Bautista "Les presentamos a Rodolfo J. Walsh". *Mayoría* 11/12/1958

Campra, R., Tarquini, F. "Rodolfo Walsh". In Campra, R. *America Latina: la identidad y la máscara* Rome, Editori Riuniti, 1982. Interview conducted in 1973 in Buenos Aires

Covarrubias, I. "Unas preguntas a Rodolfo J. Walsh sobre la novela policial". *Leoplan* 20/10/1954

Fosatti, E. L. "Operación Rodolfo Walsh". *Primera Plana* 13/6/1972

"Oficios terrestres de Rodolfo Walsh". *Análisis* 8/6/1968

"La novela geológica", *Primera Plana* 22/10/1968

"Rodolfo Walsh: Lobo estas?" *Siete Días Ilustrados* 16/6/1970

"Entrevista a Rodolfo Walsh", *Alma Mater*, August 1970

Joint interview with Rodolfo Walsh and Miguel Briante, *La Opinión Cultural*, 11/6/1972

Lugones, Piri "Hablaron de teatro". *Tiempos Modernos*, July 1965

Piglia, Ricardo "Hoy es imposible en la Argentina hacer literatura desvinculada de la politica". In Walsh (1996) see above.

"He sido traido y llevado por los tiempos". *Crisis* November 1987

"Walsh y el comisario Laurenzi". *Vea y Lea* 14/9/1961

Rivera, J. B. "Respuestas", [an interview culled from past interviews and autobiographical notes] in *El relato policial en la Argentina*, EUDEBA, 1986, co-ordinated by Jorge Lafforgue

Work included in collections

"La muerte de los pájaros". *Veinte cuentos infantiles ilustrados por niños*, Kraft (1954) pp. 109–116. Reprinted in Crisis magazine, pp. 68–71 March 1989

"Variaciones en rojo". In *Las mas famosas novelas policiales* Santiago de Chile, Compania Chilena de Ediciones, 1955

"Las tres noches de Isaias Bloom" and "En defensa propia". In *Tiempo de puñales* Seijas y Goyanarte, 1964. Prologue by Donald Yates.

"Los dos montones de tierra". In Bajarlía, Juan Jacobo (comp) *Cuentos de crimen y de misterio* Jorge Alvarez, 1964

"Esa Mujer". In Constenla, Julia (comp) *Crónicas del pasado* Jorge Alvarez, 1965. Also published in *Los mejores cuentos argentinos*, after it received the highest vote by critics and writers selecting the best Argentinian short stories of the 20th century. Extra Alfaguara, 1999.

"La máquina del bien y del mal". In *Los Diez mandamientos*, Jorge Alvarez, 1966. Selection by Piri Lugones

"La mujer prohibida". In Achaval, Horacio (comp) *Buenos Aires de la fundación a la angustia* Ediciones de la Flor, 1967

"Elección de un cuento" [Walsh explains why he chose "La cólera de un particular" by an anonymous Chinese author] in *El libro de los autores* Ediciones De la Flor, 1967

"Guevara". In *Cuba para argentinos* Merlin, 1968

"El 37". Lugones, Piri (comp) *Memorias de la infancia* pp. 53–60 Jorge Alvarez, 1968

"La literatura argentina del Siglo XX". In *Panorama de la actual literatura latinoamericana* pp. 193-210 Havana, Casa de las Americas, 1969 [conversation with Rodolfo Walsh, Francisco Urondo and Juan Carlos Portantiero]. Madrid, Fundamentos, 1971

"Cuento para tahures". In Jorge Lafforgue and Jorge B. Rivera Asesinos de papel pp. 192–197 Calicanto, 1977. Also in *Crímenes perfectos. Antología de relatos* pp. 205–213, Selection, prologue and notes by Ricardo Piglia. Planeta, 1999

"Nota al pie" *El cuento argentino* (1959–70) Centro Editor de América Latina, 1992

"Simbiosis" *El cuento policial argentino* Plus Ultra, 1986

"La aventura de las pruebas de imprenta" in Rivera, Jorge B. (comp) *El relato policial en la Argentina* pp. 45–118 EUDEBA, 1986 [inc biographical information].

"Transposición de jugadas" in Ferro, Roberto (selection and prologue) *Policiales. El asesino tiene quien le escriba* pp. 89–98 Desde la Gente, Ediciones Instituto Movilizador de Fondos Cooperativos, 1991

"Irlandeses detras de un gato" in Orgambide, Pedro (selection, prologue and notes) *Compañeros del alma. Memorias, cuentos, poemas* pp. 27–48 Desde la Gente, Ediciones Instituto Movilizador de Fondos Cooperativos, 1993

In English

Committee to Save Rodolfo Walsh, (1977) "A year of dictatorship in Argentina, March 1976–March 1977. An open letter to the military junta from Rodolfo Walsh", London

McCaughan, M., "Revolutionary revealed power of the word", *Irish Times*, 28/3/1998

Yates, D. (1972) "Gambler's tale" and "Shadow of a bird" in *Latin Blood. The Best Crime and Detective Stories of South America*. Herder and Herder: New York (Translation of *Cuento para tahures and La sombra de un pájaro*).

Adaptations

La Granada was performed in the Teatro San Telmo on 22/4/1965 by the
Grupo del Sur, directed by Osvaldo Bonet. Reprised by Teatro el Vitral in
1993, again in 1994 by the Fundación Banco Patricios and in Washington
Gala Hispanic Theatre in 1999, Dir. Jose Carraquillo.
Operación Masacre Film, Dir. Jorge Cedrón, script by Cedrón and Walsh.
Starred Norma Leandro, Zulema Katz and Julio Troxler. Premiered in 1973.
Asesinato a distancia Dir. Santiago Oves. Based on Walsh short story of the
same name. Starred Héctor Alterio and Patricio Contreras, 1998
Rodolfo J Walsh Dir Gustavo Gordillo. Documentary featuring interviews with
Osvaldo Bayer, Mario Firmenich, Rogelio García Lupo, Patricia Walsh and
others, 1998
Lluvia para tahures Dir. Tamara Binez. Adapted from Walsh short story "Tres
portugueses bajo un paraguas..." Video 1998

Books and magazines dedicated to Walsh

El Gato Negro, crime fiction magazine, December 1994, including a letter from
Yates to Walsh.
El Matadero Revista crítica de literatura argentina, Instituto de Literatura
Argentina Argentino "Ricardo Rojas", UBA, year one, issue one, 1998. Edited
by David Viñas
Nuevo Texto Critico Stanford University, July 1993–June 1994. Director Jorge
Ruffinelli.
Tramas para leer la literatura argentina. Córdoba, Ediciones del Caminante, 1995

Studies and reviews

Bayer, O. "Rodolfo Walsh, un historiador del presente" *Fin de Siglo* 10/4/1988
Bruschtein, L. "Una casa en la isla. Historias con Rodolfo Walsh 19 años despues
de su muerte" Primer Plano, cultural supplement of *Página/12* 31/3/1996
Burgos, C. A. "Rodolfo Walsh, un hombre que se anima" *Cambio*, Mexico
July–Sep 1978
Capdevila, A. "Los casos del comisario Laurenzi" *El País Cultural*, Montevideo
14/6/1996
Casullo, N. "Walsh y su pensamiento politico en 1976" *Controversia*, Mexico
Feb 1980
D'Anna, E. "Rodolfo Walsh: novela policial, sistema policial" *El lágrima trifurca*,
Rosario June 1975
Dalmaroni, M. "El último caballo blanco. Rodolfo Walsh en La Plata" *Página/12*
supplement 17/2/1990
Eloy Martínez, T. "Vidas, pasiones y muertes" *Página/12* Primer Plano cultural
supplement 31/5/1992
Feinmann, J. P. "Rodolfo Walsh. Carta a la Junta Militar. La Sangre Derramada.
Ensayo sobre la violencia politica" *Ariel* 1998 pp. 99–106
Fernandez Vega, J. "Antologia de las notas periodisticas de Rodolfo Walsh"
Crisis, March 1987 pp. 26–27
Ferreyra, L. "Esa carta" Radar, *Página/12* supplement 21/3/1999.
"Los Caballos de Walsh" Radar, *Página/12* supplement 23/5/1997
Ferro, R. "Las ediciones de Operación Masacre" Facultad de Filosofia y Letras,
UBA, Nov–Dec 1988
"Rodolfo Walsh. La operación de Operación Masacre" *Página/12*, 18/12/1988
"Prologue to 'Yo tambien fui fusilado... y otros textos" 1999
"Variaciones en púrpura" *Oasis*, May 1990 pp. 50–59

"La literatura en el banquillo. Walsh y la fuerza del testimonio" *Historia Critica de la Literatura Argentina*, (ed) Noe Jitrik, pp. 125–145 Emece 1999

Ford, A. "El Vandorismo", [bibliographical review of *Quien mató a Rosendo?*] Los Libros, September 1969

"Walsh, la reconstrucción de los hechos" Nueva Novela Latinoamericana, in Lafforgue, J. pp. 272–322 Paidos, 1972

"Ese Hombre" *Navegaciones, Comunicación, cultura y crisis.* pp. 90–91 Amorrortu Editores, 1994

Galeano, E. "Walsh (1977, Buenos Aires) y se dan de baja los libros quemados de Walsh y otros autores" (1977, Rio Cuarto. *Memoria del fuego III, El siglo del viento* Madrid, Siglo XX1 Spain, 1986

Gandolfo, E. "El caso Walsh" *El País Cultural*, Montevideo, 10/3/1995

García Lupo R. "Para los jóvenes de hoy, apenas 34 muertos" *El Periodista de Buenos Aires*, 22/9/1984

Garcia Márquez, G. "Rodolfo Walsh: el escritor que se le adelantó a la CIA" in Walsh (1994) *Rodolfo Walsh, Vivo*, anthology and prologue by R. Baschetti, Ediciones de la Flor

Gonzalez Toro, A. "Rodolfo Walsh y la aventura de un libro. Operación Masacre 20 años despues" *El Periodista de Buenos Aires*, 27/6/1986

Huasi, J. "El periodismo clandestino de Rodolfo Walsh" *El Periodista de Buenos Aires*, 15/11/1985

Jurado, A. Review of "Antología del cuento extraño" May–June 1957

Lafforgue, J. "RJW: informe para una biografia" *Página/12* Primer Plano cultural supplement 7/6/1992

"Noticia" pp. 111–119 and "Ficha" pp.120–121 in Walsh (1992) *La máquina del bien y del mal*, Clarín/Aguilar

"Walsh en y desde el género policial", by Jorge Lafforgue and Jorge B. Rivera, pp. 140–146 Colihue 1996

Lago, S. "Rodolfo Walsh: el violento oficio del escritor" *Brecha* Montevideo

Lerda, M. A. and Martin Viñas, I. "El periodismo comprometido: Rodolfo Walsh" No date given

Link, D. "Rodolfo Walsh, otra deuda interna. Una obra dispersa que se reedita de a poco" *Nuevo Sur*, p.26 16/4/1989

"Rodolfo Walsh y la crisis de la literatura" Letras Contemporaneas, Florianopolis, 1997

"Los diez mandamientos" *Confirmado* 3/11/1966

"Los sesenta, Walsh y la novela en crisis" *Graffiti*, Rosario 1988

Medina, A. "Literatura y política, una relación violenta" *Nuevo Sur* 7/1/1990

Mercado, T. "El último viaje" *Tiempo*, México 9/4/1979

Murga, C. M. "Nuevo periodismo: Rodolfo Walsh, un precursor" Congreso Nacional de Literatura Argentina, Universidad Nacional de Tucumán, 18–20 August 1993

Newman, K. E. "The Argentine Political Novel. Determinations in Discourse" Michigan University Press, 1983

Orgambide, P. "La narrativa de Walsh" *Plural*, México, June 1981 pp. 78–79

"Rodolfo Walsh. El escritor entre todos" in *Entre Todos*, 16/4/1988

"Prólogo" (pp. 9–13) and "Un hombre de verdad" (pp23–25), in *Compañeros del alma*

Pacheco, J. E. "Nota preliminar. Rodolfo J. Walsh desde México" in Walsh (1981) *Obra Literaria Completa*, Siglo XXI: México

Paulinelli, M. "Quien mató a Rosendo? Tramas para leer la literatura argentina" Córdoba, 1995 pp. 33–42

Pesce, V. "Rodolfo Jorge Walsh, el problemático ejercicio de la literatura" in Walsh (1987) *Cuento para tahures y otros relatos policiales*, Puntosur

Piglia, R. "Rodolfo Walsh y el lugar de la verdad" p.35 *Fierro*, Sep 1987
"La mejor tradición argentina de la militancia intelectual" Article with María
Seoane in *Caras y Caretas*, 1984
Rama, A. "Walsh en el tiempo del desprecio" *Marcha*, Montevideo 18/3/1966
Rodolfo Walsh: Literatura y clase social pp. 195–230 Mexico, Folios Ediciones
1984
Righi, N. "Un kilo de oro, por Rodolfo J. Walsh" *La Arena*, Santa Rosa, 31/12/1967
Rios, R. "El teatro de Rodolfo Walsh" pp. 78–79 *Crisis* May 1988
Rivera, J. B. 'La reconstrucción de los hechos" *El País Cultural*, Montevideo
10/3/1995
"Rodolfo Walsh: del cuento a la dramaturgia" [article about the premiere of *La
Granada*]. *El Mundo* 25/4/1965, no by-line
"Rodolfo Walsh: el delito de opinar" *Primera Plana* 16/5/1972, no by-line
"Rodolfo Walsh: le reclaman una novela" *El Mundo* 8/10/1967, no by-line
Ruffinelli, J. "Ferocidad de la experiencia" *Marcha*, Montevideo 3/3/1967
Saidón, G. "Una nueva colección argentina" *El País Cultural*, Montevideo
6/11/1992
Samperio, G. "Walsh". Mexico 1980, (a speech)
Sarlo, B. "Una alucinación dispersa en agonía" pp.1–4 *Punto de Vista* Aug 1984
Sasturain, J. "Rodolfo Walsh: Variaciones en Negro" pp. 26–29 *El Porteño*
19/7/1983
"Un texto desconocido de Rodolfo Walsh. El violento oficio de escritor"
pp. 28–29 *El Periodista de Buenos Aires* 20/3/1987
Soares, N. "Quien mató a Rosendo? El ejemplo de Walsh" *Acción*, February 1985
Sosa, N. "Reeditan Operación Masacre. Homenaje a Rodolfo Walsh" *Clarín*,
3/8/1984
Torre, J. "Presentación de "Tres Cuentos de Walsh" *Crisis*, April 1987
Umbral F. "Rodolfo Walsh" *El País*, Madrid, 6/6/1980
"Un Kilo de Oro" por Rodolfo Walsh, review in *La Nación* 18/2/1968. No by-line
"El homenaje a Rodolfo Walsh" *La Razón* 5/4/1987
Verbitsky, H. "El facundo de Rodolfo J. Walsh" pp. 30–33 *El Periodista de Buenos
Aires*, 22/9/1984
"La identidad de Rodolfo Walsh" *Caras y Caretas* July 1984
"Quien mató a Rodolfo?" *El Periodista de Buenos Aires*, Nov 1984
"Una charla con García Márquez. Gabo habla de Walsh" pp. 37–42 *Humor*
Sep 1985
"Rodolfo Walsh: actual nueve años despues" p.14 *Madres de la Plaza de Mayo*,
March 1986
"El pecado no es hablar, es caer" p.52 *Fin de Siglo*, April 1988
"Etica y estética de Rodolfo J. Walsh" in Walsh (1993) *Cuentos*, Biblioteca
Página/12
Viñas, D. "Dejame hablar de Walsh" pp. 147–149 *Casa de las Americas*
Havana, Nov–Dec 1981
"Walsh y Borges" p.24 *Página/12* 12/7/1988
"Rodolfo Walsh, el ajedrez y la guerra" *Nuevo Sur* 8/3/1990
"Rodolfo Walsh y las danzas de la muerte" p.8 *Página/12* Primer Plano
supplement 31/1/1993
"Rodolfo Walsh. Quince hipótesis" *Página/12* Primer Plano supplement
4/7/1995
"Mafia y política en Rodolfo Walsh" *Página/12* 15/9/1995
Wainfeld, M. "Walsh" *Página/12* 26/3/1991
Walsh, L. "Rigor e inteligencia en la vida de Rodolfo Walsh" p.15 *Controversia*,
Mexico Feb 1990

"Mas alla del rio, entre las casas blancas" p.28 *El Periodista de Buenos Aires,* 22/9/1984

Zendejas, F. "Algo más sobre Rodolfo Walsh" p.2 *Excelsior,* Mexico DF 21/2/1981

Denunciations and homages

"Alegatos: La mafia sindical. Rodolfo Walsh: Quien mató a Rosendo?" p. 57–58 *Primera Plana,* May 27–June 2 1969

Angel, R. "Estrenan obra de Walsh. La batalla tan temida" pp. 20–21 *Nuevo Sur* 19/10/1989

"Aprobado en literatura. Quien mató a Rosendo? Por Rodolfo Walsh" p. 57–58 *Análisis,* June 3–9, 1969

"Aquella noche de junio de 56" [interview with Jorge Cedrón], *Panorama* 23/8/1973 No by-line

"Con la presencia de su hija Patricia. Trabajadores y familiares unidos en el homenaje. Ongaro fue uno de los oradores". p.16 *La Voz,* 25/3/1984 No by-line

"En homenaje a Walsh" p.20 *Tiempo Argentino* 8/8/1984 No by-line

García, L. A. "Recuerdan a Rodolfo Walsh, a cuatro años de su secuestro en la Argentina" *El Día,* Mexico 24/3/1981

Gelman, J. "Desaparecidos, la clara dignidad" p.25 Mascaro, May 1986
"Walsh, Urondo: los críticos de la patrulla perdida" in Mero, *Conversaciones con Juan Gelman. Contraderrota. Montoneros y la revolución perdida.* Contrapunto, 1987

Salazar, J. "Circular de contrainformación, 2" Oficina de Prensa y Difusión del Partido Montonero, 19/4/1977

"Gestión en favor de Rodolfo Walsh" p.6 *La Nación,* 25/11/1977 [a public letter on behalf of Walsh, signed by Juan Goytisolo, Roland Barthes, Italo Calvino and others].

"Una ex-detenida vio objetos de Walsh en poder de un grupo de tareas naval" [testimony of Lila Pastoriza before the Cámara Federal]. p.11 *La Voz* 20/7/1985 No by-line

Rodolfo Walsh. Secuestrado por la Junta Militar Argentina. Madrid, Ediciones del Rescate, 1981. inc texts by Julio Cortázar, Eduardo Luis Duhalde, Eduardo Galeano, Carlos María Gutierrez et al.

UTPBA (Unión de Trabajadores de Prensa de Buenos Aires) "Rodolfo Walsh: Diez años del Punto Final", Buenos Aires 1987

Verbitsky, H. "Reportaje al único testigo" [interview with Martin Gras, survivor of the Navy School of Mechanics] *El Periodista de Buenos Aires* 24/11/1984
"Walsh.' *Página/12,* 25/3/1992

Viñas, D. "Entre los perros y la Thatcher" p.19 *Nuevo Sur,* 1/4/1990

Index